British Communism and the Politics of Race

Historical Materialism Book Series

The Historical Materialism Book Series is a major publishing initiative of the radical left. The capitalist crisis of the twenty-first century has been met by a resurgence of interest in critical Marxist theory. At the same time, the publishing institutions committed to Marxism have contracted markedly since the high point of the 1970s. The Historical Materialism Book Series is dedicated to addressing this situation by making available important works of Marxist theory. The aim of the series is to publish important theoretical contributions as the basis for vigorous intellectual debate and exchange on the left.

The peer-reviewed series publishes original monographs, translated texts, and reprints of classics across the bounds of academic disciplinary agendas and across the divisions of the left. The series is particularly concerned to encourage the internationalization of Marxist debate and aims to translate significant studies from beyond the English-speaking world.

For a full list of titles in the Historical Materialism Book Series
available in paperback from Haymarket Books, visit:
https://www.haymarketbooks.org/series_collections/1-historical-materialism

British Communism and the Politics of Race

Evan Smith

Haymarket Books
Chicago, IL

First published in 2017 by Brill Academic Publishers, The Netherlands
© 2017 Koninklijke Brill NV, Leiden, The Netherlands

Published in paperback in 2018 by
Haymarket Books
P.O. Box 180165
Chicago, IL 60618
773-583-7884
www.haymarketbooks.org

ISBN: 978-1-60846-998-7

Trade distribution:
In the US, Consortium Book Sales, www.cbsd.com
In Canada, Publishers Group Canada, www.pgcbooks.ca
In the UK, Turnaround Publisher Services, www.turnaround-uk.com
All other countries, Ingram Publisher Services International, ips_intlsales@ingramcontent.com

Cover design by Jamie Kerry and Ragina Johnson.

This book was published with the generous support of Lannan Foundation and the Wallace Action Fund.

Printed in the United States.

10 9 8 7 6 5 4 3 2 1

Contents

Acknowledgements

This book started off as a PhD project over a decade ago and has transformed immensely in the postdoctoral period until now – and it is finally ready to be read. Firstly I would like to thank David Lockwood as former doctoral supervisor for his guidance, his assistance and his steadfast Menshevism. My other colleagues at Flinders University, during both my PhD tenure and my time as a Vice-Chancellor's Postdoctoral Research Fellow, have also been a tremendous help – Matt Fitzpatrick, Andrekos Varnava, Peter Monteath, Catherine Kevin and Marinella Marmo.

This book could not have been written without the wonderful source that is the Communist Party of Great Britain archive at the Labour History Archives and Study Centre in Manchester and I would very much like to thank Darren Treadwell for his help over the years with this. Alongside this, my thanks go to the very helpful staff at the numerous other archives visited for this project: the Working Class Movement Library in Salford, the Modern Records Centre at the University of Warwick, the School of Oriental and African Studies archive, the Birmingham City Archives, the Black Cultural Archives in Brixton, the Marx Memorial Library in London, the Glasgow Caledonian University archives and the National Archives at Kew. I would also like to thank Christian Høgsbjerg for his assistance in obtaining documents from the Billy Strachan papers at the Institute of Commonwealth Studies Special Collections.

Many people provided information, advice and materials over the years that were incorporated into the book in some way, so I would like to thank the following for their input and assistance: David Renton, Ian Birchall, Matthew Worley, Satnam Virdee, Kevin Morgan, Richard Cross, Ian Goodyer, Lawrence Parker, Nigel Copsey, John Callaghan, Sean Creighton, Anandi Ramamurthy, Graham Stevenson, Martin Jacques, Joan Bellamy, Christabel Gurney, Mike Squires, Paul Flewers, Rob Marsden, Phillip Deery and Mark Perryman.

I would also like to thank Sebastian Budgen and Danny Hayward from the Historical Materialism series at Brill/Haymarket for their initial interest in my project and their support through to publication.

Thanks should also go to Keith Flett and John Callow who allowed me to present papers on my research in London at the Institute of Historical Research to the London Socialist Historians' Group and at the Marx Memorial Library respectively.

My special thanks goes to those who read sections of the book over the years, including Laura Butterworth, Nick Atanasoff, David Brooks, Aliese Millington and Lauren Piko. Any errors are my own. Thanks also to Paul Morisset for copy-editing my footnotes and compiling the bibliography.

My eternal gratitude is reserved for those family and friends (and friends of friends) who opened up their homes to me while I travelled around Britain and Australia conducting research for this book: Richard and Margaret Meredith, Laura Butterworth and Mark Seibert, Tom Meredith, Peta and Glen Dyke, Phil and Jeanette Brain, Sam and Marge Brain, and David and Fiona Hercock.

I would like to sincerely thank my parents, Robert and Helen Smith, and my parents-in-law, Peter and Felicity Nixon, for their support. But most importantly, thanks and all my love goes to Zenna Nixon, and Remy and Honor Nixon-Smith for being there for me always.

Introduction

In early 1947, the Communist Party of Great Britain (CPGB) hosted the Conference of the Communist Parties of the British Empire in London, with 28 delegates from 11 countries in attendance. The conference demonstrated the optimistic belief of the Communist Party and of the international Communist movement in the late 1940s that the present system was unstable and that progressive and democratic forces were growing stronger across the globe. R. (Rajani) Palme Dutt, one of the CPGB's leading theoreticians and anti-colonial ideologues, in addressing the conference, stated with confidence that the imperial system had been greatly weakened by the Second World War, and the Soviet Union, increasing its world influence at the end of the War, was extending its leading role in the promotion of colonial liberation.[1] For Dutt, this signalled that the capitalist and imperialist system was on the verge of transformation towards a socialist and post-colonial system, stating:

> We meet at a moment when great changes are developing in all countries of the Empire and when the Communist Parties all over the Empire are playing an ever more leading part in the advance of their peoples. Today we approach the colonial question in a new context – in the world after the victory over fascism, with the enormous advance of liberation and democracy arising from that victory, with the rising consciousness of the colonial peoples and the weakening of the power of imperialist reaction. On all sides there is increasing recognition that the old basis of Empire must come to an end and must be replaced by a new relationship of free peoples.[2]

The CPGB believed that the anti-colonial movement in the British Empire/ Commonwealth was necessary to building the socialist movement in Britain, with Dutt emphasising that 'Marxism has always taught how the liberation struggle of the colonial peoples is bound up with the vital interests of the working class movement, of democratic victory and the advance to Socialism'.[3] And at this conference in 1947, both the anti-colonial movement and the socialist movement seemed to be making significant gains. The Communist Party

---

1 Dutt, 'Political Report to the Conference of the Communist Parties of the British Empire', in CPGB, *We Speak for Freedom*, 1947, London: CPGB pamphlet, pp. 8–9.
2 Dutt, 'Political Report to the Conference of the Communist Parties of the British Empire', p. 5.
3 Dutt, 'Political Report to the Conference of the Communist Parties of the British Empire', p. 7.

of Great Britain was at the peak of its political influence in this period, with two Members of Parliament and a considerable number of local councillors (mainly in the East End of London), and its membership numbers had reached their highest levels, with numbers around 40,000 for most of the late 1940s.[4] Under the newly elected Labour government, the decolonisation process was about to begin throughout the British Commonwealth, which would continue under the Conservatives, albeit reluctantly, throughout the 1950s and early 1960s.

At the same time as this decolonisation process was occurring in the colonial peripheries, the imperial metropole was experiencing the first wave of large-scale migration from the Commonwealth, first from the West Indies and West Africa, then from the Indian sub-continent and East Africa, as well as millions from Ireland, Australia, New Zealand, Canada, South Africa and Rhodesia. The onset of large-scale black immigration, symbolised by the arrival of the *ss Empire Windrush* with 492 West Indians aboard at Tilbury in June 1948, can be seen as the beginning of what Mike and Trevor Phillips have described as 'the irresistible rise of multi-racial Britain'.[5] The Communist Party was one of the few political organisations, alongside the Labour Party and the Movement for Colonial Freedom (MCF), that these black migrants to Britain joined in the postwar period. The 1940s and 1950s saw a significant number of black immigrants gravitate towards the CPGB, as the Party's anti-colonial and anti-fascist legacy attracted many black workers who had been politically active or trade union members in their home countries. In this period, the Communist Party had the potential to be an important organisation in the anti-racist/anti-colonial movement, as an influential force in domestic labour politics and as part of the international Communist movement.

By the mid-1960s, the decolonisation process seemed, officially at least, near completion, with only the colonies in southern Africa holding out, while the international communist movement was rocked by the split between the Soviets and the Chinese. This greatly affected the anti-colonial/anti-imperial outlook of the Communist Party in Britain, shifting the focus from campaigning for self-government for the colonies to fights against neo-colonialism and US imperialism, such as the war in Vietnam and apartheid in South Africa. The

---

4   Membership figures from this period were: 56,000 (1942), 55,138 (1943), 45,435 (1945), 42,123 (1946), 38,579 (1947), 43,000 (1948), 38,853 (1950), 35,124 (1952). 'Communist Party Membership', in CPGB archives, CP/CENT/ORG/19/04, Labour History Archive and Study Centre, Manchester (hereafter LHASC); Thompson 1992, p. 218.

5   Phillips and Phillips 1998.

MCF, which was the champion of anti-colonialism amongst the labour movement in the late 1950s and early 1960s, soon became more involved in other
internationalist solidarity campaigns with the North Vietnamese and national
liberation forces in southern Africa, particularly as CPGB occupied leadership
positions within the organisation.

At the same time as the immediacy of the anti-colonial struggle started to
wane, the issue of racial discrimination and the existence of a 'colour bar' in
Britain became a major domestic political concern for the Communist Party.
Originally viewed as an extension of the 'colour bar' which operated in the colonial sphere, racism in Britain was viewed as an increasingly everyday problem
as more colonial migrants came to the country and encountered hostility. The
Communist Party, alongside the MCF, was one of the first political organisations in Britain to come out in defence of migrant workers and to call for the
labour movement to oppose racial discrimination in all aspects of public life,
especially within the workplace. This initially attracted a significant number
of migrant workers from across the Commonwealth, such as the West Indies,
West Africa, the Indian sub-continent and Cyprus. However, as practical anti-
racist activism was primarily limited to the Party's International Department
and special 'nationality' branches, a large number of these newly arrived workers, disillusioned by the slow pace of any interest in anti-racist issues held by
the large swathes of Party members and trade unionists, were also attracted to
the Chinese form of communism promoted after the Sino-Soviet split in 1960.

As well as attempting to convince their fellow trade unionists to take a stand
against racial discrimination, the Communist Party lobbied heavily on two
anti-racist issues in the 1960s – opposition to immigration controls and the
pressuring of Labour to introduce (and then strengthen) legislation prohibiting
racial hatred and discrimination. As this book will demonstrate, by emphasising these campaigns, which depended on convincing the Labour Party to
take a stronger anti-racist stance, the CPGB attempted a balancing act between
appealing to the labour movement (where there had been hostility towards
non-white people) to be more concerned about issues of 'race' and working
with Britain's black communities, who felt the effects of racism every day, often
at the brunt of those in Labour. By the late 1960s, the 'white-led' anti-racist
organisations, such as the Campaign Against Racial Discrimination and the
Institute of Race Relations, which had significant crossover between the CPGB,
the Labour Party and the Movement for Colonial Freedom, were being abandoned by black activists who were inspired by the various strains of 'black
power' in the USA (as well as other Third World and anti-imperialist movements
that mushroomed in '1968') and starting their own organisations. Traditionally
the Communist Party had been the most radical anti-racist organisation within

the sphere of the socialist left, but by the late 1960s, it had been surpassed by black revolutionary groups and others on the far left.

Up until the mid-1970s, the Communist Party was able to ride a wave of industrial militancy and had significant influence in the labour movement as the trade unions battled the Conservative government of Edward Heath. But the focus on industrial politics often meant that the CPGB's activism in other areas, such as within the anti-racist movement, was curtailed. With the onset of the 'oil crisis' in 1973–4, the Party's industrial strategy looked momentarily victorious with the downfall of the Heath government, but Labour soon introduced the 'Social Contract', which put limits on trade union activity and led to an internal debate within the CPGB over the centrality of what Geoff Andrews has described as 'militant labourism'.[6] A number of younger Party members pushed for a greater recognition of the new social movements, including a greater emphasis on the politics of 'race', and building alliances outside the traditional structures of the organised labour movement.

The economic and political crises of the 1970s also saw the revival of the fascist far right, with the National Front gaining public notoriety through a combination of electoral politics and street marching, combining populist fears about immigration with real concerns about unemployment and cuts to social services (primarily housing). From 1974 until 1979, the anti-fascist movement hit back against the NF, and the CPGB, as the traditional bearers of left-wing anti-fascism, was involved in these campaigns. However, the militant stance taken by the Communist Party in the 1930s was appropriated by the International Socialists/Socialist Workers Party, and it was this Trotskyist group who founded the Anti-Nazi League. Although initially sceptical, the anti-racist activists within the CPGB put their weight behind the ANL and helped make the ANL one of the most successful single-issue campaigns in British political history. The ANL was not only backed by the SWP and the CPGB, but also involved significant figures from the Labour left and the trade unions, demonstrating a stronger sense of solidarity between the labour movement and Britain's migrant communities.

The other event of the mid- to late 1970s that signalled closer co-operation between the labour movement and black workers was the strike at Grunwick that lasted from 1976 to 1978. The previous decade had seen a number of strikes by black and Asian workers across the country, with probably the most infamous being the strikes at Mansfield Hosiery Mills in Loughborough in 1972 and Imperial Typewriters in Leicester in 1974, which had seen local trade union

---

6   Andrews 2004, p. 17.

representatives unwilling to support the striking workers, or being publicly
hostile towards the strike. When a group of Asian workers, including a number of women, started a non-sanctioned picket outside the Grunwick Photo
Processing Lab in North London during the long summer of 1976, they inadvert-
ently began one of the most important, and longest, strikes in British history.
Grunwick demonstrated a change in the attitudes of the labour movement
towards black workers and the strike saw several unions, such as APEX, TGWU
and the NUM (as well as the TUC), mobilise their members in support of the
striking workers. Although there were differences in the aims and emphases
of the large trade union presence (the right to recognition of the union at
Grunwick) and the striking Asian workers (to end racial discrimination at the
factory), Grunwick signified a new-found solidarity in a time of economic and
political crisis.

However, by the 1980s this solidarity had lost its momentum. The election
of Margaret Thatcher as Prime Minister in May 1979 contributed heavily to this
as the political landscape started to shift under the Conservatives. Firstly the
initial objective of the Anti-Nazi League, to prevent the National Front from
becoming an electoral force by 1979, had been achieved, as the NF failed dis-
mally at the general election to obtain any significant vote across the country.
The ANL debated whether to diversify its objectives and become a more general
anti-racist organisation, but with the primary threat of the NF gone, it became
harder to convince activists that the ANL was the best anti-racist vehicle. As
Dave Cook, the CPGB's National Organiser and leading anti-racist advocate,
wrote in the *Morning Star* in July 1980: 'Despite the significance of its past
role, the ANL has tended to become submerged in CARL [the Campaign Against
Racist Laws] and the Blair Peach Committee. It only come[s] to life in response
to a fascist mobilization'.[7]

Secondly, the winding down of the ANL allowed the trade unions and sections of the Labour Party to retreat from anti-racist activities and the public
show of support at Grunwick disappeared with an emphasis by the labour
movement on fighting the Conservatives over Thatcher's monetarist and industrial relations policies (such as during the 1980 Steel Strike). This inwards turn
by the labour movement was not limited to the Labour Party and the trade
unions, with the Communist Party and the Socialist Workers Party both reas-
sessing their strategies in the perceived 'downturn' of the organised industrial
struggles of the 1970s. By early 1981, a number of black activists were com-
plaining that the left, which had promoted black and white unity only a few

---

7   Cook, 'Racism in Britain Lies Deep', *Morning Star*, 11 July 1980, p. 2.

years before, was now far removed from the struggles that black people in Britain were fighting at the time, such as police harassment, high unemployment, and discrimination in housing and social services. These struggles then became flashpoints in 1981 for a series of riots throughout Britain, starting in Brixton in April of that year, then spreading across most cities in England in July. Although many white youth were involved, the dynamics of the riots were very much driven by the grievances of Britain's black youth. Although sympathetic to those involved in the riots, most of the leftist organisations, including the CPGB, were not present in the inner cities during the riots, but descended on these areas in their aftermath to attempt to steer the direction of the post-riot political 'agenda'.

However, the anti-racist programme offered by the Communist Party was tempered by the dissent inside the Party at the time. Recognising that Thatcher marked a significant shift to the right, both in practical political and economic terms and ideologically, a number of reformers within the CPGB, inspired by the writings of Antonio Gramsci and the concept of Eurocommunism espoused by a number of Western European Communist Parties, pushed for a 'broad democratic alliance' which sought to combat Thatcherism beyond the realms of the class struggle and embrace the new social movements that fought other forms of oppression. Originally set out in the 1977 version of *The British Road to Socialism*, the broad democratic alliance promoted working with other progressive organisations and working with the Labour left to push for socialism through democratic institutions. In practical terms, the broad democratic alliance strategy had two main impacts upon the Party's anti-racist activism. Firstly, it deferred the activism of the Party's anti-racist activists to the broader organisations that they joined, such as Liberation, the Campaign Against Racist Laws, the Indian Workers Association and the Anti-Nazi League, for example, and any Communist Party influence was subsumed by the need to be involved in broad front work. Secondly, the Party, particularly those attached to the Eurocommunist wing, supported the municipal anti-racism promoted by the local Labour-led councils, especially those in London, Manchester and Bradford, which were seen as local sites of resistance to the Thatcher government's national political agenda. While providing funds and services to local black communities, many criticised this council-led anti-racism for its conservatism and focus on racism as an individual problem, rather than the underlying socio-economic and political structures that led to racial inequality and racial discrimination. Although they acknowledged these shortcomings of municipal anti-racism, the Party's anti-racist activists pointed out that at least the councils were doing something at the local level to combat racism, especially in London, when the ruling political party was doing little to improve 'race relations'.

However, as the Communist Party disintegrated in the 1980s, it meant that any effective anti-racist action became increasingly limited in terms of the Party-led agenda.

These debates over anti-racist strategy took place as the Communist Party combusted in the mid-1980s, the victim of a number of serious splits between former comrades over the direction of the Party (and its relationship with the Soviet Bloc). In 1982–3, the Party's Industrial Organiser, Mick Costello, and the editor of the *Morning Star*, Tony Chater, led a rebellion of the industrial traditionalists who believed that the Eurocommunists linked to the journal *Marxism Today* had pushed the Party away from its class politics base. After being expelled at the 1983 National Congress, many more followed them from the Party, leaving the Communist Party without its daily newspaper and a significant portion of its trade union membership. When the Miners' Strike broke out in April 1984, the Party was in disarray over how to approach it and this only exacerbated the divisions in the Party, heading towards its decline. Despite a relaunch of the Party programme in 1989 with *The Manifesto For New Times*, its decline seemed inevitable, and in 1991 the Communist Party of Great Britain dissolved itself after more than 70 years as a political organisation.

The aim of this book is to analyse the contribution that the Communist Party of Great Britain made to the anti-racist movement from the late 1940s to the early 1980s, and how this fits into the wider changes within the CPGB and the British political landscape throughout the postwar era. It will track how, for the CPGB, the politics of 'race' and the fight against racism changed from being primarily an issue tied to ideas of colonial liberation to the domestic issue of tackling the everyday racial discrimination experienced by black people in British society. The book will show how the CPGB was one of the first labour organisations that campaigned against racial discrimination and built relationships with black migrants in Britain, but also how their anti-racist agenda was subsumed by the wider struggle for socialism and 'bread and butter' trade union issues. The CPGB can be seen as a microcosm of how the British labour movement related to the issue of 'race' in the era of decolonisation, and the book will examine the challenges faced in convincing white workers, including the Party's own members, to be actively involved in the fight against racism and colonialism. The book will analyse how the centrality of class for the CPGB was contested by the rise of new social movements, and in the anti-racist movement particularly by the rise of 'black power' and other forms of ethno-politics, and the political pluralism that surfaced from this contested space. The book will explore how an *intersectional* political agenda, which was informed by positions of class, race, gender and sexuality, emerged from the struggles of the postwar era and challenged the outlook of the Communist Party (as well as the wider labour movement), who had traditionally viewed the struggle against racism as an extension of class politics and its conventional political tactics. Overall, this book is the story of the relationship between British Communism and the politics of 'race', and how the juxtaposition between the politics of class and ethnicity has informed the contemporary debates on intersectionality, hybridity and identity politics in the twenty-first century.

Themes

The history of the Communist Party's role in the anti-racist movement in Britain is one of varying degrees of success and failure from the 1940s to the 1980s. As one of the initial political organisations to actively campaign against the racial discrimination faced by black people in Britain, it was at the forefront of the broad anti-racist movements of the 1950s and 1960s (borne out of the earlier anti-colonial and anti-imperial movements that the CPGB participated in). However, by the 1970s and 1980s, the role of the Communist Party in the anti-racist movement was surpassed, on the one hand by black activists who formed autonomous black-led organisations, and on the other by the groups of the far left, such as the IS/SWP and the IMG, who proposed a more radical political agenda, including a more confrontational anti-racist/anti-fascist programme. Although the shift towards embracing the new social movements, centred around those writing for *Marxism Today*, reinvigorated the CPGB in the 1980s and promised a potentially more nuanced anti-racist strategy, the Party was on the verge of collapse and did not translate its ideas into practical anti-racist activism. Within this narrative of long-term decline, this book will explore several themes to explain the complex relationship that the Communist Party had with the anti-racist movement and with Britain's black population.

Class before Race
The Communist Party's understanding of the concept of 'race', which was central to its anti-racist activism, was heavily informed by Marxist theory and its anti-colonial programme, developed through the interwar period in line with the ebbs and flow of Comintern policy. For the CPGB, the concept of 'race' and racial discrimination was borne out of European imperialism and entrenched within capitalist exploitation. Viewing the people in the British colonies as 'fellow fighters ... against the common enemy' of British imperialism,[8] the Party

---

8   Pollitt, *Britain Arise*, 1952, London: CPGB pamphlet, p. 18.

welcomed the black immigrants who arrived in the postwar period, declaring in 1955, 'It is most urgent that the Labour movement ... set out to welcome the coloured workers who come to this country and win them for the trade unions'.[9] Anti-colonialism was an important issue for the CPGB, but it was a foreign concept to most of the white members of the Party, who were predominantly concerned with immediate economic and domestic matters. The emphasis upon the imperialist origins of racial discrimination, while important in understanding the pervasive nature of racism in twentieth-century capitalism, served to reinforce the 'foreignness' of the immigrant workers and subordinated immediate matters of fighting racism in Britain to a much longer-term programme of colonial freedom and socialist revolution.

The falsity of 'race' led to a promotion of 'colour blindness' amongst CPGB members, where appeals to fraternal notions of class disregarded the actual experiences of racism felt by black workers and undermined practical actions to combat racism at shopfloor level. The perception of racism as a construct of the ruling class to divide the working class – 'a conscious part of the policy of the most reactionary sections of British capitalism'[10] – and its eradication tied to the ideal of socialist revolution meant that issues of 'race' and racism were subordinated to the more immediate issues of class-based politics and industrial militancy that dominated the CPGB and the wider labour movement. The Communist Party was willing to make use of its black members, but the focus of the Party was on the issues of industrial class politics, thus it became, as Trevor Carter described, a case of 'class-before-race'.[11] This focus on industrial militancy and the trade unions was an important component of the CPGB's postwar strategy that promoted the building of broad left alliances and the Party was reluctant to criticise the unions for failing to effectively combat racial discrimination.

The Limits of Labourism

The trade unions were central to the CPGB's postwar strategy, with the 'progressive alliance' between the left union membership and the Communist Party being 'key to changing the whole position of the labour movement'.[12] Unity within the labour movement, including 'trade unions, co-operatives, the left in the Labour Party and the Communist Party', was, as outlined in the 1968 edition of The British Road to Socialism, 'the key to advance on the road

---

9   'Talking Points On ... Colonial Workers in Britain', World News, 19 March 1955, p. 238.
10   Bolsover, No Colour Bar for Britain, 1955, London: CPGB pamphlet, p. 10.
11   Carter 1986, p. 62.
12   Gollan, 'Left Unity', Comment, 9 December 1967, p. 780.

to socialism'.[13] The trade unions were seen by the CPGB as vital organisations in the fight against racism and much emphasis was placed upon the 'traditions of tolerance' amongst the British working class, juxtaposed with the use of racism to 'make [a] profit for a small handful of bosses, shareholders and bankers'.[14] The Communist Party declared that the 'average trade unionist ... despises any colour bar' and described shopfloor racism as 'unusual', where 'in the occasional factory ... white workers have been misguided enough to propose discrimination against coloured workers'.[15] Since the mid-1950s, the CPGB encouraged black workers to 'join their appropriate trade unions' and 'exercise their trade union and political rights' as black and white workers had a 'common interest in waging a united fight against a common enemy – the Tory imperialists and the big monopoly firms who exploit them'.[16] However, the Party's view of anti-racism as part of the wider issue of class politics did not acknowledge that the fight against racism demanded different and immediate actions that were not addressed by the trade unions. As the CPGB stated in a 1981 Discussion Pack:

> Often the major problem with the trade union movement (seen in the left generally) is 'colour-blindness'. This may seem to have good intentions, but it means, in practice, a failure to *carry out practical policies* to undermine racism and overcome racial disadvantage at work ... For a long time the struggle against racism was taken as a low political priority.[17]

The traditional allies of the CPGB in the broad left strategy, the Labour Party and the TUC, had repeatedly spoken out against racial discrimination, but the practical anti-racism of these organisations was much less effective. The trade unions were reluctant to combat racism within the workplace; this reluctance was based on the unions' 'themes of "integration" and opposition to any special provision'.[18] This was the view that 'all immigrants should *integrate* or *adapt* to the dominant social and cultural norms and values' of white British society and this integration meant that 'immigrant workers should not be singled out for separate treatment' or that the 'trade union movement had no special respons-

---

13   CPGB, *The British Road to Socialism*, 1968, London: CPGB pamphlet, p. 22; p. 25.

14   Bellamy, *Homes, Jobs, Immigration – The Facts*, 1968, London: CPGB pamphlet, p. 8; p. 3.

15   Bolsover, *No Colour Bar for Britain*, 1955, London: CPGB pamphlet, p. 7.

16   Bolsover, *No Colour Bar for Britain*, p. 11.

17   CPGB, *Power & Prejudice = Racism*, 1981, London: CPGB Discussion Pack, Unit 4, p. 2, in Marx Memorial Library, London, YA01.07/POW, Boxed Pamphlets.

18   Miles and Phizacklea 1977, p. 16.

ibility to them'.[19] As David J. Smith wrote in the PEP Report, *Racial Disadvantage in Britain*: 'While making public declarations against racial discrimination and prejudice, unions have often connived at discrimination and have often failed to represent their minority members energetically'.[20]

Frustrated by the marginalisation of the problem of racism in the labour movement and the reluctance of the CPGB to harshly criticise the trade unions for their complicity in this, the Party lost many of its black members. As the rise of autonomous black activism and wildcat strikes demonstrated in the 1960s and 1970s, black workers did not need to organise around the CPGB and although these activists were inspired by Marxism, they were able to promote anti-racism and black militancy as the central issue, associated with wider class struggle, but not subordinated to it.

The Democratic Road to Socialism

In 1951, the Communist Party outlined its postwar strategy in *The British Road to Socialism*, which formally renounced the revolutionary insurrectionism of its 1935 programme, *For Soviet Britain*, instead promoting the Party's adherence to parliamentary democracy and working through broad left alliances within the capitalist state system, rather than operating from a point of total opposition. As the postwar strategy outlined in *The British Road to Socialism* promoted working within the parliamentary system, the CPGB accepted the functions of the institutions of the state. Instead of trying to overthrow these institutions, the Party sought to democratise them and place them under popular control. For the Party's anti-racist strategy, this acceptance of the existence of the state meant that the CPGB was willing to use the institutions of the state to combat racism, in particular the more explicit forms of racial discrimination and violence, while at the same time acknowledging the contribution of the state towards perpetuating racism in British society. The relationship of being dependent upon, but also critical of, the state in the fight against racism impacted heavily upon the Party's anti-racist activism. One of the key areas of the CPGB's anti-racist activism during the 1960s and 1970s was the campaign for the introduction, and then strengthening, of the Race Relations Act and for it to be used effectively by the state to deal with racial discrimination and incidents of racial violence. However, the dependence upon the state to act as a positive force in the fight against racism was countered by the increasingly repressive actions of the state upon Britain's black population. Throughout the postwar

---

19   Miles and Phizacklea 1977, p. 19; Miles and Phizacklea 1977, p. 16.
20   Smith 1977, p. 328.

era, black communities had come under attack from the police, the judiciary, immigration control officials and the Home Office, who often saw them as a 'threat' to mainstream (i.e. white) British society, which was exacerbated by populist racist notions of black people as illegal immigrants, criminals, dole cheats, muggers and scabs.

As demonstrated by the police tactics used in policing demonstrations, Britain's black communities and industrial relations in the 1970s, it was difficult to adequately confront the power of the repressive institutions of the state, so the reformers in the CPGB argued that anti-racist activities were better mobilised through peaceful activism in local communities and through local governments. Inspired by the Gramscian idea of the 'war of position', the CPGB increasingly saw that their part in the anti-racist movement was to be most effective at grassroots level, co-operating with local councils, the local Community Relations Commissions (CRCs) and other community and minority organisations. However, by this time, the Communist Party's potential for a significant contribution to the anti-racist movement had dissipated dramatically. Despite the development of the broad democratic alliance strategy in focusing upon local community-based activism and co-operation with other anti-racist and ethnic organisations, the black communities were reluctant to follow the lead of the CPGB (or the rest of the white left), which had continually marginalised the issue of racism within the scope of class-based politics. The CPGB itself was in a state of decline with a waning influence in the trade unions and deep divisions inside the Party over the CPGB's political strategy. Many of the Party's industrial militants saw the reformers' promotion of new social movements, including anti-racism, as a diversion from socialist politics and industrial activism. Within the Party's own anti-racist activities, there had been a reliance on the state to deal with racist agitators and acts of racial discrimination, using the Public Order Act and the Race Relations Act, but any positive contribution the state could make towards combating racism was hindered by the role of the institutions of the state in the pervasiveness of racism in British society.

Shifting Away from the Centrality of Class

By the late 1970s, the Communist Party was becoming increasingly divided over its dedication to industrial militancy, with few tangible gains, and the reluctance by some within the Party to recognise the importance of the new social movements that had emerged out of the cultural radicalism of the late 1960s and early 1970s. A campaign of industrial militancy had led to the Miners' Strike in early 1974, forcing the defeat of Edward Heath's Conservative government, but was stemmed by the Social Contract between the Labour Party and the Trades Union Congress (TUC), a voluntary agreement to counter inflation by halting further claims of wage militancy. The fact that the Social Contract was supported by many of the CPGB's traditional allies in the labour movement led to a division between them and the Party's own industrial activists, which opened up a schism in the Communist Party over the centrality of militant unionism in CPGB strategy. Some members of the Party, who were influenced by the rise of new social movements, and the political theories of the Italian Marxist Antonio Gramsci, advocated reforms to the CPGB's strategy and outlook. These reformers believed that the CPGB's emphasis on class-based industrial politics did not address other forms of oppression in British society that were 'not always directly connected with the relations of production'.[21] The reformers in the Communist Party pushed for a widening of the Party's co-operation within other social movements and organisations,[22] described in the 1977 edition of *The British Road to Socialism* as the broad democratic alliance, but by the time that these reforms were being promoted, the Party itself was in steady decline (membership had fallen to 25,293 in 1977),[23] which became terminal after the election of Margaret Thatcher in May 1979.

Despite the Party's declining fortunes, *Marxism Today* performed an important function in British leftist politics, challenging the centrality of the class-based Marxism of the CPGB and the British left, stemming from Stuart Hall and Martin Jacques's innovative analysis of Thatcherism. The nature of Thatcherism had first been analysed inside the pages of *Marxism Today* in the late 1970s, viewing Thatcherism as more than just a stricter continuation of previous Conservative governments and representing a widespread ideological shift to the right. The reformers believed that this shift to the right needed to be addressed by more than traditional class-based politics and demanded a greater emphasis on the long-term ideological aspects that had allowed this rightwards shift. For those writing in *Marxism Today*, the electoral victories of Thatcherism indicated that the sections of British society who had traditionally supported Labour (and whom the CPGB had attempted to draw towards a Communist-

---

21   CPGB, *The British Road to Socialism*, 1977, London: CPGB pamphlet, p. 29.

22   The use of the term 'reformer' within this book is to indicate those members of the CPGB who wished to reform the Party towards a wider interpretation of the class struggle, primarily those who advocated for the broad democratic alliance in the 1977 edition of *The British Road to Socialism*. It does not necessarily mean a 'reformist' position as opposed to a 'revolutionary' one, as the Leninist principles of armed insurrection had been abandoned by the acceptance of the parliamentary process in *The British Road to Socialism* in 1951.

23   'Communist Party Membership'.

Labour position) was much more fragmented and much more ideologically driven, than by just class-based politics. Within the pages of *Marxism Today* (and informed by the anti-racist struggles of the 1970s and early 1980s), Hall promoted the notion that an individual's politics are informed by a multitude of experiences and identity formations – what could be described as 'intersectionality' in contemporary theoretical terms.

Thinking Intersectionally about the CPGB and the Politics of 'Race'

One of the key arguments of this book is that the fight against racism and the demands of Britain's black communities challenged the centrality of the class struggle to the programme of the Communist Party, who envisaged all socio-political problems as stemming from the inequalities created by capitalism. As mentioned above, the CPGB invested heavily in the institutions of the organised labour movement – the Communist Party, the trade unions and the Labour Party – to help combat racism and fight for the rights of black workers. However, the campaigns that brought together the CPGB (and the wider labour movement) and the black communities often highlighted the odds between the approaches taken by the different groups involved. As the strikes by Asian workers (such as Mansfield Hosiery Mills, Imperial Typewriters and Grunwick), the campaign against immigration controls or the struggle against police harassment and violence demonstrated, the socio-economic and political interests of those involved were intersectional and not simply expressions of a politics informed by class or race or gender. Instead they were often an intertwining of all three.

Kimberle Crenshaw first used the term 'intersectional' in the late 1980s to describe the position of black women in the United States and their struggles with the US criminal justice system.[24] Over the last 25 years, the term has become a valuable concept within many academic disciplines. Looking back at the anti-racist struggles of the postwar era in Britain, it can be seen that many of these struggles were intersectional and that for those involved, their politics often combined class-based, racial and gendered perspectives. For example, at the Grunwick strike, this combined those interested in the strike as a demonstration of class unity and the fight for trade union recognition, those interested in the strike to fight racial discrimination in the workplace, and those interested in the strike as a chance to highlight the particular difficulties faced by

---

24   See Crenshaw 1989, pp. 139–68; Crenshaw 1991, pp. 124–300.

South Asian women in this 'sweatshop' environment. Although the concept did not exist at the time, it was widely understood by many, especially those who were excited by the rise of the new social movements in the late 1960s and those who pushed for their recognition in the Communist Party, that class was just part of a wider spectrum that informed someone's political identity.

The 1977 version of *The British Road to Socialism* started to acknowledge this with the promotion of the broad democratic alliance as recognition that the political struggle was moving beyond 'an expression of class forces' and had to recognise the 'other important forces in society which emerge out of areas of oppression not always directly connected with the relations of production'.[25] In the same year, Barry Hindess, at the Communist Party's annual Communist University of London (CUL) lecture series, stated, 'At any given time ... working-class politics must contain features that are not reducible to class position',[26] and as a leading reformer inside the CPGB, pointed to an article by Sam Aaronovitch from 1973 to demonstrate that this reconsideration of class politics had a longer history inside the Communist Party of Great Britain. It is worth quoting Aaronovitch beyond Hindess's initial notes here to highlight the connections between the arguments being put forward by some within the Communist Party in the 1970s and the theoretical concept we now know as 'intersectionality':

> The nature of the issues posed by contemporary capitalism brings into action (or can do so) a series of *intersecting forces* which comprise: various sections of the working class as broadly defined; ...
>
> People may be brought into action by the *way* they are affected in their different roles; workers as tenant or shopper; worker as parent.
>
> They are intersecting forces in the sense that their memberships overlap but they also interact.[27]

As the 1970s progressed, the interaction between the anti-racist movement, Britain's black communities and those pushing for reform inside the Communist Party reinforced this idea of exploring the 'networks of solidarity'[28] that could be built outside of the traditional realm of class politics and the

25   CPGB, *The British Road to Socialism*, p. 29.

26   Hindess 1977, pp. 100–1.

27   Aaronovitch, 'Perspectives for Class Struggles and Alliances', *Marxism Today*, March 1973, p. 69. Italics are in the original text.

28   See Featherstone 2012.

political vehicles offered by the organised labour movement. Although both the reformers and traditionalists within the Communist Party believed in the fight against racism, the Party traditionalists were heavily invested in the trade unions and the broader labour movement as the organs to combat racism, while it was widely understood that the anti-racist struggle needed to embrace strategies beyond this and interact with those unaffected by the world inhabited by the labour movement.

The work of Stuart Hall (and others such as Ernesto Laclau and Chantal Mouffe) in *Marxism Today* in the 1980s further promoted this idea that people were likely to be guided in their actions by notions of class, as they were to be guided by notions of ethnicity, sexuality, gender, or any other form of 'identity politics'. After their defeat at the 1987 elections, Hall wrote an important piece for the journal on Labour's shortcomings in the *ideological* battle against Thatcherism and the shifting support bases for both major parties in the 1980s, which further encapsulated the idea of the intersecting experiences and identities that form an individual's political outlook. Hall wrote:

> Electoral politics – in fact, every kind of politics – depends on political identities and identifications. People make identifications symbolically: through social imagery, in their political imaginations. They 'see themselves' as one sort of person or another. They 'imagine their future' within this scenario or that. They don't just think about voting in terms of how much they have, their so-called 'material interests'. Material interests matter profoundly. But they are always ideologically defined.
>
> Contrary to a certain version of Marxism, which has as strong a hold over the Labour 'Centre' as it does on the so-called 'hard Left', material interests, on their own, have no necessary class belongingness. They influence us. But they are not escalators which automatically deliver people to their appointed destinations, 'in place', within the political-ideological spectrum.
>
> One reason why they don't is because people have conflicting social interests, sometimes reflecting conflicting identities. As a worker a person might put 'wages' first: in a period of high unemployment, 'job security' may come higher; a woman might prioritise 'child-care'. But what does a 'working woman' put first? Which of her identities is the one that determines her political choices?[29]

---

29   Hall, 'Blue Elections, Election Blues', *Marxism Today*, July 1987, p. 33.

In 1988, Homi Bhabha wrote that the arguments put forward by Stuart Hall in 1987, alongside similar ones made in the pages of *Marxism Today* by Eric Hobsbawm and Beatrix Campbell, represented 'the "hybrid" moment of political change'.[30] 'Here the transformational value of change', Bhabha said discussing the role of women in the 1984–5 Miners' Strike, '*lies in neither the One* (unitary working class) *nor the Other* (the politics of gender) *but something else besides* which contests the terms and territories of both'.[31] Similar to the concept of intersectionality, Bhabha's notion of hybridity reflected what Hall described as people's '*conflicting* social interests'[32] and recognised that the traditional Marxist approach to the question of 'race' (or gender or sexuality) was inadequate to assist in their contemporary struggles against inequality. For Bhabha and other post-colonial thinkers, such as Ranajit Guha or Gayatri Chakravorty Spivak,[33] traditional Marxism could not adequately explain the politics of 'race' and ethnicity, or effectively uphold the notion that racism and colonialism were simply parts of the wider phenomenon of capitalist exploitation. But the inadequacies of Marxism were not merely to be replaced by other forms of identity politics, with the ideas of post-colonialism opening up spaces of political and cultural hybridity. At this point, the broad democratic alliance and the counter-hegemony discussed within *Marxism Today* transformed into what Bhabha called the 'Third Space'. For Bhabha, Hall's writing in *Marxism Today* introduced 'an exciting, neglected moment ... in the "recognition" of the relation of politics to theory'[34] and demonstrates that although the Communist Party of Great Britain's role in the anti-racist movement declined, its impact has continued to resonate in various ways since.

Situating the Party's Anti-racism within the Wider Scholarship

In the last two decades, there has been a significant increase in interest in the history of the Communist Party, by academics, former CPGB members and other activists on the left. The 'official' history of the CPGB published by Lawrence and Wishart had ended with Noreen Branson's 1985 book, which took

---

30 Bhabha 1988, p. 13.
31 Ibid.; Italics are in the original text.
32 Hall 1987, p. 33; Italics are in the original text.
33 See Guha and Spivak (eds.) 1988; Spivak 2003. For a critical overview of the relationship between Marxism and subaltern studies, see Lal 2001, pp. 135–48.
34 Bhabha 1988, p. 8.

the story of the Party up until 1941.[35] Between 1997 and 2004, three new volumes were produced by Branson, John Callaghan and Geoff Andrews, which covered the period from 1941 to 1991.[36] Only Callaghan's volume, focusing on the period from 1951 to 1968, had a section dedicated to the Party's anti-racist and anti-colonial politics (during its early high point). Ending with the campaign against Enoch Powell in 1968, Callaghan looked at a period where the Communist Party still dominated the anti-racist movement and had not been significantly challenged by black power or the Trotskyist/Maoist left.

As well as these histories from Lawrence and Wishart, there have been several single volume narrative histories of the Party,[37] as well as a few specialist studies on various areas of the CPGB's history. Several of these studies have focused on the local 'grass-roots' level, which have emphasised that the history of the CPGB is about 'real' people and not merely 'Moscow and all that'.[38] However, these studies have mainly focused upon the interwar period and there is only a brief mention of 'race' within them. The only exceptions to this have been Hakim Adi's chapter on the West African branch in the CPGB in the 1950s in the *Opening the Books* collection, and the section on national and international identities in the book by Morgan, Cohen and Flinn.[39]

Other studies have addressed the role of black and Asian activists involved in (and around) the Party, but these have been limited to the interwar period and the 1950s, such as John Callaghan's biography of Rajani Palme Dutt, Marika Sherwood's biography of CPUSA exile, Claudia Jones, or Hakim Adi's study of West African activist Desmond Buckle.[40] While including some discussion of the wider political landscape in which these communists operated, these biographies have tended, naturally, to focus on the individual.

Other studies of the history of British anti-racism and anti-fascism have only mentioned the CPGB briefly, preferring to concentrate on the Anti-Nazi League, Rock Against Racism and Anti-Fascist Action on the one hand,[41] or black and Asian activism on the other.[42] Jodi Burkett has recently published *Constructing Post-Imperial Britain: Britishness, 'Race' and the Radical Left in the 1960s*,[43]

---

35   Klugmann 1968; Klugmann 1969; Branson 1985.
36   Branson 1997; Callaghan 2003; Andrews 2004.
37   Thompson 1993; Beckett 1998; Renton and Eaden 2002.
38   Andrews, Fishman and Morgan 1995; Worley 2002; Morgan, Cohen and Flinn 2007.
39   Adi 1995, pp. 175–94; Morgan, Cohen & Flinn 2007, pp. 184–229.
40   Callaghan 1994; Sherwood 1999; Adi 2006, pp. 22–45.
41   Renton 2006; Goodyer 2009; Hann 2012; Richardson (ed.) 2013.
42   Shukra 1998; Alleyne 2002; Sivanandan 2008; Ramamurthy 2013; Bunce and Field 2015.
43   Burkett 2013.

but this book does not actually deal with the British radical left in terms of the Communist Party and the Trotskyist groups. Instead Burkett focuses on various social movements, such as the Campaign for Nuclear Disarmament, the Anti-Apartheid Movement, the Northern Irish Civil Rights movement and the National Union of Students, showing how these extra-parliamentary movements were affected by decolonisation and the establishment of the 'multi-racial' Commonwealth in the 1960s.

Most recently, Satnam Virdee published *Racism, Class and the Racialized Outsider*, which looks at the interaction between ethnic minorities and the English working class since the time of the Chartists and shows that the concept that separates the working class on one side and ethnic minorities on the other (something which has been a constant feature of discussions on 'race relations' since the 1940s) is a misnomer. For Virdee, since the 1780s, the working class in England (the Scottish and Welsh working classes having differing trajectories) has been a 'multi-ethnic formation'.[44] Virdee's history prominently features the CPGB, describing it as 'at the centre of most organized campaigns against imperialism and racism',[45] but the Communist Party is not the main focus of the book and discussion of its anti-racist activities beyond the 1950s is only mentioned in passing, compared with the rise of left-wing and black activist groups.

As mentioned above, in histories of the Communist Party in the postwar period, which is quite limited in itself, there has been scant mention of anti-racism and it is a neglected area of study that needs to be uncovered. To examine the CPGB's anti-racist work is not merely 'history for history's sake', but helps to make known an important part of the Party's cultural history and the history of post-colonial Britain. The purpose of this book is to chart how the Party reacted to a massive increase in the number of black workers in Britain in the postwar period and how it used its influential role within the labour movement to attempt to win a wider commitment to anti-racism by 'white' British workers and their representative organisations. The history of anti-racism in Britain between the 1940s and 1980s is difficult to tell without reference to the Communist Party and the broader progressive groups that it collaborated with. Although its success on the issue of combatting racism was sometimes limited, the impact of the CPGB on the British anti-racist movement was significant and this book will outline the main ways in which the movement interacted with and was affected by the Communist Party of Great Britain.

---

44   Virdee 2014, p. 3.
45   Virdee 2014, p. 89.

A Note on Methodology

This book is based primarily on the documentary evidence of the Communist Party of Great Britain, either published in the Party's various journals, newspapers or pamphlets or the unpublished archival documents located at the CPGB archives at the Labour History and Study Centre at the People's History Museum in Manchester. Other documents have been accessed at the Working Class Movement Library in Manchester, the Merseyside Records Office in Liverpool, the Modern Records Centre at Warwick University and the National Archives in London. These documents have been valuable resources in understanding the inner workings of the Communist Party, which, for the most part, maintained meticulous records. Especially in the case of anti-racist actions within the Communist Party, which remained limited to a small number of Party members, these archival documents have been able to divulge how the issue of racism was discussed within the CPGB and can be contrasted with the official, published views of the CPGB on this issue. The arguments in this book are therefore based primarily on the Party's publications and its internal documentation, which provides a contemporary, although not complete, account of the Communist Party's anti-racist activities.

The book acknowledges that the reliance upon published and unpublished documents has meant that many people who are the subjects of study in this book, primarily the black worker, the unemployed youth, the local anti-racist campaigner, are, more or less, 'silent'. Their voices are not publicised in the mainstream press, CPGB literature, labour movement documents or, in some cases, by the traditional organisations (and publications) of the black communities. As the book will demonstrate, this is one of the reasons for the disillusionment of black people with the traditional organs of the white labour movement and this inability to be 'heard' is a contributing factor for the rise in autonomous black politics. Their lack of a publicised voice has meant that others, such as the white left or black activist journalists, have often claimed to have spoken for all of Britain's black population. Particularly the political and social actions undertaken by black people have been construed as either signs of an emerging class consciousness or as manifestations of ethnic-based politics.[46] This book recognises that these actions can be categorised neither by class nor by ethnicity exclusively, and that in the history of British Communism and the politics of 'race', the intersecting notions of class and ethnicity (as well as gender and sexuality) could not be easily reconciled and competed for primary attention.

---

46   See Smith 2010, pp. 18–33.

There also needs to be clarification of some terms used within this book. The term 'black' is used in this book to describe both Afro-Caribbeans and Asians as, in most literature from the period studied, this is the term used, although it is recognised that the use of this term does not allude to a homogenous community between non-white Britons. Authors such as Peter Fryer and Ron Ramdin have used the term 'black' to describe all non-white Britons in their histories of black people in Britain.[47] The term is also used to describe a political definition of Afro-Asian unity in the contemporary literature in response to the racism of white British society, which seemed to regard 'the racial characteristics of both "Paki" and "nigger" as being equally worthy of hatred'.[48] Kalbir Shukra's quote seems an apt explanation of the usage of the term in this book: 'I retain "black" not to bestow any authority upon it, but because it is the term most commonly preferred by those who were the focus of this project'.[49] In CPGB literature, the term 'coloured' was preferred in the 1950s and up until the mid-1960s, before 'black' became common usage in the 1970s. In the 1981 CPGB Discussion Pack, *Power & Prejudice = Racism*, co-written by National Race Relations Committee member and sociologist Gideon Ben-Tovim, it was acknowledged that the terms 'black' and 'white' were 'biologically inaccurate' and it was 'for social-political reasons that we use the terms'.[50] For the CPGB, the term 'black' was used to denote 'all those who are victims of Britain's main form of racism today'.[51]

Following this, the use of the terms 'black community' or 'black communities' does not assume that the entire black population of Britain is a homogenous whole or can speak with one voice. David Renton has claimed that the main purpose of the term has been 'to provide the representatives of the state with an excuse for their failure to win the trust of all sections of the urban poor'.[52] This is not the case in this book, but refers to the common experience of nearly all non-white immigrants in Britain, as described by A. Sivanandan, 'created in the postwar years by a culture of resistance to racism in the factories and the neighbourhoods of the inner cities to which the Afro-Caribbeans and Asians had been condemned to work and live'.[53] Located in 'the same ghetto', Sivanandan states that Afro-Caribbeans and Asians had 'found common cause against a racism

---

47   See Fryer 1984; Ramdin 1987.
48   Gilroy 2002, p. 36.
49   Shukra 1998, p. 125.
50   CPGB, *Power & Prejudice = Racism*, Unit 1, p. 2.
51   Ibid.
52   Renton 2006, p. xi.
53   Sivanandan 1985, p. 2.

that denied them their basic needs ... and brought them up against racist landlords, racist teachers, racist social workers and racist policemen'.[54] The common problems and interests of the black people in Britain 'led to a common
culture of resistance' and what Sivanandan calls 'a community'.[55] These black
communities of the 1960s and 1970s were defined by their struggle for political
recognition and a political voice, as well as oppression by the capitalist state
system, which was experienced by nearly all black people in postwar Britain,
but this book recognises that there were many different experiences in different ethnic groups, classes, ages and localities within these wider communities.
The Communist Party stated that the term had become common usage in Britain 'at precisely the time in our history when local government changes and
changes in patterns of work have broken up groups of people who saw themselves as groups' as the term 'pulls emotional chords of warmth, humanity and
closeness'.[56] Following the same argument as Sivanandan, the Party argued that
black people in Britain were '[f]aced with a common oppression' and formed
organisations 'to support black people living near each other'.[57] 'In this sense',
the Party recognised, 'a black community exists'.[58]

The terms 'racialism' and 'racism' are both used when quoting from contemporary Communist Party literature. The term 'racialism' was used almost
exclusively in CPGB literature up until the early 1970s, when the term 'racism'
became more common, primarily coming from the American influence of
black power. Some have made a distinction between the two terms. Kum-Kum
Bhavnani outlined in a 1982 article in Spare Rib that 'racism' referred to the
'institutionalised practices and patterns which have the overall effect of developing the system which places Black people at a disadvantage', while 'racialism' referred to 'individual acts of discrimination that many people carry out in
an attempt to "put down" and harass and humiliate Black people'.[59] In a letter to Marxism Today in 1986, a reader made the distinction between 'racism',
referring to 'a belief that there are significant distinctions (whether moral,
intellectual and cultural) between races' and 'racialism', referring to the belief
that these perceived differences 'provide adequate grounds for different treatment'.[60] However, this book makes no distinction between the two, as it is

---

54   Ibid.
55   Ibid.
56   CPGB, Power & Prejudice = Racism, Unit 1, p. 3.
57   Ibid.
58   Ibid.
59   Bhavnani 1982, p. 49.
60   'Letters', Marxism Today, September 1986, p. 43.

difficult to differentiate between the various degrees of intent and perpetration of racial discrimination and racist ideology within British society. Therefore the term 'racism' is used throughout this book and 'racialism' is only used when quoting directly from contemporary sources. This point was also raised by the CPGB in *Power & Prejudice = Racism*, acknowledging that 'some analysts distinguish between *racism* as the theory and *racialism* as the practice', but declared that 'the two are usually connected and so we prefer to use the single term racism'.[61]

Book Structure

This book is separated into five chapters that examine the history of the Communist Party's anti-racist activism and its relationship with Britain's black communities between the late 1940s and early 1980s. Chapter 1 looks at the period from 1945 to 1960, which was arguably the first high point of the Party's anti-racist activism. Tied closely to the Party's anti-colonial programme of the inter-war period, the Communist Party openly advocated for decolonisation during this period and saw migrants from the colonies arriving in Britain as 'brothers in the fight for a better life'[62] – fighting the common enemies of imperialism and capitalism. Many colonial workers who came to Britain were attracted to the Communist Party as it was one of the few political organisations that promoted combating racial discrimination and welcomed immigrant members. However, the Party's anti-racist programme was seen through the prism of anti-colonialism and many of the Party's initial black membership felt sidelined in the 1950s, so that when the Party started to lose its members after the events of 1956, many black members left at the same time.

Chapter 2 follows on from this mass exodus of people from the Communist Party and explores how the Party sought to build itself in the 1960s as a 'mass party', which helped to attract a wide range of people (including a considerable number of young people). With this broader recruitment pool came an enthusiasm for the newer political movements that the Communist Party had not previously contended with (such as the students' movement, women's liberation, black power and progressive youth culture), which challenged the centrality of the industrial trade unionist base it had developed over the last three decades. The chapter shows that until the mid- to late 1960s, the CPGB was

---

61   CPGB, *Power & Prejudice = Racism*, Unit 1, p. 2.

62   CPGB, *Brothers in the Fight for a Better Life*, 1954, London: CPGB pamphlet, p. 1.

still a significant player in the anti-racist movement, but its activism was heavily tied to the Labour left and the trade union movement, and a number of younger activists (particularly black activists) were deterred by this, forming new (and sometimes more militant) organisations. As well as its apprehension towards the radical black power groups, the challenge the Party faced within the anti-racist movement in the 1960s was highlighted by the lack of consensus over how to fight back against the popular support for racist Tory Enoch Powell, and this episode concludes the chapter, depicting a Party more comfortable organising militant trade union activities than helping grassroots actions against racism.

Chapter 3 focuses on the period of the early to mid-1970s when the Party was experiencing its 'Indian Summer'[63] as the labour movement fought the Heath government over the Industrial Relations Act and other collective bargaining matters, eventually leading to the fall of the Conservatives in February 1974. But while the labour movement was greatly mobilised to fight the government over its industrial relations policy, this chapter shows that it was difficult to mobilise the same kind of enthusiasm to fight the highly discriminatory Immigration Act 1971 or combat the racial discrimination endured by black workers in many workplaces. The chapter examines two infamous episodes where the trade unions failed to assist its black workers when they decided to strike over issues of racial discrimination and exploitation, the strikes at Mansfield Hosiery Mills in 1972 and Imperial Typewriters in 1974. Although the CPGB still represented the more radical end of the labour movement and was particularly influential in organisations such as the Indian Workers Association, it was blamed for its alleged inertia over confronting racism within the trade unions. For many it seemed that the labour movement only started to take the issue of racism seriously when the National Front started to emerge as a significant political threat in mid-1970s. To its credit, the Communist Party took the threat of the NF very seriously and evoked its anti-fascist legacy, but was unable to spearhead the anti-fascist movement on a national scale like it had in the 1930s. The chapter looks at the early attempts to build the anti-fascist response to the NF in the 1970s, and the Party's role within this, setting the scene for the rise of the Anti-Nazi League portrayed in Chapter 4.

Chapter 4 charts the escalation of the anti-fascist movement in the late 1970s as the economic and political crises deepened and the National Front changed its tactics from attempting to build an electoral presence to one of 'controlling the streets'. This increased NF presence on the streets led to a rise in cases of racial harassment and racial violence (including murder) that brought two

---

63   Thompson 1992, p. 160.

organisations into being – the Anti-Nazi League and the Asian Youth Movements, both of which attracted a new wave of radical youth that avoided the Communist Party. Between 1974 and 1977, the CPGB and the IS/SWP had differed on whether the movement should confront the NF (and the police) on the streets, as demonstrated by the 'Battle of Lewisham' in August 1977, but by 1978, the Communist Party was supportive of the ANL, a co-initiative between the SWP and the Labour left. On the other hand, the AYMs were apprehensive towards the 'white left' who were sympathetic to each other's causes, but the AYMs were wary of the SWP or the CPGB (or the IMG) taking over the agenda. At the same time, a long-running strike by Asian workers was happening in North West London at Grunwick, which saw the trade union movement mobilise behind the initial strike and promote solidarity between black and white workers in the face of a very ideologically-minded business owner, supported by the pre-Thatcherite wing of the Conservatives and other neo-liberals. This chapter looks at the possible zenith of the anti-racist movement in that period with the solidarity expressed at Grunwick and the successful campaign against the National Front in the lead up to the 1979 election. However, the chapter also notes that there were large negatives that occurred during this as well that undermined the achievements of the anti-racist/anti-fascist movement – the failure of the Grunwick strike, the election of Margaret Thatcher as the Prime Minister and the death of Blair Peach at the hands of the police during an anti-fascist counter-demonstration in April 1979. In the background of this, the chapter also outlines the internal debates that the Communist Party was having over its strategy and this led to significant divisions over its role within the anti-racist movement and its broader interaction with progressive social movements, which fed into much larger schisms in the 1980s.

Chapter 5 concludes the book, taking the story from the 1979 electoral victory by Thatcher into the mid-1980s, where the Communist Party has been internally wounded by a series of splits by rival factions and externally attacked by the Thatcherite assault on the trade unions and other progressive movements. The chapter examines how, two years after the 'victorious' expression of solidarity between black and white workers at Grunwick and through the ANL, the black communities felt increasingly isolated and bearing the brunt of Thatcher's early assaults on the welfare state, leading to rioting by black (and white) youth across Britain in 1981. The Communist Party, like the rest of the British left, were caught out by this wave of rebellion across the country and, although they were in no way responsible for these outbreaks of disorder, tried (unsuccessfully) to harness them in the aftermath. After the redrafting of *The British Road to Socialism* in 1977, there were some within the Party who saw that the way in which the 'broad democratic alliance' could be incorporated into the anti-racist movement was by working through the local (usually Labour Party led) councils. This building of alliances between various social movements and the Labour left at council level was described as 'local' or 'municipal socialism',[64] and the anti-racist programmes enacted by local councils in London, Manchester, Sheffield, Liverpool and Bradford (amongst other places) was disparagingly referred to as 'municipal anti-racism' by critics such as Paul Gilroy.[65] Like other criticisms of those attached to the journal *Marxism Today* and the Eurocommunist influences of the 'broad democratic alliance', municipal anti-racism was criticised for being focused on the ideological and individual aspects of racism and unwilling to challenge the underlying structural reasons for racial discrimination and inequality, as well as being reformist and bound to the structures of the state. However, it was difficult for the Communist Party to offer much more as an organisation, as the splits deepened in 1983 (with the *Morning Star* breaking away from the Party after a disastrous National Congress at the end of that year), leaving individual CPGB members to be involved in anti-racist initiatives – often as members of broad-based progressive organisations – but there was minimal reward for the CPGB from this. Although it had been an influential part of the anti-racist, anti-fascist and anti-colonial movements in Britain since the 1920s, by the mid- to late 1980s, the Party had almost faded into irrelevancy.

Through these chapters, it is hoped that a better understanding can be achieved of the impact that the Communist Party of Great Britain had upon anti-racist politics in Britain from the 1940s to the 1980s. This is important because many of the significant individuals and organisations involved in the anti-racist movement had some link (in one way or another) to the CPGB and the role of the CPGB has often been minimised in other accounts of British anti-racism. But the book also shows that in tandem with the wider fortunes of the Party, its role as part of the anti-racist movement diminished over the four decades, despite a significant section of the Party encouraging a re-evaluation of the relationship between the CPGB and the new social movements, including the anti-racist movement. The history of the CPGB's anti-racist activism shows that taking the issue of racism seriously often challenged its viewpoint of the centrality of class to its political activity and presented the difficulty of getting many white workers within the labour movement to recognise the importance of combating racism. Despite the official statements of leftist organisations and the trade unions, the lack of recognition by the labour movement of the

---

64   Payling 2014, p. 604.
65   Gilroy 2002, pp. 172–99.

problems facing black workers led to a divide between the left, including the Communist Party, and black activists. This divide, while it hindered practical political action from occurring in the 1970s and 1980s, also led to the development of thinkers from a new post-colonial and post-Marxist left proposing an 'intersectional' or 'hybrid' approach that transcended the need for either class or ethnicity (or sexuality or gender) to be considered the primary ground for struggle and recognised that the political agendas of individuals was determined, in a non-hierarchical manner, by a series of oppressions, rather than the old CPGB adage of 'class before race'.

The End of Empire and the *Windrush* Moment, 1945–60

The late 1940s were a promising time for the Communist Party of Great Britain, but while there was much to be confident about, the early postwar period also highlighted the obstacles ahead for the Party. The Communist Party came out of the Second World War with membership numbers near their peak and its best electoral result ever – two MPs elected to the House of Commons (Phil Piratin in Stepney and Mile End and Willie Gallacher in West Fife) and over 200 councillors in municipal elections.[1] The postwar welfare state plan set out by the Labour government seemed to indicate that the ideals of social redistribution and nationalisation were popular amongst the British public and possibly favourable conditions for the promotion of socialism and Marxism. In the colonial sphere, the British imperial project had been severely weakened by the War and talk of self-government and colonial independence seemed more and more realistic.

However, at the same time, the beginnings of the Cold War signalled turbulent times ahead for the CPGB. The occupation of Eastern Europe and the actions of the Stalin regime, which were for the most part defended (if not celebrated) by the CPGB, fostered anti-Communist sentiment within Britain at many different levels, which was compounded by a fear that Communists were causing the British Empire (now Commonwealth) to fall apart, as seen with the Malayan emergency. Two of the Communist Party's 'natural' allies, the Labour Party and the trade unions, witnessed anti-Communist 'witch hunts' occur within their ranks, often encouraged by the leadership of Labour and the unions.

By the 1950s, the domestic political situation had stabilised and the window for the push towards socialism looked to be shutting as the 1951 General Election ushered in 13 years of Conservative rule. The Cold War and the threat of nuclear war isolated the Communists from other sections of British society and exacerbated the ideological constraints that the Party worked under, inspired by the zig-zagging influence of Moscow. The lowest period for the CPGB came in 1956, when Nikita Khrushchev (Stalin's eventual suc-

---

1 Callaghan 2003, p. 185.

cessor as General Secretary of the Communist Party of the Soviet Union) delivered a 'secret speech' at the 20th Congress of the CPSU that denounced the crimes of the Stalin era and the cult of personality that surrounded Stalin. The refusal of the CPGB leadership to discuss the Party's uncritical support of the Soviet Union during the Stalin era caused much resentment in the Party and led to internal dissent and resignations. The Soviet invasion of Hungary in October 1956 worsened the situation for the international Communist movement and the CPGB's support of the invasion led to a mass exodus from the Party, with over 8,000 members leaving between February 1956 and February 1958.

Despite this, one area where the CPGB was enthusiastic and looked likely to make in-roads was the anti-colonial struggle, inspired by the anti-colonial rebellions in South-East Asia, the granting of independence to India and the Chinese Revolution. After the Party's poor results in a by-election in St Pancras North in 1949, Harry Pollitt was alleged to have commented, 'We may not have won St Pancras, but we've got China'.[2] The anti-colonial struggle also had a domestic dimension for the Communist Party in the era of decolonisation, as thousands of Commonwealth migrants flocked to the British shores, with many having been involved in trade union and anti-colonial politics in their home countries. The CPGB was deemed to be the 'natural home' for many of these migrant workers and was one of the few political organisations that attempted to foster connections with the migrant communities.

The Communist Party's Anti-colonial Traditions

As a number of scholars have discussed, the CPGB had been heavily involved in anti-colonial activism since its inception in 1920.[3] As part of the Communist International (Comintern), as well as the party being at the epicentre of the largest imperial power at the time, the CPGB attempted to co-ordinate and promote anti-colonialism and solidarity with national liberation movements throughout the British Empire. Throughout the interwar period, the focus of the Party's anti-colonial activism was India, with significant resources and personnel sent to India, along with extra assistance from the Soviet Union and the Comintern in Berlin, to help the communist movement on the sub-continent, with the Communist Party of India founded in 1925. At one stage, this led to

---

2 Macleod 1997, p. 16.
3 Callaghan 1995, pp. 4–22; Sherwood 1996, pp. 137–63; Callaghan 1997–8, pp. 513–25.

the imprisonment of several British and Indian anti-colonial activists, including one CPGB member, by the British authorities in 1929, known as the Meerut
Conspiracy Trial.[4]

In the 'Third Period' (roughly between 1928 and 1934), when the Comintern
encouraged greater working-class militancy and non-co-operation with social-
democratic parties, it also promoted stronger anti-colonial activism (but not
with 'bourgeois' elements of the national liberation movements). The rhetoric
of the 'Class Against Class' position of the Comintern was highly motivating
for many communists worldwide – initiatives such as the League Against
Imperialism (LAI) and the International Trade Union Committee of Negro
Workers (ITUCNW) were established, but the practical effect that it had upon
most Communist Parties (including those in the colonies and dominions) was,
overall, quite negative. As Matthew Worley has noted:

> Far from advancing the communist cause, it has been argued that the
> policies of the Third Period threw the movement into disrepair, with
> national parties being driven underground, marginalised within their
> respective labour movements, or shattered by a mixture of internal dis-
> pute, worker disinterest and often bloody repression.[5]

The ITUCNW was able to mobilise many black communists in the United States,
the Caribbean and Africa, but was undermined by a lack of investment by
the Comintern in the organisation and the general sectarianism of the era.
Hakim Adi argues that the ITUCNW pursued a 'Pan-Africanist approach' in
uniting black workers from across the globe, but, as part of the sectarianism
of the Third Period, were opposed to working with the other Pan-African
groups that followed the teaching of Marcus Garvey.[6] Similar problems befell
the League Against Imperialism, set up in 1927 to build links between the
international communist movement and the anti-colonial movements that
were beginning to emerge in the interwar period. Frederik Petersson shows that
by 1933, intra-party rivalries and shifting directives from Moscow had derailed
the LAI and was effectively wound up when its base in Berlin was threatened
by the installation of the Nazi government (although it existed on paper until

---

4   See articles on the Meerut trial by Ali Raza, Michele L. Louro, Carolien Stolte, Franziska Roy
    and Benjamin Zacharia in the special issue of *Comparative Studies of South Asia, Africa and
    the Middle East*, 2013, 33, no. 3: 210–377.
5   Worley 2004, p. 2.
6   Adi 2013, p. xxii.

1937).[7] The sectarianism of the 'Third Period' also affected the CPGB, both in its domestic and international work, but as John Callaghan has argued, the Party still managed to have a robust anti-colonial programme during a politically difficult time.[8]

In 1935, the Seventh Congress of the Comintern pronounced a new direction for the international communist movement and the position of 'Class Against Class' was replaced by the Popular Front, which directed communists to work with other progressive bourgeois and social-democratic forces against fascism and war.[9] Some scholars, such as Neil Redfern, have claimed this greatly hindered the anti-colonial movements as the Western Communist Parties, particularly the CPGB, were encouraged to align themselves with the British bourgeoisie, who were predominantly pro-empire, and broke the anti-colonial alliances built during the 1920s.[10]

However, by the end of the Second World War, the situation had changed dramatically and the national liberation movements across Africa and Asia were buoyed by the precarious position in which the European powers found themselves in the late 1940s. Despite this, some of the Western Communist Parties still abided by the non-confrontational Popular Front outlook adopted over the last decade, disparagingly referred to as 'Browderism' after the position taken by the CPUSA's General Secretary Earl Browder in the early 1940s.[11] However, communists in other parts of the world, primarily in Asia, were forging ahead and heavily involved in national liberation movements in countries such as China, Korea, India, Indonesia, Indochina and Malaya. This policy of confrontation was heightened in 1947 when the Soviets announced the 'two camps' thesis,[12] which claimed that there were irreconcilable differences between the imperialist/capitalist Western bloc and the anti-imperialist/communist Soviet bloc. This hostile approach by the Soviets contributed to the outbreak of the Cold War, which pushed most Communist Parties to the left, even though the CPGB was far less revolutionary in this period (working at this time towards developing the democratic path to socialism thesis outlined in *The British Road to Socialism*) than other Western communists. Some within the na-

---

7   Petersson 2014, pp. 49–71.
8   Callaghan 1995, pp. 18–19.
9   Dimitrov 1945, *The United Front Against Fascism: Speeches at the Seventh Congress of the Communist International*, Sydney: CPA pamphlet.
10   Redfern 2004, pp. 117–35. For an alternative view, see Branson 1985, pp. 121–4.
11   See Branson 1997, pp. 85–7; Redfern 2002, pp. 360–80.
12   See Zhdanov, 'Report to the Conference of the Nine Parties', *World News and Views*, 1 November 1947, pp. 493–502.

tional liberation movements in the colonies, such as in India, alongside some other Communist Parties, such as the Australian Communist Party, declared that this approach weakened the British party's anti-colonial resolve.[13] Although the CPGB insisted that anti-colonial politics was central to its programme and that 'as the Party in the ruling centre of the Empire', it held 'the greatest responsibility ... to combat the vicious and harmful policies of imperialism'.[14]

The CPGB and the Era of Decolonisation

The end of the Second World War saw the former colonial powers, such as Britain and France, severely weakened and the balance of power repositioned between Moscow and Washington. The Communist Party of Great Britain, boosted by the popularity that it enjoyed during the Second World War, entered the postwar period with great optimism and had high expectations for the colonial struggles in the wake of a weakened British Empire. As Britain entered the postwar period in a 'devastated economic state', it seemed that the British government 'did not have sufficient manpower and economic resources for a world role', with its administrative responsibilities in foreign countries a severe restraint upon the country.[15] The Communist Party was initially enthusiastic to work with the Labour government under Prime Minister Clement Atlee to implement socialistic policies (such as nationalisation of key industries and the establishment of the welfare state), and between 1945 and 1947, the Party seemed to suggest that Labour with Communist support had established the foundations of socialism in Britain. The problem was that while the CPGB was supportive of many of Labour's domestic policies, Britain's foreign policy saw the maintenance of empire in places like Malaya, close ties with the United States (and the joining of NATO) and intervention in the Greek civil war on the side of the Royalists.

By 1947, the Party was becoming disillusioned with the Labour government in the domestic sphere, particularly as Chancellor Sir Stafford Cripps called for

---

13   See the correspondence between the Communist Party of Australia and the British Party in the CPGB archives, CP/CENT/INT/34/02, LHASC, as well as 'Exchange of letters between the Australian and the British Communist Parties', *World News and Views*, 31 July 1948, pp. 332–9.

14   Dutt, 'Political Report to the Conference of the Communist Parties of the British Empire', in CPGB, *We Speak for Freedom*, 1947, London: CPGB pamphlet, p. 24.

15   Ovendale 1984, p. 3.

the trade unions to consider wage freezes and sections of the Labour Party, as well as the trade unions, began to publicly advocate for the removal of communists from the labour movement. The Party, which had held out on strike activity during the War and early postwar era, was now agitating for a more confrontational stance against the government. This new militancy was also partially inspired by the hostilities arising on the international stage between the West and the Soviets. In September 1947, the Soviets founded the Communist Information Bureau (known as the Cominform) and Andrei Zhdanov gave a speech in Poland declaring that the world now fell into two camps, 'the imperialist and anti-democratic on the one hand and the anti-imperialist and democratic on the other'.[16] Zhdanov argued that the USA, Britain and France were the leading forces of the imperialist camp, supported by other colonial powers (such as Belgium and the Netherlands) and 'reactionary anti-democratic regimes' (such as Greece and Turkey), with the 'basic aim of the imperialist camp' being:

> the strengthening of imperialism, the preparation of a new imperialist war, the struggle against Socialism and democracy and all-round support for reactionary pro-Fascist regimes and movements.[17]

The Soviet Union and the Eastern Bloc made up the 'anti-imperialist and anti-Fascist' camp, with Indonesia and Vietnam (as countries undergoing anti-colonial struggle) also supposedly belonging to the camp and Zhdanov claiming that India, Egypt and Syria also sympathised with the anti-imperialist camp.[18] Claiming the support of workers' and anti-colonial movements across the globe, Zhdanov stated that the aim of the anti-imperialist camp was 'the struggle against the threat of new wars and imperialist expansion, the consolidation of democracy and the elimination of the remnants of Fascism'.[19]

The Cominform was to guide the direction of the international communist movement through the production of a regular bulletin, *For a Lasting Peace, For a People's Democracy*, but no *formal* orders were to be given by the Cominform to individual Communist Parties, unlike the situation of the Communist International in the interwar period. As a gesture towards the Allies during the Second World War, the Communist International had been dissolved in 1943, and after this dissolution the Communist Party in each country was offi-

---

16   Zhdanov, 'Report to the Conference of the Nine Parties', p. 495.
17   Ibid.
18   Ibid.
19   Ibid.

cially an independent organisation, with no *direct* links to Moscow (although many scholars have argued that the leadership of Communist Parties, such as the CPGB, internalised their adherence to Moscow, so that only issuances from the Cominform or the Soviet Union were necessary for the 'correct line' to be interpreted). Outside of the Eastern Bloc and Yugoslavia, only the mass Communist Parties of Italy and France were members of the Cominform, with Britain dependent on the PCF for Cominform communiques. This meant that anti-colonial movements were not directly in touch with the Soviet Union, with the Communist Party of China taking a more active role in organising national liberation movements in Asia (where decolonisation was advancing the quickest) and the Communist Parties in Britain and France acting as guiding forces for anti-colonial movements in their respective empires.

Without the Comintern providing a direct link to the independence struggles, the CPGB became an influential leader for various anti-colonial organisations across Asia, Africa and the Middle East. These organisations 'acquired the habit of looking to London for guidance' and 'in the absence of direct links with Moscow, the CPGB remained the nearest authoritative resource'.[20] For example, in 1952, the newly reformed South African Communist Party requested discussion for the 'establishment of contacts and rendering of support' from the Soviet Union through the CPGB and the Soviet Embassy in London.[21] However, Rajani Palme Dutt, as a leading theoretician on anti-colonialism within the Party and connected to the Party's International Department, complained that the Party was 'frequently approached for advice on matters on which it lacked the necessary authority or expertise' and which left the CPGB vulnerable to accusations of 'political naivety and ignorance' by their colonial allies.[22] For the Communist Party, its directives on anti-colonial matters were handled by the International Department and the focus of this department in the late 1940s and 1950s was on liaising with national liberation movements across the British Commonwealth, as well as promoting the importance of anti-colonialism to the British labour movement. Several key members of the CPGB's International Department, such as Jack Woddis, Kay Beauchamp, Idris Cox and Tony Gilbert, were also involved in the London Area Council of the Movement for Colonial Freedom (MCF), started by Labour MP Fenner Brockway in 1954, which publicised the anti-colonial campaign to the Labour Party and the trade unions.

As chief theoretician of the Party and an expert on anti-colonial affairs, Dutt was able to shape the outlook of the Communist Party on anti-colonialism and

---

20   Callaghan 1994, p. 256.
21   Shubin 1999, pp. 34–5.
22   Callaghan 1994, p. 256; Sherwood 1999, p. 62.

how it related to the wider struggle for socialism in Britain. In 1947, Dutt published his treatise on the postwar situation in the British Empire, *Britain's Crisis of Empire*. Envisaging that Britain was on the verge of economic crisis, he wrote that the cause of this crisis was '*the parasitic metropolis of a world empire*' and that the solution could not be separated from the 'central necessity to advance a new non-imperialist basis'.[23] The political and economic demands that colonial occupation created for Britain – Dutt noted that between the end of 1945 and the summer of 1953, the net deficit on the balance of payments had been £471 million, while overseas military expenditure had been £1,238 million[24] – was part of a wider viewpoint of the burgeoning collapse of monopoly capitalism,[25] which the CPGB predicted throughout the late 1940s and 1950s. Britain had to 'recognise the new world situation and carry through a corresponding radical transformation of policy', such as abandoning imperialism, granting independence, disengage in wars and rearmament and 'reconstruct Britain's economy on a non-imperialist basis', or Dutt predicted that Britain would attempt 'ever more desperately to endeavour to maintain and shore up the crumbling imperialist basis', which would further Britain's economic decline.[26] For Dutt, 'the cause of the colonial peoples is to-day more than ever indissolubly linked with the cause of the working class and of socialism in Britain'.[27] As the Communist Party had declared in their 1946 resolution on the colonial question, 'a break with imperialism and the adoption of a Socialist policy towards the colonies will create the most favourable conditions for the advance towards Socialism in this country'.[28]

In the era of postwar decolonisation, the Communist Party's policy was that for the 'further advance of British industry and standard of living', Britain, hopefully under a socialist form of government, had to enter a 'new, voluntary, fraternal association' with the former colonies, 'coming together with equal rights for *their mutual benefit* [emphasis added], exchanging their products on the basis of value for value and without exploitation'.[29] This was based on the premise, developed during the interwar period, that Britain, if free of its colonies, would still require raw materials and goods from its former colonial territories and the assumption that these former colonies would want to

23   Dutt 1957, p. 424; p. 15, original emphasis.
24   Dutt, 'Britain and the Colonies', *World News*, 2 January 1954, p. 10.
25   Callaghan 1994, pp. 237–8.
26   Dutt 1957, p. 13.
27   Dutt 1957, p. 415.
28   'The Colonial Resolution', 1946, in CPGB archives, CP/CENT/CONG/05/07, LHASC.
29   Mahon 1953, p. 223.

be involved in trade with its former colonial power and become consumers of British-made goods. A 1938 pamphlet by J.R. Campbell stated that granting self-determination to the colonies 'would not deprive the British workers' government of the possibility of obtaining colonial food-stuffs, and raw materials in exchange for British manufactured products',[30] while a 1933 book by Ralph Fox stated:

> Not only would the granting of freedom to the Colonies mean that every factory in England would be kept busy supplying them with textiles and articles of consumption, but it would also mean that the industrialisation of these countries would for many generations keep British heavy industry working to capacity.[31]

This assumption that a colonial-like relationship between Britain and its former colonies would continue after decolonisation had occurred was entrenched in the International Department's outlook throughout the 1940s and was reiterated in the first version of *The British Road to Socialism* in 1951. But as will be explored later in this chapter, it became a point of contention between the Party leadership and the ethnic minority members of the Party that came to a head at the 1957 Special Congress.

Left Nationalism and the Postwar CPGB

One of the criticisms made of the Communist Party of Great Britain in the early postwar era, particularly by the Party's Trotskyist critics, is that during the Popular Front period and the Second World War, the CPGB draped itself too heavily in the Union Jack, with left nationalism overtaking its pre-Popular Front proletarian internationalism.[32] In 1943, the Communist International was wound up and each Communist Party was to determine its own national path to socialism. Since 1947, with the publication of the pamphlet *Looking Ahead* by the Party's General Secretary Harry Pollitt,[33] the CPGB had started to envisage a 'British road to socialism' that would be built upon the democratic and parliamentary structures that were unique to Britain, which was developed

---

30   Campbell, *Questions & Answers on Communism*, 1938, London: CPGB pamphlet, p. 12.
31   Fox 1933, p. 118.
32   Flewers 1995; Bornstein and Richardson 2007, pp. 20–56.
33   Pollitt, *Looking Ahead*, 1947, London: CPGB pamphlet.

throughout the late 1940s and became the Party's manifesto in 1951 with *The British Road to Socialism*.

During this period, the Party was keen to demonstrate its patriotic credentials. Even before the outbreak of the Cold War, it was eager to show that it was 'loyal' to Britain and was not merely an agent of Moscow. It also fed into an emerging anti-Americanism where the Party played up its fight for 'independence' from American imperialism.[34] In several major Party documents, the subject of 'communist patriotism' was discussed. In 1948, J.R. Campbell, editor of the CPGB's *Daily Worker* newspaper, spoke about this at the Party's 20th National Congress and remonstrated with critics for saying that the CPGB was 'not a British Party', writing:

> It is a queer kind of patriotism that bleats about the British Way of Life, but rejects the possibility of our great people, with their own skill, their own resources, discipline and working-class leadership, working out their own salvation in the modern world.[35]

To Campbell, patriotism was not about 'wrapping the Union Jack around oneself to conceal the dollar sign' or the 'desire to oppress others', but a 'willingness to work for the freedom, welfare and happiness of the common people of this land', and under this definition of patriotism, the Party claimed 'to be the patriotic British Party above all others'.[36] Harry Pollitt, in a 1952 pamphlet titled *Britain Arise*, made a similar appeal to 'all patriots and lovers of peace in Britain' and declared that 'Britain can be great, strong and independent once the American shackles are broken and friendly relations established with all peace-loving countries'.[37] It seemed, as Ian Birchall has argued, that 'American – not British – imperialism was the main enemy'.[38]

This patriotic appeal, while promoting national liberation in the colonies, sometimes sent out mixed messages about the Party's allegiances and priorities in building a socialist Britain. In trying to allay the fears of working-class Britons who had some attachment to the traditional British Empire, the Communist Party at times downplayed the importance of the anti-colonial struggle, which then disheartened Party members from the colonies. The prime example of

---

34   See Kartun, *America – Go Home!*, 1951, London: CPGB pamphlet; Callaghan 1994, pp. 239–42.

35   Campbell, *A Socialist Solution for the Crisis*, 1948, London: CPGB pamphlet, p. 8.

36   Campbell, *A Socialist Solution for the Crisis*, p. 9.

37   Pollitt, *Britain Arise*, 1952, London: CPGB pamphlet, p. 10; p. 13.

38   Birchall 2014, p. 191.

this was in the section on national independence in the 1951 edition of the
Party's postwar programme, *The British Road to Socialism*, which stated:

> The enemies of Communism declare that the Communist Party, by under-
> hand subversive means, is aiming at the destruction of Britain and the
> British Empire. But it is a lie, because it is precisely the Tories and the
> Labour leaders who are doing this by their policy of armed repression and
> colonial exploitation.[39]

There is no doubt that the Party believed in rejuvenating Britain's socio-economic conditions, but the claim that it did not *aim* for the destruction of the
British Empire (despite the criticisms that it failed to take productive actions
to support this aim) is refuted by its activities and statements made since the
1920s.

The Response of the Communist Party to Commonwealth Migration

The Communist Party was one of the few political organisations that openly
welcomed Commonwealth migrants into Britain in the late 1940s and throughout the 1950s. In *Staying Power*, his pioneering 1984 work on the history of
Britain's black population, Peter Fryer wrote that in the late 1940s, 'the door
stood open' for those coming from the Commonwealth (particularly from the
West Indies and West Africa at this point) as the British economy, 'short of
labour, needed these willing hands'.[40] In 1948, when the ss *Empire Windrush*
landed with over 490 West Indian migrants at Tilbury, Fryer was a reporter for
the *Daily Worker* and proclaimed that 'five hundred pairs of willing hands' had
now arrived in Britain, 'every one of whom was eager to work'.[41] The Communist Party welcomed these immigrants, emphasising that the reason they left was
'unemployment and low wages' back in the Caribbean[42] and that the reason
these immigrants had come to Britain was 'because life has become impossible
for them in their own country – after 300 years under British rule'.[43] In a follow-
up article written a fortnight later, Fryer positively wrote that 'all but 30 of these

---

39   CPGB, *The British Road to Socialism*, 1951, London: CPGB pamphlet, p. 11.
40   Fryer 1984, p. 372.
41   *Daily Worker*, 23 June 1948.
42   Ibid.
43   Bolsover, *No Colour Bar in Britain*, 1955, London: CPGB pamphlet, p. 4.

[immigrants had] found work'.[44] Fryer did recognise that 'some Jamaicans have, it is true, come up against colour prejudice', although he depicted that it was experienced 'from a café proprietor here, a landlady there' and not the widespread prejudice against black people that Fryer wrote of in his later history.[45]

By the mid-1950s, the Communist Party acknowledged that racial discrimination was evident in Britain, but for the most part, this was attributed to a 'prejudiced, stupid and sometimes vicious minority', identified as 'fascists', 'Tories and employers' and 'Leaders of the Government'.[46] This largely absolved the working class from acts of racial discrimination as 'race prejudice is a conscious part of the policy of the most reactionary sections of British capitalism'.[47] However, the Party did admit that 'amongst a minority of workers, some racial feelings still exist'.[48] In the 1955 pamphlet, *No Colour Bar in Britain*, the CPGB welcomed immigration from the Commonwealth, claiming that the arrival of 'colonial workers' was a 'great opportunity before British working people'.[49] In a declaration of CPGB policy, the pamphlet stated that the 'attitude of the Communist Party is clear … It welcomes the arrival of colonial immigrants'.[50] The Party stressed that 'colonial people are British subjects' and were entitled to enter Britain freely.[51] This free movement of persons seeking employment within the Commonwealth was something that the CPGB wished to keep intact, although this was to be along the lines of the voluntary relationship between Britain and the former colonies, as mentioned above. For immigrants from outside the Commonwealth, the Party's attitude was much more divisive, which can be seen with the CPGB's campaign against Polish miners in 1946.

The Campaign Against Polish Resettlement

At the end of the Second World War, around 100,000 displaced Poles travelled to Britain in the early postwar years, with the UK receiving the second largest

---

44   *Daily Worker*, 14 July 1948.
45   Ibid.; Fryer 1984, p. 374.
46   Bolsover, *No Colour Bar in Britain*, p. 10.
47   Ibid.
48   CPGB, *Brothers in the Fight for a Better Life*, 1954, London: CPGB pamphlet, p. 11.
49   Bolsover, *No Colour Bar in Britain*, p. 3.
50   Bolsover, *No Colour Bar in Britain*, p. 11.
51   Bolsover, *No Colour Bar in Britain*, p. 10.

amount of 'Stalin's Poles' (as described by Paul Sendziuk)[52] after Germany and Austria.[53] This added to the over 100,000 soldiers from the Polish Armed Forces stationed in Britain at the end of the War, with many of these soldiers nominally under the control of anti-Soviet General W. Anders, who felt betrayed by Britain's capitulation to Stalin regarding the independence of Poland.[54] By the end of 1945, only 23,000 Poles stationed in the UK had expressed interest in returning to Poland and the Atlee government had promised that no Pole would be repatriated against their will,[55] so the British attempted to use the remaining Poles to address labour shortages in vital industries, such as the coal mines.

In May 1946, the Labour government announced the formation of the Polish Resettlement Corps, a 'noncombatant military unit ... in which Polish veterans were encouraged to enrol by promise of resettlement' to direct Polish workers into 'essential' industries, such as construction, agriculture and coal mining.[56] The TUC and various unions 'voiced suspicions about threats to jobs and conditions of employment', as well as the 'potential threat' to British working-class politics and culture posed by these European recruits.[57] The Communist Party was heavily involved in opposition to the migration and settlement of Poles and other Eastern Europeans in the late 1940s. As the polarisation of the Cold War began to take place, the CPGB greeted the establishment of the People's Democracies and was, in the words of socialist journalist Paul Foot, 'upset that anyone should not volunteer to enjoy the rigours of Stalinism in the Russian satellites of East Europe'.[58]

The Polish workers were labelled 'fascist Poles' and were treated with 'accustomed shabbiness and chauvinism' by the Party.[59] In the Parliamentary debate on the Polish Resettlement Bill in early 1947, the two MPs who opposed the bill were Phil Piratin and Willie Gallacher. Piratin declared that the Polish Resettlement Corps was 'an affront to the Polish government and a hindering of its progress', and a 'dangerous move for this country to maintain a body of men under a reactionary leadership'.[60] In a 1946 leaflet titled 'No British Jobs for Fas-

---

52   Sendziuk 2015, p. 41.
53   Edele 2015, p. 19.
54   See Anders 1981.
55   Conclusions of Cabinet Meeting, 20 November 1945, CAB 128/2/7, NA; Paul 1997, p. 68.
56   Paul 1997, p. 68.
57   Lunn 1999, p. 74.
58   Foot 1965, p. 118.
59   Pollitt, *No British Jobs for Fascist Poles*, 1946, London: CPGB flyer, in Working Class Movement Library, Manchester, Ref. 35/3, CPGB Leaflets; Foot 1965, p. 118.
60   *Hansard*, 12 February 1947, col. 428.

cist Poles', the CPGB claimed that 'at least a third' of the 160,000 Polish troops in Britain 'actually fought for Hitler', while 'the remainder are fascists who do not wish to return to their own country'.[61] The CPGB claimed that 'nearly 2 million organised British workers have expressed their opposition to the presence in this country of these Polish troops' and the Party proposed repatriating them to Poland where 'they should accept the democratic will of the majority of the people and work for the reconstruction of their own country'.[62]

Accusations of anti-Semitism and collaboration with the occupying German forces towards Anders's soldiers and those displaced persons who came to the UK after the War were not limited to the CPGB and the trade unions. Don Watson has shown that the UK Foreign Office had been receiving complaints about these exiled Poles since 1940 and this 'raised suspicions that there was something fascist, or at least politically dubious, about Poles who were unwilling to return to build their new nation'.[63] David Cesarani has suggested Eastern European and Baltic labour recruits suspected of collaboration were actively chosen because of their ardent anti-communism, while Linda McDowell has argued that in most cases, any suspicions were merely overlooked as they were seen as 'suitable' migrants, compared with Irish and Commonwealth migrants.[64] While anti-Semites and former Nazi collaborators may have made up a small part of those Polish (and other Eastern European) workers in the UK, the Communist Party viewed all migrants from places behind the 'Iron Curtain' as suspect and potentially dangerous.

As well as these 'political' objections, the Party press made other accusations towards the Poles, particularly the sexual threat of the Polish migrants to British women and the Poles taking vacant housing away from homeless Britons during a shortage of adequate housing. The *Daily Worker* accused Polish officers of fraternising with young girls at a Polish Army camp in Yorkshire, with the 'majority of the girls [being] between 14 and 18 years of age'.[65] A few months earlier, at the height of the Squatters Movement led by the CPGB,[66] the paper reported that Poles were being given accommodation at various camps, while

---

61   Pollitt, *No British Jobs for Fascist Poles*.

62   Ibid.

63   Watson 2014, p. 108. For further information on Polish collaboration with the Germans, see Friedrich 2005.

64   Cesarani 2001, pp. 143–4; p. 229; McDowell 2003, pp. 870–1.

65   *Daily Worker*, 16 December 1946.

66   For further information on the Squatters' Movement, see Hinton 1988, pp. 100–26; Branson 1997, pp. 118–28.

squatters were being fined and removed from housing.[67] Syd Abbott declared in the December 1946 issue of the *Communist Review*:

> if the Government would send home Anders and his Poles, many of them fascists, a further 265 camps occupied by 120,000 Polish troops, could be freed, and made available to house the people.[68]

These accusations were similar to the racist falsehoods that numerous people directed at Commonwealth migrants, which the Communists routinely refuted in their anti-racist activities.

The CPGB saw the Polish Resettlement Corps, with its ties to Anders, as an 'anti-Soviet [and] anti-democratic' force, whose presence in Britain was 'obviously insincere'.[69] While depicted by the British government and British industry as a solution to the postwar labour shortage, the Communist Party claimed that the Poles of the Resettlement Corps had no desire to 'be absorbed as loyal citizens of this country', but looked to 'use Britain as a temporary base from which to pursue, at some future date, an armed crusade against the U.S.S.R. and the new Poland'.[70] The *Daily Worker* quoted a statement by the Polish Embassy in London, saying that the resettlement of Poles was 'nothing but diplomatic eyewash', adding 'No sensible person … can understand why training for civilian jobs should be carried out according to units and arms'[71] – evidence for the Communist Party that Poles in Britain were organising resistance to the Polish government.

The Welsh miners' leader and member of the CPGB's Executive Committee, Arthur Horner, announced in 1945 that the Communist Party would 'not allow the importation of foreign – Polish, Italian, or even Irish – labour to stifle the demands of the British people to have decent conditions in British mines'.[72] In the 1946 leaflet, the Party declared that there was 'no room in Britain for fascists' and that there was 'no reason why British jobs should be given to these Poles'.[73] In her biography of Horner, Nina Fishman writes that he had an

---

67   *Daily Worker*, 23 August 1946.
68   Abbott, 'The Mood of the People', *Communist Review*, December 1946, p. 7.
69   *Daily Worker*, 18 December 1946.
70   Ibid.
71   *Daily Worker*, 22 August 1946.
72   Horner, 'The Communist Party and the Coal Crisis', 25 November 1945, in *Marxist Internet Archive*, available at: http://www.marxists.org/archive/horner/1945/11/coal.htm.
73   Pollitt, *No British Jobs for Fascist Poles*.

'uncompromising insistence on a liberal, tolerant attitude to foreign labour',[74] but looking at his public statements (as well as other sections of the CPGB leadership) during this period, this does not appear to be the case. In February 1947, Horner, now General Secretary of the National Union of Mineworkers (NUM), spoke against foreign workers in the mining industry, declaring that the government 'might get Poles or displaced persons but not coal'.[75] The Party declared that the Poles 'should be sent home, to work out their own salvation' and, according to Paul Foot, Piratin and Gallacher 'never missed an opportunity to point out that the Poles were dirty, lazy and corrupt'.[76] In Parliament, Piratin routinely asked the government whether Polish workers were trade union members or willing to work as directed by the Ministry of Labour. Piratin was accused of having a 'vendetta against Poles who want to work here rather than return to Communist Poland', but Piratin claimed that his persistent questioning was 'merely to ensure that such Poles who are in this country do not in any way scab or blackleg on British labour'.[77]

Even in 1955, while the Party tried to combat racism amongst workers against Commonwealth immigrants, Party literature claimed that the 'real menace ... comes from the far greater number of displaced Poles and Germans whose attitude is hostile to militant trade unionism'.[78] This was compared with the black immigrant workers, who were seen to have the ability to 'greatly strengthen the fight of the trade unions'.[79] The contradictory attitudes can also be seen in the oral history of CPGB member and Secretary of the Armthorpe NUM Branch, Jock Kane, originally recorded by radical journalist Charles Parker. In one section, Kane described an argument with the NUM area leaders over black workers:

> Then I'd another run-in with them about coloured labour. He wasn't going to have coloured labour. He wasn't having any 'half-caste bastards' running about the streets of his villages. I said: 'You're a Nazi. We fought a bloody war to defeat bastards like you.'[80]

74   Fishman 2010, p. 890.
75   Cited in Flewers 1996, p. 21.
76   Pollitt, *No British Jobs for Fascist Poles*; Foot 1965, p. 10.
77   *Hansard*, 19 February 1948, col. 1333.
78   Bolsover, *No Colour Bar in Britain*, p. 7.
79   Ibid.
80   Kane, with Kane and Parker, *No Wonder We Were All Rebels – An Oral History*, available at: http://www.grahamstevenson.me.uk/index.php?option=com_content&view=article& id=697&Itemid=63.

But Kane's description of the Polish miners was very different, accusing them of being work-shy and a hostile class:

> I can remember in 1947 we paid wages to thousands of Poles for months and months on end. They never came into this industry and never did a bloody day's work ... There were thousands of Polish ex-army men in camps ... A shower of arrogant bloody swine, ex-officer bloody class, and the coal board paid them wages for months on end.[81]

In a 1961 pamphlet, John Moss wrote that immigration had little effect on the total population increase that Britain had experienced in the early postwar period,[82] but the Party still objected to the presence of around 100,000 Poles and other Eastern Europeans and their apparent drain on resources. This campaign against Polish immigration and settlement ran counter to the very arguments the CPGB had been using to convince British workers that immigrants from the Commonwealth were *not* in competition for employment, housing or welfare.

Back in 1947, R. Palme Dutt discussed the 'crucial shortage of man-power',[83] linking the CPGB's anti-colonial programme with opposition to the Polish workers. As Dutt argued continually through the late 1940s and into the 1950s, Britain's maintenance of its colonies, its role in NATO and its other activities during the Cold War caused a huge drain on its economy, resources and manpower.[84] Dutt cited that in November 1946, over 1.5 million men were in the armed forces, while another 474,000 were 'engaged in making equipment and supplies for the armed forces' – 'a total of close on two millions [sic] or one-tenth of the available man-power'.[85] Meanwhile more than half a million workers were needed in British industry to assist with reconstruction, with the British government enthusiastically recruiting European labour, including the Poles. Dutt lamented the fact that the government's solution was 'sought to be found in the settlement of Polish fascists in Britain or the retention of German prisoners of war'.[86] For Dutt, decolonisation and end of Britain's involvement

---

81   Kane, *No Wonder We Were All Rebels.*
82   Moss 1961, p. 8.
83   Dutt, 'Britain and Empire', *Labour Monthly*, February 1947, p. 34.
84   See Dutt, *Crisis of Britain and the British Empire: Marxist Study Themes no. 7*, 1953, London: CPGB pamphlet; Dutt 1957.
85   Dutt, 'Britain and Empire', p. 34.
86   Ibid.

in 'imperialist commitments in the Near East or the Far East' was the solution to Britain's labour shortage, rather than recruiting Polish 'fascists'.[87]

The Communist Party were also sceptical as to whether the deployment of the Polish Resettlement Corps to the mines would actually have any impact upon the labour shortage, with the *Daily Worker* reporting that fewer than 2,000 Polish workers – 'not half of whom are trained miners' – would be available by mid-1947.[88] In an interview with the *Evening Standard*'s Industrial Reporter, Arthur Horner, under the headline 'Foreigners: Mr. Horner Says NO', stated that '[e]ven if the Poles were willing to come into the industry they could not be taught English and be trained to work in the mines in less than six months'.[89] Thus the *Daily Worker*'s Industrial Reporter, George Sinfield, asked rhetorically, 'Is this infinitesimal force worth the big and detrimental repercussions it might have if it were used?'[90] If this was the case, the implication the Communists were making was that the British government was not interested in recruiting Polish workers to fill the gaps in the labour market, but for a more sinister political purpose, possibly to rein in militancy amongst the miners or provide assistance to anti-Communist forces in the early manoeuvres of the Cold War. The *Daily Worker* posed the rhetorical question of whether the Labour government's moves to nationalise coal production ought to be counter-balanced by 'the introduction of men who hold trade unionism in contempt' or 'the introduction of men who are avowed opponents of their own Government, which is backed by all working-class parties in Poland'.[91]

The reasoning that the CPGB opposed the Polish migrants purely on the grounds that the CPGB was devoted to the Soviet Union and the Peoples' Republics in Eastern Europe can only be part of the reason for the hostility towards the Poles. While this can be an easily identifiable target for criticising the CPGB, it doesn't explain why anti-Polish sentiment was expressed by a large number of trade unionists and why the TUC voted against the settlement of Polish soldiers in 1946. As Paul Burnham wrote, '[t]his was not just a campaign of the Communist Party'.[92] At the TUC Congress in 1946, the General Council of the TUC demanded that 'no Poles should be employed in any grade in any industry where suitable British labour was available', with a bloc majority of

87   Dutt, 'Britain and Empire', pp. 34–5.
88   *Daily Worker*, 23 December 1946.
89   Arthur Horner, interviewed by Anne Kelly, *Evening Standard*, February 1947, from Security Service file on Arthur Horner, KV 2/1527, National Archives, London (hereafter NA).
90   *Daily Worker*, 23 December 1946.
91   *Daily Worker*, 18 December 1946.
92   Burnham 2004.

884,000 voting for this.[93] Although the TUC is not a monolithic organisation and cannot be seen as interchangeable with the various policies and actions of the entire labour movement, some authors have seen a convergence at this point between the protectionist nationalism of the TUC and the sentiments put forward by the CPGB. Both Keith Tompson and Robert Winder have used a quote from Harry Pollitt to demonstrate the hostility of the labour movement towards the Poles and a reflection that the unions were 'traditional opponents of migrant workers' in general:

> I ask you, does it make sense that we allow 500,000 of our best young people to put their names down for emigration abroad, when at the same time we employ Poles who ought to be back in their own country ...?[94]

But it would be rash to conflate the attitudes and motives of the Communist Party with those of the Trades Union Congress. Although the CPGB was influential in some trade unions, it would not have been able to influence the decisions of the TUC General Council. It is also important to note that it was during this time that the Cold War was taking shape and that anti-communist sentiment started to grow within the British trade union movement, specifically within the higher echelons of the TUC. As Richard Stevens has demonstrated, during the late 1940s and throughout the 1950s, '[t]he TUC remained deeply involved in anti-Communist activity'.[95]

Neville Kirk has argued that in the early postwar period, in comparison with the explicit racism of the Australian labour movement, the British labour movement 'adopted a predominantly positive attitude to the issues of immigration and "race"', stating that the TUC 'prided itself on its efforts to promote trade unionism and worker solidarity, irrespective of colour'.[96] But the fact is that the TUC did support immigration controls[97] and in the case of the Polish workers, called explicitly for Poles to be prevented from entering the British job market, or if they were employed, that the Poles would be the first dismissed. The trade unions may have 'opposed on economic grounds' the introduction of the Polish workers, as 'trade union leaders and members feared alike the return of the mass unemployment of the 1930s', but Diana Kay and Robert

---

93   TUC, *The General Council's Report to the 78th Annual Congress*, 1946, Brighton: TUC, p. 171; p. 364.
94   Cited in Tompson 1988, p. 71; Winder 2005, pp. 323–4.
95   Stevens 1999, p. 171.
96   Kirk 2008, p. 64; p. 67.
97   See Miles and Phizacklea 1977.

Miles have also suggested that there was also a 'vigorous nationalism [that] ran through the trade union movement'.[98] Citing Kay and Miles, Kenneth Lunn noted that the argument has been made that the British labour movements' response to European immigration was 'not racist'.[99] A similar argument is made by Stephen Catterall and Keith Gildart in their study of trade union reactions to Polish and Italian miners in the postwar era, arguing that, rather than racism or xenophobia:

> [h]ostility from rank and file members arose from the perceived 'threat' that the workers posed as a result of prodigious output performance and the mining skills they brought or through domestic and social tensions.[100]

While fears about job security and unemployment may help to explain why racist sentiments were expressed by trade union members, it cannot excuse that Polish workers faced discrimination based on their nationality. As Kenneth Lunn declared, '[b]y any reasonable definition, a policy of "Poles out first" is racist'.[101]

In 2004, Paul Burnham stated that '[t]he response to the Polish migrants is not an episode that reflects any credit on the left in Britain'.[102] The opposition to the Polish workers in Britain in the late 1940s by the Communist Party had been interpreted in several ways. Some have conflated the TUC and the CPGB opposition to portray both organisations as nationalistic protectionists, while others have used the CPGB's opposition to demonstrate their loyalty to Stalinism and their descent into nationalism, following the Popular Front era and the Second World War. Opposition to the Polish workers has not been contrasted with their acceptance of West Indian migrants. This presents a dilemma for those who want to essentialise the CPGB as either inherently racist or inherently Stalinist, as both inclinations can be found within the Party's disparate approach to postwar migration. The Party's support for the Soviet Union did affect their position on Polish workers who did not want to return to the Soviet bloc, but it doesn't explain why they were receptive of West Indian workers or why the TUC adopted a similar approach. The opposition to Polish workers put forward by the CPGB is a murky episode in the Party's history, but the reasons for this opposition, like that of the wider labour movement,

---

98   Kay and Miles 1992, pp. 76–7.
99   Lunn 1985, p. 24.
100   Catterall and Gildart 2005, p. 164.
101   Lunn 1985, p. 24.
102   Burnham 2004.

are much more complex than other scholars and commentators have previously suggested.

The Legacy of the 'Battle of Cable Street' and the CPGB's Postwar Anti-fascism

One area of the anti-racist struggle where the Communist Party was on much stronger grounds was the anti-fascist activities against Oswald Mosley's Union Movement, which arose out of the ashes of Mosley's British Union of Fascists (BUF). The anti-fascist work of the CPGB during the interwar period was one of the Party's highest achievements and the 'Battle of Cable Street', where the Communist Party helped lead over 100,000 people in a demonstration against the BUF in October 1936, had quickly become part of the Party's mythology. In his study of Mosley and British fascism, D.S. Lewis wrote of the importance of the 'Battle of Cable Street' in the history of British anti-fascism and the vital role the Communist Party played:

> On the day itself the CP divided responsibility for different streets amongst its members, as well as establishing first-aid posts, information posts, and runners to carry messages to other sectors of 'the front'. The rest, of course, is history.[103]

In her history of the CPGB, Noreen Branson reminded the reader that at the beginning of 1934, the BUF had around 40,000 members, which dwarfed the number of Communist Party members that stood at around 5,800 at the same time.[104] At the heart of the Communist Party's anti-fascist legacy is the 'Battle of Cable Street', when on 4 October 1936, around 100,000 blockaded the East End of London against a march by the BUF through Cable Street and Gardiner's Corner, where a large Jewish population lived. The 'Battle of Cable Street' and the CPGB's anti-fascist work during the 1930s became part of the mythology of the British left, as well as that of British Jews. For the Communist Party, it was a demonstration of the Popular Front in action, when a Party that had only 11,500 members in October 1936[105] could mobilise 100,000 people in mass anti-fascist action.

---

103   Lewis 1987, p. 125.
104   Branson 1985, p. 159.
105   Newton 1969, p. 159.

The narrative of the 'Battle of Cable Street' is largely based on Phil Piratin's book, *Our Flag Stays Red*, which was first published in 1948, while he was a Communist MP for Mile End, and is recognised for creating the 'most lasting legacy of Communist mythology of the "Battle of Cable Street"'.[106] Piratin used the Communist Party's anti-fascist legacy in his 1945 electoral campaign, with his successful election as well as that of ten CPGB members to the Stepney Borough Council in the same year, marking the 'peak of the triumphalist use of the "Battle" for party political purposes'.[107] The book was republished in 1978 to reinforce the legacy of the CPGB's anti-fascist traditions, at a time when the Party was being surpassed by the Socialist Workers Party and the Anti-Nazi League. Piratin tried to minimise the connection between the 'Battle of Cable Street' and the actions of the SWP, claiming that their 'interpretations and conclusions on the anti-fascist struggle were distorted in order to bring them into line with the outlook of that party'.[108] In the traditional narrative of the 'Battle of Cable Street', reinforced by Piratin's account, the Communist Party was central to the anti-fascist actions against the BUF.

A dissenting account of 'Cable Street' can be found in Joe Jacobs's memoir, *Out of the Ghetto*, which argued that the Communist Party were latecomers to the call for an anti-fascist mobilisation at Cable Street and that the Party leadership only supported the mobilisation at the eleventh hour after members of the local Stepney branch coaxed them into doing so.[109] In her history of the CPGB, Noreen Branson described Jacobs's account as 'manifestly untrue',[110] while Trotskyists have used it to show how the apparent reformism of the CPGB's Popular Front strategy encroached upon their willingness to be involved in militant anti-fascism. Sam Bornstein and Al Richardson have written, 'It was not that the Party's leaders were lacking in either courage or anti-fascist feeling, but the Popular Front line predisposed them to respectable protest rather than direct militant action'.[111] However, Elaine R. Smith has declared, 'whatever the truth' of Piratin's and Jacobs's differing accounts, 'there is no doubt that the Communist Party played a leading role at Cable Street'.[112]

The legacy of the 'Battle of Cable Street' and the CPGB's anti-fascist work of the 1930s was discernable in three main areas. The first was the use of

---

106   Kushner, 2000, p. 138.
107   Ibid.
108   Piratin 1978, p. ix.
109   Jacobs 1978, pp. 235–69.
110   Branson 1985, p. 171.
111   Bornstein and Richardson 2007, p. 47.
112   Smith 2000, p. 50.

direct militant action to stop fascist organisations assembling in public areas, a precursor to the 'No Platform' tactic of the 1970s against the National Front (see chapters 3 and 4). The second is the use of the state to prevent fascists from organising in public, despite the state's hostility towards the left. The state's reaction to 'Cable Street' was the introduction of the 1936 Public Order Act, which allowed the state to use the Act to contain public demonstrations by the left, much more than against the far right. Lastly, the CPGB emphasised that to prevent support for fascist organisations, the Party should tackle the socio-economic pressures that drove people to fascism.

The Communist Party saw that the BUF was using violence to intimidate opponents and incite anti-Semitic activities and, as Piratin explained, 'the authorities ... did not deal with the fascists', instead they deployed police 'by the score and the hundred to protect them from the growing opposition of both Jew and Gentile alike'.[113] Under the slogan 'they shall not pass', the decision to block the streets against the BUF march allowed the Communist Party to portray itself as 'capable of leading the working class in keeping the fascists off the Stepney Streets'.[114] As James Klugmann wrote in the *Morning Star* in the days after the 'Battle of Lewisham' in August 1977, the 'main lesson' of Cable Street 'stood out a mile', that 'Fascism could be deflected, but not by "keeping off the street," not by appeasement, not by retreat before their threats'.[115]

Before the CPGB endorsed the blockade of Cable Street, the London District Committee supported a petition with 100,000 signatures that was presented to the Home Office, which urged the banning of the BUF march.[116] The Communist Party appealed to the state to ban fascist activities, which (as will be seen in chapter 4) became the basis for their strategy against the National Front. In 1978, Dave Cook declared that socialists who do not co-operate with the state in banning racist and fascist organisations 'should do well to read the account of Phil Piratin in *Our Flag Stays Red*' which argued that even if defeated, a call for a ban is a powerful piece of propaganda, in case of counter-demonstration.[117]

Richard C. Thurlow saw the 'Battle of Cable Street' as 'the straw that broke the camel's back', which acted as a 'trigger mechanism for the decision by the National Government to introduce the Public Order Act'.[118] Although the Act

---

113   Piratin 1978, p. 17.
114   Piratin 1978, p. 25.
115   *Morning Star*, 26 August, 1977.
116   Branson 1985, p. 162.
117   Dave Cook, *A Knife At The Throat Of Us All: Racism and the National Front*, CPGB pamphlet, London, 1978, p. 17; Piratin 1978, p. 19.
118   Thurlow 2000, p. 74.

curtailed the BUF's highly provocative marches through London, it also severely hindered popular action by the left.[119] Nigel Copsey has written that the 'Battle of Cable Street' was 'not a clash between fascists and anti-fascists, but between anti-fascists and the police'.[120] It is worth noting that there were around 6,000 police present that day, compared with the BUF members and supporters, who numbered around 3,000. 'Cable Street' represents the beginning of the contradictory nature of the CPGB's anti-fascist strategy, using the state to intervene in combating fascist activity. However, the state was not sympathetic in this struggle and therefore used its power just as much against the left as it did against the far right.

The everyday issues that affected people during the economic crises of the 1930s created the socio-economic conditions in which fascism could thrive. The Communist Party in Stepney turned the Party from a 'mainly propaganda organisation into a campaigning body, working closely with, and rooted deeply among, the local people in factories and streets'.[121] In struggles such as the tenants' movement, the CPGB was able to demonstrate to those sympathetic to fascism amongst the lower classes, that the Party was willing to act at the local level, which in turn gave them greater support against the fascists. As Piratin wrote in *Our Flag Stays Red*, Mosley's BUF 'struck a chord' with the working class in East London, because the people 'were living miserable, squalid lives', either unemployed or in low-paid jobs and living in slums.[122] The Communist Party urged that they 'should help the people to improve their conditions of life, in the course of which [they] could show them who was really responsible for their conditions, and got them organised to fight against their real exploiters'.[123]

The main aim for the anti-fascist movement, Phil Piratin wrote in his 1978 preface, 'must be to rally masses of people for a struggle which will eliminate the festering social and economic conditions in which fascism can thrive', which would encourage people to 'understand that fascism, in all its various forms, is incompatible with social advance and must be destroyed'.[124] As Colin Sparks, the SWP's most prominent writer on fascism, wrote in *International Socialism* in 1977:

---

119 Ibid.
120 Copsey 2000, p. 58.
121 *Morning Star*, 26 October 1978.
122 Piratin 1978, p. 18.
123 Ibid.
124 Piratin 1978, p. xi.

The Communist Party went into areas which were known to be strongly influenced by the fascists. They took up the very little issues like repairs, rents, lighting, etc, and organised the tenants to fight collectively around them ... The Communist Party proved to ordinary working people that, over tiny issues which really mattered, the Communist Party's politics and militancy could deliver the goods, make a real difference to their lives, while the fascist had nothing to offer but rhetoric.[125]

The legacy of the CPGB's involvement in the 'Battle of Cable Street' was important for the Party's postwar anti-fascist/anti-racist activism. But this legacy of militant anti-fascism became increasingly inconsistent with its practical postwar programme. Despite any internal dissent in the Party before 'Cable Street' in the 1930s, the CPGB established itself as a monolithic and important organisation that was central within the anti-fascist movement. By the late 1940s, the Party leadership had left militant anti-fascism to a smaller group of working class (and predominantly Jewish) activists, such as the 43 Group, who promoted confrontation with Mosley's newly formed Union Movement.

Anti-Fascist Action against the Fascist Revival of the Union Movement, 1945–51

Mark Neocleous wrote in his study of fascism, 'seeing fascism as a historical phenomenon that ended in 1945 or thereabouts ... encourages a dangerous forgetting'.[126] While Mosley and leading members of the BUF, as well as the leader of the tiny Imperial League of Fascists, Arnold Leese, were interned during the Second World War, this did not happen to the majority of fascists. Although the War and internment were huge blows to British fascism, it did not end in 1940.[127] Richard Thurlow correctly pointed out that the fascist organisations that existed in the interwar period did not survive the War, but that did not stop Mosley and other fascists from attempting to adapt fascism to the postwar period.[128] From 1945 to 1951, Mosley's Union Movement, alongside other fascist organisations and agitators, revived a campaign of violence and intimidation, with a programme that still 'smacked of fascism', despite attempts

---

125 Colin Sparks, 'Fighting The Beast: Fascism – The Lessons of Cable Street', *International Socialism*, 1/94, January 1977, p. 12.
126 Neocleous 1997, p. xi.
127 Renton 2000, p. 23.
128 Thurlow 1987, p. 233.

by the Union Movement to distance itself from the BUF.[129] As the majority of British people were clearly hostile to fascism in the aftermath of the Second World War, the Union Movement was 'always doomed to failure', but as James Eaden and David Renton acknowledged, anti-fascists, including the CPGB, 'can also claim some credit for having helped to hasten fascism's demise'.[130] In the postwar period, the Communist Party was a leading organisation in the anti-fascist movement after the 'failure of the Labour Party to take a lead in the street campaigns against Mosley'.[131] Alongside the CPGB were Jewish organisations, such as the Association of Jewish Ex-Servicemen and the Board of Deputies of British Jews, progressive organisations, such as the National Council for Civil Liberties (NCCL), and the radical organisations, such as the Trotskyist Revolutionary Communist Party (RCP) and the 43 Group.

Despite the decision of the state to intern fascists during the Second World War, the postwar Labour government was reluctant to act decisively against fascist agitators, believing the existing laws would contain the negligible fascist elements that existed in postwar Britain.[132] However, the state was far from neutral on the issue of postwar fascism, with Noreen Branson recounting:

Home Secretary [Chuter] Ede had imposed a temporary ban on all polit-ical processions in London ... Yet, as the Communist Party Executive pointed out, hundreds of police were being used to protect meetings by the fascist Oswald Mosley who was trying to re-establish his anti-semitic organisation.[133]

As E.P. Thompson wrote in a 1947 pamphlet, *Fascist Threat to Britain*, 'It is quite clear that the fascists welcome the police at their meetings – not as a warning, but as protection from the justice of the people'.[134] This did not prevent the Communist Party from demanding that the state be used to contain fascist activity. Arguing against the common assumption that 'the police already have enough powers to deal with [the fascists]', Thompson declared, 'If they have, they should use them. If they have not, they should be given the powers they need'.[135] As the Labour government was viewed as not dealing effectively with

---

129   Lewis 1987, p. 239.
130   Eaden and Renton 2002, p. 108.
131   Ibid.
132   Renton 2000, p. 74.
133   Branson 1997, p. 203.
134   Thompson, *Fascist Threat to Britain*, 1947, London: CPGB pamphlet, p. 12.
135   Ibid.

the fascist resurgence, the Communist Party, with its 'reputation for anti-fascist work going back to Cable Street', began anti-fascist work against Mosley and the Union Movement.[136]

However, there was a move by the CPGB leadership away from the direct militant action of the 1930s, such as that witnessed at Cable Street, to a position of reliance upon the state. In Thompson's pamphlet, the actions advocated by the Party did not include direct action, instead demands were made that 'spreading of specifically fascist doctrine ... be outlawed', 'spreading of racial hatred and anti-Semitism ... be made a crime' and that 'existing laws ... be strictly enforced'.[137] Alongside this, the Party urged that other organisations 'go on record for the outlawing of fascism' and more immediately, 'If the fascists come into your locality, get all the inhabitants to sign a petition of protest to the Home Secretary'.[138] Nigel Copsey suggested two reasons for this move away from direct militant action. The first was that the 'decisive action taken by the state' against the British fascists *during* the Second World War led the CPGB leadership to believe that a 'non-confrontational policy towards fascism was the most appropriate'.[139] Secondly, the cautious postwar policy by the Communist Party should be read as a result of their support for the Labour government in the early postwar years.[140] As part of the transformation by the CPGB to adjust to Britain's postwar conditions, the Party leadership 'officially discouraged any anti-fascist activity likely to give the Communist Party a bad name'. By demanding a state ban on fascism, the CPGB attempted to appear as a respectable political party.[141] This reliance on the state and reluctance to be involved in militant actions contributed largely to the Communist Party anti-fascist campaigns throughout the postwar period.

In the 1945 General Election campaign, the CPGB had proposed that anti-Semitism become a criminal offence, an attempt to attract support from the local Jewish circles and emphasise the Party's anti-fascist stance.[142] While a proposal for banning anti-Semitic propaganda and agitation was a practical task to deal with the immediate threat of fascism, the total banning of fascist organisations by the state was much more problematic. As seen with the 1936 Public Order Act, while the government stressed that 'any legislation would

---

136   Renton 2000, p. 80.
137   Thompson, *Fascist Threat to Britain*, p. 14.
138   Ibid.
139   Copsey 2000, p. 87.
140   Ibid.
141   Ibid.
142   Srebrnik 1994, p. 75.

apply equally to the Left as well as to the Right', in practice the state used this legislation 'almost entirely ... against anti-fascist protestors'.[143] The CPGB bore the brunt of the state's zealousness to keep the status quo and as David Renton has written, the state frequently used its laws to harass the CPGB while sympathising with the fascists.[144] In 1947, Will Wainwright wrote that even if new laws against racial hatred were not brought in, 'the Government could, if it chose, put a stop to the fascist threat in Britain today', citing the laws used to shut down the National Unemployed Workers Movement in the 1930s.[145] Wainwright concluded:

> there is still one law for the poor and one for the rich. The same powers that gagged the unemployed leaders, who fought for freedom from want and for freedom to work, could be used to stop the fascists – the enemies of all freedoms, whose very presence is an incitement to public disorder.[146]

This did not prevent all Communist members from being involved in militant action to stop the Union Movement organising, with some members of the CPGB working closely with the anti-fascist collective, the 43 Group. Formed in March 1946 as a militant anti-fascist group with the aim to 'go on the attack against the emergent fascists with a view to destroying them',[147] a 'number of prominent members of the Communist Party', David Renton wrote, 'had taken part in the discussions leading to the formation of the 43 Group' with a 'party cell' existing within the Group.[148] It was believed at the time by the police and the fascists that the 43 Group was a Communist front organisation, but as Morris Beckman, one of the founders of the Group, told *Socialist Review*:

> It was said that the 43 Group was a subversive Communist organisation ... We were not connected to any organisation, but sometimes we worked with the Communists. They wanted to take us over ... Sometimes we found ourselves attacking the same fascist meetings as the Communists. We would even pass information to them.[149]

---

143 Copsey 2000, p. 64; Thurlow 2000, p. 91.
144 Renton 2000, pp. 101–29.
145 Will Wainwright, 'Mosley', *World News and Views*, 6 December 1947, p. 554.
146 Ibid.
147 Beckman 1993, p. 26.
148 Renton 2001, pp. 176–7.
149 'Our War Against Fascism', interview with Morris Beckman, *Socialist Review*, March 1993, p. 23.

Beckman wrote in his memoir of the 43 Group, 'the enemy of our enemy was our friend, and the Communists were actively attacking the fascists'.[150] The CPGB leadership could not publicly condone the actions of the 43 Group, but there was no disciplinary action against those Party members involved. Long-time Hackney branch member Monty Goldman told Dave Hann for his book that collusion between the two groups extended to the higher levels of the Party:

> There was very close co-operation between the leadership of the 43 Group and the leadership of the Communist Party. People like Gerry Flamberg and Harry Pollitt met regularly in the Communist Party's headquarters in King Street. Harry Pollitt spoke at a mass meeting in York Hall in Bethnal Green, which was jointly stewarded by the 43 Group and the Communist Party.[151]

The Communist Party's anti-fascist work of the 1930s and 1940s has been largely identified with the Jewish population of London and the considerable Jewish membership within the Party. The relationship between the Jewish community and the CPGB has been well-documented by Henry Srebrnik, who described the Party's anti-fascist legacy and its stature among East End Jews as tapping into a 'specifically *ethnic* means of political expression'.[152] For the Jews of East End London, their attraction to the CPGB was the Party's 'self-appointed role as a steadfast opponent to all manifestations of domestic fascism'.[153] In the Stepney branch, one of the Party's biggest, around 50 percent of the 1,000 members in 1945 were Jewish.[154] As the Union Movement began to agitate in the early postwar period, Communist Party members and Jewish activists both fought against the fascist revival, utilising the memory of the Party's anti-fascist work of the interwar period. However, by the early 1950s, the Jewish Communist subculture had fallen into decline, although as late as 1965, it was estimated that around ten percent of the CPGB's membership was Jewish.[155]

There are several factors for this decline. David Renton stated that the physical destruction of London's East End by the Blitz meant that large numbers of

---

150 Beckman 1993, p. 30.
151 Cited in Hann, 2013, p. 165.
152 Srebrnik 1995, p. 136, original emphasis.
153 Srebrnik 1994, p. 53.
154 Kushner 1990, p. 66.
155 Renton 2000, p. 89; Kushner 1990, p. 66.

the Jewish population moved north and west, out of the areas where the BUF had drawn support and with the end of the war, more former East End Jews became employed in middle-class jobs, with the number of Jews in trade unions dropping dramatically.[156] Alongside this, Chimen Abramsky, Secretary of the CPGB's National Jewish Committee, suggested that in the postwar period, 'Fascism was not the main issue of the day' and the CPGB was 'more concerned with the danger of the Cold War, with the Marshall Plan, with the future of India, of the future of Palestine', believing that Mosley was 'a spent force'.[157] There was also the Communist Party's opposition to Zionism, based on Stalin's statement that Zionism was a 'reactionary nationalist trend of the Jewish bourgeoisie', as well as the Party's uncritical support for the Soviet Union when details of widespread anti-Semitism amongst the CPSU began to surface in the 1950s.[158] However, there was an uneasiness amongst some CPGB members towards the large Jewish membership in London, which is possibly indicative of the latent working-class racism that the Party had to face in the postwar period, demonstrated by this passage in Bob Darke's 1952 exposé on the Communist Party:

> Yet I never felt happy with Jewish Communists. They were too sensitive, their feelings were too close to the skin. They were certainly among the hardest-working, most active members of the Party, but they made me uncomfortable. And a great many Gentile comrades felt the same way.[159]

After six years of anti-fascist activity, the Union Movement went into decline, and in 1951 Mosley left Britain for self-imposed exile in Ireland. This can be viewed as the end of 'classical' fascism in the vein of the interwar movement, although not the end of fascism in Britain (as the rise of the National Front in the next chapter demonstrates). The defining organisation for the postwar fascist movement was the League of Empire Loyalists (LEL), formed in 1954 by former BUF Director of Propaganda A.K. Chesterton, and an organisation through which nearly all the important figures of postwar fascism passed. However, the fascists were now a response to the collapse of world imperialism and the decolonisation process. In the Cold War polarisation between Washington and Moscow, Britain had lost its significance as a world power and for the fascist organisations of the mid-1950s onwards, non-white Commonwealth

---

156 Renton 2000, p. 89.
157 Cited in Renton 2000, p. 89.
158 Stalin 1953, p. 418, fn. 131.
159 Darke 1952, p. 44.

immigrants became the new scapegoat for the supposed threat to the 'remnants of the British Empire and way of life'.[160]

After Mosley left for Ireland in 1951, the other fascist organisations that existed were more influenced by the interwar Imperial Fascist League's Arnold Leese, emphasising anti-Semitism and racism against Britain's black immigrants. What characterised British fascism between 1951 and the formation of the National Front in 1967 was a series of splits into tiny organisations featuring the same individuals, the result of attempting to adjust fascism to postwar Britain and a succession of personal clashes. From 1957 onwards, the same names – Colin Jordan, John Tyndall, Martin Webster, John Bean, Andrew Fountaine – were involved in various groups, which despite numerous splits and different organisational titles, were only superficially distinguishable from each other, primarily the White Defence League (WDL), National Labour Party (NLP), British National Party (BNP), National Socialist Movement (NSM) and the Greater Britain Movement (GBM). Despite involvement in and brief notoriety from the anti-immigrant agitation of the Notting Hill riots, these fascists achieved little during this period. Copsey remarked that, '[f]or the most part, the 1950s in Britain were quiescent years for both fascists and anti-fascists',[161] despite appealing to populist anti-black racism. The focus of anti-racist activists, including those in the Communist Party, in the 1950s and 1960s was the mainstream prejudice against newly arrived Commonwealth immigrants.

The Impact of Commonwealth Migrants upon the Party's Anti-racist Outlook

As the problem of Mosleyite fascism and explicit anti-Semitism seemed to die down in the early 1950s, prejudice against Commonwealth migrants who were now arriving in Britain in significant numbers was becoming a concern for the Communist Party. During the 1950s, although postwar immigration had been constant since 1948, the Party still viewed the issue of racism and the plight of immigrants in Britain very much in the context of the colonial struggle. In the 1958 edition of *The British Road to Socialism*, the line concerning racism in Britain – 'It [the British labour movement] needs to fight against the colour bar and racial discrimination, and for the full, social, economic and political equality of colonial people in Britain' – was attached to the

---

160   Thurlow 1987, p. 239.
161   Copsey 2000, p. 102.

section dedicated to Colonial Freedom.[162] The reason for West Indians coming to Britain was rising poverty and unemployment in the West Indies, but the CPGB highlighted that 'these conditions are the inevitable result of imperialist rule, with the extraction of huge super-profits from the natural resources of the colonial territories'.[163] For the CPGB, the problems that the newly arrived immigrants faced in Britain were intrinsically linked to the exploitation of the colonies in the British Empire. As written in a pamphlet produced by the London District Committee, 'colonial workers' (not British subjects working in Britain) faced discrimination in housing and jobs, and still faced hostilities within the trade unions, but 'friendly co-operation' with the colonial workers to deal with the problems of housing and employment was linked to 'righting the wrongs of British imperialism with the colonies themselves'.[164] Action against the colour bar was tied to support from the labour movement for 'every struggle of the colonial peoples in their fight against Imperialism for National Independence'.[165] In another CPGB pamphlet published in 1955, Phil Bolsover wrote that a 'partnership of British working people with colonial people' was now 'being offered to us on our doorsteps' against the common enemy of monopoly capitalism, 'the forces that seek to exploit us all – black or white, in Britain or in the colonies, on the Clydeside or the Gold Coast'.[166]

The early postwar migrants were seen by the Party as having dual interests – 'concern for freedom in their homeland, and for realisation of their fight for equal rights and privileges here, with all other British subjects'.[167] This is what Edward Said described as the paradox of the exile, where the 'positive benefit of challenging the system' by the migrant's position was always countered by a debilitating sense of loss and exclusion, 'between the old empire and the new state'.[168]

In 1955, the Communist Party was reporting in the *World News* that the 'presence of colonial workers in Britain has, over recent months, become an

---

162 CPGB, *The British Road to Socialism*, 1958, p. 16. Another line, slightly different from the line under the Colonial Freedom, appears under the section of the programme dedicated to Socialist Democracy – 'All forms of discrimination on grounds of race or colour need to be made illegal'. CPGB, *The British Road to Socialism*, 1958, p. 24.

163 'Talking Points On ... Colonial Workers in Britain', *World News*, 19 March 1955, p. 238.

164 CPGB, *Brothers in the Fight for a Better Life*, 1955, London: CPGB pamphlet, p. 12.

165 CPGB, *Brothers in the Fight for a Better Life*, p. 13.

166 Bolsover, *No Colour Bar for Britain*, p. 3.

167 Jones, 'West Indians in Britain', *World News*, 29 June 1957, p. 416.

168 Said 1994, p. 404; p. 403.

important political issue and a serious subject of public discussion'.[169] The
Party declared that the 'real solution to the problem [of colonial workers in
Britain] is to free the colonies and end imperialist exploitation, so that colonial
workers can freely build up their own countries and reap the benefits of the
wealth which they produce in their own countries'.[170] This statement suggests
the notion, pervasive in the 1950s, that black immigrants were *the problem*
and that by favouring struggles in the colonies, the CPGB avoided making any
serious suggestions for tackling the problems *faced* by these immigrants in
Britain and 'in doing so confounded the issues of racial discrimination and the
effects of imperialism'.[171]

Two connected issues relating to the Party's anti-colonial and anti-racist
strategies came to a head at the Party's 1957 Special Congress. The 1957 Special
Congress is well-known in the history of the Communist Party because it was
specially convened in the aftermath of Khrushchev's Secret Speech and led to
a split in the Party over the issue of inner-party democracy. However, it was
also important because the issues of the Party's anti-racist record and its idea
of post-colonial relations were raised by the ethnic minority members in the
Party. Firstly, a report from the International Department in March 1957 titled
'West Indians in Britain' complained that although two pieces of literature had
been circulated in 1955, the Party's commitment to anti-racism 'does not appear
to have penetrated deeply into the Party membership'.[172] These included the
pamphlet *No Colour Bar in Britain* and the leaflet *Stop Stirring up Race Hatred*,
both of which contained a 'Charter of Rights for coloured workers in Britain'.[173]
The Charter called for:

1. No form of colour discrimination by employers, landlords, public-
    ans, hotel proprietors, etc., or in any aspect of social, educational
    and cultural activity. Any racial discrimination to be made a penal
    offence.

2. Opposition to all Government restrictions and discrimination
    against coloured workers entering Britain.

---

169   'Talking Points On ... Colonial Workers in Britain', p. 238.
170   Ibid.
171   Sherwood 1999, p. 65.
172   International Affairs Committee, 'West Indians in Britain', March 1957, p. 6, in CPGB
     archives, CP/CENT/CTTE/02/04, LHASC.
173   Bolsover, *No Colour Bar for Britain*, p. 11; *Stop Stirring Up Race Hatred*, CPGB flyer, 1955, in
     CPGB archives, CP/CENT/INT/67/07, LHASC.

3.   Equality of treatment in access to employment, wages and condi-
     tions. To receive the rate for the job (including equal facilities for
     apprenticeship and vocational training), and the maintenance of
     full rights to social security benefits.

4.   Full encouragement to join their appropriate trade union on equal
     conditions of entry with British workers and to exercise their trade
     union and political rights.[174]

Marika Sherwood has argued that despite the positive steps made with this
Charter, the propositions made by the Party were vague and 'while advocating action, [they] sadly do not indicate what form that action might take'.[175]
The 1957 report requested a re-examination of this 'Charter of Rights', alongside
more practical and immediate measures, such as the Industrial Department to
'present an account of the problems arising' in various industries, public support for Fenner Brockway's Racial Discrimination Bill, a call for co-operation
with the Movement for Colonial Freedom (MCF) and other immigrant organisations and more prominence on the matter in the *Daily Worker*.[176]
   The second issue was related to the aforementioned assumption by the Party
that in the post-colonial era, Britain's former colonies would want to retain
some form of relationship with their former ruler and agree to the forms of
trade suggested to be 'mutually beneficial' by the Communist Party. The Party's
programme for the postwar period, *The British Road to Socialism*, was first published in 1951 and outlined a proposal for a 'new, close, fraternal association
of the British peoples and the liberated peoples of the Empire', in order to
'promote mutually beneficial economic exchange and co-operation'.[177] This
exchange would ensure Britain obtained 'normal supplies of ... vital food and
raw materials' and in return, the former colonies would receive 'the products
of British industry'.[178] Marika Sherwood has argued that what the Communist
Party promoted in the early 1950s was a 'somewhat unequal exchange' and the
Party had not considered that the 'newly-independent countries might choose
to purchase their capital and consumer goods elsewhere' or 'develop their own
industries'.[179] Trevor Carter has noted that the 'fraternal association' suggested
in the 1951 edition of *The British Road to Socialism* was not the most 'politically

---

174   Bolsover, *No Colour Bar for Britain*, p. 11; *Stop Stirring Up Race Hatred*.
175   Sherwood 1999, p. 66.
176   'West Indians in Britain', p. 7.
177   CPGB, *The British Road to Socialism*, 1951, p. 12.
178   Ibid.
179   Sherwood 1999, p. 64.

logical kind of relationship' for the colonies, where a 'Central or South American country which had become socialist would have greater real links with a socialist West Indies' than Britain.[180] Pollitt compared this 'fraternal association' to the relationship between the Soviet Union and the Eastern bloc countries, stating 'you cannot go anywhere in Peoples' China, Poland, Czechoslovakia, Bulgaria, Albania, and the German Democratic Republic without being struck by the volume of assistance that has been given to the peoples of all these countries by the Soviet Union'.[181] In a 1951 article, Dutt suggested that the main reason for this 'new, close fraternal association' was military, stating that '[t]he grounds for this proposal lie in the present world situation, with the dominant aggressive role of American imperialism in the world of imperialism'.[182] But the decolonisation process and the balance of the Cold War shifted greatly between the time of *The British Road to Socialism*'s first publication (at the height of the Korean War) and in 1957 (after the Bandung conference and the Suez Crisis), which impacted upon the Party's anti-colonial outlook.

As part of the reforms proposed by the Party leadership during the crisis of 1956, a commission was put in charge of redrafting *The British Road to Socialism* to be ratified at the 1957 Special Congress. The Party's West Indian Committee challenged the proposal of a 'new, close, fraternal association' of Britain and its former colonies as outlined in the manifesto's 1951 edition. The term, the WIC asserted, was objectionable to people in the colonies for two reasons:

(a)   Does not take into consideration that the freed colonies may wish to *associate* more *closely* with other countries for geographical and other reasons, e.g. Malaya.

(b)   Smacks of imperialism in a new way ... It is necessary to recognise the acute distrust which colonials have of British imperialism and the feeling which exists that *no* British Government can be trusted to treat colonials or coloured people fairly.[183]

'Instead of proposing a *close alliance*', the WIC stated, 'we should think in terms of *fraternal relations*, which the former colonies could enter into with any and

---

180   Carter 1986, pp. 59–60.
181   Pollitt, 'The National Independence of the Colonies', *World News*, 10 July 1954, p. 544.
182   Dutt, 'The Communist Programme and the Empire', *World News and Views*, 10 March 1951, p. 114.
183   West Indies Committee, 'Recommendations of West Indies Committee on The British Road to Socialism', n.d., p. 1, in CPGB archives, CP/IND/DUTT/07/05, LHASC.

all countries which respect their equal rights.'[184] Whilst a long-standing member of the Party leadership and agreeing with the majority position on most issues during the debates in the lead-up to the Special Congress, Dutt supported this amendment suggested by the WIC and advocated for a change in the wording of *The British Road to Socialism*. In a document outlining his position, written in August 1956, Dutt said that the 'fraternal association' proposed in 1951 was based on the assumption of 'a parallel victory of the British working people and the colonial peoples and the carrying forward of the common victory to forms of co-operation following the victory', referring to Stalin's statement of 'the victory of one is impossible without the victory of the other'.[185] But now, Dutt argued, the 'liberation of the colonial peoples has been achieved over the greater part of the colonial area in front of any victory of the working class in Britain'[186] and they could now pursue their own way forward without waiting for the socialist revolution to occur in Britain.

The majority of the commission charged with the task of rewriting the Party's manifesto rejected Dutt's arguments, although a significant majority supported Dutt and the WIC, and a debate was played out in the pages of the *Daily Worker* and the *World News*. The majority position, publicly put forward by Emile Burns, promoted keeping the wording the same, arguing that economic and military concerns, as well as historical ties, would be reasons for maintaining fraternal relations between Britain and its former colonies, using the pre-existing template of Labour's multi-racial Commonwealth. Burns argued that 'many formerly subject countries have won independence', but had chosen to remain in the Commonwealth for 'economic and political reasons, even though Britain is imperialist'.[187] Burns wrote:

It is one thing to end the present association based on domination and exploitation; it is another thing to reject association on a new basis, for this would not only create difficulties for all the peoples concerned, but it would check the future development particularly of the more backward countries.[188]

---

184   West Indies Committee, 'Recommendations of West Indies Committee on The British Road to Socialism', n.d., p. 3.

185   Dutt, 'Programme Commission Points for Consideration on Revision of Part II', 29 August 1956, p. 2, in CPGB archives, CP/IND/DUTT/07/05, LHASC.

186   Dutt, 'Programme Commission Points for Consideration on Revision of Part II', p. 2.

187   Burns, Contribution to 'From a Discussion', *World News*, 18 May 1957, p. 316.

188   Burns, 'The Case for Fraternal Association', *World News Discussion Supplement*, p. 15.

Dutt replied to the majority position by declaring that the economic reasons put forward 'inevitably creates the impression that we envisage the continuance of the role of the countries of the Empire as an agrarian hinterland for an industrial Britain', reminding readers that this was 'the very system against which the colonial and dependent peoples whose economic development has been retarded by imperialism are in revolt.'[189] Elsewhere Dutt replied that the world situation had changed dramatically since 1951, with 'the emergence, alongside the socialist world, of the new international alignment of former colonial states, revealed at Bandung in 1955, transforming the whole character of international relations'[190] and ending the military need for such a close fraternal association. Dutt added that the concept, as outlined in 1951, had 'caused disquiet and dissatisfaction' amongst 'all colonial comrades' and this needed to be taken into account, 'rather than proceed ... by lecturing colonial comrades on their backwardness.'[191] Contributing to the debate, John Williamson, a Scottish-American member of the CPGB, agreed with Dutt, claiming that 'there are still some remaining formulations which could give the impression of a paternalistic relationship, with a socialist Britain still being the "Big Brother" that must look out for the welfare of the peoples of the former colonies'.[192] At the Congress, Dutt declared:

Our Colonial comrades, including the West Indian and West African branches, in the overwhelming majority support the minority formulation ... We should not lightly ignore their opinion.

Since 1951 no Communist Party in the Empire has accepted or taken up our formulation of fraternal association. If the Communist Parties of the Empire were putting forward this proposal, that would be a different matter.

But if only the British Party, at the centre of imperialism, is putting it forward and all our brother Parties are turning away from it, then we should think twice.[193]

---

189   Dutt, 'Future Relations of Countries of the Present British Empire', *World News Discussion Supplement*, p. 18.
190   Dutt, Contribution to 'From a Discussion', *World News*, 18 May 1957, p. 315.
191   Dutt, 'Future Relations of Countries of the Present British Empire', p. 18.
192   Williamson, letter to discussion on *The British Road to Socialism*, *World News Discussion Supplement*, 26 January 1957, p. 14.
193   Cited in *Daily Worker*, 22 April 1957.

Burns answered that '[t]his is not big brotherism any more than the Soviet industrialisation of Asia was big brotherism', but the majority position was defeated by 298 votes to 210.[194] The 1958 edition of *The British Road to Socialism* thus stated that the CPGB would recognise the 'complete independence and right of self-determination' of former colonies and that a socialist Britain would 'seek to promote close voluntary fraternal relations ... between Britain and [those countries] willing to develop such relations'.[195] This colonial migrant members rebellion, predominantly in the West Indian Committee, demanded that the CPGB leadership pay more attention to the desires of those seeking independence from Britain and respect the agency of the colonial citizens in the decolonisation process. With the support from Dutt, the subsequent edition of the Party programme included a much stronger commitment to anti-colonialism and should be remembered as a rare victory of rank-and-file CPGB members in changing party policy from the grassroots level.

The Nationality Branches

The West Indian Committee of the CPGB was probably at its height in the mid- to late 1950s and was part of a network of branches under control of the London District Committee that were based upon nationality, rather than by area or workplace. Many of the members of the London District Committee were also members of the International Department and these nationality branches were established to accommodate the migrant workers who joined the Party in the late 1940s and early 1950s.

Hakim Adi has noted that a particular source of CPGB members from the Commonwealth was through the West African Student Union (WASU), with the CPGB viewed as a training ground for 'Marxists' to take the skills learned within the Communist Party back to Africa to assist in the colonial struggles, partic- ularly in Nigeria and Ghana.[196] In 1950, a 'mass influx' of Nigerians joined the Party, although Adi has admitted that 'the basis on which so many Nigerians were admitted into the party remains something of a mystery'.[197] To accom- modate these new members, the International Department established a num- ber of 'Robeson branches', based on national grouping, which was against Party

---

194   Ibid.
195   CPGB, *The British Road to Socialism*, 1958, London: CPGB pamphlet, p. 25.
196   Adi 1995, p. 179; p. 181.
197   Adi 1995, p. 181.

rules. It was hoped by the CPGB that these new recruits would assist in the 'development of a Communist movement in West Africa', but the interest in Marxism did not translate into the creation of 'disciplined revolutionaries' and the Marxism-Leninism of the Communist Party had to compete with other revolutionary ideologies, such as Pan-Africanism or 'deviant' forms of Marxism, such as Titoism.[198] These 'Robeson branches' were dissolved as recruitment of colonial 'agents' did not seem to reap the benefits the Party had hoped for, but still a series of committees, such as the West African Sub-Committee and the African and West Indian Committee, were created by the International Department, as well as various publications, such as the *Africa Newsletter* and *Colonial Liberator*.[199]

Other national branches were formed in the mid-1950s, organised around Cypriot, Indian and West Indian communities. These branches were an attempt to accommodate new immigrant members, who often had experience in their native countries' labour movements, into the Party structure, 'justified on the grounds that either language or some other temporary special circumstances necessitated exceptional organisational forms'.[200] These branches were under the direction of the International Department and in the case of the West Indian and Cypriot branches, they were 'peculiar to London', as described by Trevor Carter, therefore also under control of the LDC.[201] Only the Indian branches appeared outside of London, but these branches came into clashes with the already existing Indian Workers' Associations (IWA). Established where 'a language difficulty and … clearly defined concentrations' of immigrant members were present, the Indian branches became 'embroiled in disputes within the IWA and the wider Indian community',[202] based on the schisms within the Communist Party of India after the Sino-Soviet split. The Party did advise that it was still 'very important to note that participation in the Party branches and the groups must not be substituted for each other'.[203]

However, these groups 'gradually converted into actual party units or branches composed of Indian Party members only'.[204] The existence of these nationality branches was usually left unacknowledged by the Party leadership.

198　Adi 1998, pp. 161–2.
199　Adi 1995, p. 182; p. 180.
200　Flinn 2002, p. 61.
201　Carter 1986, p. 57.
202　Cited in Flinn 2002, p. 55.
203　Cited in 'Indian Members of the CPGB', 25 October 1966, in CPGB archives, CP/CENT/CTTE/ 38/01, LHASC.
204　'Indian Members of the CPGB'.

The fact that there were branches based on nationality created an 'impossible position' for the CPGB, with these branches in 'clear violation of Party rule'.[205] The nationality branches were eventually dissolved in 1966 by the International Department, stating that 'all members must belong to a basic unit, either where they live or where they work'.[206] In his article on the nationality branches, Andrew Flinn writes that unlike the Indian and Cypriot branches, the West Indian branches were dissolved much earlier, but their fate is 'somewhat obscure'.[207] Flinn estimates that the branches were dissolved in 1955 (although Dutt referred to them in his debates with Burns in 1957), but the West Indian Committee continued to exist.[208] However, like the wider Party membership, many of the ethnic minority members of the CPGB were disillusioned with the Party after the crises of 1956–7 and membership amongst migrant communities declined in the late 1950s and early 1960s. This was further exacerbated by the Sino-Soviet split in 1960, with a number of ethnic minority members choosing the Chinese path, who seemed to be more active in the sphere of decolonisation. But a number of ethnic minority members remained in the Party, usually attached to the International Department, and slowly working towards greater prominence in the Party, as will be discussed in later chapters.

Conclusion

This chapter has looked at how the Communist Party reacted to the politics of race and immigration in the early postwar era. One of the primary concerns for the Communist Party in the late 1940s and early 1950s was the change in the international political arena in the aftermath of the Second World War. In the wake of the War, Britain's place on the world stage had altered with the world divided now between the USA and the Soviet Union, with Britain unable to maintain its hold over its colonies. The establishment of Communist governments in Eastern Europe and China, as well as the beginnings of decolonisation in Asia, Africa and the Middle East, bolstered the Communist Party in Britain and the latter's view that there was a decisive shift towards socialism worldwide. However, the Cold War and the anti-communist hysteria that broke out with the Korean War in 1950 dampened down the Party's spirits somewhat.

---

205 'Special Meeting of Leading Indian Party Members and District Representatives', in CPGB archives, CP/CENT/CTTE/38/01, LHASC.
206 'Indian Members of the CPGB'.
207 Flinn 2002, p. 58.
208 Ibid.

But despite the setback experienced by the CPGB in the domestic sphere, the Party was still buoyed by the ongoing decolonisation process, and it is within this anti-colonial context that the Party mainly interacted with Commonwealth migrants and ethnic minority workers. As this chapter has shown, the anti-colonial struggle and the fight against racial discrimination in Britain were seen by many within the Party as interchangeable and the Party's International Department took on the bulk of its anti-racist work. However, by the mid- to late 1950s, the Party's ethnic minority members, particularly those from the West Indies, were frustrated at the Party's outlook on the question of decolonisation and its practical anti-racist efforts. These saw two challenges by West Indian members to the Party leadership in 1957. The first was a report (probably written by West Indian-American member Claudia Jones) that the Party was not doing enough to address the concerns of its non-white members and that the 'Charter of Rights' it had written concerning Commonwealth migrants was too vague and hard to put into practice. The second was the assumption by the Party that in the post-colonial era, the former colonies would still want to be in a colonial-type relationship with a socialist Britain. The ethnic minority rank-and-file had an important victory on the second issue at the 1957 Congress, but it was still the case that for most of the Party's non-white membership, anti-racism and the concerns of the black workers were on the periphery of the party's agenda.

While the CPGB described the people in the British colonies as 'fellow fighters ... against the common enemy' of British imperialism and those that arrived in Britain as 'brothers in the fight for a better life',[209] it did not welcome other migrant groups in a similar way. This chapter also looks at how the Communist Party dealt with European migrants, in particular the Poles who had remained in Britain after the War and were deployed by the Labour government to work in the mines and other areas of heavy industry. The CPGB resisted the deployment of these migrant Poles, portraying them as fascist sympathisers, 'scabs' and betrayers of socialism, amongst other things. While documenting how welcoming the Communist Party was to Commonwealth migrants, this chapter shows that the Party was unpleasant in the way it treated European workers and that this should be contrasted with the Party's more general anti-racist agenda.

This chapter also shows that the Party's anti-racist outlook was shaped heavily by its anti-fascist record and that even in the postwar period, the CPGB was one of the few organisations to confront the fascist far right in public. Between 1945 and 1951, the CPGB, alongside Trotskyists and Jewish activists, was

---

209   Pollitt 1952, p. 18; CPGB, *Brothers in the Fight for a Better Life*, p. 1.

heavily involved in (physically) campaigning against Oswald Mosley's fascist Union Movement. After Mosley left for Ireland in 1951, the fascist threat seemed to decline and anti-racists shifted their focus to the 'colour bar' and anti-immigrationism. It was not until the late 1960s that the fascists would regroup under the umbrella of the National Front, but the Communist Party learned much from these anti-fascist campaigns, which will be evident in later chapters.

Although the Communist Party was one of the first political organisations in Britain to be involved in anti-racist activity and encouraged migrant workers to engage with the Party, by the end of the 1950s this was beginning to change as a greater number of 'ordinary' people interacted with non-white migrants, especially in London and other major cities. Jodi Burkett has written that it was 'in the mid-1960s, roughly 1963–64, that "race" issues came home to the British left wing',[210] which coincided with Labour's shift to the right on the matter of immigration controls and the formation of moderate 'race relations' organisations by progressives and sections of the labour movement. The next chapter will look at how the CPGB reacted to this wider recognition of issues of race and immigration on the British left and whether its pioneering work in the 1940s and 1950s allowed it to keep pace in the 1960s.

---

210   Burkett 2013, p. 194.

Anti-racism and Building the 'Mass Party', 1960–9

By the early 1960s, the CPGB looked to have recovered from the exodus of 1956 and membership reached a post-1956 peak in 1964. A number of the early Cold War anxieties about communism had abated by this time and the CPGB's position within the trade union movement was reaching an influential level. These seemingly favourable signs saw the Party push towards a 'mass party', trying to bring a wider range of people into the Party and embrace other emerging social movements in a 'broad popular alliance' against monopoly capitalism. The Party was buoyed by the initial trade union activity against the Wilson government, as well as the new social movements and single-issue organisations that grew in the 1960s, but at the same time, the Party was wary about the structure and composition of these movements and organisations, which seemed less disciplined than the traditional CPGB.

This was certainly the case with the anti-racist groups and the black political movements that developed in the 1960s. This chapter will explore how the CPGB grappled with the development of specifically 'black' political organisations and the assertion of a more militant stance amongst Britain's ethnic communities, who had been frustrated by the moderate and white-led anti-racist groups in the 1950s and early 1960s. Alongside these ethnic organisations, the Communist Party had to contend with other leftist groups, such as the International Socialists and the International Marxist Group, who pursued more militant anti-racist politics, combined with a revolutionary Marxist stance inspired by the militancy and radicalism of '1968'.

The 1960s saw a significant shift in 'race relations' in Britain and major legislative changes. For most of the 1950s, the Conservative government had wavered over the implementation of immigration controls, trying to keep a balance between the economic benefits of Commonwealth migration with concerns over the social 'problems' presented by non-white migration. By 1962, the anti-immigrationist sections of the Conservatives had won and controls were established through the Commonwealth Immigrants Act. Although opposing the implementation of controls while in opposition, Wilson's new Labour government further tightened controls in 1965, but also introduced the first Race Relations Act in the same year, which prohibited explicit racial discrimination in the public sphere. Labour introduced even tougher restrictions on Commonwealth migration in 1968 in an attempt to prevent Kenyan Asians from migrating in large numbers to Britain, but once again followed this with an amended

Race Relations Act, which now tackled racial discrimination in employment, housing and other areas.

The Communist Party found itself in a balancing act regarding these legislative reforms. On the issue of immigration controls, the CPGB opposed the implementation of 'racist' controls, but accepted that nation-states had the right to restrict immigration, calling for it to be done in a 'non-racial' way. The Party's allies in the labour movement, the Labour left and trade unions, were generally in favour of some kind of control on immigration and the Party faced an uphill battle to convince the labour movement that immigration controls as established by the government were discriminatory and unnecessary. On the other side, the CPGB was criticised for its surrender to chauvinism with its acceptance of the concept of non-racist or non-discriminatory controls by sections of the far left, such as the IS and the IMG, as well as various black political and immigrant organisations. On the issue of legislation being used to tackle racial discrimination, the Party supported the use of the Race Relations Act to prosecute cases against racism and indeed campaigned for the Act to be strengthened. This caused consternation for others involved on the far left and some militant black political organisations, who warned that the state could not be employed to fight racism as it was the perpetrator of significantly racist actions.

The Communist Party, Labour and Immigration Controls

Although the Conservatives had considered controls on Commonwealth migration since the early 1950s,[1] it was in the aftermath of the Notting Hill 'riots' in 1958 that the issue of immigration controls became more prominent.[2] Conservative MP Cyril Osborne forwarded a motion in Parliament urging the government to 'take immediate steps to restrict the immigration of all persons, ... who are unfit, idle, or criminal',[3] having argued for the 'urgent need for a restriction ... particularly of coloured immigrants' just over a month before.[4] In the CPGB weekly, the World News, Kay Beauchamp tried to counter the 'many exaggerated statements about the country being flooded with vast numbers of coloured people', stating in late 1958 that immigration from the New Commonwealth

---

1 See Carter, Harris and Joshi 1987.
2 For further information about the 1958 Notting Hill riots, see Miles 1984, pp. 252–75; Pilkington 1996, pp. 171–84.
3 House of Commons, *Hansard*, 5 December 1958, col. 1552.
4 House of Commons, *Hansard*, 29 October 1958, col. 195.

had 'fallen rapidly' since the mid-1950s.[5] In countering calls for immigration, Beauchamp claimed that although these advocates tried to argue for unbiased controls, the 'demand for controlled immigration is the sharpest expression of colour bar because it is only raised in relation to coloured immigrants'.[6] The issue of racial discrimination was seen by Beauchamp as a leftover product from Britain's imperialist past:

> Only those with very deep-seated imperialist ideas would attempt to justify a position in which British people would still go to the colonies and take the best jobs, the best houses and the most fertile land, but colonial workers would be barred from coming here, in search of the work denied them in their homeland.[7]

Beauchamp reiterated that these immigrants were British subjects and in keeping with the CPGB's position of free movement within the Commonwealth, stated that 'as long as they remain so there is no justification for depriving them of the right to come here'.[8] A document prepared by Dutt in 1961 stated that the question of 'colonials in Britain' was 'now taking on increasing importance as a field of practical solidarity and in the fight to defeat attempts to promote racial division', highlighting the campaign against 'the proposed legislation on colonial immigration'.[9]

In November 1961, the Conservative government presented the Commonwealth Immigrants Bill for debate in Parliament. The Communist Party opposed the Bill stating that despite claims by the government that the Bill would 'have nothing to do with colour ... there has been little agitation among Tories about white immigration'.[10] The Party asserted that 'make no mistake, it is a colour bar that is proposed'.[11] The aim of the Commonwealth Immigrants Bill was 'not to guarantee jobs ... but to bring in a scheme of indentured cheap labour for immigrants with the tap being turned on and off to suit the needs of British big business'.[12] The Bill was seen by the Party as the extension of the col-

---

5   Beauchamp, 'Labour Movement Must Act', *World News*, 13 September 1958, p. 557.
6   Beauchamp, 'Labour Movement Must Act', p. 558.
7   Ibid.
8   Ibid.
9   Dutt, 'End Colonialism ... Old and New', 27 October 1961, p. 17, in CPGB archives, CP/IND/DUTT/19/14, LHASC.
10 Moss 1961, p. 3.
11 Moss 1961, p. 4.
12 Ibid.

our bar which already existed in Britain used by the ruling class to 'justify the exploitation of colonial workers ... and splitting white and coloured workers'.[13] For the CPGB, the colour bar in Britain worked to divide the labour movement, aiming to create an 'unorganised pool of coloured workers defenceless against unscrupulous employers and a potential weapon for lowering all working conditions'.[14] The strategy for combating the creation of a colour bar was not to 'ban the coloured worker or to strike against his employment', but to 'organise coloured workers into the unions and encourage them to play a full part'.[15] The Commonwealth Immigrants Bill extended the colour bar to entry in Britain and would 'reverse Britain's traditional open door policy of allowing free entry to all her citizens', which the CPGB continued to argue for.[16] The 'common enemy' of the British working class, both black and white, as well as of the colonial workers was the Conservative government, which 'denies so many low paid workers decent homes to live in' and the 'big monopolies which exploit workers in the colonies and at home'.[17]

As the Conservatives had introduced the law and the Labour government had sworn to repeal the Act once elected, much of the CPGB's campaign seemed limited to waiting for the election of Labour to repeal the Act and focusing on fighting racial discrimination in Britain. The 'real way to fight the Tory racialist policy is to do as the Communists do', the *Daily Worker* editorial stated in September 1964 in the lead up to the General Election, urging readers to 'oppose all ... racial and colour discrimination, including the Commonwealth Immigrants Act'.[18]

There was an emphasis by progressive and immigrant organisations on lobbying the High Commissions and the Labour Party, rather than demonstrations on the streets. Once the Bill was passed 'the Labour Party, with an eye to the elections, had begun to sidle out of its commitment'.[19] In an article written in 1964, Claudia Jones wrote that 'all ... political parties have capitulated in one way or another way to this racialist immigration measure'.[20] The only exception was the Communist Party, which, Jones acknowledged, 'completely oppose[d]

---

13   Ibid.
14   Ibid.
15   Moss 1961, p. 14.
16   Moss 1961, p. 3.
17   Moss 1961, p. 15.
18   *Daily Worker*, 29 September 1964.
19   Sivanandan 1982, p. 12.
20   Jones 1985, p. 144.

the system of "quotas" and "controls" for *Commonwealth* immigration'.[21] The CPGB had a distinct anti-racist policy, with Jones listing at length the Party's stance on racism and immigration:

A recent statement of the Executive Committee of the British Communist Party declared its opposition to all forms of restrictions on coloured immigration; declared its readiness to contest every case of discrimination; urged repeal of the Commonwealth Immigrants Act; and called for equality of access for employment, rates of wages, promotion to skilled jobs, and opportunities for apprenticeship and vocational training. It gave full support to the Bill to Outlaw Racial Discrimination and pledged its readiness to support every progressive measure to combat discrimination in Britain. It also projected the launching of an ideological campaign to combat racialism, which it noted, infects wide sections of the British working class.[22]

The statement that Jones was referring to had declared that 'the main aim of the [Commonwealth Immigrants] Act is to cut down the number of coloured immigrants to Britain'.[23] The Party announced it was 'completely opposed to the system of "quotas" and "controls" for coloured immigrants', which was now being accepted by the Labour Party, declaring that Labour's stance 'does not differ in principle from the attitude of the Tory government'.[24]

For the CPGB, the left of the Labour Party was an important part of the transition to socialism as outlined in *The British Road to Socialism*, but the 'major obstacle' was the 'right-wing dominance in the leadership of the Labour Party'.[25] Therefore the Communist Party's strategy focused on trade union cooperation with the Labour left and the Wilson government was viewed as more of a barrier to Conservative re-election than the foundation for fundamental political change. This was demonstrated by the increasing criticism from the CPGB aimed at the Labour Party throughout the 1960s as it tightened immigration controls.

Before the 1964 General Election, the Communist Party had hoped that Labour would repeal the Commonwealth Immigrants Act, which had been

---

21   Ibid.
22   Jones 1985, p. 145.
23   *End Racialism in Britain*, 1964, London: CPGB flyer, in CPGB archives, CP/LON/RACE/01/02, LHASC.
24   *End Racialism in Britain*.
25   Thompson 1992, p. 134.

pledged by Labour Party officials on several occasions, but by mid-1964 the CPGB's political statements demonstrated their doubts that Labour would follow through on this demand. It was realised after the election that Labour was in fact just as capable of being influenced by racist and imperialist ideas as the Conservatives. In the lead up to the 28th National Congress in 1963, Trevor Carter wrote that the Labour Party had promised to repeal the 1962 Act if they won the next election and demanded that the Party 'have got to see that they keep their promise!'[26]

As the election loomed closer, the CPGB warned that the Labour Opposition also talked about a 'system of "quotas" and "controls" for coloured immigrants', which did 'not differ in principle from the attitude of the Tory Government'.[27] A White Paper that was introduced in 1965 significantly restricted the number of work vouchers available for Commonwealth migrants and this was seen by the Communist Party as the 'direct outcome of the influence of Tory racialism on Labour Government policy'.[28] Idris Cox, a leading figure in the Party's International Department, claimed that 'it seemed obvious' in October 1965 that the Labour Party's opposition to the Commonwealth Immigrants Act in 1962 was 'more a matter of political expediency than of principle'.[29] Before Wilson had become Prime Minister, Labour's opposition to the control of Commonwealth migration was 'unconditional', but soon after the electoral victory in 1964, Wilson announced that, 'We do not contest the need for control of immigration into this country' and accepted the continuation of the Commonwealth Immigrants Act.[30]

Wilson's statement that Labour now accepted the concept of immigration controls was the beginning of a growing consensus between the two major parties that Commonwealth immigration was a problem. The defeat of Labour MP Gordon Walker to Conservative candidate Peter Griffiths, primarily fought on the issue of immigration, stressed the capitulation of Labour to the acceptance of racial discrimination through immigration controls. Griffiths used the issue of immigration, supported by the Conservative Association, local anti-immigration advocates and fascist groups, to disrupt the traditional support for the Labour Party in Smethwick. The most notorious and infamous part of this campaign was the slogan, 'If you want a nigger neighbour, vote Labour', to which Griffiths commented, 'I would not condemn anyone who said that. I

---

26   Carter, 'National Liberation', *Comment Supplement*, 23 February 1963.
27   *End Racialism in Britain*.
28   Cox, 'Spotlight on Racialism', *Comment*, 2 October 1965, p. 638.
29   Ibid.
30   *Hansard*, 27 November 1963, col. 367.

regard it as a manifestation of popular feeling'.[31] The Labour Party's interpretation of the loss of Smethwick (a loss of 7.2 percent against an average swing across the nation to Labour of 3.5 percent)[32] was, according to Labour Minister Richard Crossman, that '[e]ver since the Smethwick election it has been quite clear that immigration can be the greatest potential vote-loser for the Labour Party'.[33]

The notion of the Labour Party yielding in the face of racist public opinion has been well described in the history of race relations in Britain, but as Kathleen Paul wrote, the concept of a 'hostile public push[ing] an otherwise liberal administration toward ever greater "immigration" control' is the 'picture presented by policy makers themselves'.[34] While the traditional history views the Smethwick result as the impetus for Labour's acceptance of restrictions on black immigration, Kathleen Paul's assertion that these measures were 'driven not by the explosion of "race and immigration" into the electoral arena but by imperatives internal to the governing elite' is much more convincing.[35]

The emphasis of the Labour government during this period was on the notions of 'integration' and 'absorption' of black immigrants, but the government believed that integration could not occur without immigration controls. Labour MP Roy Hattersley summarised this by declaring that 'without integration, limitation is inexcusable; without limitation, integration is impossible'.[36] By the mid-1960s, consensus had been reached by Labour and the Conservatives that Commonwealth immigration was undesirable and threatened social cohesion in Britain. As Roy Hattersley stated in Parliament in March 1965, 'I believe that unrestricted immigration can only produce additional problems, additional suffering and additional hardship unless some kind of limitation is imposed and continued'.[37] Speaking as 'a passionate opponent of the [Commonwealth Immigrants] Act', Hattersley now claimed that 'with the advantages of hindsight, I suspect that we were wrong to oppose the Act'.[38]

The Labour government believed that immigration control, alongside the Race Relations Act that they introduced in 1965, would ease the process of integration for black immigrants from the New Commonwealth into the 'Brit-

---

31   Cited in Miles and Phizacklea 1984, p. 49.
32   Miles and Phizacklea 1984, p. 50.
33   Crossman 1975, pp. 149–50.
34   Paul 1997, p. 177.
35   Paul 1997, pp. 177–8.
36   Cited in Miles and Phizacklea 1984, p. 57.
37   *Hansard*, 23 March 1965, col. 380–1.
38   *Hansard*, 23 March 1965, col. 380.

ish way of life'. This process of integration, reinforced by legislation against the most overt forms of public racial discrimination, would help 'stamp out the evils of racialism'.[39] As Peter Alexander wrote, 'Immigration control was expected to reduce racism. The reverse happened. And with increased racism came further controls'.[40]

The General Election of 1964 and in particular the upset that occurred at Smethwick, has traditionally been viewed as the turning point for the Labour Party in the acceptance of immigration controls (although an increasing amount of scholarship contradicts this thesis). On this issue, it is clear from contemporary Communist Party literature that there was a suspicion that Labour would not repeal the Commonwealth Immigrants Act once elected and demonstrated a lack of conviction over any legislation concerning racial discrimination. The Party's London District Committee proposed four factors that led to the electoral result at Smethwick:

i)   Continuous agitation by an unscrupulous anti-immigrant organisation.
ii)   Publicity for its activities in the press.
iii) Tories adopted the same policy.
iv)   Labour Party did not fight on principle and was put on the defensive.[41]

These factors, particularly the last one, the Communist Party warned were 'more and more becoming applicable to the whole country' and that Labour had 'succumbed' to the Conservative's 'attack on coloured people'.[42] On the issue of the legislation against racial discrimination, the LDC warned:

> The Labour Government has also retreated on the Bill against racial discrimination and prejudice which it is proposed to pass in an emasculated form. This means that the Tories are allowed to make the running. They can always claim that Labour is not doing enough to restrict coloured immigration and Labour is put on the defensive.[43]

---

39   Ennals, 'Labour's Race Relations Policy', *Institute of Race Relations Newsletter*, November/December 1968, p. 437.
40   Alexander 1987, p. 34.
41   'Racialist Threat to London Labour Movement and How to Meet It', 1964, p. 1, in CPGB archives, CP/LON/RACE/01/05, LHASC.
42   Ibid.
43   Ibid.

In a 1965 CPGB pamphlet, Harry Bourne wrote that there was no justification for the Labour Party to 'surrender to Tory racialist clamour' for 'electoral reasons'.[44] 'Such yielding to an enemy demand does not strengthen the Party that surrenders', wrote Bourne, 'but only serves to strengthen the hand of the original promoters of the demand'.[45] This enemy was identified as the 'Tory landlords, bankers and factory owners' who promoted racism to divide the working class.[46]

Despite the increasing capitulation to popular racist attitudes by the Labour government in the 1960s and 1970s, the CPGB still looked to the Labour Party to implement anti-racist legislation, appealing to notions of leftist unity and not proposing total opposition to Labour. Racism amongst the labour movement was overlooked in favour of praise for the trade unions and the 'leading part' they were to play in future anti-racist campaigns.[47] Racism was still described as a 'Tory trick to split the working class'[48] and the actions of the Labour Party were passed off as mere capitulation to racism amongst the Conservatives, with little analysis of Labour's notions of 'race' and tradition of imperialism. Despite the opposition to the Commonwealth Immigrants Act under Gaitskell, Labour's traditional views on 'race', immigration and imperialism were not entirely liberal or progressive. As Paul Foot wrote, Labour's attitude towards immigration 'falls very clearly into an established historical pattern', with the Labour Party in opposition bitterly opposing controls, but once elected, they had 'manipulated these controls much more ruthlessly than had [their] political opponents'.[49]

The Principle of Immigration Controls

The Communist Party always maintained its opposition to racially biased immigration controls, and from 1962 onwards it called for the repeal of each increasingly racist amendment to legislation concerning immigration. However, on the principle of immigration controls, the Party's line was much more populist. This was defined in 1965 in a Party statement on the 1962 Commonwealth Immigrants Act:

---

44   Bourne, *Racialism: Cause and Cure*, 1965, London: CPGB pamphlet, p. 10.
45   Bourne, *Racialism*, p. 11.
46   Bourne, *Racialism*, p. 14.
47   Ibid.
48   Ibid.
49   Foot 1965, p. 186.

Every government, whatever its character, and whatever the social system, will naturally make regulations concerning immigration and emigration. This is an understandable exercise of its power by any sovereign government. The Communist Party has never stood for general unrestricted immigration, but has always opposed racialism and racial discrimination into Britain.[50]

Before the introduction of legislation restricting Commonwealth immigration, the Party, like the shadow Labour government, opposed immigration controls on the principle that 'colonial people are British subjects' and should retain the right to enter, settle and work in Britain.[51] In the lead up to the 1962 Act, the Communist Party opposed imposing restrictions, declaring that the Act would 'reverse Britain's traditional open door policy of allowing free entry to all her citizens'.[52]

The Party's policy statement on 'race relations' simply stated that the 'Communist Party stands for ... the repeal of the Commonwealth Immigrants Act, and complete opposition to all forms of restriction (open or concealed) ... against coloured immigrants'.[53] By 1965, the Party was conceding ground, like the Labour Party, in its opposition to controls. In a statement on the 1965 White Paper, the Party declared that 'Every government makes regulations concerning immigration and emigration' as this was 'an understandable exercise of its sovereign rights'.[54] But as Harry Bourne wrote in a CPGB pamphlet published at the same time, this right was 'not a cover for the practice of racial discrimination'.[55] The CPGB called for the repeal of the 1962 Act, because it was 'not an Act introduced for normal immigration purposes [a concept Bourne did not elaborate on] but designed to introduce an element of racial discrimination into the system of immigration'.[56]

Tony Chater was one of the few to elaborate on the Party's position in CPGB literature. 'Restrictions on immigration should never have a racialist bias and in any case are only justifiable if immigration is threatening the country with political, economic and social harm', wrote Chater, '[and] no-

50   'Draft Statement on Commonwealth Immigrants Act of 1962', 1965, in CPGB archives, CP/LON/RACE/01/10, LHASC.

51   Bolsover, *No Colour Bar in Britain*, 1955, London: CPGB pamphlet, p. 10.

52   Moss 1961, p. 3.

53   *End Racialism in Britain.*

54   'Immigration', 1965, in CPGB archives, CP/LON/RACE/01/09, LHASC.

55   Bourne, *Racialism*, p. 9.

56   Bourne, *Racialism*, p. 11.

one can seriously maintain that this applies today'.[57] This asserted that there
was no need for immigration control *at all at that moment*, rather than the
usual Party line, which accepted controls, if they were not applied on racial
discrimination. Chater was much more concerned about socialist planning
to fix the housing and employment problems facing Britain, stating that the
'only real solution is socialist policy, not immigration control'.[58] Overcrowding
in South-East England was 'due to movements of population within Britain
itself, rather than to immigration from outside', claiming that as a 'result of
deliberate Tory policy ... Industry [had] been allowed to develop too quickly in
the South-East'.[59] For Chater, to combat overcrowding, what was needed was
'not immigration control, but a real National Plan for the development of the
country as a whole'.[60] The Commonwealth Immigrants Act was described as
a 'dangerous charade', stating that 'it solved no problem because there was no
problem to solve'.[61]

The Campaign for Legislation against Racial Discrimination

As mentioned in the previous chapter, the International Department published
the 1955 pamphlet *No Colour Bar in Britain*, which contained the 'Charter of
Rights' for Commonwealth migrants coming to Britain. The first point of this
Charter called for:

> No form of colour discrimination by employers, landlords, publicans,
> hotel proprietors or any aspect of social, educational and cultural activity.
> Any racial discrimination to be made a penal offence.[62]

This meant support for Fenner Brockway's attempts to pass legislation that
would ban racial discrimination and the 'colour bar' in Britain. In June 1956,
Brockway introduced a Bill 'to make illegal discrimination to the detriment
of any person on the grounds of colour, race and religion in the United Kingdom'.[63] Brockway acknowledged that 'there must be a limitation to the powers

---

57   Chater 1966, p. 62.
58   Chater 1966, p. 42.
59   Chater 1966, p. 39.
60   Chater 1966, p. 40.
61   Chater 1966, p. 50.
62   Bolsover, *No Colour Bar in Britain*, p. 11.
63   *Hansard*, 12 June 1956, col. 247.

of legislation', but cited three main areas where legislation was 'justified and necessary' – public areas, housing and employment.[64] At this time, Brockway was also National Chairman of the Movement for Colonial Freedom, founded in April 1954.[65] Between 1956 and the introduction of the Race Relations Act in 1965, Brockway proposed a bill on racial discrimination a number of times, all defeated by the Conservative majority. Kay Beauchamp wrote in *Marxism Today* in 1967 that Brockway had introduced a Bill on racial discrimination 'no less than eight times', and this had been supported by the MCF, the National Council for Civil Liberties (NCCL) and other progressive organisations, as well as the Communist Party itself.[66]

There were two main arguments made by the Communist Party for the introduction of the Race Relations Act. The first was a continuation of the CPGB's anti-fascist stance, calling for a ban on the incitement to racial hatred. The other was the wider argument for legislation to combat racial discrimination that was much more widespread and institutionalised than that explicitly perpetrated by the fascist far right minority. The CPGB argued that this was not an issue of free speech, but stated that preventing race hatred was a 'guarantee of peace, democracy and progress'.[67] To defend these ideals, the Party demanded that fascist organisations, such as Mosley's Union Movement, be banned from using public halls, and that workers should 'oppose every form of colour discrimination' and make 'such discrimination or propaganda for it, a criminal offence'.[68]

This argument was raised again in July 1962, when anti-fascists, in what were the beginnings of the Yellow Star Movement, battled in Trafalgar Square against the fledgling National Socialist Movement (NSM), led by Colin Jordan and future National Front leader, John Tyndall. According to *The Guardian*, the first public meeting of the NSM 'ended with 20 arrests, fights, bleeding faces, abuse, and tears'.[69] In the weeks following, the CPGB demanded that 'racial incitement be made illegal ... as a result of the widespread and deep indignation aroused by the recent re-activisation of fascist organisations in Britain'.[70] The Party repeated that Fenner Brockway had been proposing legislation against racist

---

64   *Hansard*, 12 June 1956, col. 248–9.

65   Howe 1993, p. 231.

66   Beauchamp, 'Racialism in Britain Today and How to Fight It', *Marxism Today*, July 1967, p. 203.

67   'Stop Racial Propaganda', n.d., Manchester: CPGB flyer.

68   'Stop Racial Propaganda'.

69   *The Guardian*, 2 July 1962.

70   Jones, 'Outlaw This Incitement to Racial Hatred', *Comment*, 11 August 1962, p. 381.

propaganda for years and declared that it, along with the British working class, would 'give its wholehearted support to the efforts being made for the carrying of such legislation in Parliament'.[71]

However, the Party was wary about the state using the 1936 Public Order Act to combat public racist agitation. In the same article, it warned that a 'Tory MP, incidentally, has seized the opportunity to propose a ban on ALL political meetings in [Trafalgar] Square',[72] which would have had a much harder impact on the left and other progressive movements than the fascist far right. The fact that the Public Order Act had been 'mainly used against those who resent and protest against provocative racialist propaganda' was one of the reasons why the Communist Party supported Brockway's Bill, rather than amending the 1936 Act.[73] In a memorandum presented by the London District Committee in December 1964, the Party declared:

> There should be no question of amending the Public Order Act (1936) instead of introducing a Bill. The Public Order Act is an Act directed *against* the working class movement and any strengthening of it will tend to be used not against fascists, but as in the past, against anti-fascists.[74]

The other side to the campaign for legislation against racial discrimination was the much more widespread and institutionalised racism that black people in Britain faced in public places, in employment, in seeking housing and in their interactions with the state. Any legislation brought in could not eliminate all racism within British society, but Fenner Brockway's aimed to 'end, by legislation, the practice of race discrimination in … *public* relations'.[75] Despite the very real instances of racial discrimination that were experienced by blacks in Britain, the Conservatives opposed any legislation, declaring that 'it would be almost impossible to prove that a person had been turned away on the grounds of colour and on the grounds of colour alone'.[76] Describing Brockway's proposals as 'badly drafted and ill-conceived', Conservative MP Bernard Braine claimed during a Parliamentary debate on the Bill that 'a large number of coloured people … have not experienced any form of discrimination', and

---

71   Ibid.
72   Ibid.
73   Zaidman, 'Fight Race Hate Here Too', *Comment*, 5 October 1963, p. 631.
74   London District Committee, 'Memorandum on a Bill against Racial Discrimination and Incitement', 16 December 1964, in CPGB archives, CP/LON/RACE/01/01, LHASC.
75   *Hansard*, 30 April 1958, col. 388.
76   *Hansard*, 24 May 1957, col. 1604.

that 'discrimination, therefore, is something which ought not to be tackled by legislation, but ... by education'.[77]

The Communist Party countered these claims by the Conservatives in the *Daily Worker* and other CPGB literature. In a memorandum submitted to the Labour government by the London District Committee in March 1965, the Party declared that racism was 'widespread in relation to employment, housing and recreational facilities' with 'many examples of refusal to serve coloured people in restaurants, public houses and other public places'.[78] To counter this, the Party proposed that discrimination should be made illegal:

(a) by a keeper of a Hotel, Public House, Café or Restaurant ...;
(b) by a keeper of any kind of Boarding House, Common Lodging House or in granting a tenancy;
(c) by a keeper of any public place of entertainment ... to which the public are admitted.[79]

In the sphere of employment, the Party proposed legislation making it illegal for 'employers or workers to refuse employment, apprenticeship, training or promotion' on the grounds of race, along with attempts to 'pay a lower rate to a worker' on racial grounds.[80] The Party proposed that any public incitement of racial hatred or contempt should be an offence, to be applied to the spoken word and that used in leaflets, newspapers or any other printed or duplicated material. The Party reiterated that 'existing legislation is inadequate with this menace' of explicit racial prejudice and 'the matter cannot be effectively dealt with by amending the Public Order Act'.[81]

Throughout the Communist Party's campaign to support the creation of what became the Race Relations Act, there was the acknowledgement of the limitations of legislation without wider education and efforts made at local grassroots level. 'No one would pretend that such legislation, by itself alone, would be sufficient to wipe out colour-bar practices', wrote Kay Beauchamp, 'let alone to rid people's minds of the racial ideas which more than three hundred years of capitalist rule have plated there'.[82] But it was hoped that the Race

77   *Hansard*, 24 May 1957, col. 1602; col. 1606.
78   London District Committee, *Against Racial Discrimination & Incitement: What Should Be in the Bill?*, March 1965, p. 2, in CPGB archives, CP/LON/RACE/01/04, LHASC.
79   London District Committee, *Against Racial Discrimination & Incitement*, p. 5.
80   London District Committee, *Against Racial Discrimination & Incitement*, p. 6.
81   London District Committee, *Against Racial Discrimination & Incitement*, pp. 8–9.
82   Beauchamp, 'Colour Bar', *Comment*, 11 January 1964, p. 22.

Relations Act would 'deter those who at present practice racial discrimination' and 'restrain those ... who deliberately incite racial hatred', as well as preventing 'the more open forms of their insidious propaganda'.[83]

The Race Relations Acts Under Labour, 1965–8

In November 1965, the Race Relations Act was enacted by the Labour government. On the issue of discrimination, the Act made it illegal for places of public resort to 'practise discrimination on the ground of colour, race, or ethnic or national origins against persons seeking access to or facilities or services at that place'.[84] In the sphere of housing, tenancy could not be withheld on the grounds of race, but this only applied to freestanding properties and not to lodgings where the landlord also lived.[85] The Labour government established a Race Relations Board to investigate complaints of violations of the Act and facilitate conciliation between the parties concerned. Punishment for violation of the Act could only be delivered by the Attorney General, to whom the Race Relations Board would report. While racial discrimination was now in violation of *civil* law, it made racial incitement, published, distributed or publicly spoken, a *criminal* offence. However, the final clause of the Act also amended the 1936 Public Order Act, extending it to any words or writings deemed 'threatening, abusive or insulting, with intent to provoke a breach of the peace' and not limited to the issue of 'race'.[86]

The Race Relations Act was a significantly weaker Act than the one that had been proposed by Fenner Brockway, and, as Dilip Hiro noted, it was 'criticized by liberal opinion both inside and outside Parliament', including criticism from the Communist Party.[87] The Act was described as being 'marred by weakness which represented a dangerous concession to the most reactionary and racially

---

83   Ibid.
84   *Race Relations Act*, 1965, 1(1).
85   In most discussions of the shortcomings of the first Race Relations Act, it is generally mentioned that 'it did not apply to the areas of employment and housing'. While employment was not included in the Act, some mention of housing was included, but this is commonly overlooked. Even contemporary reports in the Communist Party press generalised about the weaknesses of the Act, stating that, 'Discrimination in the important fields of employment and housing is not within its scope'. Miles and Phizacklea 1984, p. 57; Hiro 1992, p. 210; Moore 1975, p. 103; Chater 1966, p. 62; *Daily Worker*, 29 April 1965.
86   *Race Relations Act*, 1965, 7.
87   Hiro 1992, p. 210.

prejudiced of the Tory Party'.[88] Tony Chater claimed that the Act worked as a 'barrier against prosecution for incitement to racial hatred' as it relied on the Attorney General to initiate any proceedings.[89] Conciliation machinery was viewed as 'very desirable, but only within the framework of criminal proceedings', not as a substitute for legislation.[90] 'If such machinery becomes a substitute for legislation against racial discrimination', warned CPGB member Harry Bourne, 'then full licence will be left to the racialists to carry on their foul work'.[91]

In July 1967, Beauchamp wrote in *Marxism Today*:

> The Race Relations Board recently reported that out of 309 cases referred to it, 224 referred to matters outside its powers, including 97 on jobs and 23 on housing. Of the remaining 87, 17 had been settled out of court, 2 had been referred to the Attorney General and 31 were being looked at.[92]

The amendments to the Public Order Act in the 1965 Act were claimed by the CPGB to have 'nothing to do with race relations' and its extensions argued to go 'beyond the intention' of the Act, with the possibility of it being 'used to curb the normal political activities of the people'.[93] Despite its weaknesses, the Communist Party saw the Act as 'a first limited step to combat the spread of racial discrimination and incitement' and called for support for it 'in principle by all progressive people'.[94] The CPGB continued to call for 'amending of the Race Relations Act to make it more effective against incitement to race hatred and against discrimination, particularly in housing and employment'.[95] It also proposed that 'it should be easier for a victim … to have recourse to law without having to seek the Attorney General's intervention'.[96] However, when the Act was strengthened by the Labour government in 1968, this happened as more severe restrictions were placed on black immigration in Britain.

---

88   'Political Committee Statement on Race Relations Bill', in CPGB archives, CP/LON/RACE/ 01/02, LHASC.
89   Chater 1966, p. 62.
90   Chater 1966, p. 63.
91   Bourne, *Racialism*, p. 12.
92   Beauchamp, 'Racialism in Britain Today and How to Fight It', p. 203.
93   'Political Committee Statement on Race Relations Bill'.
94   'Political Committee Statement on Race Relations Bill'.
95   Beauchamp, 'Racialism in Britain and the Fight Against It', p. 617.
96   Bourne, *Racialism*, pp. 12–13.

The CPGB's Concept of 'Race' in the Post-colonial Era

By the mid-1960s, the Party's literature on race and racism had developed two concepts that dominated discussion on the issue of race relations. These had repercussions on the practical anti-racist campaigning taken up by the CPGB. One was that 'race' was purely a sociological construct, demonstrated by the promotion of the CPGB slogan, 'one race, the human race'.[97] While 'race' has no basis in biological science, this notion detracted from the fact that ideas of 'race' were used for the very real purpose of oppression and discrimination; the denial of 'race' was a gesture that could be made by white people, but did not alter the actual experience by non-white people of racial discrimination. The other concept followed on from this, emphasising that racism was an ideological weapon created by capitalism for imperial exploitation and the division of lower class rebellion. As Jack Woddis stated, 'the root and fruit of racialism is profit'.[98] The emphasis on racism as an ideological falsity allowed for a subordination of race below the 'immediate' issues of the class struggle, which led to a failure to attract black workers to the CPGB, who were more likely to join the black power organisations (especially young blacks), or in the case of Asians, organisations such as the Indian Workers Association.

Before the 1960s, there had been a tendency to view black immigrants as a colonial product, the 'alien' or 'outsider', a view that was pervasive in wider British society. By the mid-1960s, black immigration had occurred on a large scale for nearly twenty years. The black population was more visible, especially in the larger cities, and regarded as unexceptional, although racial prejudice still faced them in many areas of British society. For those in the Communist Party involved with anti-racism, the perception was changing from a colonial viewpoint to that of an indigenous and everyday issue, although a paternalist attitude was still apparent in the CPGB's relationship with its black members and the wider black communities. The Party acknowledged that there was 'already considerable colour prejudice' in Britain, described as 'latent for the most part', but since the General Election, racism had been brought to the surface, 'inflamed by political exploitation' through the Conservatives and

---

97   *One Race, the Human Race ... Two Classes, Workers and Bosses*, CPGB flyer, 1968; *One Race, the Human Race: A Communist Party Broadsheet on the Menace of Racism*, CPGB flyer, 1974; 'One Race – the Human Race', draft of CPGB flyer, in CPGB archives, CP/CENT/CIRC/52/07, LHASC; 'Fight Racialism', Merseyside Area CPGB statement, in Merseyside Record Office, M329COM/10/15.

98   Woddis 1960, p. xii.

the far right.[99] This latent racism existed, Harry Bourne explained in a CPGB pamphlet, because of Britain's imperialist history and the capitalist economic system, asserting that racial prejudice was not 'natural or inborn', but 'man made ... based on lies and thriv[ing] of ignorance'.[100]

Daily Worker writer Tony Chater's *Race Relations in Britain* furthered the Communist Party's emphasis that race was a sociological construct with no definite basis in biological science. The 'mythology of racialism' was the belief that 'the white man stands at the pinnacle of evolution', but Chater stated that 'even from a strictly biological angle, the concept of racial superiority is untenable'.[101] Adding to Chater's analysis, Kay Beauchamp declared in *Marxism Today* that 'there are no pure races', instead that a 'mixture of races' existed.[102] Beauchamp stated in her article, 'there is only one human species with one common origin and in that strict sense we all belong to one human race'.[103] Beauchamp's prominence as an anti-racist campaigner for both the CPGB and the MCF saw both organisations using the slogan, 'one race, the human race', with Beauchamp writing a pamphlet for Liberation under the same title.[104]

The CPGB emphasised that race was not a biological fact and logically there was 'no scientific basis for racial prejudice'.[105] However, this reliance on anthropological and scientific definitions of race ran into the very real problem that race as a political and sociological phenomenon did exist. As Robert Miles has written, '"races" are socially imagined rather than biological realities', with racism being 'an ideology which identifies individuals as belonging to a group on the basis of some real or imaginary biological or inherent characteristic'.[106] Thus, racism can be used to 'constitute the foundation for discriminatory and unfavourable treatment of all individuals identified as belonging to the group' or 'be employed to justify such a course of action after it has occurred'.[107] Therefore a denial of the importance of race and racism under the slogan 'one race, the human race' reduced the problems experienced by blacks in Britain to a

99   Bourne, *Racialism*, p. 8.

100   Ibid.

101   Chater 1966, p. 20.

102   Beauchamp, 'Race and Human Society', *Marxism Today*, June 1966, p. 167.

103   Beauchamp, 'Race and Human Society', p. 171.

104   See Beauchamp, *One Race, the Human Race*, 1979, London: Liberation pamphlet.

105   Beauchamp, 'Race and Human Society', p. 170.

106   Miles 1991, p. 71; Miles and Phizacklea 1984, p. 10.

107   Miles and Phizacklea 1984, p. 10.
          For more discussion on the ideology of 'race', see Miles 1982, pp. 7–92; Gilroy 2002, pp. 1–40; Solomos 1989, pp. 1–25; Anthias, Yuval-Davis and Cain 1993, pp. 1–20.

purely abstract position that conflicted with practical anti-racist campaigns and the rise of the concept of 'black power'.

As written by the Educational Committee for YCL branch meetings, the Communist Party's ideological position on the origins of racism asserted that although 'many people attribute race prejudice to a natural instinctive reaction against strangeness', the real cause of racism was to 'justify the slave trade and the rape of India'.[108] The Party's account of the cause of racism was based on a historical materialist account, which stated that racism 'did not exist before the sixteenth century'[109] and it was the expansion of the European imperial powers into the Americas and Africa in the 1500s that led to the development of the concept of racial superiority and therefore racial prejudice. 'Intolerance based on culture and religion' had existed for thousands of years, but Tony Chater stated that 'until modern times there is no evidence to suggest that it was justified by feelings of racial superiority'.[110] The discovery of the Americas in 1492 was described by Chater as the 'turning point' where definitions of racial inferiority started to emerge as British and Dutch merchants later joined the Spanish and Portuguese in a 'lust for gold' that ended the ideal of 'universal conversion'.[111] This elaborated a 'theory denying human status and human rights to the coloured races' for the purpose of a 'source of cheap labour for European capitalism'.[112] For Chater, 'race prejudice therefore serves the interests of capitalist exploitation'.[113]

As racism was a 'product of and a justification for ruthless exploitation' in the colonies,[114] it was necessary for ideas of racial superiority to be propagated within the lower classes. These ideas were generally accepted amongst the upper and middle classes because, according to Chater, 'they were in line with the general ideology ... to explain the exclusion of the working class from the fruits of the bourgeois revolution'.[115] Racism amongst the lower classes in Britain was the result of 'woggism', the philosophy disseminated within the colonial armies, made up of the working class and lower middle class, who had to use force against 'coloured workers demanding the very rights for which their

---

108   YCL Education Committee, 'Racialism', in CPGB archives, CP/LON/RACE/01/05, LHASC.
109   Chater 1966, p. 7.
110   Chater 1966, pp. 8–9.
111   Chater 1966, pp. 12–3.
112   Chater 1966, p. 13.
113   Chater 1966, p. 17.
114   Central Education Department, 'Racialism', Comment, 8 March 1969, p. 159.
115   Chater 1966, p. 16.

fathers had fought back home'.[116] The 'insidious concept' of racism and white racial superiority was the 'main weapon' of the British imperialist armies and thus had been 'bred deep into the British consciousness'.[117]

Chater admitted that his work was not a 'definitive statement on party policy' or an academic work,[118] with his argument weakened by his notion that racism was something that could be controlled by the capitalist ruling class, rather than a particular aspect of the capitalist process. The fact that Chater's arguments were considerably toned down or dropped in subsequent literature demonstrates that the Communist Party began to understand the complexities of anti-racism, not only as part of the wider struggle for socialism, but as one of the new social movements that created an awareness of (and resistance to) exploitation in other areas than the class struggle. The fact that Chater was part of the traditional industrialist wing of the Party further explains the class reductionism that formed his historical analysis of the evolution of racism.

Before the alternative of black revolutionary organisations began to appeal to a wider black population in the late 1960s, the Communist Party of Great Britain still commanded a position of authority amongst black workers and intellectuals, as the only party that seemed to be dealing with racism.[119] Up until the mid-1960s, the prevailing attitude of the Party's anti-racist activist cohort was the notion that the fight against racism in Britain was inherently a colonial issue. Dutt's 1958 statement that the 'real foundation of the colour bar and racial discrimination is the colonial system' is an indication of the mindset of the Party's anti-racist agenda in this period.[120] Most CPGB members involved in anti-racist activism had first taken up the struggle against imperialism during the interwar period and the arrival of migrants from the Commonwealth led to them constructing an anti-racist programme based around an already existing anti-colonial framework. Even in 1961, it was assumed that colonial subjects in Britain would eventually return to their countries of origin and the Party encouraged the 'development of Marxist training among colonials in Britain ... [to] help prepare cadres for development of the movement in countries to which they will return'.[121] This approach to issues of race and immigration was mainly developed by members within the Party's International Department,

---

116   Chater 1966, p. 17.
117   YCL Education Committee, 'Racialism'.
118   Letter from Tony Chater to Jack Woddis, 27 July 1966, in CPGB archives, CP/LON/RACE/ 01/11, LHASC.
119   Carter, CPGB Biographical Project, tape 04.
120   Dutt, 'Britain's Colonies and the Colour Bar', *Labour Monthly*, December 1958, p. 532.
121   Dutt, 'End Colonialism ... Old and New', p. 17.

and there was an attempt to spread these ideas through work with other anti-colonial groups, with the largest in the 1950s and 1960s being the Movement for Colonial Freedom (MCF).

The Movement for Colonial Freedom and Moderate Anti-racism

As mentioned above, a significant section of the anti-racist movement in Britain was borne out of previous organisations that championed anti-colonial politics and the rights of indigenous people abroad. This was certainly the case with the Movement for Colonial Freedom (MCF), which was the largest anti-colonial organisation in Britain, with broad support from progressive and labour circles. The CPGB saw the MCF as an important organisation for gathering support within the Labour Party and the trade unions for 'the struggle for national liberation in Africa, Asia and elsewhere', as well as its efforts to combat racism in Britain.[122] For the CPGB, the strength of the MCF was in its base in the labour movement and with 3,050,431 affiliated union members in the Movement in 1964–5,[123] the Party argued that the MCF's effectiveness would 'depend on the degree of support' it received from the trade unions.[124] In the Party's anti-racist campaigning of the 1950s and 1960s, the CPGB emphasised that 'British imperialism is the common enemy of the colonial people and of the British working class', which demanded a 'resolute and united struggle', a notion that was shared with the Movement for Colonial Freedom.[125] To this end, the Party declared in a 1964 flyer that it gave 'its complete backing to the positive campaigns of the Movement for Colonial Freedom', alongside pledging 'Full support for Fenner Brockway's Bill against Racial Discrimination'.[126]

Although CPGB members appeared in numerous leadership roles within the organisation, the political inspiration of the Movement for Colonial Freedom was 'drawn from the radical-liberal heritage', rather than Marxism, as the MCF, wrote Howe, 'refused to define its aims in specifically socialist terms'.[127]

---

122 'Racialist Threat to London Labour Movement and How to Meet It', in CPGB archives, CP/LON/RACE/01/05, LHASC.

123 Howe 1993, p. 241.

124 'Racialist Threat to London Labour Movement and How to Meet It'.

125 Moffat, 'Unite the Struggle for Colonial Freedom', *World News*, 29 April 1961, p. 321; Callaghan 2003, p. 138.

126 *End Racialism in Britain*, 1964, London: CPGB flyer, in CPGB archives, CP/LON/RACE/01/02, LHASC.

127 Howe 1993, p. 235.

However, the Communist Party's programme for decolonisation, despite its adherence to the Leninist theory that the end of imperialism would be the catalyst for socialist revolutions in the former colonies, was not a detailed strategy and did not dramatically differ from that proposed by the MCF. The objects of the Movement for Colonial Freedom, as defined in the MCF Constitution that was published in April 1961, were:

(a)   The right of all peoples to full independence (including self-determination and freedom from external political, economic and military domination).

(b)   The principle of international mutual aid by the extension to underdeveloped territories of economic aid free from exploitation or external ownership, technical assistance in the economic, social and political fields, and assistance in the development of trade unions and co-operative organisations.

(c)   The application of the Four Freedoms and the Declaration of Human Rights to all peoples, including Freedom from Contempt by the abolition of the Colour Bar.

(d)   The substitution of internationalism for imperialism in all political and economic relations.[128]

In a draft resolution published in the Party's weekly journal, *World News*, for the National Congress in April 1961 the same time as the publication of the aforementioned MCF pamphlet, the Party declared:

It is also in the interests of the British people to support the national liberation struggle of the colonial peoples against imperialist rule and of the newly-independent peoples against the attempts of imperialism to maintain or restore in new forms economic or strategic domination. This requires the withdrawal of military occupying forces; the cancellation of imperialist military treaties for strategic rights; and the redistribution of economic assets held by overseas monopolies. Only by ending colonialism and by recognition of full economic and political independence can new relations be established of mutual benefit.[129]

---

128   Movement for Colonial Freedom, *Objects and Constitution*, MCF pamphlet, London, 1961, in CPGB archives, CP/IND/KAY/01/01, LHASC.

129   CPGB, 'Draft Political Resolution', *World News Supplement*, January 1961, p. 10.

The above statements by the MCF and the CPGB seem very similar, with both organisations stressing the right to political and economic self-determination by the colonies. The long-term socialistic aspects of the Communist Party's anti-colonial programme seemed to be limited, with emphasis placed upon the immediate measures of decolonisation.[130] The Communist Party asserted that there was general consensus, 'at least on all the immediate issues' between the CPGB, large sections of the Labour Party and many trade union organisations on the issue of colonial freedom, meaning that there was 'an agreed programme on which wide sections [could] co-operate'.[131] This consensus on the immediate issues of decolonisation amongst sections of the labour movement was at the basis of the Movement for Colonial Freedom.

As the decolonisation process was nearing completion in the late 1960s, critics started to question the relevancy of the Movement for Colonial Freedom and some MCF members were apprehensive towards the MCF's foray into more general anti-racist activism and campaigns against immigration controls. Josiah Brownell has argued that this shift in the agenda of the MCF (to become Liberation in 1970) coincided with the domination of the MCF National Executive Committee and its London Area Council by members of the Communist Party.[132] Brownell has shown that when Fenner Brockway was Chairman of the MCF, there was a strong push to keep the Communist Party away from the organisation, with affiliation to the MCF denied to the CPGB in line with Labour's proscription.[133] Communists had to join the MCF as individual members and were instructed to keep recruitment or the promotion of CPGB policy to a minimum. But by the late 1960s, and certainly after the organisation became Liberation, the original goal of the MCF had been replaced with a more

---

130   In response to the Political Resolution put forward, George Thomson, a strong supporter
       of traditional Marxism-Leninism (and the Chinese Revolution) within the CPGB, wrote in
       a pre-Congress discussion in *World News*, 'Have we no aims or demands to put forward
       in the struggle against British imperialism? ... The truth is, surely, that we shall never win
       socialism in Britain ... until we show far greater solidarity with the colonial peoples than
       appears in this document'. However, Thomson did not propose what aims or demands the
       Communist Party should have included, other than 'making it clear to them [the people
       in the colonies] that we recognise that we and they are bound together in a common
       struggle, the brunt of which still falls on them'. Thomson, 'Have We Forgotten The Colonial
       Peoples?', *World News*, 4 February 1961, p. 63.
131   Beauchamp, 'The Common Struggle of the British and Colonial Peoples', *Marxism Today*,
       March 1960, p. 77.
132   Brownell 2007, p. 256.
133   Brownell 2007, p. 244.

generalised anti-racist agenda and with the Communist presence in the leadership roles, this took on certain types of campaigning, such as anti-fascist activism. This came to a head when the LAC organised a counter-demonstration against the National Front in June 1974, resulting in the death of one protestor, which will be discussed at length in the next chapter.

The Beginnings of the 'British Upturn' and the Radicalism of '1968'

The 1960s saw a transformation in British society, described by Chris Harman as the 'British upturn',[134] and this had an enormous effect on the outlook of the Communist Party, including the Party's anti-racist work. The period from 1964 to 1970, under the Prime Ministership of Harold Wilson, has been described as the high point of the 'permissive society', with significant steps taken in social legislation dealing with abortion, homosexuality, divorce and the abolition of the death penalty, as well as the introduction (and amendment) of the Race Relations Act. At the same time, there was 'a shift towards an authoritarian response to so-called "threats" to society' – the student movement, the anti-Vietnam War movement, trade unions and Irish Republicanism, with black immigrants being viewed as a 'subversive' element.[135] The CPGB had originally hoped for the building of a mass party through electoral co-operation with Labour, but this had not reaped the political dividends the Party had expected, while the efforts made by Labour to implement an incomes policy brought the Party back to a strategy of confrontation through the trade union movement. This 'business of opposition', as described by John Callaghan,[136] in the industrial sphere was also seen in the increasingly critical nature of the Party towards the Labour government's immigration policies.

Trade unions were central to Communist Party strategy and the Party leadership saw the importance of the unions and the labour movement to the anti-racist struggle. The Party stated that the 'fight to defend black workers is a fight to defend the whole trade union movement',[137] and that 'all sections of the [labour] movement must unite and fight together against every manifestation of racialism'.[138] This united movement against racism was linked to the wider alliances supported in *The British Road to Socialism*, described as the 'key to

---

134   Harman 1988.
135   Solomos, Findlay, Jones and Gilroy 1982, pp. 22–3.
136   Callaghan 2003, p. 193.
137   Bellamy, *Unite Against Racialism*, 1971, London: CPGB, p. 9.
138   Bourne, *Racialism*, p. 14.

winning the people's economic and social demands, making decisive inroads into capitalist power, and advancing to the construction of the new socialist system in Britain'.[139]

The strategy outlined in *The British Road to Socialism* was based around a 'strong Communist Party working in full association with the Labour Party, trade unions and Co-operative movement',[140] which meant collaboration with the Labour left in the trade unions and in the electoral process. In elections, the Party stated it would 'always work for a Labour Government against the Tories', but it also pursued an independent electoral presence, fighting for 'Communist representation in Parliament and on the local councils, in order to strengthen the whole working class'.[141] Commitment to this strategy in the industrial and electoral fields was the beginning of what was described by CPGB historian Willie Thompson as the attempt to build a 'mass party'.[142]

Building a 'mass party' around the strategy of *The British Road to Socialism* meant an increase in election work, both for its independent candidates and in support of the Labour Party. The failure of the Party in the electoral field in 1964, and then again in 1966, contributed to a shift in emphasis towards industrial opposition to the Labour Party. As John Callaghan wrote in his history of the CPGB, 'by the summer of 1966 all introspection [on the election results] was in any case put aside as the Communists got back to the business of opposition ... and the Party's instruction to militants was unequivocal – mobilise and destroy'.[143]

One of the major concerns for the CPGB was its position on the left and its relationship to the Labour Party as it opposed the right-wing Labour government, but co-operated with the Labour left within the trade union movement. The Communist Party was occupying the political space to the left of the Labour Party and was by far the biggest Party of the left, but was also 'separate and distinct from the hard-left diaspora',[144] the various Trotskyist and Marxist-Leninist (Maoist) organisations. The central theme for the CPGB was building 'Labour-Communist unity ... to advance on the road to socialism', which demanded 'common action, without reservations, between the various sections of the labour movement'.[145]

---

139   Ibid.
140   CPGB, *The British Road to Socialism*, 1958, p. 30.
141   CPGB, *The British Road to Socialism*, 1958, p. 13.
142   Thompson 1992, p. 133.
143   Callaghan 2003, p. 193.
144   Cross 2003, p. 42.
145   CPGB, *The British Road to Socialism*, 1968, p. 25; p. 22.

It was the appointment of Bert Ramelson as Industrial Organiser in 1966 that consolidated the CPGB's Broad Left strategy.[146] It was Ramelson's concept that the Party should be 'strong at the top as well as the bottom' of the unions, placing emphasis on building from the shopfloor to secure its own candidates in trade union offices and executive levels.[147] The decade of heightened industrial militancy began in 1966 as the new Labour government attempted to introduce a Price and Incomes Policy, which Harold Wilson called 'a necessary condition of maintaining full employment' because 'if incomes rise faster than production unemployment is threatened'.[148] Wilson claimed that it was only through a 'conscious assertion of social responsibility in the matter of incomes of all kinds' that Britain could achieve 'full employment [and] price stability at home and abroad'.[149] The general view of economists was that the only way this legislation could be implemented was by 'outfacing the trade unions on some big national wage struggle'.[150] In June 1966, the CPGB supported the seamen's strike against this incomes policy, when Harold Wilson denounced the Communist Party union leaders as a 'tightly knit group of politically motivated men … determined to exercise backstage pressures … endangering the security of the industry and the economic welfare of the nation'.[151] In September 1966, the Liaison Committee for the Defence of Trade Unions (LCDTU) was formed to connect the CPGB's industrial activists with non-Communists in the wider labour movement, opposing the incomes policy legislation. The CPGB's Broad Left strategy brought it influence in a number of the larger unions, supporting both Communist and sympathetic non-Communist officials, who were all generally opposed to the Labour government's attempts to control wage increases and union activity.

The Donovan Report, published in 1968, stated that a major deficiency in trade union legislation was in the 'present methods of collective bargaining and especially our methods of work-shop bargaining, and … the absence of speedy, clear and effective disputes procedures'.[152] A White Paper, *In Place of Strife*,

---

146   McIlroy 1999, p. 218.

147   McIlroy 1999, p. 220; Callaghan 2004, p. 393.

148   Address by Harold Wilson, in Scottish Trade Union Congress, STUC *Annual Report*, 1966, p. 405, in STUC Archive, Glasgow Caledonian University Archives.

149   Parliamentary Report by Harold Wilson, in Labour Party, *Report of the 65th Annual Conference*, 1966, London: Labour Party publication, p. 168.

150   *The Economist*, 15 January 1966.

151   *The Times*, 21 June 1966.

152   Royal Commission on Trade Union and Employers' Associations, *Report on Royal Commission on Trade Unions and Employers' Associations, 1965–1968*, 1968, p. 128, in HMSO, NA.

was presented by Secretary of State for Employment and Productivity, Barbara Castle, in early 1969 and based on the recommendations of the Donovan Report, proposed reforms curtailing 'unofficial' strike action. In using legal action against strikes deemed 'unofficial', the White Paper proposed powers enabling 'the Secretary of State by Order to require those involved to desist for up to 28 days from a strike or lock-out which is unconstitutional'.[153] In reaction to the government's attempts to establish state intervention in regulating strike activity, the trade union movement mobilised massive strike action and the LCDTU was used to co-ordinate this industrial action against the proposed legislation. This action by the labour movement contributed to Wilson and his Cabinet withdrawing the legislation in June 1969.

This was seen as a major victory for the labour movement and the CPGB celebrated the importance of the Party within the LCDTU's campaign. However, the reality of left unity in the labour movement was that Communist union leaders were frequently forced to compromise with the non-Communist unionists and industrial action became more concerned with defensive measures against restrictive legislation and in favour of wage militancy than any progressive or radical measures. As Richard Hyman wrote, the strikes were 'overwhelmingly a reflection of immediate economic issues', while 'political' stoppages, 'designed to influence or challenge government social policy', were infrequent.[154]

The CPGB's industrial policy was primarily wage militancy and defensive measures against state restriction, which depended on the Party working within wider broad left alliances in the trade unions. The Party leadership's reluctance to upset these fragile alliances prevented the proposal of any major radical or socialist reforms, although within the boundaries of its broad left coalition, the Party had an 'appreciable if minority role'.[155] This unity meant 'common action on the immediate issues' of the working class and the 'daily battle conducted by the trade unions for the defence of living standards and workers' rights is a decisive part of the opposition to capitalism'.[156] In recent scholarship on the CPGB's industrial policies, it has been claimed that the Party was shown to be 'greater in building trade unionism rather than moulding its politics' and its involvement in the trade union movement seemed 'subordinated to electoral manoeuvres' rather than creating a 'politically developed

---

153   Department of Employment, *In Place of Strife: A Policy for Industrial Relations*, 1969, p. 37 in HMSO, NA.

154   Hyman 1990, p. 157.

155   McIlroy 1999, p. 218; p. 245.

156   CPGB, *The British Road to Socialism*, 1968, p. 22.

membership'.[157] The industrial wing of the Party had been given prominent status, but the entrenchment of its members in union bureaucracy meant that the Party's unionists were 'largely concerned with industrial issues' and not with daily work within the Party.[158] While the CPGB was able to gain some influence in the trade unions at the executive level, they were unsuccessful in creating a 'national community of political branches' around which the Party could decisively steer the labour movement, with the reality being a 'shallower, personalized network of trade union militants'.[159] The optimism of the Party that it could influence major industrial action in the trade unions was negated by the fact that it was 'simply absent from many regions and industries and its presence was patchy in the centres of its strength'.[160]

Amongst those who have written on CPGB industrial policy, there has been disagreement on how far the Party was willing to push its own agenda within the trade unions. Thompson asserted that the strategy undertaken by the CPGB's union leadership was to 'mobilise its members at large to support action by workers rather than to instigate workers to industrial action in pursuit of its own policies and aims'.[161] On the other hand, McIlroy claimed that this view was 'plainly mistaken', arguing that the Party sought to mobilise workers, but towards 'calculated, limited objectives'.[162] However, it is unclear what objectives the Communist Party successfully agitated for which had not already gathered popular support within the unions. In *Endgames and New Times*, Andrews quoted from both Thompson and McIlroy, not commenting exclusively on either statement, but stated that CPGB industrial influence was 'one of pragmatism and low-profile politics' and that any success in *political* mobilisation 'must be doubted'.[163]

John Callaghan has demonstrated that the mid-1950s, when 22,503 of its 32,681 members belonged to a trade union, were essentially the peak of the Party's promising industrial position.[164] From 1957 onwards, the Party's presence in the factories diminished rapidly and according to Callaghan, 'it proved an uphill struggle to maintain the Party's factory branches throughout the 1950s

157   McIlroy 1999, p. 236; p. 246.
158   McIlroy 1999, p. 222.
159   Ibid.
160   Callaghan 2003, p. 226.
161   Thompson 1992, p. 136.
162   McIlroy 1999, p. 243.
163   Andrews 2004, p. 117.
164   Callaghan 2003, p. 34.

and 1960s in all parts of Britain'.[165] Between 1957 and 1963, the number of factory branches fell by around 36 percent, with only 3,249 members in factory
branches in 1963.[166] At the same time, the Party was experiencing its highest
membership since 1956, with a total membership of 33,008 in 1963 and up to
34,281 in 1964.[167] However, the number of members in factory branches continued to decline throughout the decade, so that by 1968, there was only 2,576
members, or 8.5 percent, in these branches.[168] The factory branches were seen
by the CPGB leadership as 'decisive for generating the mass movement for
change in government policy and for building left unity',[169] but the number of
these branches continued to decline into the 1970s, at a time when the Party's
industrial action would have been expected to deliver some numerical gains.

The problem the Party faced was the fact that it 'was not recruiting young
workers and had not been doing so since at least the crisis of 1956'.[170] Since
1967, the Young Communist League's membership had dropped from 6,031 to
2,576 in 1974.[171] This added a generational aspect to the strategic and ideological divisions that were beginning to divide the CPGB. A large number of the
young members who had begun joining the Party in the late 1960s had been
radicalised by the student activist and feminist movements, reacting against
what they viewed as a 'narrow "workerist" position', which 'tended to ignore
the wider and crucially important aspects of working class youth life, outside
the workplace'.[172] The period from 1968 to 1974 has been described by Willie
Thompson as the Party's 'Indian Summer', where it became 'briefly a national
political force', with its industrial and student leaders being elected to leading positions within the trade unions and the National Union of Students.[173]
However, John Callaghan contends that the Party in this period was under an
'illusion of influence',[174] where it concealed the weaknesses of its industrial
base and rapidly declining membership at factory level by focusing on wider
industrial activism that was occurring.

---

165   Callaghan 2003, pp. 32–3.
166   Callaghan 2003, pp. 36–7.
167   Thompson 1992, p. 218.
168   Callaghan 2003, pp. 36–7.
169   McLennan, 'Left Unity in Action for an Alternative Policy', *Comment*, 9 December 1967,
       p. 777.
170   Callaghan 2004, p. 406.
171   Stevenson n.d.
172   Bell, 'Youth: Report to the Communist Party EC', *Comment*, 2 October 1976, p. 310.
173   Thompson 1992, p. 160.
174   Callaghan 2004, p. 407.

The Trade Unions and Race

In retrospect, it seems that the Party's efforts towards building a Broad Left unity with the Labour Party through the trade union movement was, in line with the criticisms made by reformers during the 1970s, essentially an 'economist' relationship that had very limited and economic-based aims, with no real influence over social policy, which would include the issues of race and immigration. As detailed in *The British Road to Socialism*, the trade unions were integral to creating a radicalised Labour Party, which would form part of a 'united Labour movement' in the 'fight for the common interests of the working class', all 'working to end capitalism and win socialism'.[175] Further outlined in the 1968 edition, the strategy for the transition to socialism depended upon a 'socialist Labour and Communist government', with the aim to 'win a Parliamentary majority, pledged to decisive socialist change'.[176] In the 1960s, the Communist Party sought to establish a 'mass party' by creating 'Broad Left' unity with the Labour left and the labour movement, attempting to gain influential positions within individual trade unions and the executive union body, the Trade Union Congress (TUC). Although the TUC is not a monolithic organisation and cannot be seen as interchangeable with the various policies and actions of the entire labour movement, it is one of the most important guides for observing broad trends within the British trade union movement. The role of the TUC in the British labour movement illustrates why the Communist Party attempted to disrupt the 'right-wing majority of the TUC' and for Party members, as well as sympathetic left leaders, to gain positions within the upper echelons in the Congress.[177] In the anti-racist struggle, the CPGB continually maintained that the 'trade union movement has a leading part to play'.[178] However, the reality of the TUC's efforts in the struggle against racism was not straightforward and its policy on 'race' and immigration can be seen as a 'muddled position'.[179] The general policy of the TUC, as Barry Munslow wrote, had been to 'play down the subject, stress the need for immigrants to integrate and oppose special provisions'.[180]

---

175 CPGB, *The British Road to Socialism*, 1958, p. 29.

176 CPGB, *The British Road to Socialism*, 1968, p. 50; p. 48.

177 Gollan 1975, p. 239. A list of important Communist and sympathetic left leaders in the unions that had been achieved by the early 1970s is recorded in Gollan 1975, p. 257.

178 Bourne, *Racialism*, p. 14.

179 Radin 1966, p. 161.

180 Munslow 1983, p. 204.

The trade union movement, symbolised by the statements of the TUC, actually 'paid little attention to issues of race and immigration in the 1950s until the Notting Hill disturbances'.[181] Before 1958, the TUC did briefly condemn racial discrimination, but 'implicitly accepted that the "problem" was ... the very presence of immigrants' and the General Council expressed the need for immigration controls.[182] The 1958 Congress was the 'first instance of an open recognition at Congress that "our people" [trade unionists] were racially prejudiced' and that the unions 'had a direct responsibility to deal with this prejudice and its manifestations'.[183] However, they stated that the TUC still implicitly accepted that it was 'the attitude and behaviour of the immigrants which was "the problem" and [the] view that immigration should be controlled flowed logically from that premise'.[184] As Kay Beauchamp noted, although they had 'gone on record against racial discrimination, this opposition is often very perfunctory'.[185] The issues of 'race relations' and immigration were 'consistently muddled together' by the TUC and while the Congress opposed, on paper, racial discrimination, their position on immigration was that 'black immigrants were a problem and their arrival in Britain should consequently be controlled'.[186]

Between 1958 and 1964, immigration was barely mentioned by the TUC, with the 'only matter of substance' being opposition to the Commonwealth Immigrants Act, which was in line with the Labour Party's opposition in Parliament and Congress's stance against racial discrimination.[187] As the first Wilson government was elected in 1964, the TUC and the Labour Party were entering together into a 'formal, close relationship' and the corresponding period saw the TUC's policy on immigration move 'directly in line with that of the Labour Government'.[188] Although it routinely passed resolutions at Congress condemning racial discrimination, the TUC's position became to 'control immigration in order to permit "integration"'.[189]

The Communist Party continued to look to the labour movement to lead the anti-racist struggle. While the Party called for stronger anti-racist action at

---

181 Lunn 1999, p. 77.
182 Miles and Phizacklea 1977, p. 7.
183 Miles and Phizacklea 1977, p. 10.
184 Miles and Phizacklea 1977, p. 11.
185 Beauchamp, 'Racialism in Britain Today and How to Fight It', p. 205.
186 Miles and Phizacklea 1977, p. 2.
187 Miles and Phizacklea 1977, p. 14.
188 Fishman, TUC History Online, http://www.unionhistory.info/timeline/1960_2000.php, accessed 18 June 2006; Miles and Phizacklea 1977, p. 17.
189 Miles and Phizacklea 1977, p. 37.

shopfloor level to co-ordinate with resolutions passed at national level, there was no criticism of the TUC's official support for immigration control, unlike that aimed at the Wilson government. The fact that two of the major bodies within the labour movement with which the CPGB endorsed co-operation either implicitly supported or were actively involved in creating immigration controls challenged the Communist Party's opposition to the Commonwealth Immigrants Act. Despite how much rank-and-file opposition there was, nonetheless the official TUC policy on immigration was 'more or less identical with that of the Labour Government'.[190] In his study of Asian workers in Britain's foundry industry, Mark Duffield wrote that in the Amalgamated Union of Foundry Workers, 'official AUFW policy on immigration was opposed to restriction until 1966', but then fell 'in line with the closing of ranks in the labour movement', favouring control.[191] Those AUFW members who led the opposition were mainly Communists, although this opposition, as demonstrated in the following chapter, was unable to make much headway in the union and the wider labour movement until the mid-1970s, when the TUC began to shift its position.

The Rise of New Social Movements and Black Radicalism

The ties of the Communist Party, as well as the Movement for Colonial Freedom, to the trade unions and the Labour Party made black workers and activists start to look for other political organisations to support.[192] During the mid-1960s, the main path for black political action was through race-related organisations, such as the Campaign Against Racial Discrimination (CARD), Institute for Race Relations (IRR) and the United Coloured People's Alliance (UCPA). These organisations were seen as respectable, moderate and included significant middle class and white sections. But by the late 1960s, these organisations started to lose significance as a black militant position started to emerge – 'black power', the idea that 'black people needed to redefine themselves by asserting their own history and culture to project an image which they would develop without white people'.[193] But as Kalbir Shukra noted, black power was a 'diffuse political identity', often leading to 'constant conflicts, splits

---

190   Ibid.
191   Duffield 1985, p. 161.
192   See Huntley 1982, p. 71.
193   Shukra 1995, p. 6.

and new formations' within the black militant movement.[194] Black militancy, which included both black separatist organisations and a Marxist-inspired black radicalism, 'captured and reactivated many of the disaffected activists'[195] that had been neglected by the labour movement or felt compromised by working within official race-related bodies. The existing black communities, both Afro-Caribbean and Asian, came to have an important function and to recognise the importance of social rather than political ties, although, as Carter states, 'the dividing line is difficult to draw'.[196] For the emerging black organisations, the Communist Party's denial of 'race' was rejected in favour of an active acceptance of the political and cultural definition of 'race', the basis for black militancy.

For the Communist Party, black power was 'seriously compromised by the lack of class analysis implied in the concept'.[197] The Party was also suspicious of black militancy due to its revolutionary approach outside the established trade union movement and its inclusion of violent revolutionary rhetoric. In an internal document prepared by the International Affairs Committee, the Party lamented the various black groups who 'expressed their opposition to integration within the British community and advocated ... more militant action against white racialism'.[198] The Communist Party saw the links between black militants and Trotskyist and Maoist organisations as 'strongly anti-Communist' and associated 'black power' with 'the "thoughts of Mao tse Tung" [sic], with the writings of Che Guevara and with confused versions of Trotskyism'.[199]

The Communist Party stated that immigrant organisations 'advance ... on the basis of genuine unity' that could only come through 'close co-operation with the Labour and progressive movement', with black militancy, as advocated by organisations such as the Black Power Alliance, seen to 'embark on the dangerous path of "all blacks against all whites" [that] could lead to serious consequences'.[200] In a letter from Jack Woddis to the Party's Press and Publicity Department, it was proposed that in CPGB literature, black power organisations should not be mentioned by name, instead broadly stating that 'immigrant

---

194   Ibid.
195   Carter 1986, p. 62.
196   Carter 1986, p. 63.
197   Thompson, 'Black Power', p. 4.
198   International Affairs Committee, 'Racialism and "Black Power"', 10 May 1968, in CPGB archives, CP/LON/RACE/02/01, LHASC.
199   Ibid.
200   Ibid.

organisations themselves have an important role to play'.[201] However, these 'immigrant organisations' mentioned by Woddis almost certainly meant the progressive-liberal and race relations bodies that the CPGB approved of and not the revolutionary groups with connections to the far left or black separatism.

The Communist Party was also worried that the radicalism of the black power movement in Britain would bring confrontation with the authorities. At a demonstration against police harassment in Notting Hill in August 1970, organised by the Action Committee for the Defence of the Mangrove Nine and the British Black Power Movement, there was a series of confrontations between demonstrators and the police, with more than 700 police officers involved in overseeing the 150 people on the march.[202] In the days following the demonstration, the CPGB's Political Committee complained in its weekly letter that the violent rhetoric used by some of the black radical activists would 'play into the hands of racialists and all others who are trying to stir up trouble.'[203]

In a 1969 article, Scottish Communist Party member Willie Thompson reiterated the traditional Party line that racism was a result of capitalism and 'not from any inherent biological antagonism between races'.[204] However, Thompson also acknowledged, aside from his assertion that black power was 'unscientific', that what justifies black power is 'power to combat persecution' because the 'racial line represents certain social facts'.[205] This constituted a significant step within the Communist Party's attitude towards race after coming into contact with the rise of black militancy – that despite its falsity as scientific fact, 'race' was a political and social classification that formed a necessary partner in the struggle against exploitation and could not be ignored. Campaigns against racial discrimination were publicised by the Communist Party and other organisations in the labour movement, but practical anti-racist action was hindered for a number of reasons, including a lack of understanding of the issue of racism amongst the primarily white membership and the Party's inability to recruit black members.

The shift towards more militant organisations was replicated amongst many of the emerging social movements and there a general radicalising of youth interested in moving past the 'old axis of the unions, Labour Party and CP', as

---

201   Letter from Jack Woddis to Nora Jeffrey, 30 April 1968, in CPGB archives, CP/LON/RACE/ 02/01, LHASC.

202   Bunce and Field 2014, pp. 106–7.

203   CPGB PC Weekly Letter, 13 August 1970, p. 3, in CPGB archives, CP/CENT/PC/11/17, LHASC.

204   Thompson, 'Black Power', p. 4.

205   Thompson, 'Black Power', pp. 4–5.

described by John McIlroy.[206] There was a perception among the younger radicals that these traditional organisations were too culturally conservative. Many of them therefore joined the International Socialists (IS) and the International Marxist Group (IMG), who competed with the CPGB for support among young people and influence amongst the new social movements. While the concerns of these wider social movements were being recognised within the CPGB as important political issues, the Party had extremely limited success in recruiting black workers and the problem of few black members made it difficult to recruit others, which created practical and ideological problems for anti-racist activism. These problems became more prominent in the 1970s as the Communist Party became divided over which course of action to take as the radicalism of the 'British upturn' rescinded, as will be shown in the following chapters.

The Link with International Issues

The origins of the Communist Party's anti-racist agenda lay in its anti-colonial work that began in the 1920s and, as mentioned in the previous chapter, this anti-colonial outlook informed how the Party viewed issues of racial discrimination in Britain – in the era of postwar migration, the colonial 'colour bar' was now being enforced in the 'mother country'. The International Department oversaw the nationality committees (and branches) that were the most dedicated to raising the question of 'race' in the Party and the majority of those who wrote about the subject in the Party press were from this department. By the early 1960s, coinciding with the campaigns against the Commonwealth Immigrants Bill and for a bill against racial discrimination, the issue of racism became seen more as a domestic issue and in the Party press, there was less mention of issues of imperialism and colonialism in discussions of immigration and 'race relations' in Britain. Imperialism and colonial rule was still portrayed as the root of racism, but the Party stressed that racism must be tackled by immediate steps in Britain. Racism was to be confronted without having to wait for success in the colonial sphere – and that success of the anti-colonial revolutions across the British Commonwealth did not have a bearing on the issue of racism inside Britain.

However, the International Department continued to manage the affairs of those members involved in anti-racism campaigning, with members involved in organisations, such as the Movement for Colonial Freedom, the Campaign

---

206   McIlroy 1999, p. 224.

Against Racial Discrimination and the Indian Workers Association all reporting to Jack Woddis and Idris Cox, who ran the Department. By the mid- to late 1960s, the anti-colonial movement had, more or less, been successful, with very few European colonies remaining. Dutt wrote in *Marxism Today* in early 1964:

> When Lenin wrote his thesis on the national and colonial question in 1920, the colonies, semi-colonies and Dominions and dependencies accounted for 77.2 per cent of the territory and 69.2 per cent of the population of the world. In 1963 only 7.7 per cent of the world's area and 1.7 per cent of its population remain under the direct domination of colonial rule.[207]

The Portuguese colonies in Africa and Asia, as well as Southern Rhodesia and South Africa, became the focus of the anti-imperialist struggle for many on the left, including the CPGB, and alongside the anti-Vietnam War movement, this was the focus of the Party's anti-imperialism during the late 1960s (and early 1970s). From this perspective, the International Department was keen to emphasise the links between the fight against imperialism overseas and the fight against racism in Britain.

In *Marxism Today* in 1966, Kay Beauchamp argued that racialism was 'one of the main and most frequent methods' used by the imperialist powers to maintain power, pointing to the racism evident in South Africa and the United States, and therefore argued that 'the struggle against racialism is an essential part of the struggle against imperialism.'[208] Beauchamp continued: 'It is necessary for all anti-imperialists to expose the false racial doctrines and to show the common interest of those who suffer from imperialism.'[209] Beauchamp's colleague at the International Department, Joan Bellamy, wrote something similar a few years later in the same Party journal, stating that 'the struggle for independence links with the issue of the struggle against racialism.'[210] The arguments for national liberation and against racism both were, according to Bellamy, 'about peoples' right in general to determine their own lives', and this meant that the working class in the imperialist countries needed to 'accept the principle of racial equality', or else they could be 'isolated by their respective ruling classes from the national liberation struggles.'[211]

---

207 Dutt, 'National Liberation Today', *Marxism Today*, January 1964, p. 10.
208 Beauchamp, 'The Roots of Racialism', *Marxism Today*, November 1966, p. 332.
209 Ibid.
210 Bellamy, 'Politics and Race', *Marxism Today*, October 1969, p. 313.
211 Ibid.

While the importance of fighting 'everyday' racism in Britain was recognised by the Party, the reliance on the International Department to co-ordinate the Party's anti-racist work allowed the Department to emphasise using internationalist bodies, such as the Movement for Colonial Freedom, which was about building solidarity networks, rather than taking the lead of a domestic protest campaign. As mentioned earlier, this approach was eventually abandoned after the events at Red Lion Square in June 1974 and the creation of a National Race Relations Committee in the mid-1970s.

Capitulating to Racism: Labour and the Commonwealth Immigrants Act 1968

While Labour had brought in restrictive quotas of work vouchers granted to Commonwealth migrants in 1965, it was generally felt that the Commonwealth Immigrants Act 1962 was largely working as intended, and there would be no substantial legislative changes under a Labour government. However, the increase in the mid- to late 1960s of Asian migrants from East Africa, as well as Conservative fear-mongering around the issue, led Labour to capitulate further to anti-immigrationism and create the Commonwealth Immigrants Act 1968, which introduced new restrictions on Commonwealth migrants from the former colonies, rather than the Dominions.

After Kenya won independence in 1963, an 'Africanisation' campaign had 'prompted many [Kenyan Asians] to migrate to Britain rather than face continued discrimination'.[212] A 'steady flow' of Kenyan Asians had migrated to Britain between 1965 and 1967. In 1967, the Kenyan government passed a law under which these British citizens of Asian descent could reside and work in Kenya only on a temporary basis. This created an increase in migration to Britain and a response from sections of the media and Conservative MPs, such as Enoch Powell, demanding that restrictions be applied to these Kenyan Asians.[213] Powell claimed that the number of Asians arriving from Kenya would be around 200,000, but the reality was a much smaller 66,000 out of a potential 95,000, with 29,000 already settled in Britain by February 1968.[214]

In late February 1968, the Labour government 'steamrollered through Parliament in three days of emergency debate' the 1968 Commonwealth Immig-

---

212 Paul 1997, p. 179.
213 Solomos 2003, p. 60; Hiro 1992, p. 213.
214 Alexander 1987, p. 36; Hiro 1992, p. 214.

rants Act with the 'sole purpose of restricting entry into Britain of Kenyan Asians holding British passports'.[215] According to the Act, British citizenship was determined if a person or one of their parents or grandparents were born in Britain. This effectively eliminated the Kenyan Asians, or any other black citizens of the Commonwealth, from being deemed British citizens. Despite the rhetoric of the 1968 Act remaining impartial and not racially biased, the practical reality of this amendment was the Labour government's intention to prevent further black immigration into Britain.

Zig Layton-Henry described the 1968 Act as the 'logical outcome of appeasement that the Labour government had adopted in order to achieve the bipartisan consensus with the Conservatives and to reduce the electoral salience of the issue'.[216] However, this was more than just a pragmatic issue of 'appearing weaker than the Conservatives on the issue of immigration controls',[217] but a longer reassessment of the idea of British nationality that had become more apparent as the British Empire collapsed. White British citizens born abroad were 'never referred to as "immigrants" under any circumstances'. The term 'immigrants' was reserved for black migrants, and by the late 1960s the equation of 'immigrant' with 'black' had become the prevailing attitude.[218] The Labour Party had originally opposed immigration controls on the grounds of the ideal of the free movement of people and trade within the Commonwealth. However, the right to enter and live in Britain without restriction did not mean that Commonwealth immigrants were 'regarded as British in any other sense'.[219] For Labour, the 'Commonwealth ideal had never been intended as a defence of [unrestricted] black immigration to Britain' and as Caroline Knowles stated, the increasingly tough controls on black immigration during the 1960s demonstrated that Labour 'reconstructed immigration away from commonwealth and labour needs', perceiving immigrants as 'an invasive and oppositional political community to indigenousness'.[220]

In 1968, Robert Moore wrote that 'Racialists have nothing to lose and everything to gain by pressing the Labour Government even harder'.[221] The long-term effect of the 1968 Commonwealth Immigrants Act was to create a distinc-

---

215   Fryer 1984, p. 383.
216   Layton-Henry 1992, p. 79.
217   Ibid.
218   Dummett and Nicol 1990, p. 201.
219   Knowles 1992, p. 94.
220   Knowles 1992, p. 96; p. 103.
221   Moore, 'Labour and Colour – 1965–8', *Institute of Race Relations Newsletter*, October 1968, p. 390.

tion between the predominantly white British citizen who could claim lineage within Britain and the predominantly black Commonwealth citizen who could no longer claim to be 'British', which in turn barred the Commonwealth immigrant from entering Britain. As Paul Foot wrote in his 1969 book, *The Rise of Enoch Powell*: 'One of the most constant rules in the history of immigration control is that those demanding controls are encouraged, not silenced, by concessions'.[222]

The 1968 Act was called the 'White Passport' Act by Vishnu Sharma in the Communist Party weekly, *Comment*, and blame was directed at the Labour government, especially Home Secretary James Callaghan, for the 'first incontestably racialist law to be placed on the Statute Book'.[223] Joan Bellamy called the Act a 'capitulation to racism', claiming that some Labour MPs were worried about losing their seats 'if they become identified as "immigrants" candidates'.[224] 'The answer', Bellamy argued, 'is not capitulation but struggle'[225] against racial discrimination. Continuing on this theme in another *Comment* article in the following months, Bellamy asserted that 'racialists are not appeaseable' and that it was 'not time for concessions to racialists and their sympathisers',[226] which the Communist Party claimed the Labour Party had made. Calling for a 'vigorous counter-attack' to racism, bolstered by Labour's immigration policies and the racist speeches by Conservative MP Enoch Powell, Bellamy emphasised that while the CPGB would continue to call for changes to be made to legislation, it was much more important to fight racism through the trade unions and the 'need for grass roots campaigning to fight for the hearts and minds of the people', through 'social measures and the education of public opinion'.[227] However, as the Labour government came under intense criticism for the passing of the 1968 Commonwealth Immigrants Act, the initial pressure came from Conservative MPs and the entire issue of 'race relations' and immigration was dominated in 1968 by the racism of the Conservatives, primarily Enoch Powell after his 'rivers of blood' speech in April.

---

222   Foot 1969, p. 111.
223   Sharma, 'The "White Passport" Act', *Comment*, 4 May 1968, p. 281.
224   Bellamy, 'Shutting the Door on British Citizens', *Comment*, 9 March 1968, p. 147; p. 149.
225   Bellamy, 'Shutting the Door on British Citizens', p. 149.
226   Bellamy, 'Racialists are not Appeaseable', *Comment*, 27 July 1968, p. 467.
227   Bellamy, 'Racialists are not Appeaseable', pp. 467–8.

Integration and 'Good Race Relations': The 1968 Race Relations Act

As mentioned earlier, Labour sought a twin-track approach to race and immigration, accepting the consensus that strict immigration controls were necessary
for 'good race relations', but also attempting to ensure that migrants integrated
into mainstream British society by legislating against the more explicit forms
of racial discrimination. The Race Relations Act was amended in November
1968. It extended the legislation to cover property and housing, employment,
including hiring, training, promotion and dismissal, as well as the provision
of goods, facilities and services in areas, such as banking credit, education,
entertainment and travel.[228] The workings of the Race Relations Board were
revised, but the responsibility of enforcing the Act was still given to 'weak
quasi-governmental bodies', with their ability to combat racial discrimination
'severely limited'.[229] Although the areas covered by the Act had been extended, correcting what was seen as one of the major reasons for the weakness of
the 1965 Act, the CPGB still saw that the government bodies established to deal
with complaints of discrimination were 'without "teeth", severely restricted in
effectiveness'.[230]

The Communist Party pointed out that there were still 'considerable weaknesses' in the amended Act, with conciliation still preferred by the government
to fines and criminal punishment, along with the fact that 'only the Race Relations Board can take legal proceedings'.[231] The Party also took issue with the
fact that the bodies established by the Act had appointed members only and
made 'no provisions for coloured immigrants ... trade unionists to serve on
them'.[232] The Act was seen as a 'modest step in the right direction', with the
Party warning that it would 'need constant care to see that it is operated prop-
erly'.[233] The Communist Party objected to the fact that despite incitement to
racial hatred being criminalised by the Act, Enoch Powell, after his 'rivers of
blood' speech, had no action taken against him, declaring that it was 'disgrace-
ful that leading Tory politicians have repeatedly flouted the law in blatantly
racialist speeches'.[234]

---

228   Hiro 1992, p. 219.
229   Solomos 1988, p. 39.
230   Bellamy, 'Racialists are not Appeaseable', p. 467.
231   Bellamy, 'Race Relations', *Comment*, 30 November 1968, p. 756.
232   Bellamy, *Homes, Jobs, Immigration – The Facts*, 1968, London: CPGB pamphlet, p. 13.
233   Ibid.
234   Bellamy, 'Race Relations', p. 755.

The Labour government had passed an amended Commonwealth Immigrants Act in February 1968, with greater restrictions over entry into Britain for black immigrants from the Commonwealth. In a statement on the Race Relations Bill prepared by the International Department, the Communist Party stated that 'Government policy operates in two conflicting directions'.[235] Along with strengthening the Commonwealth Immigrants Act, the government also amended the Race Relations Act, solidifying Labour's attempt to integrate the black population in Britain, while restricting entry of more black immigrants at the same time. The 1968 Commonwealth Immigrants Act reiterated the belief of the government that black immigration was undesirable and a problem, while the Race Relations Act attempted to integrate these immigrants, although they were seen as undesirable. 'No wonder that coloured people are regarding all government-sponsored efforts to improve race relations as suspect', declared Asquith Gibbes in a report to the CPGB's Executive Committee.[236] The CPGB stated that despite the government passing an amended Race Relations Act, the fact that the 1968 Commonwealth Immigrants Act remained, had 'undermined confidence in the Labour Government's sincerity towards coloured people', claiming there was now 'widespread disillusionment' amongst Britain's black population.[237]

A much more controversial clause of the 1968 Race Relations Act concerned racial discrimination in employment. Complaints against discrimination in employment were not investigated by the Race Relations Board, but through the Department of Employment and Productivity. The reason for this, the CPGB noted, was because of collaboration between employers and the Trade Union Congress (TUC), who both 'declared against legislation on the grounds that they were against interference in industrial relations'.[238] The TUC had an increasing interest in integration and an unfavourable reaction to proposals to legislative control over discrimination in the sphere of employment, 'a reaction that at times verged on outright opposition'.[239] The TUC favoured voluntary conciliation rather than legislation and feared that legislative control 'might allow bodies outside the trade union movement to pursue issues in an industrial situation, for which they had no responsibility'.[240] This stemmed from

---

235   'Memorandum on the Race Relations Bill', April 1968, in CPGB archives, CP/LON/RACE/
      02/01, LHASC.
236   Gibbes, 'Racial Discrimination in Britain', Comment, 6 April 1968, p. 215.
237   'Memorandum on the Race Relations Bill'.
238   Bellamy, 'Race Relations', p. 756.
239   Miles and Phizacklea 1977, p. 21.
240   Miles and Phizacklea 1977, p. 22.

the traditional hostility of the TUC towards legislation being used in industrial matters and as Robert Miles and Annie Phizacklea noted, the TUC 'feared that legislation to control racial discrimination in industry was the thin end of the wedge'.[241]

This lack of support for the 1968 Act by the TUC, disputed Trevor Carter, 'cannot be put down simply to traditional ... union resistance to workplace matters being resolved through the intervention of the law'.[242] For Carter, racist feelings and fears that immigrants were abusing 'the system' were not untypical in black people's experience, both outside and within the labour movement.[243] The CPGB feared that if the union movement failed to take the issue of racism seriously, 'those coloured workers who do not understand the essential class character of discrimination will feel that British working-class organisations are irrelevant' and this would lead to black workers joining black power organisations, 'who pose the solution as the successful struggle of all coloured peoples against all white peoples'.[244]

Despite the hostility to legislation at the executive level of the trade unions, the Communist Party still saw the labour movement as vital to the struggle against racism. The unions were important in resisting attempts by employers to divide black and white workers to make it 'easier to resist demands for better wages and conditions and make higher profits', Joan Bellamy explained.[245] However, this anti-racism was still viewed within the wider struggle for socialism, based on a 'Marxist understanding of the racial question'.[246] While it was important to fight to 'end all discrimination and win equal rights and opportunities irrespective of race, colour and religion', this was part of a wider 'social and economic fight requiring the unity of all working people in bringing an end to the social and economic inferiority imposed by capitalism'.[247] This position was viewed by some black activists as having a negative effect on black workers, with Trevor Carter writing in his book, *Shattering Illusions*:

> My impression was always that the left was genuinely concerned to mobilise the black community, but into *their* political battles. They never had time to look at *our* immediate problems, so it became futile to refer to

241   Miles and Phizacklea 1977, p. 24.
242   Carter 1986, p. 79.
243   Carter 1986, pp. 79–80.
244   Gibbes, 'Racial Discrimination in Britain', p. 216.
245   Bellamy, *Homes, Jobs, Immigration – The Facts*, p. 14.
246   Gibbes, 'Racial Discrimination in Britain', p. 216.
247   Ibid.

them. So blacks ended up in total isolation within the broad left because of the left's basic dishonesty.[248]

There were doubts amongst the anti-racist activists within the Party that the struggle against racism would be taken up as wholeheartedly as the industrial struggles at the time. As Asquith Gibbes explained, 'If we cannot win our industrial members to take up this struggle as a workers' struggle, defending coloured workers and cementing the unity of the working class, then we shall not be able to win the movement as a whole for a correct attitude'.[249]

Powellism and the Rise of the National Front

While Labour and the Conservatives dominated the issues of race and immigration in the 1960s, fear of the era's radicalism, combined with old racist prejudices, led to a revival of fascist agitation in Britain, as well as a mobilisation of a new generation of anti-fascists, which, as will be shown in the following chapters, caused a conundrum for the CPGB. In February 1967, the League of Empire Loyalists and the British National Party, along with several smaller anti-immigration groups, including members of the Racial Preservation Society (RPS), merged to form the National Front (NF). The National Front was 'an attempt to synthesize the mass politics and economic and political programme of the BUF with the ferocious anti-Semitism and racial populism of Arnold Leese', presented in a 'more respectable and seemingly rational guise'.[250] With A.K. Chesterton as its chairman, the NF tried to appear as a legitimate political party, although divided between Chesterton's elitism and support for mass politics by John Bean and Andrew Fountaine, two leadership figures from the BNP. Chesterton saw the NF as 'a pressure group, rather than as a potential mass movement', while others, such as those who had joined from the BNP as well as the GBM leadership of John Tyndall and Martin Webster, 'insisted that the NF's sights be set on a mass membership, a nation-wide and popular movement'.[251] The leadership of the National Front was hesitant to include Tyndall and Webster's Greater Britain Movement, who were viewed as neo-Nazi extremists, but as Martin Walker explained, amongst the rank-and-file NF members, it had been 'long expected and desired that any coalition of the Right would

---

248   Cited in T. Carter 1986, p. 140; Italics are in the original text.
249   Gibbes, 'Racial Discrimination in Britain', p. 218.
250   Thurlow 1987, p. 277.
251   Walker 1979, p. 188.

have to include Tyndall'.[252] The disparate groups involved in the amalgamation brought different membership numbers, properties and finances, along with several publications – *Spearhead* from Tyndall's NSM and GBM; *Candour* from Chesterton's LEL; and *Combat* from Bean's BNP, which merged with *Spearhead* in 1968.[253] Membership numbers were hard to define throughout the existence of the NF, but it is estimated that it had around 1,500 members at its inception.[254]

Although concerns over the social impact of non-white immigration had been expressed in parliamentary and extra-parliamentary discourses since the 1940s, a major turning point in the discourse was Enoch Powell's 'rivers of blood' speech in April 1968, who brought the populist tone of the far right to a mainstream audience. Speaking at a local Conservative Party meeting in Birmingham, Powell launched a tirade against non-white migration, stating:

> We must be mad, literally mad, as a nation to be permitting the annual inflow of some 50,000 dependants, who are for the most part the material of the future growth of the immigrant-descended population. It is like watching a nation busily engaged in heaping up its own funeral pyre ...
>
> We are on the verge here of a change. Hitherto it has been force of circumstance and of background which has rendered the very idea of integration inaccessible to the greater part of the immigrant population ... Now we are seeing the growth of positive forces acting against integration, of vested interests in the preservation and sharpening of racial and religious differences, with a view to the exercise of actual domination, first over fellow immigrants and then over the rest of the population ...
>
> As I look ahead, I am filled with foreboding. Like the Roman, I seem to see 'the River Tiber foaming with much blood'.[255]

Powell's speech alluded to the views of the 'ordinary British citizen' on race relations, immigration and 'alien cultures', appropriating the 'crude and inconsistent racism expressed in the factories, shopping centres and pubs ... endorsed

---

252 Walker 1977, p. 68.
253 'Spearhead' was originally the name of a paramilitary elite corps formed by John Tyndall and Colin Jordan in 1962 while both were in the National Socialist Movement. It gained them notoriety when Tyndall, Jordan and two others, Kerr Ritchie and another NSM/NF member Denis Pirie, were jailed for breaches of the Public Order Act, pertaining to the formation of a paramilitary organisation. Thurlow 1987, p. 267.
254 Lewis 1987, p. 248.
255 Powell 1991, p. 375; pp. 378–9.

by a politician who had the authority of education, political office and a position in the Shadow cabinet'.[256] Powell attributed one of the most controversial remarks of the speech to an anonymous constituent, 'a middle-aged, quite
ordinary working man', exploiting the anxieties of a large section of the British
population in his declaration: 'In this country in fifteen or twenty years' time
the black man will have the whip over the white man'.[257] Although dismissed
by Edward Heath from the shadow cabinet, Powell's exploitation of popular
racism generated much support for him, with a Gallup Poll in May 1968 reveal-
ing that '74 per cent of those questioned agreed in general with his views and
24 per cent said they would like him to be leader of the Conservative Party
if Edward Heath retired'.[258] In the week following Powell's speech, a series of
strikes occurred across Britain, most prominently amongst the London dock
workers, in support of Powell, either for his racist views or his right to free
speech.

It was also Powell's 'Rivers of Blood' speech that allowed the National Front
to exploit popular racist attitudes as Powell 'brought the language and arguments of the neo-fascist political fringe into the heart of the establishment'.[259]
'There can be little doubt', Richard Thurlow wrote, 'that the NF would not have
survived if Enoch Powell had not unwittingly given it such a helping hand in its
infancy'.[260] Powell's speech gave the NF a massive boost, with it claiming 10,000
members in April 1968, although *Searchlight* editor, Gerry Gable,[261] estimated
that it was probably around 7,000 'fully paid up' members.[262] However, Powell
was still seen as part of the Conservative establishment, which the NF tried to
distance itself from. This led to a clash between Chesterton and the more militant members, who were 'desperate ... to capitalize on support for Enoch Powell' – a strategy that Chesterton, who eschewed the populism of Powell, had 'res-

---

256   Miles and Phizacklea 1984, p. 64.
257   Powell 1991, pp. 373–4.
258   Miles and Phizacklea 1984, p. 64.
259   Thurlow 1987, p. 276.
260   Thurlow 1987, p. 279.
261   *Searchlight* was an anti-fascist journal that was published briefly in the early 1960s by anti-
      fascists involved in the 62 Group before it was resurrected in 1975 as a monthly magazine.
      Two of its co-founders, Maurice Ludmer and Gerry Gable, had been CPGB members. Gable
      had left the Communist Party 'over its apparent reluctance to tackle organised fascism',
      which the 62 Group did through direct confrontation on the streets in the early 1960s, but
      also in regards to the CPGB's official opposition to Zionism. Collins, 'Smashing Against
      Rocks', interview with Gable, *The Australian/Israel Review*, February 1999, p. 12.
262   'Rightist and Fascist Developments', 2 May 1969, in CPGB archives CP/CENT/SUBS/04/16,
      LHASC.

olutely opposed'.[263] This clash resulted in Chesterton resigning in October 1970, with John O'Brien, a recent convert from the Conservative right via the National Democratic Party (NDP), becoming chairman in February 1971.[264] Of the other founding members, Andrew Fountaine had earlier been expelled by Chesterton in mid-1968 and John Bean publicly disassociated himself from those who ousted Chesterton, despite being suggested for the post, and withdrew from active politics.[265] O'Brien attempted to purge the NF of its neo-Nazi elements, represented in the leadership by Tyndall and Webster and throughout 1971 the factional fighting continued, but Tyndall was able to survive. In early 1972, O'Brien and his supporters defected to the National Independence Party (NIP), with Tyndall replacing him as chairman.[266]

The formation of the National Front in February 1967 largely escaped protest from anti-fascist forces, with Nigel Copsey explaining that 'opposition to the NF in the late 1960s was mainly restricted to a small amount of militant anti-fascists who followed the pattern of covert activity undertaken against the NF's immediate predecessors'.[267] This covert anti-fascist strategy, as well as the National Front's relative obscurity, saw the Communist Party not particularly involved in anti-fascist action against the NF. The CPGB, symptomatic of the left in Britain as a whole, was 'more concerned about the racial populism of Enoch Powell than the National Front'.[268]

Enoch Powell's speech had encouraged 'vicious racialist and fascist forces' into 'stirring up hatred against coloured people' and 'trying to whip up mass fear and hysteria', but the 'real enemy of all working people', the Communist Party stated, was capitalism and the 'Tory and right wing Labour Governments [who] keep the system going'.[269] Powell was described by Joan Bellamy in a 1968 CPGB pamphlet as 'a diehard Tory who has never done anything to help the working people', but this did not mean he was a fascist.[270] However, by using the racist language normally associated with the fascist far right, Powell had 'deliberately chose[n] to use words that would fan the flame of hatred, words that help to create an atmosphere in which people no longer listen to rational

263   Walker 1977, p. 94.
264   Shipley 1978, p. 14.
265   Anti-Fascist Research Group, *Anti-Fascist Bulletin*, 5, March–June 1971, p. 27.
266   Lewis 1987, p. 252.
267   Copsey 2000, p. 116.
268   Ibid.
269   Bellamy, *Homes, Jobs, Immigration – The Facts*, pp. 2–3.
270   Bellamy, *Homes, Jobs, Immigration – The Facts*, p. 3.

argument and facts'.[271] Joan Bellamy stated that, 'Leading fascists were quick
to recognise what Powell was doing', noting that Colin Jordan, Oswald Mosley
and Dennis Harmston of the Union Movement were in public agreement with
Powell's argument.[272]

The Communist Party relied on reports from Jewish organisations, the anti-
fascist journal *Searchlight* and its own intelligence for knowledge on the fascist
far right. The most detailed CPGB document on the NF in the early period was a
May 1969 internal memo on 'Rightist and Fascist Development', which outlined
the major figures in the NF and the structure of the organisation.[273] This report
claimed that the 'most serious and dangerous organisation appears to be the
National Front ... trying to take over right groups' and able to 'mobilise people
quickly'.[274] However, as an article in *Comment* in July 1969 stated, for the CPGB,
'Enoch Powell emerges ever more clearly as the most reactionary influence in
British politics today', with the author declaring that the Party must 'redouble
our efforts to defeat Powellism'.[275]

However, Powell's speech tapped into existing feelings of popular racism and
in the week following, a series of strikes occurred across Britain, most prominently amongst London dockworkers, in support of Powell, either for his racist
views or his right to free speech. The response by the Communist Party was
to emphasise who Powell was and what his politics were, stating that Powell was a 'diehard Tory who has never done anything to help working people'
and a 'declared enemy of the trade unions'.[276] At the executive level of the
labour movement, where the CPGB held significant influence, the *Morning
Star* reported on official motions of opposition to racism by the trade unions,[277] but at shopfloor level, the Party's presence was less prominent. John
Callaghan described the Communist Party members on the docks, who distributed leaflets denouncing Powell and 'bravely addressed hostile mass meetings',
but acknowledged that the support for Powell demonstrated how marginal the
Communist Party's influence could be.[278] With its members on the docks put
'clearly on the defensive' by the Powellite strikes,[279] CPGB and LCDTU member

271   Ibid.
272   Ibid.
273   'Rightist and Fascist Developments'.
274   'Rightist and Fascist Developments'.
275   Barnsby, 'Wolverhampton and Powell', *Comment*, 12 July 1969, p. 442.
276   Bellamy, *Homes, Jobs, Immigration – The Facts*, p. 3.
277   *Morning Star*, 25 April 1968.
278   Callaghan 2003, p. 112.
279   Lindop 2001, p. 91.

Danny Lyons 'decided to bring in one of the Catholic padres to speak at the dock-gates' in a hastily organised meeting.[280] While this action was felt to be misguided by other Communist dockworkers, Jack Dash, a leading Party member on the docks, stated retrospectively, 'I thought it was wrong but then they had to do something',[281] which turned out, in the end, to be very limited. The Party's limited influence on the docks at rank-and-file level and its dependence on its broad left allies in the labour movement had a significant impact upon its ability to fight racism during the Powellite strikes, but what the strikes did reveal was the level of popular racism still existing within the organised labour movement and the difficulties ahead for the Party in the struggle against racism.

In the wake of this, there was a push in late 1968 and early 1969 to emphasise the campaign against racism by the Party and the YCL. A memo from the National Organiser at the time, Gordon McLennan to Frank Stanley, the London District Secretary, in May 1969 called for greater activity, particularly amongst the labour movement. This was to include '[t]he distribution of a Party leaflet on a wide scale at factories, trade union meetings, houses, etc', as well as '[f]actory gate and street meetings in which the fight against racialism will feature'.[282] Most of the Party's anti-racist literature produced between 1968 and 1970 concentrated on Enoch Powell and the influence that he had over sections of the Conservatives. The Communist Party was anxious over the continual tightening of controls as both Labour and the Conservatives made tougher proposals. As John Hostettler wrote, the Labour government was 'trying to show it [was] not to be outdone by Mr Heath who [was] trying to show he [was] not far behind Mr Powell'.[283] However, while Powell enjoyed wide popularity as an individual between 1968 and 1974,[284] his political momentum stalled as he became a Tory backbencher and decided not to join one of the many anti-immigrant or far right groups that supported him (or form a party of his own). 'Powellism' and its anti-immigration message was soon overtaken by the Conservatives with the Immigration Act 1971, and then by the fascism of the National Front – and in the end, this racist populism was imbibed by early Thatcherism.

---

280 Jack Dash, interview by Fred Lindop, 1984, MSS.371/QD7/Docks 2/10/1, Trade Unionism in British Docks, in Modern Records Centre, University of Warwick.

281 Ibid.

282 Letter from Gordon McLennan to Frank Stanley, 28 May 1969, in CPGB archives, CP/LON/RACE/02/02, LHASC.

283 Hostettler, 'Immigrants, Race Relations and the Law', Comment, 12 July 1969, p. 438.

284 Schofield 2013, p. 317.

Conclusion

The 1960s was a transformative time for the Communist Party, for 'race rela-tions' in Britain and British society in general. The Communist Party started off the decade reeling from the exodus of 1956, with allegations of ballot-rigging in the trade unions and the victory of the Macmillan government on the domestic front, while on the international stage, the international communist movement was divided over the Sino-Soviet split. By 1964, it had made up the membership losses that it had incurred after 1956 and started attempts to build the 'mass party', so that by the end of the decade, the Communist Party seemed to occupy an important and influential role in the British labour movement, riding on the success of the Liaison Committee of the Defence of Trade Unions' victory over the Wilson government and the *In Place of Strife* White Paper. The Party entered the 1970s wary that while the trade unions had secured a victory over income policies in the short term, a Conservative victory in an election to be held in the next two years would be a different challenge altogether.

While the British labour movement finished the decade on an upward tra-jectory, the same cannot be said for Britain's ethnic minorities and migrant population. The 1960s saw the implementation of immigration controls against those coming from the Commonwealth, so that by 1968, there was a clear divide between desirable (i.e. white) migrants from the Dominions and undesirable (i.e. non-white) migrants from the former colonies of Africa and Asia. While Labour introduced and amended the Race Relations Act in 1965 and 1968 to improve 'race relations', these pieces of legislation only addressed the most explicit forms of racial discrimination and the onus lay with the Attorney-General to prosecute cases, which meant that the Act was infrequently used to its full potential. By the end of the 1960s, anti-immigrationist rhetoric had shifted from the fringes of the fascist far right to the mainstream with Enoch Powell's 'Rivers of Blood' speech, which then prompted a resurgence in the for-tunes of the fascist fringe, with the National Front entering the 1970s as a threat to British democracy and to the nation's ethnic minorities. This coincided with a rise in black political militancy and a more general anti-racist awakening, making the 1970s a turbulent decade for 'race relations', as will be shown in the next two chapters.

These intertwining narratives of victory and misfortune greatly affected how the Communist Party related to issues of race and immigration throughout the 1960s. At the start of the decade, the Party was one of the few organisations that embraced migrant workers and advocated a principled anti-racist position, but as the decade wore on, the Party's anti-racist work, performed by an older cadre of members in the International Department, started to lag, based on the politics of anti-colonialism, which was losing its immediacy in the mid-1960s. The Party found itself competing with other groups on the far left, primarily the IS and the IMG, and more radical black organisations that eschewed the trade union/Labour Party links offered by the Communist Party and the Movement for Colonial Freedom. As long as the CPGB supported working with the Labour Party and the trade unions, both of whom advocated some form of immigration control over Commonwealth migrants, the Communist Party faced a tough battle in winning over ethnic minorities and migrant workers. The 1970s would see the 'old axis' of the CPGB, Labour and the trade unions challenged by the far left and by the new social movements, which would re-energise the Party's anti-racist work over the next ten years, but also highlight some of its major weaknesses. The next chapter will look at how the 'British upturn' turned into 'crisis' and the effects that this had upon the Communist Party, Britain's ethnic minority communities and the CPGB's anti-racist work.

The Crisis Emerges, 1970–5

In between the 'hey-day' of 1968–9 and the upsurge in trade union militancy and political radicalism of 1971–4, the 1970s began for the British left as a period of a political plateau, only shaken up by the unexpected election of the Conservatives under Edward Heath. Although Harold Wilson had faced several political problems in the dying days of the 1960s, such as increased trade union militancy, the 'Troubles' in Northern Ireland, a burgeoning anti-war movement against Vietnam and some economic woes, it was still expected that Labour would win the 1970 General Election, probably with a reduced majority of seats. However, once the Conservatives were elected to power, Heath introduced two pieces of legislation that would transform the labour movement and the anti-racist movement in Britain for the first half of the decade – the Industrial Relations Act 1971 and the Immigration Act 1971. The Industrial Relations Act created a groundswell of resistance to its implementation and in 1972, the trade union movement, with the lead taken by the National Union of Mineworkers (NUM), undertook a strategy of continual strike action, which led to paralysed industries, arrested trade unionists and the most days lost to strike activity since the General Strike of 1926. The Immigration Act 1971, on the other hand, reinvented the immigration control system, removing any special status granted to Commonwealth subjects and categorising all migrants into those who could demonstrate ancestral ties to the UK (patrials) and those who could not (non-patrials). This effectively ended any labour migration from the Commonwealth and meant that the only two major groups of migrants to Britain throughout the 1970s and 1980s were women and children from the Commonwealth seeking to join their male family members in the UK and citizens of the European Economic Community (EEC), who, after 1 January 1973, were allowed free movement across all countries within the EEC, which now included Britain.[1]

The Communist Party was heavily involved in the strike action of the early 1970s and it has been argued the CPGB's union membership created a framework for easy organisation and mobilisation, but, as discussed in the previous chapter, other scholars have claimed that the importance of the Communist Party in this period of industrial militancy was the presence of numbers,

---

1   See Smith and Marmo 2014.

not leadership or agenda-setting. The success of this strike activity in making the Industrial Relations Act unworkable enthused the CPGB greatly and while membership was falling, the Party seemed to believe that a breakthrough could be made from the alliances formed with sections of the trade union leadership and the Labour left. The previous decade seemed to show that the Communist Party had found its winning strategy and the focus of the Party was placed upon industrial militancy and broad left activity within the labour movement. Several people, including CPGB members, have written that this emphasis on trade union matters was at the expense of other political campaigns and that the Party's anti-racist work was not able to mobilise much enthusiasm for demonstrations against the Immigration Act.

However, Britain was thrown into disarray over the next few years, beginning in late 1973 when the Oil Crisis plunged the Western world into economic shock and the re-election of Harold Wilson as Prime Minister in 1974. The Oil Crisis emanating from the Middle East in October 1973 caused massive energy problems for the Western world, particularly in Europe and North America who were facing the start of winter, which impacted upon industry, causing a rise in inflation and living costs. The Heath government, concerned about conserving energy now that the price of oil had risen exponentially, instigated a three-day business week, but was also concerned about an ongoing pay dispute with the NUM, which threatened access to coal stocks. To break this deadlock, Heath called a snap election in February 1974 with the campaign promise to be tough on trade unions that held the nation to 'ransom', with the NUM calling a strike a few days later. The outcome of the February election was a hung parliament with no clear majority to either Labour or the Conservatives and thus another election was held in October 1974, which Labour won with a majority of three. After the February election, Labour ruled momentarily as a minority government and the NUM called off its strike, but Wilson, not wanting a return to the industrial action he faced in the late 1960s and fearing that any strike activity would hinder Britain's economic recovery, negotiated a 'Social Contract' with the Trades Union Congress that agreed to a voluntary wage freeze and a cessation of strike activity for the short-term future. Many felt that the victories of the early 1970s had not produced their desired effects and that the end result of years of militant industrial struggle was a return to the same old Labour government that had preceded Heath and had now restrained the unions with the Social Contract.

This caused a high level of debate within the Communist Party over the strategy that it had pursued since the late 1960s. Many of those who had joined over the last decade (predominantly students and those involved in the new social movements) were disapproving of the emphasis placed on industrial action by the Party's Industrial Department under Bert Ramelson and the lack of results gained from attaching themselves to the broad left figures of Jack Jones and Hugh Scanlon, who ended up supporting the Social Contract. This led to a series of debates over whether the Party needed to maintain its emphasis on seeking influence with the trade union leadership or move towards embracing those 'alienated' by industrial action and radicalised instead by the new social movements and other issues.

But the crisis that Britain faced in the mid-1970s was not remedied by reinstallation of a Labour government. Despite Labour's best efforts, unemployment and inflation still rose and productivity declined. The economic crisis compounded the feelings that a political crisis was impending. Wilson suspected that a right-wing conspiracy, with sections of the military and intelligence services involved, was out to unseat him from being Prime Minister. The National Front, as well as the Monday Club, started to agitate for stricter immigration controls and the repatriation of non-white Britons, as well as the elimination of trade unions and the monitoring of those considered 'communists' or 'socialists'. In 1976, the International Monetary Fund agreed to loans to assist the Labour government, but only on the condition of strict public spending cuts, which exacerbated the problem further and turned many sections of British society away from Labour. This, alongside the view that the Social Contract agreed between the TUC and Labour was on the verge of collapse, saw Wilson resign in March 1976, with James Callaghan becoming Prime Minister. Increasingly it looked to many observers that Britain was experiencing a crisis of the postwar social-democratic consensus and that the bipartisan framework constructed by both major parties in the early 1950s was now falling apart. As Stuart Hall and others from the Centre for Contemporary Cultural Studies wrote, the crisis of the mid-1970s was 'a crisis in political legitimacy, in social authority, in hegemony, and in the forms of class struggle'.[2]

The 1971 Immigration Act and Opposition to the Conservative Government

After winning the 1970 General Election, viewed by many observers as an unexpected victory, Heath stated that the Conservatives had been 'returned to office to change the course and history of this nation, nothing else'.[3] Rallying against

---

2   Hall et al. 2013, p. 319.
3   Cited in Butler and Kavanagh 1974, p. 10.

the mixed economy of the Wilson era and against the 'permissive society' that allowed the explosion of cultural radicalism and industrial militancy, Heath launched a campaign for a less restricted market economy, while strengthening state structures against the 'enemy within'.[4] The radicalism and militancy of the late 1960s created a perception amongst the Conservatives that to prevent British society drifting into 'violence' and 'disorder', a transition towards a more repressive role for state institutions was needed.[5] A 'clear tendency in the fields of industrial relations, social welfare, and race relations' towards the use of repression was accepted by the state in combating the perceived crisis that faced Britain. The 1971 Immigration Act needs to be viewed in the wider context of the Conservative government introducing legislation to create greater control by the state over those who were deemed to be threats to 'the nation'. The introduction of the Industrial Relations Act to combat the militancy of the trade union movement had been prefigured by Labour's 1969 White Paper, *In Place of Strife*,[6] just as the Immigration Act was prefigured by Labour's 1968 Commonwealth Immigrants Act, which separated black and white Commonwealth citizens. Both Acts worked in the same way, by identifying and isolating an element of society considered 'subversive', regulating and controlling them by legislation and the threat of repressive state action.

The 1971 Immigration Act replaced both the 1962 and 1968 Commonwealth Immigrants Acts and all legislation concerning the immigration of aliens, basing control around the single distinction between 'patrials' and 'non-patrials'.[7] The concept of the 'patrial' had been prefigured by the 1968 Commonwealth Immigrants Act, but had been more strictly defined under the Immigration Act. The most important categories of 'patrial' were:

(a) ... a citizen of the United Kingdom and Colonies who has that citizenship by [their] birth ... in the United Kingdom.
(c) ... a citizen of the United Kingdom and Colonies who has at any time been settled in the United Kingdom and Islands and ... been ordinarily resident there for the last five years or more.[8]

All those considered 'non-patrials', both alien and Commonwealth citizens, needed permission to enter Britain, except for those who migrated within the

---

4   Solomos, Findlay, Jones and Gilroy 1982, p. 23.
5   Solomos, Findlay, Jones and Gilroy 1982, p. 25.
6   Lyddon and Darlington 2003, p. 129.
7   Miles and Phizacklea 1984, p. 69.
8   *Immigration Act*, 1971, Part 1, 2, (1); Solomos 2003, p. 63.

European Economic Community.[9] The voucher system that had existed under the Commonwealth Immigrants Acts was abolished and the right of abode was now determined by the possession of an annually renewable work permit.[10] The traditional right to settlement was no longer available to 'non-patrials' as work permits had to be renewed annually and 'only after four years of working in *approved* jobs could they apply for the lifting of restrictions and settle' in Britain.[11] During the 1970 General Election campaign, the Conservatives had promised, influenced by the rise of 'Powellism', that there would be 'no further large scale permanent immigration', and accordingly, under the Immigration Act, 'primary immigration [of new workers] was effectively halted'.[12]

Alongside the tightening of controls on entry, immigration officials were given a 'wide range of discretionary powers, including ... the right to deport people and to refuse entry'.[13] Those suspected 'with reasonable cause' to have entered Britain illegally or overstayed their time could be arrested without warrant under the new discretionary powers given by the Act.[14] Under the new Act, the immigration control system also encompassed other government agencies, such as the police, the Department of Social Security and the National Health Service, which created a complex web of organisations that could cross-check data and detect 'bogus' or 'illegal' immigrants within the UK. All 'non-patrials' residing in the UK for more than six months had to report to the police whilst in the country, and it also became part of police operations during the 1970s to enquire into people's citizenship status, which made the police an integral part of the border control system for post-entry controls. As A. Sivanandan wrote, 'from the village in the Indian subcontinent to the British social security office, blacks are checked and scrutinised'.[15]

For the CPGB, the Conservatives were on a 'collision course with practic-ally every section of working-class and progressive opinion on a wide range of economic, social and political issues'.[16] The Conservatives blamed marginal-ised elements of British society for 'what is wrong with Britain' and considered

---

9   Solomos 2003, p. 63.
10   Ibid.
11   Hiro 1992, p. 223, my emphasis.
12   Solomos 2003, p. 62; Alexander 1987, p. 39.
13   Miles and Phizacklea 1984, p. 69.
14   Sivanandan 1982, p. 27.
15   Sivanandan 1982, p. 134.
16   *Morning Star*, 25 March 1971; Bellamy, *Unite Against Racialism: Defeat the Immigration Bill,* 1971, London: CPGB pamphlet, p. 2.

them 'responsible for the country's economic problems'.[17] The strategy of confrontation and state repression, which the Communist Party saw as inherent
in the Industrial Relations Act, also prompted the Immigration Act under the
'classic tactic of divide and rule'.[18] At the CPGB's National Congress in December 1971, the Party declared that the Immigration Act was 'a primary weapon in
the hands of reaction to disarm the struggle of the working class ... introduced
at a time when unemployment is mounting and serious attacks are being made
on living standards and trade union rights'.[19] Both Bills were considered attacks
on the working class and while the Industrial Relations Bill attacked 'the Trade
Unions head on', the Party stated that the 'Immigration Bill attacks the unity of
black and white workers',[20] pivotal to opposition to the Conservative government's reforms. In a report to the Executive Committee in March 1971, Jimmy
Reid wrote that the Conservatives believed that 'if they can effectively place
the trade unions in a legal straitjacket controlled by the capitalist state, then
the road is clear for their class to ride roughshod over the British people'.[21] Part
of this attempt to curb the militancy of the labour movement was isolating and
restricting sections of the working-class base, which the Communist Party saw
the Immigration Act as doing to black workers.

The Immigration Act created these legal controls 'in the hope of dividing
[black workers] from the rest and cutting them off from working class struggle
for a better life'.[22] The threat of deportation was enshrined in the Immigration
Act, for either being an illegal immigrant or in much more sinister terms, for
'acting in ways not "conductive to the public good"'.[23] One of the conditions
of the right of abode under the Act was suitable employment, which Bellamy
pointed out, meant that if an immigrant lost their job, they ran the risk of being
deported and if the immigrant did not do what their employer requested, the
threat of 'the sack' effectively meant the threat of deportation.[24] The CPGB
emphasised that this threat restrained the black immigrant worker from taking
part in the militancy of the labour movement, stating that if an immigrant 'joins
the fight for better wages, takes an active part in trade union life, becomes a

---

17   *Morning Star*, 25 March 1971.
18   *Morning Star*, 10 February 1972.
19   'Branch and District Resolutions Adopted by Congress: Racialism', *Comment*, 18 December
     1971, p. 484.
20   *Kill This Bill Too*, 1971, London: CPGB flyer, in CPGB archives CP/CENT/CTTE/02/05, LHASC.
21   Reid, 'Clear Out the Tories!', *Comment*, 27 March 1971, p. 151.
22   Bellamy, *Unite Against Racialism*, p. 3.
23   Sivanandan 1982, p. 28.
24   Bellamy, *Unite Against Racialism*, p. 4.

shop steward, joins a picket line in a strike, take his rightful place in the British trade union and working class political movement, he will be at risk'.[25] The hope of employers and the government, the Executive Committee stated in a resolution on the Immigration Bill, was to 'create a docile pool of labour, deprived of normal democratic rights, insecure, and consequently cut off from the rest of the working class'.[26]

As well as applying to new applicants for immigration, the Act was retrospective and gave the state the power to deport illegal immigrants and arrest those suspected of evasion. This effectively put every black person in Britain under suspicion. 'In effect', wrote Bellamy in early 1972, 'the new law says "black is alien" and the atmosphere of suspicion which it generates will serve to add yet more racialist pollution to the atmosphere of British life'.[27] Once again, the Party emphasised the divisive nature of the Immigration Act on the labour movement as 'the black worker on the picket line, or a demonstration, will be the one picked out by the police' and 'harassed to prove his right to be here'.[28] The Act made 'no contribution whatever to improving race relations', wrote Bellamy, and only served to 'increase fear and insecurity' and 'encourage racialists'.[29] The aim of the Act was, according to Party member and local community worker Winston Pinder, 'to harass black working people and make life intolerable for them, so that for those who break under the strain the doors of repatriation will be open'.[30]

The Communist Party and the Reaction of the Trade Unions to the Immigration Act

The Communist Party emphasised that 'unity' was needed to 'kill the bills' and attempted to gather support amongst white workers by explaining that the Immigration Act was part of the wider Conservative campaign to curb the labour movement.[31] Strike action against the Industrial Relations Act had generated great solidarity amongst the labour movement and the CPGB hoped to

---

25   Ibid.
26   'The Immigration Bill', Executive Committee resolution, 13 March 1971, in CPGB archives, CP/CENT/CTTE/02/05, LHASC.
27   *Morning Star*, 10 February 1972.
28   *Morning Star*, 25 March 1971.
29   Bellamy, *Unite Against Racialism*, p. 7.
30   *Morning Star*, 11 October 1971.
31   *Black and White Unity Needed to Kill Both Bills*.

tap into this support in campaigning against the Immigration Act. 'For trade unionists to concentrate only on defeating the Industrial Relations Bill', the Party warned, would be a 'great mistake', and it emphasised that black workers, who had demonstrated against the Industrial Relations Bill, needed the white labour movement to also fight for rights of blacks.[32] One of the continuing problems the Communist Party had was conveying to white workers the problems faced by black people in Britain and the Party stated it was 'not sufficient to call upon the black people alone to organise against racist immigration laws'.[33] The Party demanded that workers attend marches against both Acts and also join the CPGB, 'the only revolutionary organisation with militant working class leaders fighting the class struggle in every field'.[34]

However, while action against the Industrial Relations Act was widespread, elements of the wider labour movement had not shown a commitment to opposing the Immigration Act. The disparity between the two campaigns was that the militancy of the trade unions in the early 1970s was narrowly focused on protecting collective bargaining and industrial action rights and opposing legislation that would threaten this. Despite their influence with the trade unions at this point of heightened industrial militancy, the CPGB were unable to advocate more far-reaching reforms, including opposition to racist immigration controls, relying on supporting the immediate (and primarily economic) demands of the labour movement. The fact that important elements of the trade union movement had not come out in vocal opposition to the Act was noticed by Winston Pinder, who asked in the *Morning Star*, 'why is the trade union movement so conspicuously silent about this Bill?'[35] The labour movement, Pinder argued, was 'too preoccupied with the Industrial Relations Act and the Common Market' and failed to realise that the Immigration Act was 'only another part of the capitalist attack on all working people'.[36] It was up to the trade unions to defend their black members from 'discrimination and ... attacks on their democratic rights',[37] just as the unions had come out to defend the right to strike and collective bargain.

While calling for trade union action against the Immigration Act, in conjunction with the Industrial Relations Act and to 'clear the Tories out', the Party's suggested anti-racist strategy called for workers to 'win a promise that the next

---

32   *Kill This Bill Too.*
33   *Black and White Unity Needed to Kill Both Bills.*
34   Ibid.
35   *Morning Star*, 11 October 1971.
36   Ibid.
37   Bellamy, *Unite Against Racialism*, p. 8.

Labour Government will repeal all racist immigration laws'.[38] The Communist Party still saw the Labour government, who had upheld and strengthened
Conservative immigration controls before, as central to their anti-racist campaign. In 1971, the Labour Party had voted against the Immigration Bill. James
Callaghan had described it as 'a badge of respectability to prejudice', promising to repeal it once Labour was elected.[39] The Industrial Relations Act was
repealed by the Labour government soon after its election in 1974. Although
Labour had opposed the Immigration Act while the Conservatives were in
power, the CPGB noted in 1975 that the 'Labour government has, so far, failed to
repeal the 1971 Immigration Act'.[40]

Facing the Limits of Industrial Militancy

In 1973, the CPGB published the pamphlet *Time to Change Course*, authored by
Secretary of the Party's International Department, Jack Woddis, which capital-
ised on the major strike action of the early 1970s and expounded the role of the
Communist Party within this period of heightened industrial militancy.[41] Central to its argument was the Party's position within the wider labour movement
and its relationship with the Labour left. Woddis argued that 'Britain today
is run *by* big business *for* big business' and despite some reforms, the right-
wing Labour Party 'fundamentally acted no different than the Tories'.[42] For this
reason, Woddis proposed that, '*The entire labour and progressive movement has
to face the fact that ... it cannot advance decisively without a much bigger and
more influential Communist Party*'.[43] However, since the majority of the trade
unionists in Britain associated themselves with the Labour Party, the CPGB
adhered to the strategy dependent on a 'Labour Government committed ... to
carry[ing] out left policies'.[44] Despite attempting to 'reiterate the party's independent political position', Geoff Andrews, among others, has argued that the

---

38   *Equal Rights for British Citizens*, 1972, London: CPGB flyer, in CPGB archives, CP/CENT/
      CTTE/20/05, LHASC; *Kill This Bill Too*.
39   Alexander 1987, p. 39.
40   *Racialism at Work*, 1975, London: CPGB broadsheet, in CPGB archives, CP/LON/RACE/02/
      07, LHASC.
41   Woddis, *Time to Change Course: What Britain's Communists Stand For*, 1973, London: CPGB
      pamphlet.
42   Woddis, *Time to Change Course*, p. 48; Italics are in the original text.
43   Woddis, *Time to Change Course*, p. 136; Italics are in the original text.
44   Woddis, *Time to Change Course*, p. 126.

Party's agenda was 'essentially reformist' and that there was almost no discernable variance in short-term objectives with the Labour left.[45]

The Party's industrial demands of free collective bargaining and opposition to state restrictions on union activity were defensive measures that did not propose any progressive radical or socialist policies. The 'fixity of wage militancy'[46] and the commitment to unrestrained collective bargaining was wholeheartedly accepted by the Party's Industrial Department, which led it into direct conflict with the newly elected Labour government over the Social Contract in 1974. The Social Contract was agreed to by the Trades Union Congress (TUC) and Labour before the October General Election as a 'voluntary restraint on free collective bargaining' and was proposed as the 'only alternative to long-term inflation'.[47] The acceptance of the Social Contract by the TUC caused divisions between the Party and the wider labour movement, with trade union leaders and former Communist Party allies, such as Hugh Scanlon and Jack Jones, supporting the Social Contract. The CPGB's Industrial Department opposed the Social Contract, with Bert Ramelson asserting that this policy was no different from the Conservative government's Industrial Relations Act, as it had the 'same objective – the inhibiting of strikes and industrial action by workers to improve their real earnings'.[48] 'The greatest harm of the Social Contract', wrote Ramelson, 'is that ... by supporting wage restraint it is an encouragement to resort to the old policy of trying to solve the crisis of capitalism by cutting the workers' living standards'.[49] Ramelson chastised those left union leaders who supported the Contract, declaring that 'in advocating the Social Contract they are causing incalculable harm to their members, the economy, and helping the right wing core in the government'.[50] This opposition brought an end to the alliance between Ramelson, Jones and Scanlon, as well as the 'beginning of the demise of the Party's influence' as it depended on 'sustaining a close relationship with the same left trade union leaders who were architects of the contract'.[51]

This schism between those who supported the Social Contract and the CPGB's emphasis on maintaining the focus upon unrestrained collective bargaining is important because it allowed those who sought to reform the Party an opportunity to draw attention to the stress placed on economic industrial

---

45   Andrews 2004, p. 121; p. 122.
46   Callaghan 2004, p. 398.
47   Thompson 1993, p. 106.
48   Ramelson, *Social Contract: Cure-All or Con-Trick?*, 1974, London: CPGB pamphlet, p. 16.
49   Ramelson, *Social Contract*, p. 17.
50   Ramelson, *Social Contract*, p. 8.
51   Andrews 2004, pp. 131–2.

130

issues at the expense of other political concerns. Debates over the relevancy of pursuing a total opposition to wage restraint began to appear inside the CPGB, proposed by some young economists associated with the Gramscian trend that was emerging amongst those who had joined in the late 1960s, most notably David Purdy and Mike Prior. In a debate over economic policy in *Marxism Today* in 1974, Purdy argued that, 'Inflation has become too profound a social and economic problem for us to remain satisfied with a purely defensive line'.[52] Purdy claimed that 'incomes policy in the sense of a collectively and democratically agreed plan for the development of prices and incomes is an essential part of socialist economic planning'.[53] Prior summarised the situation as a 'choice between accepting a vague "squeeze the rich" and "social contract" incomes policy of the Labour Party and an alternative "revolutionary" policy of pursuing increasingly unrealistic wage demands'.[54] 'The acceptance of a *working-class* incomes policy with increasing working-class control over the economy', argued Prior, would 'simultaneously raise its [the working class's] political understanding and will begin to make it the hegemonic class within society'.[55] Although the debate over the validity of opposition to the Social Contract did not begin the move away from the centrality of class conflict towards the inclusion of wider social movements and cultural politics, it did establish an alternative to the primacy of industrial militancy, now that the CPGB was in disagreement with its traditional allies in the trade unions and the Labour left.

The Ugandan Asian 'Controversy' and the Rise of the National Front under the Conservatives

The crisis conditions allowed the far right to start to make inroads into the mainstream as anti-immigrationists looked for a scapegoat for the socio-economic problems facing Britain. After being sacked from the shadow cabinet for his 'Rivers of Blood' speech, Enoch Powell continued to dominate Conservative

---

52 Purdy, 'Some Thoughts on the Party's Policy Towards Prices, Wages and Incomes', *Marxism Today*, August 1974, p. 252.

53 Purdy, 'Some Thoughts on the Party's Policy Towards Prices, Wages and Incomes', p. 250.

54 Prior, 'Inflation and Marxist Theory', *Marxism Today*, April 1975, p. 124.

55 Prior, 'Inflation and Marxist Theory', p. 125. Prior advocated that the working class should attempt to extend its influence and control over 'the area of resource allocation and investment decision', which was 'the heartland of capitalism' and 'controls precisely those factors which affect the realisation of working class aspirations and needs'. Prior, 'Inflation and Marxist Theory', p. 124.

thinking about immigration and there is a suggestion by scholars that the Conservatives were eventually convinced by Powell's argument, leading to the introduction of the Immigration Act 1971.[56] However, before the Act came into effect on 1 January 1973, the Heath government faced a new 'problem' regarding Commonwealth immigration that allowed the far right to capitalise on populist anti-immigrant sentiment.

In 1972, Idi Amin expelled the Asian community from Uganda and as Uganda was a former British colony, many of these Asians had United Kingdom passports. However, the passports were mainly issued prior to 1968, when the law was changed to nullify these overseas-issued passports and made residential entry to Britain for Commonwealth migrants reliant upon an ancestral link to the country. Therefore many Ugandan Asians were displaced persons, expelled from Uganda and ending up in India, with most trying to enter Britain (often via another European country). The Conservative government found itself in a difficult position – it did accept many of the Ugandan Asians (feeling obligated to accept a significant quota as former colonial subjects and unofficial 'refugees'), but did not want to encourage further Ugandan Asians in India and elsewhere to come to Britain.

The Attorney-General, Peter Rawlinson, told Edward Heath's Cabinet in September 1972 that '[u]nder international law a State had a duty to other States to accept within its territory those of its nationals who were expelled from their country of residence and were not admitted to any other country', which 'applied notwithstanding the controls imposed' by the Commonwealth Immigrants Act 1968, which denied East African Asians (from Kenya in 1968) entry into Britain.[57] Rawlinson cited the precedent offered by James Callaghan, Labour Home Secretary in 1968, who 'publicly acknowledged an obligation to receive such individuals if they were expelled with no prospect of any alternative refuge'.[58] Over the next two years, around 23,000 Ugandan Asians migrated to Britain, with around another 17,000 distributed between India and other Commonwealth countries.[59] This caused much outrage amongst anti-immigrationists, with the National Front, as well Enoch Powell and the Monday Club, campaigning against this intake of migrants.

By criticising the 'soft' approach towards the Ugandan Asians by the government, the NF appeared to many as an extreme extension of traditional

---

56   See: Ben-Tovim and Gabriel 1982, pp. 150–1; Miles and Phizacklea 1984, pp. 68–9; Turner 2008, p. 27.

57   Cabinet Meeting Conclusions, 7 September 1972, 3, CAB/128/50/42 in NA.

58   Ibid.

59   Gupta 1974, p. 321.

Conservative ideals. This period saw the NF attempt to capitalise on anti-immigrant sentiment amongst 'disillusioned, largely middle-class Conservatives', reinforced by 'growing links with the reactionary Conservative Monday Club'.[60] The attempts at closer ties with the Conservative right brought the NF significant numbers and members, such as Roy Painter and John Kingsley-Read. Membership numbers reached their highest during 1973–4. While not exact, membership was estimated at being between 14,000 and 17,500.[61] However, there was still apprehension amongst the Nazi elements of the leadership, such as John Tyndall and Martin Webster, that the NF was becoming too close to the Conservatives. The National Front's strategy with the Monday Club was appropriation of members and infiltration, 'aimed to win over its support and, ultimately, destroy it'.[62] What characterised the NF during the period from 1968 to 1974 was its use of Conservative opposition to black immigration and its extreme position on traditional Conservative ideas. However, when the economic crisis set in after 1974, the NF moved away from trying to appeal to middle-class Conservative voters to attempting to siphon Labour Party supporters and appealing to the working class, exploiting the dire economic situation by blaming black immigration for shortages in employment, housing and welfare.

While the NF was appealing to Conservative voters, the Communist Party made much of the association between Enoch Powell and the National Front, trying to break the 'respectable' racism of Powell and the Monday Club. In a flyer distributed by the Westminster CPGB branch, it announced that 'fascism is on the march again', warning that it 'wears the "respectable" face of Enoch Powell', as well as appearing in 'its most naked form in the National Front'.[63] The flyer called for the banning of a NF march in London, but also warned against Powell, 'who pours out racialism whenever he appears on the telly' and 'publicly stated that whenever he sees a rich man he thanks God!'[64] For the CPGB, the NF were 'working to strengthen the capitalist system', blaming black immigrants for the problems of capitalism and despite any appeal to the interests of the working class, 'racialism plays into the hands of the capitalist class'.[65] The aim of the NF was 'to smash the trade union movement

---

60   Eatwell 1997, p. 336.
61   Eatwell 1998, p. 1200; Thurlow 1987, p. 288.
62   Miles and Phizacklea 1984, p. 121.
63   'Westminster Communists Say ... Outlaw the Racists', n.d., London: CPGB flyer, in CPGB archives, CP/LON/EVNT/03/07, LHASC.
64   Ibid.
65   'Don't Be Fooled By The National Front!', n.d., London: CPGB flyer, in CPGB archives, CP/IND/KAY/03/05, LHASC.

and make it servile to the state in the interests of state monopoly capital', with 'racialism ... only the most obvious of their anti-working class policies'.[66] Essentially this was viewed as the same agenda as Enoch Powell, who Joan Bellamy described as 'a declared enemy of the trade unions'.[67] The consensus was that Powell's speech had given the fledgling NF valuable exposure that allowed the fascist fringe to exploit popular racism and anti-immigration sentiment. ' "Enoch is Right" became the slogan of everyone from the Tory Monday Club through the National Front out to every tinpot little nazi sect', Bob Campbell wrote in the *Morning Star*, linking Powell, the NF, various anti-immigration groups and the Orange movement.[68] However, there were differences between the various elements of the far right. Powell, as a traditional Conservative, 'warned of the dangers of a corporate state emerging from the relationship between the Labour Government, the TUC and the CBI', while the NF 'tend toward[s] corporate statism ... and *suggest* they are opposed to capitalism'.[69] But 'what unites all the elements of the ultra right in Britain', he wrote, 'is the racist campaign on the question of immigration, and against black people as a whole'.[70] Although in private correspondence with Vishnu Sharma, a CPGB and IWA member, Joan Bellamy, criticised Campbell for elevating the danger of these far right organisations when 'the major enemy is racialist attitudes among people who do not have a consistent fascist or even right wing position, and the cowardly connivance of Tory and Labour politicians with right wing demands'.[71]

During this period, the National Front was increasing its electoral participation, attempting to appropriate middle-class support away from the 'soft' Conservative government, playing down its notorious neo-Nazi elements. Alongside this electoral push by the NF, several other anti-immigrant and far right organisations attempted to exploit popular racism to make gains, following the Ugandan Asians controversy. Campbell warned the readers of the *Morning Star*:

---

66   Trade Union Committee Against Racialism, 'National Front – Election Campaign Notes', in CPGB archives, CP/CENT/CTTE/02/05, LHASC.

67   Bellamy, *Homes, Jobs, Immigration*, p. 3.

68   *Morning Star*, 22 February 1973.

69   *Morning Star*, 1 March 1973, my emphasis.

70   Ibid.

71   Letter from Joan Bellamy to Vishnu Sharma, 15 March 1973, in CPGB archives, CP/CENT/CTTE/02/05, LHASC.

Beware. If anyone stands in your area as a national independent, a national democrat, or even 'something' against the Common Market, this
can be a shield for straightforward ultra-right policies.

These people will claim that they are not fascist, but their racial attitudes are those which aided the rise of Hitler and the massacre of those
other 'aliens,' the Jews ...

Remember the anti-fascist slogan of the '30s – 'They Shall Not Pass'.[72]

The 'No Platform' Strategy

As the National Front grew after the Ugandan Asians controversy and contested
more seats in elections leading up to the 1974 General Elections, the anti-
fascist movement developed the 'no platform' strategy to deny the NF venues to
hold meetings or public addresses. Essentially 'no platform' was an extension
of the successful anti-fascist strategy that had been developed since the late
1940s. As well as physically combating fascist agitation in the streets, one
of the major strategies was campaigning for local governments and other
institutions to prevent fascists from using public places to speak or meet. After
the Race Relations Act was passed, a significantly stronger case was made
for state intervention against fascist agitation, but the decision to hire out
meeting venues rested primarily with local government, becoming an issue of
pressuring councils to prevent this from occurring.

Nigel Copsey claimed that despite being the largest group on the left, the
CPGB was 'seemingly preoccupied with trade union work' and therefore unable
to initiate a significant anti-fascist agenda and instead 'it was the more militant
groups that first began to vocalise opposition to the National Front'.[73] Copsey
notes that it was the International Marxist Group (IMG) who 'advocated a "no
platform" policy for fascists' in the lead up to the February 1974 General Election.[74] In fact, as early as September 1972, at the height of the Ugandan Asians
controversy, the IMG's paper, *The Red Mole*, had the headline, 'No Platform for
Racists'.[75] Between 1972 and 1976, the 'no platform' concept dominated anti-
fascist strategy, supported by the Communist Party, the International Socialists
(IS) and the IMG, as well as becoming policy for the National Union of Students
(NUS), which was considerably influenced by the IMG and the CPGB. The 'no

72   *Morning Star*, 1 March 1973.
73   Copsey 2000, p. 118.
74   Copsey 2000, pp. 118–19.
75   *The Red Mole*, 18 September 1972.

platform' strategy was not limited to petitioning local councils and institutions to deny the NF access to meeting places, but included physical opposition to the NF organising in public. As *The Red Mole* declared, 'the only way to deal with fascist type organisations like the National Front is to break up their activities *before* they grow to a size where they can begin to smash the activities of the working class'.[76] The 'no platform' strategy was about denying the NF venues to speak and was not interchangeable with the opposition on the streets, which occurred later with the SWP at places such as Lewisham and Ladywood. The street battles of the late 1970s were primarily the result of the NF switching tactics (after its failure to garner electoral support) to provocative demonstrations through areas with large immigrant communities, which some, particularly the SWP, thought should be physically opposed, in the tradition of the 'Battle of Cable Street'. 'No Platform' was essentially about the denial of access for the NF to public venues, either by petition or by physically preventing NF members from entering, where petitioning had failed.

The policy of 'no platform' promoted by the NUS in April 1974 sparked debate over the issue of free speech and the use of violence to defeat fascism. At a conference held in Liverpool in April 1974, the NUS passed a motion calling for universities and student unions 'to prevent any member of these [fascist] organizations, or individuals known to espouse similar views from speaking in colleges *by whatever means necessary*'.[77] This position was criticised for its denial of freedom of speech and it was argued by some that the way to fight racist and fascist ideas was through debate. The NUS's National Secretary Steve Parry argued in *Labour Monthly* that to allow this would be giving fascists a platform and 'surely this is the danger to freedom, not the determination of the NUS to oppose racism and fascism at every opportunity'.[78] The freedom of speech was not absolute, Parry argued, as it was 'already limited by such laws as the Race Relations Act' and denying fascist and racist ideas a platform was 'fighting for a freedom of even greater importance: the freedom to live without discrimination on the basis of race'.[79] The National Student Organiser of the CPGB, Dave Cook, pledged the Party's support for the NUS's position in the *Morning Star*, stating that 'it is correct to argue that student unions should seek to deny racists a platform'.[80] Cook attempted to make it clear that Conservative

---

76   Ibid; Italics are in the original text.
77   Cited in 'Dialectics of Freedom', *Patterns of Prejudice*, 8/3, May/June 1974, pp. 12–13, my emphasis.
78   Parry, 'Students Against Racism and Fascism', *Labour Monthly*, June 1974, p. 259.
79   Ibid.
80   *Morning Star*, 24 May 1974.

ideas, while 'repugnant', were 'political views which [students] can accept or reject', but racist attacks 'on grounds of his or her colour' were 'against that person as a human being, against something they cannot change'.[81]

The Communist Party supported the NUS position, stating that the 'principal argument of N.U.S. policy is correct, it is necessary to fight to deny racist and fascist organisations a platform in the colleges'.[82] However, the Party had difficulty with the inclusion of the Monday Club in this category. In a statement by the Political Committee, the Party argued:

> Its target is the expression of organised racialism and fascism. No matter how nauseous we find the views of *individuals* who are not members of such organisations ... or the views of the *right wing of the Tory Party*, e.g. the *Monday Club*; the fact is that both of these differ significantly from organisations whose aim is *declaredly* racialist.[83]

The CPGB were wary of the militancy of some on the far left who supported the 'no platform' position, with Cook warning that it was 'important that direct action does not become a substitute for the often more difficult task of winning the majority'.[84] 'Physical thuggery' was seen as counter-productive which created sympathy for those attacked and demonstrated 'the sort of bigotry and intolerance that alienates potential supporters'.[85] For the CPGB, the decision to deny fascists a platform should 'seek to involve the largest possible number of students' and not 'resort to individual terroristic acts'.[86]

The aim of the Communist Party was 'to unite the broadest forces possible against racialism', with the Political Committee believing that the application of the 'no platform' strategy was a tactical question for local bodies and 'whether one can argue for the total position is for each branch or body of comrades to decide in the concrete situation'.[87] This was reiterated in the YCL's pamphlet produced in late 1974, *The Fascist Threat*, acknowledging that 'the fight must not only be confined to the Socialist students and the Left within the labour

---

81   Ibid.

82   'The Fight Against Racialism and Fascism', in CPGB archives, CP/CENT/PC/13/05, LHASC.

83   Ibid; Italics are in the original text.

84   *Morning Star*, 24 May 1974.

85   LSE CPGB Branch, 'Thuggery & Fascism & Exit of Socialism', in CPGB archives, CP/CENT/STAT/03/02, LHASC.

86   'The Fight Against Racialism and Fascism'.

87   'Racialism and No Platform', in CPGB archives, CP/CENT/PC/14/06, LHASC.

movement'.[88] The author, Mike Power, recognised that the NUS had 'played an important part in this fight, by its decision to refuse a platform to fascist speakers', as the 'poisonous doctrine of racialism is as much an offence to humanity as crimes of violence'.[89] However, there was a feeling amongst some Communist Party members that students and the far left were leading the anti-fascist movement, while the trade union movement was not active enough. 'I appreciate the role of the students in this struggle', wrote Frank Watters in *Comment*, '[b]ut because we need the involvement of the labour movement any committees set up to organise this struggle must have the aim of the winning of the organised working class'.[90] The student activists, though radicalised and influenced by the far left, were felt to be disassociated from the traditional labour movement and the anti-fascist bodies organised beforehand were described by Watters as '"ad hoc" committees ... set up ... by a handful of people with little or no influence, in the labour movement'.[91] In a veiled attack on the far left, Watters claimed that these committees 'expect the [labour] movement to respond to calls which are not designed to secure the fullest possible mobilisation of anti-fascist forces' and 'instead are geared towards "confrontation"'.[92]

The IMG took exception to the Party's support of the 'no platform' strategy only while the current laws against incitement to race hatred were inadequate.[93] 'The "no platform" position ... cannot be made dependent on the legal situation', argued the IMG's John Kilbane, reiterating that 'mass action will remain necessary'.[94] The argument for direct action, with the potential for physical confrontation, was also made by the International Socialists, who criticised those on the left, such as the CPGB, who 'end up ... talking of "peaceful pickets" and implying that the police can "stop the fascists"'.[95] 'For the left to call upon the police force to deal with the fascists', it was asserted in the journal *International Socialism*, 'is to provide it with a chance to enhance its own powers for attacking the left'.[96] The 'peaceful picket, pious resolutions, rational arguments alone' would not stop the fascist threat as fascists 'have to be driven

88   Power, *The Fascist Threat: A Young Communist Review of Fascist and Authoritarian Trends*, n.d., Manchester: YCL pamphlet, p. 11.
89   Ibid.
90   Watters, 'Birmingham's Lead in Fight Against Racialism', *Comment*, 10 August 1974, p. 250.
91   Ibid.
92   Ibid.
93   *Red Weekly*, 29 March 1974.
94   Ibid.
95   'Fists Against Fascists', *International Socialism*, 1/70, June 1974, p. 5.
96   Ibid.

physically from the streets'.[97] While in its journal, the International Socialists argued that 'only mass mobilisation on the streets can defeat fascism', internally it accepted that 'elections are the main demonstration of Front support', which required different tactics than the street battles of the late 1970s.[98]

For the CPGB though, the emphasis was on 'unity and discipline' amongst the broad sections of the labour and progressive movement that organised against the National Front. What concerned them was, as London District Secretary Gerry Cohen stated, 'the defence by such a colossal demonstration of police power, of organisations and policies which are so abhorrent to the wishes of the great mass of ordinary, decent people'.[99] The issue of 'no platform' and direct action, the far left, the police and the NF first came to a head on 15 June 1974, when an anti-fascist demonstration in Red Lion Square in London ended in the death of a demonstrator, Kevin Gately.

Red Lion Square and the Death of Kevin Gately

On 15 June 1974, the National Front had organised a march through London, ending at Conway Hall in Red Lion Square. Liberation (formerly the Movement for Colonial Freedom) organised a counter-demonstration that was to end with a meeting outside the hall, which was supported by the CPGB, the IS, the IMG and many other groups within the labour movement. The Communist Party had supported the counter-demonstration organised by the London Area Council of Liberation. The Liberation/MCF Area Council had been staffed by several CPGB members, including Jack Woddis, Kay Beauchamp, Tony Gilbert, Dorothy Kuya, joint CPGB/AKEL member George Pefkos, Billy Strachan and joint CPGB/SACP member Sam Kahn.[100] Brownell has described this presence of Communists (mainly from the International Department and from the London District Committee) as 'the single most powerful bloc in the MCF/Liberation organization'.[101] As mentioned previously, Brownell argues that once these Communist Party members gained control of the Liberation leadership, the organisation started to shift away from its original mandate, becoming involved in 'general anti-racism and immigration-related campaigns'.[102] It could be that

---

97   Ibid.
98   Ibid; International Socialists, *IS Internal Bulletin*, June 1974, p. 18.
99   *Morning Star*, 27 March 1975.
100   MCF, *AGM Report*, February 1970, in CPGB archives, CP/IND/KAY/01/04, LHASC.
101   Brownell 2007, p. 256.
102   Brownell 2007, p. 256, fn. 115.

the Communist bloc within the London Area Council leadership of Liberation chose to call for the counter-demonstration under the banner of Liberation, which would bring a wider audience than the CPGB, but this divided Liberation between those on the LAC and the non-Communists involved in the organisation. In the aftermath of the counter-demonstration, Fenner Brockway angrily wrote to the General Secretary of Liberation and LAC member, Steve Hart:

> I understand the project was initiated by officers of the London Area Council. Who gave Head Office the authority to participate? The leaflets calling for the march were in the name of Liberation and not of the London Area Council and you, as General Secretary, were active.
>
> In the past Head Office has always been expected to consult with Liberation's officers when action not already endorsed by the E.C. or the Central Council was contemplated. I understand that the Chairman was informed only in general terms ... I was not consulted. I was asked six days before the march only if I would speak. I then expressed my dissent.[103]

However, as Nigel Copsey noted, 'Unbeknown to Liberation ... was the determination of the IMG to organise a mass picket at the main entrance of the hall thereby denying the NF access'.[104] The police, with what Lord Scarman later described as a 'concern ... with maintenance of public order', attempted to disperse the IMG contingent that were blocking the NF's access to Conway Hall.[105] The IMG members refused to be dispersed and, according to Lord Scarman's report, 'when the IMG assaulted the police cordon there began a riot, which it was the duty of the police to suppress, by force if necessary'.[106] It was in this initial violent clash between police and militant anti-fascists, lasting for less than fifteen minutes, that Kevin Gately, a student from Warwick University, was fatally injured. Gately died from a brain haemorrhage stemming from a blow to the head.[107] Further clashes between police and anti-fascist demonstrators occurred throughout the day, with the end result being that 'one person died,

---

103   Letter from Fenner Brockway to Steve Hart, 23 June 1974, in Liberation Papers, LIB/04/08 File 21, School of Oriental and African Studies Archives, London.

104   Copsey 2000, p. 120.

105   Lord Justice Scarman, *The Red Lion Square Disorders of 15 June 1974: Report of Inquiry by the Rt. Hon. Lord Justice Scarman, O.B.E.*, 1975, p. 8, in HMSO, NA.

106   Ibid.

107   Copsey 2000, p. 120; Scarman, *The Red Lion Square Disorders of 15 June 1974*, p. 11.

46 policemen and at least 12 demonstrators were injured, 51 people arrested and the whole police operation had cost an estimated £15,000'.[108]

In the *Morning Star* on 15 June 1974, an article urged people to support the counter-demonstration, including an appeal by leading trade unionists, stating that the NF's 'poisonous ideas are a threat to all that is best in our society'.[109] In the aftermath, the *Morning Star* declared that 'blame for what occurred ... must be placed where it belongs – on the authorities for permitting it, and the police for brutality'.[110] The march by the NF was in violation of the Race Relations Act, the CPGB claimed, and on these grounds the march should have been banned.[111] Appealing to the repressive apparatus of the state, such as the police, the judiciary and the Home Office, to deal with fascists, plus criticism of the police, showed an inconsistency in the Communist Party's strategy, which believed the state could be utilised to counter the NF, while the police were hostile to the left and far from impartial. As London District Secretary Gerry Cohen wrote in the *Morning Star*, 'The police, like the National Front, are on the side of the exploiting class. They operated on that side with thoroughness and with fury on Saturday in Red Lion Square. And Kevin Gately died'.[112] The CPGB and Liberation emphasised the peaceful nature of their march, quoting Gilbert as saying, 'At least 99.9 per cent of the 2,000 people there were absolutely peaceful and they were attacked'.[113]

The IMG were condemned by the CPGB for aiming at confrontation. The anti-fascist movement needed to appeal to the broader progressive and labour movements, according to Cohen, 'but what this small section of the march did was to make this more difficult', as the IMG 'played into the hands of all those in the key positions of establishment ... aimed at destroying our basic democratic rights'.[114] In a press release by the CPGB's London District Committee, the CPGB declared that it had 'by far the largest number of individuals of any single organisation involved in the demonstration', with approximately 500–600 numbers involved.[115] The press release stated that, 'At no time did our Party

108 Copsey 2000, p. 120.

109 *Morning Star*, 15 June 1974.

110 *Morning Star*, 17 June 1974.

111 Ibid.

112 *Morning Star*, 22 June 1974.

113 Ibid.

114 Ibid.

115 London District Communist Party, 'Copy of Statement for the Public Enquiry Sent to the Treasury Solicitor on Events in Red Lion Square, June 15th 1974', 15 August 1974, in CPGB archives, CP/LON/EVNT/03/07, LHASC.

contemplate, nor did it take part in any discussions that contemplated of bringing about any physical confrontation with the police or anybody else at this demonstration'.[116] According to the Party, there was 'absolutely no reason why the police could not have contained the situation *peacefully at all times*' and the police had 'undoubtedly mishandled the situation'.[117] For Cohen, this was the lesson of the Red Lion Square demonstrations: 'For the sake of humanity don't let the adventurist tactics of a minority, and the way they are seized on by the media, divert from the main question ... Root out this evil'.[118]

In the days following, there were calls for an inquiry into Gately's death. NUS President John Randall was quoted in the *Morning Star* as saying, 'We now know that Kevin Gately died as a direct result of police violence'.[119] By the end of the month, Lord Scarman had been placed in charge of the inquiry, conducting a tribunal with witnesses throughout September 1974, and a report was eventually produced in February 1975. Scarman's conclusions strongly defended the police force's actions and criticised the demonstrators, primarily the IMG and the naivety of Liberation, for the violence. The report was 'unable to make any definite finding as to the specific cause of the fatal injury which Mr Kevin Gately suffered'.[120] Scarman largely absolved the police of any wrongdoing.

Scarman concluded that the police were 'right not to ban the National Front demonstration', but recommended that the Race Relations Act needed 'radical amendment to make it an effective sanction'.[121] As Scarman could not discover the direct cause of Gately's death, in his judgement he found that 'those who started the riot carry a measure of moral responsibility for his death', namely the IMG, who he believed had 'initiated the disorder by their inexcusable assault on the police cordon'.[122] The overall lesson that Lord Scarman had for the anti-fascist movement was 'co-operate with the police'.[123]

---

116   Ibid.

117   Ibid.

118   *Morning Star*, 22 June 1974. In the days following Gately's death, a march was organised by the NUS and Warwick University's Student Union in memory of Gately and in protest against the police brutality. In a memo to the CPGB's National Student Committee members, Dave Cook announced that 'the Demo organisers are insisting on a silent march without banners', with a pointed reference to the IMG: 'You know who disagree'. Memo from Executive Committee to National Student Committee, 18 June 1974, in CPGB archives, CP/CENT/CIRC/60/01, LHASC.

119   *Morning Star*, 18 June 1974.

120   Scarman, *The Red Lion Square Disorders of 15 June 1974*, p. 44.

121   Scarman, *The Red Lion Square Disorders of 15 June 1974*, p. 44; p. 46.

122   Scarman, *The Red Lion Square Disorders of 15 June 1974*, p. 44; p. 43.

123   Scarman, *The Red Lion Square Disorders of 15 June 1974*, p. 43.

The CPGB were critical of Scarman's dismissal of the failure to ban the National Front march under the Race Relations Act. Demonstrations that 'conflict with the law ... should be banned', Gerry Cohen stated, as the incitement to race hatred had been outlawed by the Act, and he warned that if 'Fascists are allowed to parade, and propagate racist views', then 'members of the public are going to react in a hostile way'.[124] To remove the threat of conflict from anti-fascist/racist protestors, the CPGB recommended strengthening the Act, which would 'immediately remove one of the major sources of conflict situations giving rise to issues of public order and demonstrations at the time'. In a pamphlet published by the NUS, the Scarman inquiry was criticised for providing 'a political platform for the police prosecutor' and 'permitted in a legal sense a continuation of the police action in Red Lion Square'.[125] In the aftermath of Red Lion Square, the number of anti-fascist demonstrators increased dramatically and continued to rise throughout the mid- to late 1970s. As Nigel Copsey wrote, 'despite adverse publicity that the Red Lion Square disorder had generated for the left, more anti-fascists than fascists could be mobilised at street level'.[126]

After Red Lion Square, Liberation's role as a national body that could organise an anti-fascist response to the NF diminished, even though the anti-fascist movement was increasing in size. One of the prominent reasons why Liberation could not continue as an effective vehicle for anti-fascist action was that it was essentially an anti-imperialist pressure group, which focused upon international issues and relied on building international alliances, not locally based anti-fascist groupings. The objectives of Liberation were aimed towards the 'abolition of imperialism and neo-colonialism',[127] which attracted different activists who were not involved in domestic anti-fascist work. In the IMG's *Red Weekly*, the Group described Liberation as a 'CP dominated organisation', which now had 'refused to put out any public call for a counter-demonstration', leaving 'all the initiatives in the hands of the NF and the police'.[128] In mid-1975, the IMG had noted that there was a void 'in terms of a national anti-fascist focus' left by Liberation and the Communist Party, partly filled by the relaunch of the

---

124 Gerry Cohen, 'Scarman Enquiry – Part 2', 28 October 1974, in CPGB archives, CP/CENT/PC/ 13/10, LHASC.

125 NUS, *The Myth of Red Lion Square*, 1974, London: NUS pamphlet, p. 14.

126 Copsey 2000, p. 122.

127 Liberation, *Liberation Annual Report (October 1975–October 1976)*, 13 November 1976, p. 7, in CPGB archives, CP/IND/KAY/01/02, LHASC.

128 *Red Weekly*, 29 August 1974.

anti-fascist journal *Searchlight* earlier that year.[129] Even in 1976, the Communist Party's National Race Relations Committee still regarded Liberation, at London level at least, as 'the co-ordinating body for anti-racialist activities'.[130] In his history of militant anti-fascism in Britain, Dave Hann has described how in the wake of the Red Lion Square episode, there were several calls and attempts to create a single anti-fascist organisation,[131] which would not be created until November 1977 with the formation of the Anti-Nazi League.

The Trade Union Response to Fascism and Racism in the 1970s

Trade unions were central to Communist Party strategy, and the Party leadership placed great importance on the unions and the labour movement in the anti-racist struggle in general. In a 1971 pamphlet, Joan Bellamy stated that the 'trade unions must become the pivot of the struggle against racialism'.[132] It was seen by the Party that the 'fight to defend black workers is a fight to defend the whole trade union movement',[133] and that 'all sections of the [labour] movement must unite and fight together against every manifestation of racialism'.[134] This united movement against racism was linked to the wider alliances supported in *The British Road to Socialism*, described as the 'key to winning the people's economic and social demands, making decisive inroads into capitalist power, and advancing to the construction of the new socialist system in Britain'.[135]

But the trade unions were reluctant to take the issues of immigration and racial discrimination seriously until the mid-1970s. As Miles and Phizacklea point out, '[i]t was not until 1973 that a motion from the floor of [the TUC] Congress was carried which requested the next Labour Government repeal the racist legislation of 1971'.[136] This re-evaluation of policy and practice, Miles and Phizacklea suggest, was a reaction to increasing industrial action by black workers, dissent amongst the rank and file 'voiced regularly at the annual congress' and the rise of the National Front, who exploited popular racism amongst the

---

129   'A New Period of Fascist Revival', in IMG Papers, MSS.419 Box 3, Modern Records Centre (MRC), University of Warwick.

130   NRRC Minutes, 21 June 1976, in CPGB archives, CP/LON/RACE02/08, LHASC.

131   Hann 2013, pp. 44–249.

132   Bellamy, *Unite Against Racialism*, p. 9.

133   Ibid.

134   Bourne, *Racialism: Cause and Cure*, 1965, London: CPGB pamphlet, p. 14.

135   Ibid.

136   Miles and Phizacklea 1977, p. 35.

working class.[137] In a 1973 pamphlet, the CPGB acknowledged that some unions were now 'making efforts to break away from a formal routine approach in tackling the problem of racism within the labour movement',[138] although it did not mention that the TUC had previously supported immigration controls. Lunn claims that the TUC was still reluctant to become involved in 'race' issues, 'except on very narrow labourist concerns'.[139] But as Satnam Virdee has written, trade unions were 'essentially defensive organisations established ... *within* the confines of the capitalist social formation' and therefore the anti-racist actions were certainly limited by the 'pursuit of material concerns' and not aimed at 'the creation of a new socialist order'.[140]

Despite the reluctance of sections of the trade union movement to get involved wholeheartedly in anti-racist campaigns, the Communist Party put great stock in trying to get the anti-racist message out to the trade union membership. One of the primary vehicles for disseminating an anti-racist message to the trade unions was through its paper the *Morning Star*, and it can be seen as one of the Party's achievements that it was a daily newspaper that regularly highlighted issues of racism and the fight against it. Although sales of the newspaper had fallen since the early 1970s, the paper's editor, Tony Chater, reported to the Executive Committee in May 1976 that daily sales between July and December 1975 averaged 41,235.[141] Communist Party membership at the same time was 28,519[142] (and not every member would have bought a copy daily), so it is highly likely that a significant number of copies were read by fellow trade unionists (although Francis Beckett claims that the Soviet Union ordered around 12,000 copies daily).[143] In his book, Geoff Andrews claims that because the *Morning Star* was 'the only national newspaper to consistently carry sympathetic coverage of trade union issues, it became a vehicle not only of the more militant section but of the more mainstream viewpoint'.[144] The consistent featuring of issues of racism and racial discrimination in the newspaper allowed the anti-racist message of the Communist Party to be read by a considerable cross-section of the British labour movement – even though it is difficult to assess how much of this

---

137   Miles and Phizacklea 1978, p. 195.
138   CPGB, *The Fight Against Racialism in Britain*, 1973, London: CPGB pamphlet, p. 16.
139   Lunn 1999, p. 84.
140   Virdee 2000, p. 548; p. 560.
141   Chater, 'The Morning Star', *Comment*, 15 May 1976, p. 151.
142   Thompson 1992, p. 218.
143   Beckett 1998, p. 226.
144   Andrews 2004, pp. 116–17.

message was taken on board by the trade unions. As Satnam Virdee has written, 'Socialist opinion by the early 1970s was forced over and over again to concede that it had greatly underestimated the depth of racist sentiment within the British working class'.[145]

Although the trade unions were slow to put together an anti-racist programme in the 1970s, trade unionists were able to mobilise more readily against the National Front in the mid-1970s. Believing that the ultimate goal of fascism in Britain was the destruction of the working class, the trade union movement started to build a campaign against the NF in 1974. A rank-and-file member of the Transport and General Workers Union, Brian Nicholson, wrote a pamphlet, *Racialism, Fascism and the Trade Unions*, which proclaimed that the TGWU was now taking a stand against the National Front and other forms of racism, such as that promoted by Enoch Powell. The pamphlet warned against the NF infiltration of the trade union movement and against trade unionists supporting Enoch Powell, stating that '[r]acialism and fascism ... represent true dangers for the trade union movement'.[146] The pamphlet was endorsed by TGWU leader Jack Jones, who wrote in the foreword:

> Opposition to the policies of the trade unions, opposition to the democratic advance of the Labour Party, hatred of the tolerance for which our movement stands is characteristic of the National Front and its allies. Our answer must be more enlightenment, increased educational activity, the strengthening of the trade union movement. Not least we must do everything we can to develop greater respect for our democratic institutions and oppose racial, religious and political discrimination ... This pamphlet should spur us on to be vigilant and active against fascism in all its forms.[147]

A few months earlier, Hackney CPGB member Tony Gilbert, in his capacity as member of Liberation's London Area Council, wrote a pamphlet for the organisation also to warn workers of the dangers of the National Front, the Monday Club and Powellism. Gilbert's pamphlet was much more in-depth than Nicholson's and was much more forthright in its call to arms for white workers to support their black co-workers. In one section, Gilbert declared:

---

145   Virdee 2014, p. 128.
146   Nicholson, *Racialism, Fascism and the Trade Unions*, 1974, London: TGWU pamphlet, p. 3.
147   Jones, 'Foreword', in Nicholson, *Racialism, Fascism and the Trade Unions*, p. 1.

Until the labour and trade union movement challenges every examination of [racial] discrimination vigorously and consistently, a really united
struggle of black and white workers for working class advance cannot
develop. To get this united struggle ... the movement must wage an all-
round and consistent battle for equal opportunity for black people, for
the rooting out of racist ideas, for bringing more black workers into the
trade unions and providing the service they need and for the repeal of all
racist laws.[148]

Gilbert also highlighted that the TGWU, the Amalgamated Union of Engineer-
ing Workers (AUEW) and the Association of Scientific, Technical and Mana-
gerial Staffs (ASTMS) had all announced initiatives to combat racism and fascism within the trade union movement and urged the TUC to take similar steps.
Jack Jones again wrote the foreword to Gilbert's pamphlet, which pronounced:

The disgrace of discrimination and racialism clearly acts against all that
is meant by trade unionism. It is surely right, therefore, that all good
trade unionists should set their face against those who attempt to stir up
trouble by trying to set worker against worker ... In my view active trade
unionists must do all they can to rebut and rebuff racialists, anti-semitic
and discriminatory tendencies ...[149]

According to a report in *Marxism Today*, 1,000 copies of the Liberation pamphlet were being distributed by the TGWU and a number of other unions had
made bulk orders, which the CPGB saw as 'a sign that trade unionists are beginning to see that racialism not only harms those against whom it is directed
but confuses, divide and corrupts those who accept its ideas'.[150] Despite this
campaign on paper against the National Front, some felt that the unions were
making their presence felt within the practical anti-fascist movement and on
the streets. For example, in September 1975, the Hackney Communist Newsletter complained about 'the small Labour Movement representation' at a recent
anti-fascist demonstration.[151]

While the trade union movement were moving towards a more comprehensive anti-fascist and anti-racist programme, other sections of the trade unions

148   Gilbert, *Danger – Racialists at Work*, 1974, London: Liberation pamphlet, p. 13.
149   Jack Jones, 'Foreword', in Gilbert, *Danger – Racialists at Work*, p. 1.
150   'Editorial', *Marxism Today*, December 1974, p. 356.
151   Joe Noble, 'They Shall Not Pass', *Hackney Communist Newsletter*, September 1975, in CPGB
      archives, CP/IND/KAY/03.07, LHASC.

were reluctant to pursue this anti-racist agenda. This was evident at several strikes in the early 1970s where black workers came up against resistance from their fellow white workers and the local trade union bureaucracy. The following section will look at the two most infamous incidents, the Mansfield Hosiery Mills strike in Loughborough in 1972 and the 1974 strike at Imperial Typewriters in Birmingham.

Asian Workers and the Trade Unions in the Early 1970s: Mansfield Hosiery Mills and Imperial Typewriters

Feeling isolated from the trade union movement, Asian workers were also mobilising and engaging in strike action outside the traditional organisations of the labour movement and the white left. This built on the black militant organisations of the late 1960s and early 1970s that showed that there were other options for political activism away from the Labour Party, the Communist Party or other Trotskyist/Maoist groups. Black militancy, as expressed in *Black Liberator* in 1974, was concerned with the white left's 'pervasive need to "integrate" the Black class struggle under their organizational/political domination'.[152] As Avis Brown wrote for the influential *Race Today* journal, black militancy was 'subsumed to the white working class strategy' because of the 'confused historical position in which black people find themselves in white capitalist society'.[153] 'The capitalist exploitation of blacks is veiled by racial oppression', wrote Brown, and the result is a contradictory consciousness, 'as a class and as a race'.[154]

Although autonomous black industrial action had been occurring since the mid-1960s, it was in the mid-1970s that the strike activities started to gain momentum and increasingly demonstrate the gulf between the traditional labour movement and the demands of black workers. The Mansfield Hosiery Mills strike is cited as an important example of conflict between the white labour movement and the interests of black workers and is significant because it occurred at the height of the labour movement's industrial action against the Heath government, what Dave Lyddon and Ralph Darlington have described as the 'Glorious Summer' of class struggle in Britain.[155] At the height of the unions' national battle to protect workers' right to strike and collectively bargain,

---

152 Cambridge and Gutzmore 1974, p. 199.
153 Brown 1973, p. 169.
154 Ibid.
155 Lyddon and Darlington 2001.

the unions were unable to muster any solidarity with black workers at the local level in the fight against racial discrimination. Alex Callinicos, a leading theoretician in the SWP, wrote:

> When the [working] class is engaging successfully in battles with the bosses, then white workers are more likely to place their confidence in workers' self-organisations to defend their interests, and to see themselves as part of the same class as their black brothers and sisters.[156]

However, in 1972, when the labour movement was causing major problems for the Conservatives' Industrial Relations Act, the black workers on strike at Mansfield Hosiery Mills were hindered by the non-commitment of the local union leadership to their own struggle.

In October 1972, Asian workers went on strike at the Mansfield Hosiery Mills factory in Loughborough against the racist practices used in promoting workers, after an initial complaint by an Asian worker to the Race Relations Board in March 1972 had not been resolved. The factory had no union branch for the National Union of Hosiery and Knitwear Workers (NUHKW) and as the Commission on Industrial Relations reported, the union 'did not seek to regulate conditions of employment in the factories on a comprehensive or regular basis'.[157] After the initial strike, the union and the company agreed to a small pay increase, but not to the immediate promotion of any Asian workers, so as not to agitate the white workers. This led to a bigger walkout, in which time the company 'recruited 41 white trainee knitters'.[158] The journal *Race Today* complained that the 'progress of the strike has not been materially assisted by the National Union of Hosiery and Knitwear Workers, to which all the strikers belong' and reported that the Race Relations Board had found that the union 'connived with management to prevent Indian workers' advancement in training'.[159] The Race Relations Board stated in its findings that the 'Asian members did not seem to feel that the union was as interested in their special problems as it might have been'.[160] An internal TUC memo noted that a

---

156   Callinicos 1993, p. 61.
157   Commission on Industrial Relations, *Mansfield Hosiery Mills Limited: Report No. 76*, 1974, p. 36; p. 29, in HMSO, London.
158   Commission on Industrial Relations, *Mansfield Hosiery Mills Limited*, p. 1.
159   'Don't Ask the Price', *Race Today*, December 1972, p. 385.
160   Department of Employment, *Report of a Committee of Inquiry into a Dispute Between Employees of the Mansfield Hosiery Mills Limited, Loughborough and Their Employer*, 1972, p. 16, in HMSO, London.

report by the Runnymede Trust on the dispute had found the following issues of disagreement:

(1) Almost all the best jobs are held by British workers, although 20 per cent of the labour force are coloured immigrants.

(2) Ensuing resentment prevents joint action on industrial disputes.

(3) Joint consultation machinery does not exist

(4) Consequently management can set piece-work rates arbitrarily, and the rates at different firms show a great deal of variation.

(5) The union is rather undemocratic with little rank and file participation preventing unskilled workers from putting their point of view.

(6) There is a language barrier between the groups and many workers would welcome courses in English and in industrial relations.

(7) The resentment of Asian workers arising from lack of promotion may well lead to future industrial action.[161]

However, the TUC, as well as the NUHKW, were reluctant to take action over these issues.

Satnam Virdee wrote that it was 'not until the strikers occupied the union offices that the union finally made the strike official'.[162] In a leaflet by the Mansfield Hosiery Mills Strike Committee produced after the strike, it was stated that 'the white workers did not support the official strike',[163] but does not clarify whether this meant the white NUHKW members or the non-union labour brought in by the company during the strike. In his article, Virdee is much more explicit in his account, declaring that while the union made the strike official, 'it still refused to call out its white membership'.[164]

Those on strike at Mansfield Hosiery Mills declared that 'this was not a fight against the White Workers but a struggle for equal job opportunity', viewing themselves as part of 'one brotherhood in the struggle for the improvement in their working conditions'.[165] A report to the TUC warned that Mansfield was 'not an isolated case' and that the discrimination that Asian work-

---

161   Letter from J.A. Hargreaves to Victor Feather, 5 December 1972, MSS.292D/253.109, in TUC papers, Modern Records Centre, University of Warwick.

162   Virdee 1999, p. 137.

163   Mansfield Hosiery Mills Strike Committee, 'A Brief History of the Mansfield Strike', in CPGB archives, CP/CENT/CTTE/02/05, LHASC.

164   Virdee 1999, p. 137.

165   Narendra D. Patel, 'A Report on the Asian Strikers at Mansfield Hosiery Mill', 3 January 1973, p. 1, MSS.292D/253.109, in TUC papers.

ers faced at the Loughborough factory was faced by many immigrant workers across Britain.[166] The report advised that this discrimination might have
pushed immigrant workers away from the labour movement and cautioned
against 'the danger of these immigrant workers forming their own Trade Union
organisations, because of the frustration they come across in the existing Movement'.[167]

In April 1973, *Race Today* reported that the strikers had returned to work,
'but the causes of their strike against discriminatory practices are not solved'.[168]
What was significant about the Mansfield Hosiery Mills strike was the juxtaposition between the militant action taken by black workers and the resistance they encountered from the official union machinery and, as Virdee wrote,
the fact that 'the Asian strikers had to rely on the support they received from
the Asian community rather than the trade union movement to sustain the
strike'.[169] This was a phenomenon that had been increasingly demonstrated
in the industrial actions taken by black workers over the past decade and one
that continued with the strike at Imperial Typewriters in the summer of 1974.
In fact, the Imperial Typewriters Strike Committee commended the strikers at
Mansfield Hosiery Mills for their inspiration to other black workers, proclaim-
ing:

> We pay tribute to the Asian workers of Mansfield Hosiery Mills who beat
> out a path of determined and consistent struggle for Black workers in
> Britain. They have made things so much easier for us. They pointed out
> what was happening to Black workers on the shop floor.[170]

The Communist Party was one of the groups that were shocked out of com-
placency by the events at Mansfield Hosiery Mills, and in early 1973 several
members of the Party (Winston Pinder, Tom Sibley and Peter Jones) formed the
organisation, Trade Unionists to Combat Racism (TUCR). Closely connected to
the Liberation London Area Council, Liberation and the TUCR held an initial
conference in March 1973 and then another 'regional' conference in July of the
same year.[171] Inviting representatives from the Birmingham-based IWA (Avtar

---

166   Patel, 'A Report on the Asian Strikers at Mansfield Hosiery Mill', p. 1.
167   Patel, 'A Report on the Asian Strikers at Mansfield Hosiery Mill', p. 3.
168   'More From Mansfield', *Race Today*, April 1973, p. 101.
169   Virdee 1999, p. 137.
170   Imperial Typewriters Strike Committee, *Strike Bulletin*, 1, p. 1, MS 2142/C/1/17, in Avtar Johul
      papers, Birmingham City Archives.
171   Liberation/TUCR invitation to delegate conference, MS 2142/C/1/17, in Avtar Johul papers;

Johul), CPGB trade unionists (such as UCATT's Terry Heath) and the Labour MP
Norman Atkinson, the March conference adopted a resolution that stated:

> The struggle against all aspects of racial discrimination and the divisive
> and corrupting influence of racist ideas must be led by the labour move-
> ment. It is therefore of primary importance to win the London labour
> movement for consistent and militant anti racialist [sic] activity.[172]

As part of this activity, the resolution called for the TUC to hold a regional
conference on the issue of anti-racism, for the TUC to establish a Race Relations
Committee and closer links between the TUC and Liberation/TUCR.[173] The
resolution also demanded that the TUC seriously address the issue of racism,
urging the Congress to:

(a) Work more consistently and vigorously to combat racialism and to
     develop solidarity with black workers struggling against its effects.
(b) Expose the National Front and other fascist groups as enemies of
     the whole working class and oppose National Front activities in the
     workplaces and localities.
(c) Develop forms of organisation capable of giving this work detailed
     and consistent attention ...[174]

The TUCR was rivalled by another initiative set up in 1973 called the Trade Unions Against Racialism that held a national conference in June 1973, which was
attended by representatives from the IWA, the IMG, the CPGB (the Secretary
of TUCR, Tom Sibley) and *Searchlight* magazine. According to A. Sivanandan,
over 350 delegates attended this national conference and called for more pressure to be put upon the TUC to act against racism in the workplace and within
the labour movement.[175] This pressure was felt by the TUC who reported in
1974 that the Mansfield Hosiery Mill Strike Committee had linked up with the
Trade Unionists Against Racialism and complained that this group were 'making propaganda', which meant that the controversy over the 1972–3 strike was

---

TUCR Greater London Regional Conference report, July 1973, in Alvaro de Miranda Papers,
        Modern Records Centre, University of Warwick.
172   'TUCR/Liberation Conference Resolution', March 1973, MS 2142/C/1/17, in Avtar Johul pa-
        pers.
173   Ibid.
174   Ibid.
175   Sivanandan 1982, pp. 35–6.

'by no means over'.[176] Despite these campaigns to fight racism in the trade unions, black workers still faced an uphill battle to get trade union recognition of the issues of racial discrimination in the workplace and within the labour movement. The Imperial Typewriters strike that occurred for three months in the middle of 1974 demonstrated that the trade unions had not fully addressed the problems raised by the Mansfield Hosiery Mills strike the year before.

In May 1974, over 500 Asian workers went on strike at the Imperial Typewriters factory in Leicester; their grievances, like those at Mansfield Hosiery Mills, had come from the lack of opportunities for promotion for Asian workers and unpaid bonuses. The striking workers saw the local TGWU as complicit in their underpayment and as the strike got underway, they felt that 'the struggles being waged by them were not merely unsupported but were actively opposed by their union'.[177] The strikers demanded 'their own shop-steward to be elected by their section' to negotiate promotions and pay matters, but also to negotiate 'on all the important restrictions that made up their daily working lives compared to those of white workers', such as 'washing time, tea breaks, lunch breaks, [and] toilet breaks'.[178] Originally a number of Asian workers made a complaint against the managers at one of the factories, citing:

(1)   Racial discrimination against Asian operators such as giving chances to whites first, as an off line operator, that is we as coloureds.
(2)   Always we have difficulty with the Wage claim.
(3)   The foreman does not allow us to see the higher authority to make complaints.
(4)   His attitude is rude towards Asian operators and he treats us like slaves.[179]

However, this was allegedly rejected by a local TGWU representative and this resulted in the walkout by Asian workers. From then on, the Strike Committee pushed for a number of short-term demands and stated 'there could be a return to work on the basis [of] (1) absolutely no victimization (2) continuous employment [and the] (3) democratic election of shop stewards'.[180] But these demands, the Strike Committee said, had to be tied to 'a serious attempt to

---

176   'Mansfield Hosiery Case', 6 May 1974, MSS.292D/253.109, in TUC papers.
177   Dhondy 1974, p. 202.
178   Ibid.
179   Imperial Typewriters Strike Committee, *Strike Bulletin*, 3, p. 8.
180   Imperial Typewriters Strike Committee, *Strike Bulletin*, 3, p. 5.

resolve' the wider problems that had frustrated the Asian workforce previously, the issue of 'equality of opportunity' and 'bonus backdating' from the start of the strike period.[181]

While both Imperial Typewriters and the local TGWU denied any racial discrimination, the strikers claimed that the 'white workers don't suffer from the same degree of discipline as blacks do', although they were quoted in *New Society* as stating, 'This discrimination is quite peculiar because it is so hard to nail. It is the racialism that you feel but cannot overtly see, that exists at Imperial'.[182] The representative of the TGWU for Imperial Typewriters was George Bromley, who objected to the unofficial nature of the strike and the demands being made. In an interview in *Race Today* in October 1974, Bromley stated, 'As fast as these demands were being put we investigated and every time we could find nothing in it'.[183] Bromley criticised the unofficial measures being taken by the Asian strikers and their apparent disregard for the 'proper disputes procedure', stating that the strikers 'have got to learn to fit in with our ways' and then claiming, 'the way they have been acting ... means they will close factories and people won't employ them'.[184] Bromley did concede that, 'It may well be true that a white worker would have a slightly better chance of having his case heard than an Asian worker', but the 'extraordinary behaviour' of those on strike would, he believed, 'make matters worse, creating racial tension'.[185] In a letter to TGWU headquarters, Bromley wrote that '[t]o continue this dispute will settle no problems whatsoever and will only inevitably lead to hardship to both the Asian community and the vast majority of workers who are still working at Imperial Typewriters.'[186] Further, Bromley accused the strike leaders of having (yet unnamed) ulterior motives and recommended that 'those people out on strike ... think about the motives of those leading them'[187] and declined to call out the rest of the workforce at Imperial Typewriters, particularly the white workers. The Strike Committee claimed that '[m]any ... [white] workers are sympathetic to the strike but because the strike had not been made official they have not come out' and argued that Bromley should have done this immediately – 'to recognise the legitimacy of the strikers'

---

181   Ibid.

182   Taylor, 'Asians and a Union', *New Society*, 30 May 1974, p. 511.

183   'Two Worlds in Conflict', interview with George Bromley, *Race Today*, October 1974, p. 274.

184   Cited in Dhondy 1974, p. 201; 'Two Worlds in Conflict', p. 275.

185   'Two Worlds in Conflict', p. 275.

186   Letter to TGWU Headquarters from George Bromley, 13 May 1974, MS 2142/C/1/17, in Avtar Johul papers.

187   Ibid.

demands and to have taken those steps which would have rallied the whole work force behind the strikers'.[188]

In 1973, a study of trade unions and racism in *Race Today* that looked back on the 'lessons' of the Mansfield Hosiery Mills strike, stated:

> Yet despite the obvious deficiencies of union organisation in the area, it is interesting to note that not one leading black militant involved in any of the above disputes is in favour of forming separate structures outside the trade union movement. Despite the apparent failure of the official organisation to support black workers in struggle, leading figures still want to fight on inside the present union set-up.[189]

And this sentiment was explicit in the statement of the Imperial Typewriters Strike Committee, who stated that they did not see the strike 'solely for the benefit of Black Workers', instead viewing it as a fight for 'the general interests of the whole working class in Britain', of which black workers were a part.[190] In another strike bulletin, the Strike Committee claimed that from the beginning, 'we did not regard our dispute as fundamentally a racial one but as a workers' dispute'.[191]

However, the refusal of Bromley and the TGWU to fully support the industrial action at Imperial Typewriters led to the strikers relying on the black community, instead of the solidarity of their fellow unionists. The *Morning Star* and *Socialist Worker* did report on the strike, but Hasmukh Khetani, one of the leaders of Imperial Typewriter Strike Committee, wrote, 'One got the impression that the white left organisations ... were more concerned about a fascist threat [the National Front had organised a demonstration against the striking Asians] ... than actual support for Black workers' struggle'.[192] This ties in with the scenario mentioned above that the trade unions were more interested in fighting the presence of the National Front amongst trade unionists than dealing with more 'ordinary' examples of racial discrimination in the labour movement. When the strike was over, a report in *Race Today* blamed the 'white left' for their poor response to the strike, describing the Heaylite Workers Revolutionary Party as opportunist for their calls for revolution 'instead of addressing ... the concrete problems and perspectives of the strike' and alleging

---

188   Imperial Typewriters Strike Committee, *Strike Bulletin*, 3, p. 5.
189   'The East Midlands: A Cameo in Conspiracy', *Race Today*, August 1973, p. 239.
190   Imperial Typewriters Strike Committee, *Strike Bulletin*, 1, p. 2.
191   Imperial Typewriters Strike Committee, *Strike Bulletin*, 3, p. 1.
192   Khetani 1974, p. 287.

that the Communist Party had 'hinted that the behaviour of the strikers alienated much of the goodwill which existed among white workers'.[193] The International Socialists were named as 'the one group who might have had the capacity to win over some of the white workers inside the factory', but were chastised for their non-involvement and little reportage featured in *Socialist Worker*.[194]

The support for the strike, as Robert Moore wrote, 'reached right down into the community', not amongst the white working class or within the union, but amongst 'members of the local Asian society'.[195] *Race Today* reported the 'move away from trade union directives' had given the striking workers 'a source of political strength', with the strikers' autonomy bringing the strike 'a spirit, an approach, a willingness to try any tactic'.[196] This autonomy and reliance on the black community presented a challenge to the labour movement, which promoted the traditional path of union politicisation as the key to affecting change for Britain's black population, although black workers were wary of what use the trade unions had in asserting their political rights. However, as Robert Moore stated in his 1975 work, *Racism and Black Resistance in Britain*, 'Community power alone is not enough to achieve significant political changes',[197] and what the strike at Imperial Typewriters demonstrated was that black workers needed the solidarity of the wider labour movement, but not at the expense of their own agenda. The Strike Committee stated in May 1974:

> It is through [the union] that workers (black and white) get together to protect their common interests. The union must educate all its members in the principle of working class unity ... For this reason also there can be no question of Asian workers or any other section of the working class forming its own union. It must and can only work through the existing trade union structure.[198]

To realise this meant that the trade unions themselves had to undergo a reassessment of their approach to their black members and how their demands were incorporated into wider union actions.

---

193 'Back to Work at Imperial', *Race Today*, September 1974, p. 251.
194 Ibid.
195 Moore 1975, p. 81; p. 83.
196 Dhondy 1974, p. 205; 'Imperial Typewriters Strike: The Continuing Story', *Race Today*, August 1974, p. 223.
197 Moore 1975, p. 83.
198 Imperial Typewriters Strike Committee, *Strike Bulletin*, p. 2.

The strike action which united the white left, the British labour movement and Britain's ethnic minority workers was that which occurred at Grunwick in North London between 1976 and 1978. Satnam Virdee has written that Grunwick 'crystallised ... how, in the space of less than a decade, parts of the working class had undergone a dramatic, organic transformation in their political consciousness' and that the 'language of class' of socialist activists 'now encompass[ed] racialised minority workers as well'.[199] As will be demonstrated in the next chapter, the strike at Grunwick, led by Asian women, but backed by the entirety of the British labour movement, was a turning point for the British left and the fight against racism, although the convergence between the white left and ethnic minority workers diverged again soon after.

Conclusion

While the 1970s had seemed to begin on a positive note for the Communist Party, with the British labour movement at the height of its influence, the economic and political crises which followed the Oil Crisis in October 1973 saw the country (and the CPGB) thrown into disorder. The labour movement had been able to make the Industrial Relations Act unworkable and help unseat Heath from power, but was unable to push forward and influence substantial reform from the newly elected Labour government, instead agreeing to a halt to industrial action with the Social Contract. But as the crises continued throughout the mid-1970s, it was difficult for many workers to continue to support a Labour government that was freezing wages, cutting public spending and unable to curb inflation and unemployment. The Communist Party was stuck between supporting Labour and the trade unions, who had endorsed the Social Contract, and trying to win the trade unions back to a position of militant labourism, but also stuck between those who celebrated the Party's achievements through the trade unions over the last decade and those who questioned whether the Party had made any tangible gains from their support of the labour movement during the 'British upturn'. This would lead to much internal strife within the Communist Party and eventual splits, which will be covered in the next chapter.

The Heath government and then the socio-economic crisis of the mid-1970s were not so positive for Britain's ethnic minorities. The aftereffect of Powell's 'Rivers of Blood' speech was that the Conservatives reacted to the public show-

---

199   Virdee 2014, p. 357.

ing of populist racism and anti-immigration sentiment by promising that they would put an end to labour migration from the Commonwealth, and they did so with the Immigration Act 1971. The Act put severe restrictions on people trying to enter Britain (particularly from developing countries), but also created a complex and interlocking web of state institutions, such as the police, the DHSS and the NHS, to detect any 'illegal' immigrants inside the country. Anti-immigration sentiment and suspicion of non-white people in Britain intensified with the onset of the 1973 crisis. Stuart Hall and others described this as 'black panic', where the issues of race and immigration became synonymous with the idea that Britain faced an insurmountable crisis – 'the arena in which complex fears, tensions and anxieties, generated by the impact of the totality of the crisis ... can be most conveniently and explicitly projected'.[200] From 1972 onwards, the National Front, as well as other fascist and far right groups, publicly campaigned for an end to non-white immigration, the repatriation of Britain's ethnic minorities and other authoritarian measures. And in the factories, ethnic minority workers were subject to poor conditions and wages as the crisis plunged the British economy into a downward spiral, with little help from the trade unions.

The result of this was that there seemed to be two parallel responses to these problems. On the one hand, the left, including the Communist Party, mobilised heavily against the National Front, and the anti-fascist movement became a significant political force throughout the 1970s, although the CPGB found itself increasingly shut out as other left-wing groups (most prominently the SWP) took the initiative. On the other hand, Asian youth and factory workers were organising themselves at the grassroots level, opposing the National Front on the streets of London, Bradford and Manchester (amongst other places) and helping defend their communities from racist violence, or becoming involved in unofficial strikes that opposed the racial discrimination of both management and trade union officials, relying on the local migrant communities for support. By 1976, these two parallel responses started to converge and there was increased understanding between the left, the labour movement and the ethnic minority communities in Britain. This increased understanding is perhaps best demonstrated by the strike at Grunwick and the campaign against the National Front, both of which intensified in the late 1970s and will be discussed in the following chapter.

---

200   Hall et al. 2013, p. 333.

The Great Moving Right Show, 1976–9

With the anti-racist struggle looking to increase in intensity in mid-1976, the Communist Party's Executive Committee formulated a six point policy on the issues of 'race' and racism that was distributed throughout the Party. Cited in the newsletter of the Putney and Roehampton Branch, the programme stated:

1. Demand a ban on all racist activity and strengthen the Race Relations Act against incitement to race hatred.
2. Stop police harassment of ethnic minority groups.
3. Develop the broadest united campaign of all anti-racist forces to resist racist activities and work for positive policies to end discrimination.
4. Develop the demands for increased resources to end the acute social problem of the inner urban areas of our major cities.
5. Campaign to win the trade union and Labour movement to policies to defend black workers, to win them into the organisations of the working class, and to use its full power to resist racism and for the adoption of positive policies against discrimination.
6. Campaign for the ending of the 1971 Immigration Act and its replacement by a policy based on equal opportunity and full social rights for all immigrant workers.[1]

This programme presented several immediate aims that would form the basis of the Communist Party's anti-racist work and were goals that could be worked towards, in conjunction with other socialist, progressive and anti-racist organisations. Although the Communist Party still held the belief that 'racialism can only be ended by socialism', those involved in the Party's anti-racist work accepted that immediate anti-racist measures had to be taken as racism was an ideological construct that would 'not cease to exist automatically' with the building of a socialist society.[2] This acknowledgement was a move away from earlier CPGB discussions about the relationship between capitalism and racism,[3] but

---

1 Cited in Putney & Roehampton Branch, *Communist Party Newletter*, n.d., p. 2, in CPGB archives, CP/LON/BRA/17/11.
2 Beauchamp, *Black Citizens*, 1974, London: CPGB pamphlet, p. 13.
3 See Smith 2008, pp. 455–81.

the programme put forward also reveals how the fight against racism became a central and immediate issue for the Party in the late 1970s and early 1980s, with detailed points about how the ordinary rank-and-file membership could get involved.

Central to the Party's anti-racist work, as well as the wider broad democratic alliance put forward in 1977, was the promotion of co-operating with other organisations to achieve more immediate goals, rather than waiting for the establishment of socialism. This chapter shows that the broad democratic alliance strategy was taken up wholeheartedly by anti-racist activists within the CPGB, but at the same time, the Party's engagement with other organisations and movements diluted its own specific (anti-racist) agenda and allowed other socialist groups, such as the Socialist Workers Party, to occupy the space that the CPGB used to occupy from the 1930s to the 1960s. At the same time, there were tensions within Britain's ethnic minority communities over whether to co-operate with predominantly 'white' organisations, such as the various left-wing parties (including the CPGB, the SWP and the Labour Party), the trade unions and other progressive organisations (such as Liberation, CARF and the JCWI). Many of the older people within these communities, such as the Indian Workers Associations, were willing to continue working with the Labour Party, the CPGB and the trade unions, but others, such as those affiliated with the *Race Today* Collective, the reconstituted Institute for Race Relations under A. Sivanandan and the Asian Youth Movements, believed that the actions of many of these organisations over the last decade meant that autonomous black activism was more desirable.

However, while there were differences, some of the distance between ethnic minority activists and workers and the traditional organisations of the left was being reduced in the mid- to late 1970s. Two of the biggest events in the history of anti-racism in Britain in the 1970s demonstrate this bridging of the gap – the Grunwick strike that lasted from 1976 to 1978, in which the trade union movement supported an unofficial strike by migrant workers and the rise of the Anti-Nazi League, which motivated a broad-based campaign against the fascist National Front from 1977 to 1981. In his book, *Racism, Class and the Racialized Outsider*, Satnam Virdee wrote that these two phenomena 'helped crystallize how – in the space of less than a decade – parts of the organized working class had undergone a dramatic, organic transformation in their political conscious-ness', with a 'process of Asian, black and white working class formation' taking place amidst the crisis that faced British capitalism in the 1970s.[4]

---

4   Virdee 2014, p. 135.

160   CHAPTER 4

This chapter will look at how Grunwick changed the relationship between ethnic minority workers and the organs of the British labour movement (heavily supported by the Communist Party) from one of mutual suspicion (extending from the stand-offs at Mansfield Hosiery Mills and Imperial Typewriters in the early 1970s) to one of co-operation. At the height of the mass pickets outside Grunwick in mid-July 1977 (when the NUM brought down sympathetic miners from Yorkshire and other regions), there were around 12,000 people on the mass picket, followed by a demonstration of around 20,000 marchers,[5] creating significant bonds between Asian striking workers and trade unionists from across the country. But while these bonds were being created, the way that the strike was being operated by the trade union organisations came under criticism from both black activists and sections of the left, who felt, respectively, that the issue of trade union recognition was overtaking other aspects of the strike, such as the issue of racial discrimination, and that the strike was being waged in a too cautious manner.

Similar plaudits and criticisms were also directed towards the Anti-Nazi League, an anti-fascist mass movement that began in late 1977 as a campaign to prevent the National Front from gaining a foothold on the streets and in electoral politics. While the left had been divided previously over how to approach the rise of the NF during the 1970s, demonstrated by the conflict between the CPGB and the SWP at the 'Battle of Lewisham' in August 1977, the ANL offered an anti-NF front on the broadest possible platform that tried to overcome the left's traditional sectarianism. Launched by members of the SWP and the Labour Party, the ANL was soon supported by the Communist Party and the International Marxist Group (although Militant and the Healyite Workers Revolutionary Party did not get involved).[6] Between 1977 and 1979, the ANL was very successful with getting the message out to the public that the NF were 'Nazis' and the threat that these fascists presented to British society, particularly Britain's ethnic minorities, and can be partially credited with the dismal results that the NF had at the 1979 election, as well as disseminating an anti-racist consciousness amongst many British youth. In an obituary for ANL activist David Widgery in 1992, Paul Foot wrote in *New Left Review*:

In a brilliant and moving tribute to David at the SWP's memoria meeting in December [1991], Darcus Howe said he had fathered five children in

---

5 Dromey and Taylor 1978, p. 144.
6 Crick 1984, p. 72; Gale, *The Anti-Nazi League and Fascism*, 1978, London: News Line pamphlet, p. 4.

Britain. The first four had grown up angry, fighting forever against the racism all around them. The fifth child, he said, had grown up 'black at ease'. Darcus attributed her 'space' to the Anti-Nazi League in general and to David Widgery in particular.[7]

But others criticised the ANL for its populism and its unwillingness to be too confrontational. As this chapter will show, a number of black and left-wing activists felt that the focus of the ANL was too narrow and that it should have had a wider remit to tackle all different forms of racism in British society, rather than concentrating on the explicit fascism of the National Front. Other groups, such as some within the Asian Youth Movements and localised anti-fascist squads (who later became Red Action/Anti-Fascist Action), felt that the ANL was about public gestures and playing to the media, rather than actively confronting the NF on the streets.[8]

Although the Grunwick strike and the momentary success of the Anti-Nazi League showed that the British labour movement could be mobilised around issues of 'race' and anti-racism (and both have been celebrated for this in the intervening years), these achievements came on the cusp of a watershed moment in British history, which upended much of the positive work achieved in the late 1970s. The election of Margaret Thatcher as Prime Minister in May 1979 signalled the beginning of a decade-long struggle for both the labour movement and Britain's black communities. And despite a connection being made between migrant workers and the labour movement at places like Grunwick, many of the younger generation of the ethnic minority communities were still suspicious of left-wing and progressive groups and felt that their problems were not being represented in the political arena. Against this background of disillusionment with the traditional political vehicles open to ethnic minority communities, large numbers of Afro-Caribbean and Asian youth were involved in public disorder across the country in 1980 and 1981 (which will be discussed in the following chapter).

One of the ironies of this period is that some within the Communist Party recognised that the rise of Thatcher, particularly from 1978 onwards, presented a different challenge for the British left, with Stuart Hall writing in *Marxism Today* that Thatcherism was not 'a temporary swing in the political fortunes', but a more sustained 'swing to the right'.[9] However, the schisms within the Party

7 Foot 1992, p. 122.
8 Ramamurthy 2013, pp. 47–51; Hann 2013, pp. 280–1; Birchall 2010, p. 36.
9 Hall 1979, p. 14.

over its direction that had been brewing since the mid-1970s now engulfed the
Party in the early 1980s and it became less and less effectual as a practical organisational force – individual Party members could still make a difference, but
this was *in spite* of the Party. At the same time, the Communist Party threw
its weight behind initiatives such as the Anti-Nazi League and Grunwick strike
(as well as other broad-based movements), largely coinciding with the points
of the Party's anti-racist programme referred to earlier, but it was unable to
influence the direction of these initiatives or benefit from them in terms of
membership or paper sales. By the late 1970s, the Party had developed a more
sophisticated understanding of the issue of 'race' and racism in British society, but its position within the labour, progressive and anti-racist movements
had slipped, for a variety of reasons, and its influence waned. On the anti-
racist and progressive front, it was left to individual members, such as Dave
Cook, Tony Gilbert, Kay Beauchamp, Vishnu Sharma and Gideon Ben-Tovim
(as well as a number of others), to engage with other organisations and promote co-operation between them and the CPGB in a 'broad democratic alliance'.

Looking at the six points of the anti-racist programme that the Party's Executive Committee drew up in 1976, this chapter will show that the Communist
Party campaigned heavily around these topics in the late 1970s within the wider
anti-racist movement, and that some positive steps were made, such as the
campaign to prevent the NF from using public places to hold meetings, the
establishment of the ANL as a broad and united anti-fascist campaign and the
significant shift in attitudes towards 'race' in the trade unions. However, the
impact of the CPGB *as a party* on these anti-racist campaigns was less significant. This meant that although the Party had a better understanding of 'race
relations' issues during this period, it did not have the *organisational* ability to
convert this understanding into substantial *practical* activity.

The Building of the Broad Democratic Alliance

The development of the Party's anti-racist strategy cannot be divorced from
the wider trends in the CPGB that underwent significant change in the postwar
period. Most significant was the acceptance of parliamentary democracy in *The
British Road to Socialism* and the emphasis on leftist unity between the CPGB,
the labour movement, the Labour left and other progressive forces. The rise of
the new social movements, combined with a decline in industrial militancy,
saw increasing emphasis being placed on wider social forces by reformists
within the Party as a way of radicalising people outside the traditional labour

movement. This was not a rejection of the importance of the trade unions, but an acknowledgment that trade union militancy only addressed one section of British society and that other social movements could be used to build a broad democratic alliance towards the implementation of socialism. The creation of a coherent anti-racist programme in the late 1970s is to be observed against the background of the extension of democracy at the centre of Communist Party strategy, as seen in the 1977 edition of *The British Road to Socialism*. Despite this shift towards the broad democratic alliance, the reality of the CPGB's decline in the late 1970s and into the 1980s hindered effective political activity within the anti-racist movement. It is only through an examination of the wider ideological shifts within the CPGB in the postwar period that it is possible to understand the process of development of a coherent anti-racist policy by the Party.

As mentioned in the previous two chapters, the CPGB had invested heavily in working in a broad left alliance with the trade unions and Labour left in the period between 1966 and 1974, when the miners' strike brought down Edward Heath's Conservative government. Despite this, a number of CPGB members saw the 'Social Contract' entered into between the TUC and the newly formed Labour government as evidence that this strategy had not produced the desired results and called for alternative strategies to put forward. Party intellectuals and activists, such as Martin Jacques (future editor of *Marxism Today*), Mike Prior, David Purdy, Dave Cook, Sarah Benton, Willie Thompson and Jon Bloomfield (amongst numerous others), used the ideas of Italian Marxist Antonio Gramsci and Eurocommunism to challenge the perceived wisdom of the CPGB leadership and ignite a debate about the future of the CPGB.

Most importantly, the rediscovery of the ideas of Antonio Gramsci opened up for a significant part of the CPGB membership a stream of socialist politics that moved beyond the industrial militant strategy favoured by the Party in the late 1960s and early 1970s. Eric Hobsbawm, in a discussion of Gramsci's political theories in *Marxism Today* in 1977, explained that Gramsci argued that 'societies are more than structures of economic domination and political power' and 'have a certain cohesion even when riven by class struggles' – this was the process of hegemony, where the ideas of the dominant social group are reinforced through the institutions of civil society.[10] Or as Stuart Hall and several other fellow travellers wrote in the influential *Resistance Through Rituals*, '[h]egemony works through *ideology* ... It works *primarily* by inserting the subordinate class into the key institutions and structure which support the

---

10   Hobsbawm 1977, pp. 209–12.

CHAPTER 4

power and social authority of the dominant order'.[11] Under the influence of
Gramsci, to upheave the present system, many of the reformers in the CPGB
and fellow travellers, such as Hall, believed that a 'counter-hegemony' needed
to be established, which would align different social forces whose identity was
not necessarily determined by the capitalist political economy.

This appeal of Gramsci was twinned with an enthusiasm for 'Eurocommunism' as promoted by the Communist Parties of France, Italy and Spain. The
Communist Parties in these Western European countries chose to distance
themselves from the Soviet Union after the invasion of Czechoslovakia in 1968
and promoted the idea of working within the framework of Western liberal
democracy, contesting elections and co-operating with the institutions of the
capitalist state. These parties argued that the Soviet model of armed insurrection was no longer an option for Western Communist Parties and that each
Communist Party needed to follow its own 'national' path. Santiago Carillo, the
General Secretary of the Communist Party of Spain, stated in his 1977 book that
Eurocommunists essentially agreed:

> on the need to advance to socialism with democracy, a multi-party sys-
> tem, parliaments and representative institutions ... and the development
> of the broadest forms of popular participation at all levels and in all
> branches of social activity.[12]

In the internal debates within the CPGB, the term 'Eurocommunism' was used
to illustrate the strategy based on the 'extension of democracy' through a 'dense
network of social, cultural and political groupings based on a voluntary commitment', accepting that the Soviet model of the October Revolution was 'inap-
propriate ... for advanced capitalist societies'.[13] This idea of the 'extension of
democracy' was used to explain that the acceptance of socialism through parliamentary democracy had been established with *The British Road to Socialism*
since 1951 and now simply widened the scope of the Party's allies against monopoly capitalism. As Dave Cook wrote in *Marxism Today* in December 1978:

> Workers (and others) are oppressed according to their sex, their col-
> our, the social services they use, their age, as young people, where they
> live, etc. In reaction to these varied forms of oppression, movements of

---

11   Clarke, Hall, Jefferson and Roberts 2006, p. 29. Italics are in the original text.
12   Carrillo 1977, p. 110.
13   Aaronovitch 1978, p. 222.

struggle have emerged (national, women, black people's etc). Because of the class structure of our society most people involved in these movements will be from the working class, broadly defined, but it is often their consciousness of oppression, rather than of their class exploitation which is the key politicising factor.[14]

In late 1976, a Commission, including reformists Peter Carter, Judith Hunt and Martin Jacques, drafted a new edition of *The British Road to Socialism* for the CPGB's 35th National Congress in November 1977.[15] This edition of *The British Road to Socialism* demonstrated many of the Gramscian/Eurocommunist ideals in its widening of the 'broad popular alliance', put forward in the 1968 edition, to the 'broad democratic alliance'. Most importantly, the 'broad democratic alliance' signified the official, yet highly disputed, acceptance that the struggle for socialism needed 'not only ... to be an association of class forces, ... but of other important forces in society which emerge out of areas of oppression not always directly connected with the relations of production'.[16] 'Capitalism', the new draft stated, 'not only exploits people at work, but impinges on every aspect of their lives', so social movements outside the traditional labour movement, such as 'black, national, women's, youth, environmental, peace and solidarity movements', were considered in the Party's wider strategy.[17] These 'democratic movements' were to be supported by the labour movement, 'because, in supporting their aims and aspirations, it becomes increasingly aware that class oppression, and the struggle against it, extend far beyond the workplace' and alliance between the labour movement and these social movements was central to 'extending democracy, improving living conditions and opening the way to socialism'.[18] The Communist Party, 'as the organised Marxist political party', imbued itself and the Labour left with a 'special role to play in developing broad left unity', acting as pivotal organisations and mediating between the traditional union movement and other social forces for building of the 'broad democratic alliance'.[19]

---

14   Cook 1978, p. 371.

15   The other members appointed to the Commission included George Matthews, Jack Ashton, Chris Myant, Dave Priscott and George Wake, with John Gollan as secretary. CPGB, *The British Road to Socialism Draft*, 1977, London: CPGB pamphlet, p. 2.

16   CPGB, *The British Road to Socialism*, 1977, London: CPGB pamphlet, p. 29.

17   Ibid.

18   CPGB, *The British Road to Socialism*, 1977, p. 33; p. 36.

19   CPGB, *The British Road to Socialism*, 1977, p. 34.

The acceptance of the new Party programme at the 1977 Congress led to the defection of a group of hardline pro-Soviet members who formed the New Communist Party, and built a pool of discontent amongst many others, which eventually led to the split between the CPGB and its paper the *Morning Star* in the early 1980s (discussed in the following chapter). Although the promotion of Eurocommunism and the notion of the 'broad democratic alliance' seemed of great importance at the time, Willie Thompson has argued that the anxiety caused by the change from 'broad popular alliance' (included in the 1968 edition) to the 'broad democratic alliance' was 'more of style and terminology than of real substance'.[20] The 1968 edition had already proposed the 'broad popular alliance' consisting of 'trade unions, co-operatives, the left in the Labour Party and the Communist Party' in alliance against monopoly capitalism, although it did acknowledge that this alliance could also include 'workers in factories, offices, professions, working farmers, producers and consumers, owner-occupiers and tenants, housewives, young people and students, pensioners, workers in the peace movement' among others.[21] In his 1992 history of the CPGB, Thompson states that the 'broad democratic alliance' did not fundamentally challenge this concept, but was more aimed at ending the 'oppression … rooted in anti-democratic structures at every level and in every sphere of society', and 'at most represented a modification of outlook rather than a fundamental alteration'.[22]

The Grunwick Strike

As has been widely noted,[23] in the mid-1970s, there was a change within the labour movement that demonstrated 'a more positive policy towards the issues raised by the presence of black workers … in Britain'[24] and a 'recognition … that working class solidarity could only be built by actively opposing the racism and disadvantages faced by black workers'.[25] This recognition was not necessarily a shift in the perception of the trade union movement by black workers, who had been disillusioned by the actions of the unions at Mansfield Hosiery Mills and

---

20   Thompson 1992, p. 171.

21   CPGB, *The British Road to Socialism*, London: CPGB pamphlet, 1968, p. 22; p. 28.

22   Thompson 1992, p. 171.

23   See Miles and Phizacklea 1978, pp. 195–207; Virdee 1999, pp. 140–4; 'Race, Class and the State (2)', *Race & Class*, 19/1, 1977, pp. 72–3.

24   Miles and Phizacklea 1978, p. 195.

25   Virdee 1999, p. 141.

Imperial Typewriters, as discussed in the previous chapter. It was a shift by the trade unions towards involving their black members in wider industrial action, but also using the labour movement to assist in fighting the struggles faced by black workers. This was recognised as an 'advance' for the unions, which, 'when compared with earlier policy and practice', was 'significant and substantial',[26] but was treated, according to Trevor Carter, 'as if it marked a great new dawning of consciousness on the part of *black* people, rather than white people's perception of black people'.[27] The shift by the trade unions did not mean that the labour movement was necessarily willing to support the industrial actions of black workers, such as those taken during previous strikes, but was the incorporation and appropriation of the struggles of black workers into the official machinery of the labour movement. As A. Sivanandan wrote, 'instead of directly sabotaging the black workers' struggle', as had happened in earlier strikes, the trade union leadership now 'attempted to contain and incorporate it, clapping a procedure on their backs'.[28] This convergence between the aims of black workers and that of the labour movement was demonstrated at the strike at the Grunwick Processing Laboratories in North-West London in the summer of 1978.

The strike at Grunwick began with a small number of Asian workers walking out 'in protest at oppressive working conditions' on 20 August 1976,[29] becoming one of the longest strikes in British history, before it was eventually defeated in July 1978. Asian workers led the strike, but the union leadership of APEX (the Association of Professional, Executive, Clerical and Computer Staffs), the Brent Trades Council and the TUC opted for negotiation through the official industrial relations machinery of ACAS (the Advisory, Conciliation and Arbitration Service), whose decisions were ignored by the owner of the Grunwick plant, George Ward. The CPGB was influential in the Brent Trades Council, Grunwick's local TUC representative, with Tom Durkin serving on the Council.

The strike drew together many elements of society, with Graham Taylor, a member of the Executive Committee of the Brent Trades Council, writing:

The Grunwick strike is focus for many different issues and struggles. For trade unionists it is a struggle for trade-union recognition; some fix on police brutality; feminists point to the oppression of female workers;

---

26   Miles and Phizacklea 1978, p. 205.
27   Carter 1986, p. 116; Italics are in the original text.
28   'Grunwick (2)', *Race & Class*, 19/3, 1978, p. 292.
29   Forbes, 'In the Wake of Grunwick', *Marxism Today*, December 1978, p. 386.

while democrats denounce gross violations of the human rights to work, to speak freely and to associate. To many, Grunwick is part of the struggle against racialism and imperialism ... Others regard the racial aspect as minimal and rally behind a simple class struggle by the under-paid. It is the importance of the Grunwick Strike that it embraces *all* these issues.[30]

Taylor, along with Brent Trades Council Secretary Jack Dromey, wrote in their account of the Grunwick strike that the significance of Grunwick was that for the first time, the labour movement could mobilise significant support for black workers, while before Grunwick, 'It would not have been capable of summoning up such solidarity for a tiny strike'.[31] This can be seen as partly the result of the policy change towards positive action on issues of racism by the trade unions that had occurred in the mid-1970s.

With Grunwick's owner George Ward dismissing the recommendations made by ACAS on recognition of trade union membership, the APEX leadership called off the strike, which ended in unclear circumstances on 14 July 1978.[32] Tom Durkin, a long-time CPGB member and Chair of Brent Trades Council, saw the defeat as the result of the domination of the right wing of the trade union movement, stating:

> It was the Right within APEX, the General Council and the Government which took the strikers into a legal morass, worked might and main to prevent the full power of our movement being used to paralyse Grunwick and which then deserted and ditched the brave men and women of Grunwick.[33]

While Durkin was the Chair of the Brent Trades Council, he was one of the few CPGB members on the Strike Committee (the other was Graham Taylor who was also Secretary of the Brent North CP branch) and was unable to influence the direction of the strike, despite, as Dromey and Taylor note, the conspiracy theories promoted by George Ward and his supporters that the strike was run by Communists.[34] Geoff Andrews asserts that despite the public portrayal of unity on the Brent Trades Council, it was plagued by internal divisions, including

---

30   Taylor, 'Grunwick', *Broad Left*, 12, n.d., p. 8; Italics are in the original text.
31   Dromey and Taylor 1978, p. 190.
32   Ramdin 1987, p. 307.
33   Durkin 2006, p. 23.
34   Dromey and Taylor 1978, p. 56.

disagreements amongst CPGB members involved.[35] In *Socialist Review*, Dai Davies suggested that this internal disunity was one of the possible reasons for the dominance of the TUC and the right wing of the labour movement over the tactics used at the strike.[36] The influence that the Communist Party had upon the strike was really its coverage of the strike in the *Morning Star* which was constant and prominent from October 1976 until the strike's end in April 1978, urging the TUC and APEX to take more drastic action.

Others, such as the Socialist Workers Party, saw the defeat as the end result of the 'increased involvement of trade union organisation in the machinery of government' and the 'involvement of senior shop stewards in the management policies of many firms'.[37] This was supported by the comments made by Jayaben Desai, one of the leaders of the Grunwick strike, when she declared in late 1977, 'The union views itself like management ... We are the real fighters ... But the union just looks on us as if we are employed by them'.[38] But for black activists and workers, it was the use of 'official channels' that had 'steered the black workers away from community based support' and towards the unions, who in the end 'finally betrayed them'.[39] The impact of the defeat upon the black workers, and the wider black communities, was that it seemed to verify that the labour movement was unable to respond adequately to the demands of the struggle against racism in the workplace and highlighted the lack of a vehicle for political agency available to Britain's black population.

Intersectionality and the British Labour Movement

Looking through the lens of critical race and feminist theory, it can be argued that the Grunwick strike was intersectional,[40] where issues of race, gender and class were all present and raised by different people involved in the strike. However, while all of these issues were present (and recognised by those involved), the approaches formulated to tackle these issues were disparate and non-inclusive. As shown above, while the trade union movement recognised racial and sexual discrimination were issues of resentment amongst those strik-

---

35   Andrews, 2004, p. 198.
36   Dai Davies, 'What Didn't Happen at Grunwick', *Socialist Review*, May/June 1979, p. 30.
37   SWP, *Grunwick*, 1978, London: SWP pamphlet, p. 16.
38   Cited in 'Grunwick (2)', p. 294.
39   'Grunwick (2)', p. 292; Sivanandan 1985, p. 7.
40   See Crenshaw 1989, pp. 139–68; Crenshaw 1991, pp. 1242–300.

ing at Grunwick, the strategy for 'victory' was a class-based approach – primarily recognition of trade union representation from the owners of Grunwick.

In the coverage of the strike in the various left-wing, feminist and black activist publications at the time, the prominence given to the various issues of class, gender and race can be seen. The SWP declared in their pamphlet on the strike that the 'issue at stake was simple: trade union recognition',[41] while the International Marxist Group (IMG) depicted the Grunwick strike as part of a longer union history:

> From Tolpuddle to Tonypandy, from the Match Girls to the Miners, working people have fought for the right to organise. Trade Unionism is now under attack at GRUNWICK. A defeat for us would be a defeat for the whole working class.[42]

However, in the journal *Race Today*, some black workers felt that to mobilise on this issue 'does not mean that white workers are there supporting a strike by black workers'.[43] Meanwhile A. Sivanandan, editor of the journal *Race & Class*, wrote that the strike was 'no longer about racism', but was now about the 'legality ... of the weapons that unions may use'.[44] In his eyes, the official union movement was not proving its commitment to black workers, but instead was 'determining the direction that the strike should take and the type of actions open to the strikers'.[45] For example, in February 1977, APEX's Grunwick Strike Committee produced a bulletin listing the demands of the strike, which stated 'What are we fighting for': the right to belong to a union, for APEX to be recognised at Grunwick, the reinstatement of those strikers that had been fired after belatedly joining APEX, 'a decent living wage, proper working conditions and an end to the abusive and tyrannical regime of our management'.[46] However, there was no mention of combating racism anywhere within these demands. What the demand for trade union representation by the white labour movement failed to recognise was that the presence of a trade union did not

---

41   SWP, *Grunwick*, p. 4.

42   *Socialist Challenge*, 3 November 1977.

43   'Grunwick Strike: The Bitter Lessons', *Race Today*, November/December 1977, p. 154.

44   'Grunwick (2)', p. 292.

45   'Race, Class and the State (2)', p. 70.

46   Grunwick Strike Committee (APEX), *Strike Committee Bulletin*, 29, 21 February 1977, G1548/9, MSS.464 Box 1, in Grunwick Dispute Archive, Modern Records Centre, University of Warwick.

actually equate to countering racism within the workplace at Grunwick. The black workers at Mansfield Hosiery Mills and Imperial Typewriters had been members of a union at these factories and these trade unions had been ineffectual in combating the racism experienced within these workplaces. The Black Women's Group Brixton protested:

> The only basis on which the trade union movement and the White left would support the struggle of Black workers was on the condition that they subordinate the main issue of racism to trade unionism, which is of importance, but not sufficient to ignore the racist issue.[47]

The feminist magazine *Spare Rib* celebrated the role taken by women, particularly Asian women, in the strike, who, according to them, made up 60 percent of strike. In January 1977, the magazine declared:

> It takes a great deal of guts for an Asian woman to come out on strike and stand on a picket line in the full glare of publicity day after day. All sorts of psychological pressures are brought to bear on her. Members of her family may gossip and deprecate her, as it is considered a dishonour for a woman to put herself in the public eye.[48]

The magazine also highlighted the particular hardships faced by women employees at Grunwick and quoted one of the women on strike:

> What I mean by slave treatment is that if a woman is pregnant, for example, she can't get time off to go to the clinic. The management says why can't we go on Saturdays, but the clinic is not open on that day.
>
> Many of our women have small children at school or in nurseries. The management tells you halfway through the day that you *must* work overtime that night – but this is terrible because you can't pick up your children and you can't contact your home.[49]

Interviewed at the height of the mass pickets in July/August 1977, Jayaben Desai talked positively about the support that came from different areas for the women on strike:

47 Black Women's Group Brixton, 'Editorial', *Speak Out*, 2, 1981, p. 3, DADZIE/1/8/3, in Stella Dadzie Papers, Black Cultural Archives, London.

48 Rossiter, 'Risking Gossip & Disgrace: Asian Women trike', *Spare Rib*, January 1977, p. 18.

49 Campbell and Charlton, 'Grunwick Women', *Spare Rib*, August 1977, p. 7.

Before the mass picketing began in June the issue was not so clear in our community, it was misty before. But now the Asian community see what we are fighting for.

And before, the trade unions in this country were felling that our community was not interested – this was always a gap in our community. But this will bring the distance nearer. We can all see the result – people coming here from all over the country were seeing us as part of the workers now.[50]

These differing perspectives on the focus of the Grunwick strike have led to much debate over whether the strike was a class-based strike or a strike against racism (or both), with the female aspect of the strike overlooked by many scholars. A. Sivanandan wrote in 1981 that the 'basic issue for the strikers was the question of racist exploitation', acknowledging that union recognition was part of this.[51] Ron Ramdin also acknowledged that racial discrimination was an issue at Grunwick, but wrote, '[w]hile low pay, racism and the oppression of women' were contributory factors, the main cause of the Grunwick strike was the 'conditions of work'.[52] Following on from this argument from Ramdin, several authors have argued that Grunwick brought black and white workers together *as a class* to fight for trade union recognition *and* to combat racism in the workplace. Gary Macfarlane stated that the strike 'demonstrated that class unity could be forged in action and racism challenged head on',[53] while Satnam Virdee wrote during Grunwick, 'key groups of workers had moved towards a more inclusive language of class that could now also encompass racialized minority workers'.[54]

Although the main emphasis of APEX and the Brent Trades Council was on trade union recognition, as mentioned above, there were moments when these organisations did not acknowledge that there was a racial aspect to the strike. In a letter from the Basingstoke General branch of APEX to the General Secretary of the TUC, there was a call for a national campaign by the TUC to highlight the struggle at Grunwick, with the letter ending, 'Let all know about the Grunwick employers' Dickensian nature of employment, mainly of Asian origin, thus making the issue additionally delicate in the matter concerning

---

50   Ibid.
51   Sivanandan 2008, p. 130.
52   Ramdin 1987, p. 288.
53   MacFarlane 2013, p. 87.
54   Virdee 2014, p. 135.

race relations'.[55] Furthermore, in a flyer produced by APEX to call for the mass pickets in mid-1977, it was stated in bold capitals at the top of the flyer:

GRUNWICKS STRIKE IS ABOUT
IMMIGRANTS WOMEN
TRADE UNION RIGHTS
WORKING CLASS SOLIDARITY[56]

However, other academics, such as Jack McGowan, have rejected that racism was an issue at Grunwick, writing that a 'race-driven narrative is a tenacious trope in the accounts of Grunwick from the Left'.[57] McGowan cited the Commission for Racial Equality as stating, 'It cannot be shown that the management at Grunwick practised racial discrimination', and further argued that the strike could not be about 'race' because the co-owner of Grunwick, George Ward, was of Anglo-Indian descent.[58] Criticising a particular BBC Radio 4 documentary on the strike produced by Melissa Benn, McGowan lamented that 'Benn's radio audience might ... misinterpret Grunwick as a case of white exploitation of ethnic workers' and argued:

[Benn] appears to conflate the profound difference between the structural, socio-economic status of a sector of the labour force – regardless of ethnicity – with an implied willingness on the part of an employer deliberately to exploit workers on the grounds of race alone.[59]

McGowan here takes a very narrow concept of racism and does not consider that Grunwick's owners and management relied on the *structural* position of the Asian manual workers (especially the female workers), largely informed by their ethnicity and recent migrant status, to treat them poorly as employees. As Pratibha Parmar and Parita Trivedi have argued, Asian women were viewed as 'passive', 'submissive' and 'meek' and 'pushed into unskilled and semi-skilled jobs' in 'small organized sweatshops or doing homeworking'.[60] These racist

---

55   Letter from APEX Basingstoke General branch to TUC General Secretary, 18 April 1977, MSS 292D/253.119/3, in TUC Papers, Modern Records Centre, University of Warwick.
56   APEX flyer, August 1977, MSS.464/20, in APEX papers, Modern Records Centre, University of Warwick.
57   McGowan 2008, p. 389.
58   McGowan 2008, pp. 389–90.
59   McGowan 2008, p. 390.
60   Parmar 1986, p. 245; Trivedi 1984, p. 45.

and sexist assumptions, along with the difficulties of trade union organising in these workplaces, made Asian female workers vulnerable to exploitation, but as the Grunwick strike has shown, these women were willing to challenge these assumptions and were able to take the lead in militant industrial action.[61]

The importance of the strike in fighting sexual discrimination has traditionally been overlooked in discussions of the strike, although since Amrit Wilson first wrote about the strike in the 1978 edition of *Finding a Voice*, it has been acknowledged by feminist scholars that the discrimination that workers faced *as women* informed the militancy of the women involved on the picket line.[62] As the quotes from *Spare Rib* above show, women at Grunwick experienced specific discrimination based upon their gender, which was often combined with discrimination based upon their ethnicity. The recent work by Linda McDowell, Sundari Anitha and Ruth Pearson suggests that previous accounts of the strike have 'neglected the complex intersections between class, gender and ethnicity' at Grunwick and therefore argue that the strike should be viewed through an intersectional lens[63] – a theoretical framework that could be applied to how to view the interaction between the labour movement and ethnic minority workers in the period under examination. For the labour movement, including the Communist Party, there was an emphasis on class, although there was an increasing acknowledgement of the extra problems faced by ethnic minorities and by women – but the strategies put forward for combating the intersecting forms of class, gender and racial oppression always emphasised *class unity* and using the tools of class mobilisation, such as the mass picket and the accession to the trade union leadership.

Although the strike ended in defeat, it has been celebrated by the British labour movement ever since because of this compelling narrative of class unity. As McDowell, Anitha and Pearson have argued:

> the strike has become constructed as a iconic moment in the history of the labour movement, the moment when the working class recognised the rights of women and minority workers to join a union as part of the British working-class movement.[64]

---

61   Although a recent study has suggested that African-Caribbean women, who also went on strike at Grunwick, have been erased from the visual and collective memory of the strike. McDowell, Anitha and Pearson 2014, p. 606.

62   Wilson 1981, pp. 60–71.

63   McDowell, Anitha and Pearson 2012, p. 134.

64   McDowell, Anitha and Pearson 2014, p. 600.

But the strike also foreshadowed a new type of policing of strikes, of scenes of public disorder and of ethnic minorities, which will be explored below.

Policing the Labour Movement

As Labour was unable to effectively deal with the worsening economic crisis, working-class resistance, through strikes for better pay and against unemployment, increased greatly, with much debate over the supposed 'British disease' of 'chaotic and adversarial industrial relations and endless strikes'.[65] This greatly intensified the belief that a national crisis loomed.[66] The National Front, amongst others, looked to exploit this fear of crisis and began to propose a fascist solution, including the forced repatriation of non-white Britons, the destruction of the labour movement and the dismantling of the institutions of parliamentary democracy. Anti-fascist confrontation, such as that endorsed by the International Marxist Group and the IS/SWP, was seen by the CPGB as providing an excuse for the state to impose further restraints. After the events of Red Lion Square, where an anti-fascist demonstrator was killed during an anti-NF rally, the Communist Party warned that confrontations between militant anti-fascists and the police could be exploited by those 'who are for authoritarian measures aimed at destroying our basic democratic rights'.[67] The actions of the IMG, fighting the police rather than NF, gave the state 'the opportunity to whip up the scare about violence on the streets', which would coerce the public into 'accepting even tougher authoritarian measures in all spheres of life'.[68]

Although the Party was concerned with the rise of the National Front, the much greater threat seemed to be from a 'new kind of popular rightism'.[69] The 'sinister reality' of a Conservative government under Margaret Thatcher was feared by the CPGB.[70] Despite the increasing shift by the government and the Conservative opposition towards the right, the Party declared that 'it would be incorrect to think that the crisis had reached such a stage in Britain' that the

---

65   Morgan 1990, p. 415.

66   Jacques, 'Thatcherism – The Impasse Broken?', *Marxism Today*, October 1979, p. 9.

67   *Morning Star*, 22 June 1974.

68   Ibid.

69   Jacques, 'Thatcherism – The Impasse Broken?', p. 10.

70   CPGB PC Weekly Letter, 30 September 1976, in CPGB archives, CP/CENT/CIRC/68/05, LHASC.

state saw 'coercion and repression' as the only way to maintain power.[71] In *A Knife at the Throat of Us All*, Dave Cook wrote that Britain was not 'on the edge of a fascist takeover' and a greater threat came from the 'more openly asserted authoritarian face of the Conservative Party'.[72]

The use of the repressive institutions of the state to engage in conflict with the 'subversive' elements of society did not begin with Margaret Thatcher's attainment of leadership of the Conservative Party. As Paul Gilroy and Joe Sim noted in a 1985 article (published in the aftermath of the 1984–5 Miners' Strike), there had been a view on the left of Thatcherism that 'dates the arrival of authoritarianism and its new right forces in the Spring of 1979'.[73] While Thatcher was explicit in her 'law and order' agenda and her willingness to enter into confrontations with dissenters, as seen in her anti-union stance, the basis for this shift to the right that was attributed to Thatcherism had existed since the late 1960s and Thatcher could not have implemented any actions without sharing a considerable amount of consensus with the British population. The view that Britain was on the verge of collapse had existed since the industrial militancy and cultural radicalism of the late 1960s and had been exacerbated by the economic crisis of the mid-1970s. Thatcherism was a response to this anxiety about the collapse of British society and was now openly willing to challenge the elements that were seen as 'threats' to Britain's economic recovery and the 'British way of life'.

As Stuart Hall explained in an interview with the Merseyside socialist publication *Big Flame*, the issues of 'law and order' had been monopolised by the right and the left had to 'grasp the importance of what they once dismissed as non-political issues'.[74] As the economic crisis continued, the police were increasingly used to deal with 'subversive' elements of British society, dissatisfied with Labour's ineffective policies. The perceived lack of initiative of the Labour government on the economic crisis and the issues of law and order allowed the Conservatives to sway traditional Labour voters with the populist notions of a strong state to deal with the trade unions, crime, illegal immigrants and other 'subversive' elements. The appeal of Thatcherite populism was part of the reason why around a third of trade unionists voted for the Conservatives

---

71   'The Fight for Democracy and Against Authoritarianism', Draft of Report to Executive Committee, 11/12 January 1975, p. 5, in CPGB archives, CP/CENT/PC/13/13, LHASC.

72   Cook, *A Knife at the Throat of Us All: Racism and the National Front*, 1978, London: CPGB pamphlet, p. 8.

73   Gilroy and Sim 1985, p. 16.

74   Interview with Stuart Hall, *Big Flame*, February 1979.

in the May 1979 General Election.[75] But these populist notions and the result of a more restrictive police presence were not merely creations of Thatcher herself. Gilroy and Sim acknowledged this, stating that 'as far as law and order, policing and criminal justice matters are concerned, the Thatcher governments do not represent a decisive break with patterns in preceding years'.[76] The elements for a centralised and militarised police force had been present in the 'fudged social democracy of the Wilson, Heath and Callaghan years',[77] but under Thatcher, the repressive institutions of the state were different, as they were *explicitly* used against certain demonised parts of society and there was *consent* for this use amongst large sections of the British public.

As the economic crisis continued in the late 1970s, the police were viewed by the left as increasingly repressive and brutal. The police were used to break strikes, particularly at Grunwick, and to protect NF demonstrations, as well as focusing on illegal immigrants and black youth, under the auspices of a concern over street crime. The CPGB questioned the reason for the police protection of NF marches, which were seen as a violation of the Race Relations Act, and concluded that the state had something to gain from the NF's explicit racism. 'It is no accident that this year of racist provocations is also the year of deepening crisis for British capitalism', the *Morning Star* claimed, 'with right-wing Labour policies pinning the burdens on the working people and mounting Tory pressure for more ruthless attacks on living standards and democratic rights'.[78] Police brutality and the state's anti-left bias were evident in the protection of NF demonstrations, most significantly with the deaths of Kevin Gately and Blair Peach (to be discussed later in this chapter).

In the union struggles under the crisis-ridden Labour government, the issue of police repression, and the increasingly repressive means of the state, was most significantly demonstrated at the strike at Grunwick. Because part of the aim of the Grunwick strike was trade union recognition, much of the strike activity was considered unofficial or illegal, which brought it into confrontation with the police, who, on several occasions, attempted to break the picket lines. The mass picket, organised in mid-1977 as official trade union negotiations broke down, was attacked by the police. One of the significant aspects of this police action was the use of the Special Patrol Group (SPG) 'for the first time

75   Hobsbawm, 'The Forward March of Labour Halted? – A Response', *Marxism Today*, September 1979, p. 265.
76   Gilroy and Sim 1985, p. 18.
77   Ibid.
78   *Morning Star*, 20 November 1976.

in British labour relations history [upon] a picket line'.[79] The result was over 550 arrests, more than in any labour dispute since the General Strike of 1926.[80] The decisions over the police and SPG actions at Grunwick 'had to be approved, implicitly or explicitly' by the Home Secretary Merlyn Rees who was criticised for introducing the SPG 'which was never intended to be brought into industrial disputes'.[81] At their 35th National Congress in November 1977, the Communist Party condemned 'the savage police attacks on pickets' and declared that Rees had 'given to the police virtually an open cheque which has heightened their brutality to trade union pickets and defence of the employer'.[82] The Party demanded 'the right to picket free of police restriction and intimidation', along with 'an open independent inquiry into the use of the police Special Patrol Group into industrial disputes'.[83] The use of the SPG by the Labour government to deal with hostile protests did not end at Grunwick, with the SPG being used at the anti-NF demonstration in Southall on 23 April 1979. By the end of the 1970s, the reputation of the SPG was 'synonymous with "trouble"' and, as Tony Jefferson and Roger Grimshaw wrote, 'the most controversial aspects of policing operations in London – "swamping" black communities, policing industrial relations and policing demonstrations – were almost reducible to three letters: SPG'.[84]

The NF's Shift to the Streets and the Rise of the Asian Youth Movements

The authorities' concern over public disorder in the late 1970s was raised by the rise of the National Front and its shift towards attempting to occupy the streets in 1976–7, as their electoral fortunes began to stall in the face of sterner anti-fascist opposition. The National Front was now the prominent anti-immigration group 'using popular discontent and anxiety about inadequate housing, growing unemployment and miserable social services' to 'stoke up their campaign' to halt black immigration.[85] While the CPGB's 33rd National Con-

---

79   Dromey and Taylor 1978, p. 114.
80   Taylor, 'Lions Leave the Zoo', *Comment*, 9 December 1978, p. 391.
81   Dromey and Taylor 1978, p. 138.
82   'Grunwick', Official Report of CPGB's 35th National Congress, 12–15 November 1977, in CPGB archives, CP/CENT/CONG/19/13, LHASC.
83   Ibid.
84   Jefferson and Grimshaw 1984, p. 108.
85   'Editorial Comments', *Marxism Today*, October 1972, p. 289.

gress in December 1973, the resolution on racism made no specific mention
of the National Front,[86] by the 34th National Congress in December 1975, the
Party acknowledged that the National Front had a 'new and dangerous significance' and was 'matched by the right wing trend of the Tory leadership'.[87]
Although the mainstream (especially tabloid) media, the right wing of the Conservative Party and state institutions, such as the police and the judiciary, all
contributed heavily to popular racism and negative views on black immigration, the National Front dominated the 'debate' about immigration during
the mid-1970s. Support and recruitment for the National Front was predominantly on the issue of immigration and it was suggested that around three-
quarters of NF members joined out of racism and concern about black immigration.[88]

The NF's fortunes had shrunk throughout 1975, although the anti-fascist
response continued to grow. In 1976, the National Front were still contesting
elections and actually increased the number of seats they contested, but by
1977, this electoral push had come to the same result as that as in 1974 – notoriety, but no tangible gains. The split by John Kingsley-Read and other 'populists'
to form the National Party, along with this electoral failure, contributed to a
short decline for the NF. However, the growing economic crisis, along with
the controversy over Asians expelled from Malawi arriving in Britain, saw the
NF reinvigorated under a new strategy. Although the NF continued to contest
elections, managing to record some relatively 'disturbing electoral successes',[89]
the main focus of the NF was now on occupying the streets with provocative
street marches and confrontation with a growing anti-fascist movement. At
the same time, the NF's campaign of intimidation saw an increase in violence
against Britain's black population, with several deaths and 'scores of other similar incidents of unprovoked and savage racist attacks'.[90]

In May 1976, the National Party won two council seats in Blackburn and both
the NF and the NP demonstrated at London airports against the arrival of the
Malawi Asians. The following month, the *Morning Star* reported that 'racial
violence has reached a level not seen at least since the events of the autumn of

---

86   'Resolution: The Fight Against Racialism in Britain', *Comment*, December 1973, p. 407.

87   'Branch and District Resolutions: Racialism', *Comment*, 27 December 1975, p. 424.

88   Renton 2006, p. 22.

89   Copsey 2000, p. 123.

90   Bethnal Green and Stepney Trades Council, *Blood on the Streets: A Report by Bethnal Green
      and Stepney Trades Council on Racial Attacks in East London*, 1978, London: BG & STC
      pamphlet, p. 4.

1958 in Notting Hill and Nottingham'.[91] As the NF and the NP revitalised their provocative campaigns, the *Morning Star* noted that these incitements to race hatred were systematic breaches of the Race Relations Act and warned that, 'Racial hatred and violence are not very far apart'.[92] On 4 June 1976, Gurdip Singh Chaggar, a Sikh youth, was stabbed to death by a gang of NF-inspired white youths in Southall.[93]

Southall had one of the largest concentrations of Asians in Greater London, originally attracted by the employment of Sikhs at Woolf's rubber factory, but then expanding to other ethnicities and job opportunities.[94] The Asian community had suffered from racism for decades, but as stated in *Southall: The Birth of a Black Community*, 'The black community of Southall ... fought against racism all along the line'.[95] With the murder of Chaggar, the Asian youth of Southall became militant, with 'no time for resolutions, nor for reliance on the goodwill of politicians', forming the Southall Youth Movement.[96] For the SYM, 'the racist attacks against young black people makes black people feel it is not safe to go out at night' and after Chaggar's murder, 'whilst leaders were saying keep calm and trying to play down "isolated incidents" ... [w]e knew it was time to organise ourselves'.[97] While the Indian Workers Associations had been important organisations for Asian workers during the 1960s, by the 1970s, the second generation Asian youth felt that the IWA had begun to 'degenerate into the position of mediator, into the posture of a support force and into downright conservative, leadership-seeking reaction'.[98] The Asian youth organised around the SYM sought a more active and militant organisation. The SYM was dedicated to 'physically keeping racism off the streets of Southall' and countering the 'lack of youth provision in the Borough'.[99]

The new militancy and self-reliance of the SYM and of Asian Youth Movements across Britain reflected the influence of 'Black Power and Third World liberation movements',[100] rather than the emphasis on class struggle and indus-

---

91   *Morning Star*, 25 June 1976.
92   Ibid.
93   Hiro 1992, p. 169; Renton 2006, p. 139.
94   Harrison, 'The Patience of Southall', *New Society*, 4 April 1974.
95   CARF/Southall Rights, *Southall*, p. 45.
96   CARF/Southall Rights, *Southall*, p. 52.
97   Bahai Purewal, cited in 'Against Racism in Southall', *Challenge*, 36, August/September 1976.
98   Race Today Collective, *The Struggle of Asian Workers in Britain*, 1983, London: Race Today Publications, p. 17.
99   CARF/Southall Rights, *Southall*, p. 54.
100   Ramamurthy 2006, p. 39.

trial politics endorsed by the white left. John Rose wrote in *International Social-ism* that the formation of the SYM 'took the entire local left by surprise', writing that they had 'already given chase to the racists on the streets ... and ultimately they will give the racists chase in the factories'.[101] However, Rose stated that the 'only long-term chance that the SYM has for growth and development is if the leadership comes to decisively adopt revolutionary socialist politics'.[102] The SYM experienced difficulties in maintaining its own identity when dealing with the left, as explained by the General Secretary of the SYM, Balraj Puriwal: 'Every time we tried to protest and give our own identity the left tried to take it over ... they gave us their slogans and placards ... our own identity was subsumed, diffused and deflected all over the place'.[103] There was sympathy for the left amongst those involved in the AYMs, but not at the substitution of their own identity. As Nermal Singh wrote in *Kala Tara*, the publication of the Bradford AYM:

> The white left tell us only the working class as a whole will be able to smash racism by overthrowing capitalism and setting up a socialist state.
> This maybe so, but in the meantime are we, as one of the most op-pressed sections of the working class, to sit by idly in the face of mounting attacks. No! We must fight back against the cancerous growth of racism.[104]

The CPGB acknowledged the anger felt by black youth who felt 'unwanted by British society as a whole', but warned against 'impulsive, un-thought-out, little supported ... reactions' that led to violence and physical confrontation.[105] 'Public demonstrations have a vital and essential role', wrote Ken Graves in the *Morning Star*, 'but the lesson surely is take to the streets, yes – but take to the streets with strength'.[106] After the death of Chaggar, the *Morning Star* reported that the slogans for the 'March of Unity' in Southall in response to the murder would be:

---

101   Rose, 'The Southall Asian Youth Movement', *International Socialism*, 1/91, September 1976, p. 5.

102   Rose, 'The Southall Asian Youth Movement', p. 6.

103   Cited in Grewal 2003, p. 21.

104   Singh, 'Racism: Time to Fight Back', *Kala Tara*, 1, p. 3, available at: http://www.tandana.org/pg/PDF/SC/SC2.PDF.

105   *Morning Star*, 24 June 1976.

106   Ibid.

'One race, the human race'; 'Say no to racism'; 'Peace through unity'; 'Together for peace and unity'; 'Together for peace and justice'; 'Black and white unite'; 'Co-operation not conflict'.[107]

These slogans, aimed at gathering broad support, were in juxtaposition with the more militant stance of the SYM, who declared, 'We shall fight like lions'.[108] The young Asian militants wanted direct action to protect themselves against racist attacks by individuals and discrimination by the authorities, with the Asian Youth Movements (AYM) across Britain taking up the slogans, 'Self defence is no offence' and 'Here to stay, here to fight'.[109] The Communist Party, as expressed by the District Secretary of the West Middlesex CPGB Branch (which encompassed Southall) in a letter to *Race Today*, wanted 'unity to challenge discrimination and racialist immigration laws ...[,] demand equal rights and opportunities for all ... [and to] call on the Government to outlaw racial incitement'.[110] The CPGB's appeals, while still significant for the long-term eradication of racism, averted direct action and looked to the state to deal decisively with racial violence, which was at odds with the experiences and demands of black youth.

The Rise of the SWP and the Revival of Militant Anti-fascism

By 1976–7, the Communist Party was at a crossroads over its anti-fascist strategy as the NF moved to campaigning in the streets. At this time, the CPGB's National Student Committee had removed 'no platform' as a slogan and acknowledged that the 'real debate on racialism had been lost in this controversy over "No Platform"'.[111] In the immediate steps to combat the NF, the CPGB called for 'a ban on all racist activity and strengthen the Race Relations Act against incitement to race hatred' and to 'develop the broadest united campaign of all anti-

---

107   *Morning Star*, 12 June 1976.
108   CARF/Southall Rights, *Southall: The Birth of a Black Community*, 1982, London: Institute of Race Relations/Southall Rights, p. 52.
109   Sivanandan, 'Asian Youth Movements: Here to Stay, Here to Fight', *Red Pepper*, June 2005, available at: http://www.redpepper.org.uk/society/x-jun05-sivanandan.htm; See Ali, 'Here to Stay – Here to Fight!', *Kala Tara*, 1, pp. 6–7, available at: http://www.tandana .org/data/pg/PDF/SC/SC2.PDF.
110   'Letters', *Race Today*, July/August 1976, p. 146.
111   National Student Committee, 'National Student Conference', 17 February 1977, in CPGB archives, CP/CENT/PC/14/06, LHASC.

racist forces to resist racist activities'.[112] However, the CPGB's Political Committee believed that there was still no 'basis for forming some new, national
anti-racialist organisation' and the Party 'should not try to form at this stage a
national organisation ... which presents the danger of being a grouping of Left
wing organisations and another area of disruptive activity for ultra-Lefts'.[113] By
the end of 1976, it looked as if the Socialist Workers Party and the Asian Youth
Movements were to provide the two forms of political organisation that would
confront the National Front on the streets in the late 1970s, although, as Anandi
Ramamurthy has pointed out, the white left and the AYMs disagreed over the
centrality of the struggle against racism and the strategies to be pursued.[114]

The CPGB had traditionally been the dominant anti-fascist force, but by
the mid-1970s, they had been overtaken by the IS/SWP. By 1976, the economic
crisis had stalled the IS/SWP's efforts to revolutionise the union's rank and file
and 'in an attempt to bolster its flagging industrial perspective, but without
losing its foothold in the union camp', the SWP launched the Right to Work
campaign.[115] The IS/SWP's concerns were now focused on Right to Work and
combating the NF, announcing that 'the twin themes of fighting racialism and
fighting for the right to work now dominate our immediate perspective'.[116] This
emphasis signalled a significant shift for the SWP, 'away from established union
and political structures and towards the young working class'.[117] In relation to
defining itself as an alternative to the CPGB, Ian Birchall explained that part
of this was an appeal to the Communist Party's heritage, which reflected two
things, 'the hunger marches ... and anti-fascist activity, especially Cable Street',
and in the 1970s, the SWP 'were the ones who were emulating the "golden age"
of the CP'.[118]

In his history of the IS/SWP, Birchall recognised the SWP's strategy against
the National Front was twofold. Firstly they emphasised that 'racism and fascism were a product of a system of crisis' and anti-racism 'had to be combined with a critique of the system as a whole'.[119] On the other hand, the NF's

112   *Morning Star*, 12 July 1976.
113   'Draft for Political Committee', 1 July 1976, in CPGB archives, CP/CENT/PC/14/01, LHASC.
114   Ramamurthy 2013, p. 38.
115   Goodyer 2002, p. 24.
116   IS Central Committee, 'The Anti-Racialist Fight and the Right to Work Campaign', *IS Post-
       Conference Bulletin*, 1976, in Alastair Mutch Papers, MSS.284, Modern Records Centre,
       University of Warwick.
117   Goodyer 2002, p. 25.
118   Email from Ian Birchall to the author, 22 May 2005.
119   Birchall 1981, p. 25.

marches were part of a fascist attempt to control the streets and build a mass organisation, so 'organised fascism had to be confronted physically'.[120] The SWP criticised the CPGB for '[m]erely shouting "One race – the human race"' as those attracted to the NF were 'fed up with rhetoric from politicians, they are impressed by action'.[121] To prevent the building of a fascist mass movement required a strategy of 'uncompromising opposition to any form of publicity, meeting or demonstration' for the NF, which meant physically confronting the NF in the streets.[122] The SWP were wary of police protection for fascist marches, but declared that 'if five or ten thousand people assembled with the clear purpose of physically stopping a nazi march – then the police would probably not allow them to march'.[123] As the SWP stepped up their anti-fascist strategy of confronting the NF in the streets, they warned, 'physical action will become the litmus test for distinguishing those who are seriously attempting to build a revolutionary alternative from those who are merely careerists and hacks'.[124] By August 1977, this 'litmus test' had come with the major street battle of the 1970s between the NF and the anti-fascist left, the 'Battle of Lewisham'.

The 'Battle of Lewisham'

The 'Battle of Lewisham' on 13 August 1977, when anti-fascist demonstrators clashed with the National Front and the police in the London borough of Lewisham, was a turning point for both the CPGB and the SWP in the anti-fascist movement. Attempting to exploit the recent arrest of a number of young blacks, the NF called for an 'anti-muggers' march, to assemble near New Cross station in Lewisham.[125] In response to this announcement, the anti-fascist movement in Lewisham called for a ban from Home Secretary Merlyn Rees and Metropolitan Police Commissioner David McNee. The Lewisham council appealed to Rees to ban the march under the 1936 Public Order Act, while

---

120   Ibid.
121   'Fascism in Leicester', *International Socialism*, 1/93, November/December 1976, pp. 18–19.
122   Evans, 'News from the Nazi Front', *International Socialism*, 1/80, July/August 1975, p. 5.
123   'Fascism in Leicester', p. 19.
124   Ibid.
125   Renton 2006, p. 57; Copsey 2000, p. 123. A police campaign in the Lewisham area had arrested a number of young blacks, who became known as the 'Lewisham 21'. During a demonstration in support of the Lewisham detainees in early July 1977, a number of demonstrators were attacked by NF members.

McNee 'suggested a three month ban on all marches'.[126] However, the *Morning Star* stated that under the Act, Rees could have ordered a 'one-off' ban, claiming that the three-month period proposed by McNee was a 'red herring' and it was only police practice to ban all marches.[127] However, Commissioner McNee stated that 'he was turning down calls to ban the NF march because to do so would be to give in to "mob rule"'.[128]

The All Lewisham Campaign Against Racism and Fascism (ALCARAF) was formed in January 1977, a broad-based alliance, including in its own words 'conservatives and socialists, church people and trade unionists, blacks and whites'.[129] Nigel Copsey has noted that at a national level, the CPGB 'had done little to counter the National Front', but its members 'were often key figures in local anti-fascist committees',[130] which was the case with ALCARAF. With the refusal to ban the NF march, the Lewisham CPGB branch announced that 'ALCARAF should encourage all Borough organisations ... to support a counter-demonstration ... calling for a peaceful, democratic, multiracial society based on social harmony', as well as 'to reject fascism and end unemployment'.[131] ALCARAF and the CPGB urged a 'powerful but peaceful demonstration', which was scheduled to take place at a different time, away from the location of the NF's march at Clifton Rise.[132] The SWP, on the other hand, announced its own demonstration at Clifton Rise, where the NF were meeting, with the notion of confronting the NF on the streets. The SWP recognised the ALCARAF march, but declared that 'it will provide no substitute for confronting the fascists directly'.[133] The *Morning Star* announced that 'it almost goes without saying that the Socialist Workers Party has prepared itself for the definitive game of cowboys and indians'.[134]

---

126   *Morning Star*, 10 August 1977.

127   Ibid.

128   *Morning Star*, 11 August 1977.

129   All Lewisham Campaign Against Racism And Fascism, *Why You Should Support ALCARAF*, 1977, London: ALCARAF flyer, in CPGB archives, CP/LON/LEW/05/04, National Museum of Labour History (hereafter LHASC).

130   Copsey 2000, p. 127.

131   Lewisham CPGB Branch, 'National Front Provocation in Lewisham', 9 July 1977, in CPGB archives, CP/LON/LEW/02/06, LHASC.

132   Lewisham CPGB Branch, 'ALCARAF Demonstration August 13th', in CPGB archives, CP/LON/LEW/02/06, LHASC; Copsey 2000, p. 126.

133   *Socialist Worker*, 13 August 1977.

134   *Morning Star*, 12 August 1977.

On the day of the demonstration, around 4,000 people attended the ALCARAF march.[135] In the flyer handed out to marchers, the CPGB called for marchers not to attend the SWP demonstration, appealing for them to resist 'violent confrontation with the National Front or the police' and remain 'united and disciplined', asserting that organisations, such as the SWP, 'who insist on the ritual enactment of vanguardist violence only damage the hard, patient work that has been put in over the years in the area by anti-racists and anti-fascists'.[136] The SWP distributed its own leaflet amongst the ALCARAF march to join the demonstration at Clifton Rise. SWP District Secretary Ted Parker described the event in Dave Renton's history of the Anti-Nazi League:

> We knew one pivotal thing was to get as many people as possible from the first march up to Clifton Rise ... The fascinating thing was that people wanted to march to Clifton Rise, but they just wouldn't line up behind a Socialist Workers Party banner ... Eventually, we found some members of some other groups like the IMG with a banner for some united campaign against racism and fascism. People agreed to group behind that. It taught me a lesson for later – many people would support a united campaign, they didn't all want just to line up behind the SWP.[137]

Around 3,000–5,000 demonstrators congregated at this point, compared with 500–600 NF marches and 'as police made snatch raids into the crowd ... counter-demonstrators retaliated with bottles, bricks, and soft drink cans'.[138] Fighting also broke out between police and counter-demonstrators on Lewisham High Street at the end of the NF march. By the end of the day, 110 people had been injured, including 56 policemen, and 210 people detained, with 204 charged with offences.[139]

The following week's *Socialist Worker*'s headline declared 'We Stopped The Nazis ... And We'll Do It Again!'[140] Thousands of people – 'black people and trade unionists, old and young, 14-year-olds and veterans of Cable Street, Rastafarians and Millwall supporters, Labour Party members and revolutionary socialists' – had come out to demonstrate against the National Front. The NF,

---

135   Copsey 2000, p. 127.
136   'A Message From Lewisham Communists to the ALCARAF Demonstration', in CPGB archives, CP/LON/LEW/02/06, LHASC.
137   Renton 2006, p. 60.
138   *The Guardian*, 15 August 1977.
139   Ibid.
140   *Socialist Worker*, 20 August 1977.

'cowering behind massive police lines', were 'forced to abandon their march before it was half completed'.[141] The SWP saw the 'Battle of Lewisham' as a major victory, when the 'Nazi Front got the hammering of their lives'.[142] Central London Organiser of the SWP, Jerry Fitzpatrick, described Lewisham as 'our Cable Street ... it was our generation's attempt to stop fascism. It was rugged, scrappy. It got bad publicity. But it was a real success. The NF had been stopped, and their ability to march through black areas had been completely smashed'.[143] The black SWP paper *Flame* called Lewisham 'the day that the Black youth gave the police a beating', and declared: 'For the black community it was a day of victory'.[144] The *Socialist Worker* reported that the 'angriest anti-fascists were not those who had travelled many miles to take on the Nazis, but the local people, the blacks especially'.[145] The paper quoted the father of one of the Lewisham 21 as saying, 'I don't agree with everything the Socialist Workers' Party says but they were the only organisation to stand up for the rights of black people here'.[146]

For the Communist Party, the 'Battle of Lewisham' demonstrated the need for widespread political pressure to ensure that the Public Order Act and the Race Relations Act were used effectively to ban provocative racist marches and, in the case of this ban not being implemented, the need for a broad-based counter-demonstration, rather than street fighting. The Party was outraged at Police Commissioner McNee's refusal to ban the NF march and asserted that instead of police mobilising 'to carve a way for a few thousand supporters of the National Front', the NF's marches 'must be stopped by police'.[147] If this did not occur, then 'political, mass struggle ... will be found to finish with the National Front and its like' and 'not the staging of ritual confrontations and street fights between the police and handfuls of protestors'.[148] The CPGB condemned the 'crass adventurism' of the SWP to assemble where the NF were marching.[149] While Dave Cook acknowledged the 'courage and determination' of those who took part in the protest at Clifton Rise, the ensuing clashes 'gave the capitalist press the chance to present that day as being a violent struggle between two sets

---

141   Ibid.
142   Ibid.
143   Cited in Renton 2006, p. 72.
144   *Flame*, September 1977.
145   *Socialist Worker*, 20 August 1977.
146   Ibid.
147   *Morning Star*, 15 August 1977.
148   Ibid.
149   *Morning Star*, 2 September 1977.

of "extremists"'.[150] What was needed for a successful anti-racist campaign was a broad-based movement including the labour and progressive movements, as well as the black communities, which had the potential to be isolated by the violent clashes of the SWP. As Dave Cook wrote, 'The problem about street fighting is that only street-fighters are likely to apply, and it is this which can make it difficult to achieve the mobilisation of the labour movement'.[151] Some members within the CPGB, particularly those involved in the militant anti-fascism of the 1930s and 1940s, defended the confrontational tactics against the NF, but this was more likely to be support for the local black community in Lewisham, than for their Trotskyist rivals. Tony Gilbert, one of the CPGB's leading anti-racist activists and a former International Brigades volunteer, 'commented on the courage of the young blacks' after Lewisham at a National Race Relations Committee (NRRC) meeting, but stated that the main lesson of Lewisham was that 'the presence of the Party must always be visible on any anti-fascist demo'.[152]

For the CPGB, the 'Battle of Lewisham' signalled the end of a 'primarily *defensive* phase' against the NF, where 'mobilisation reflected the intentions of the fascists'.[153] The need was not the 'occasional dramatic "confrontation"' with the NF, but a 'detailed, systematic, painstaking' campaign to 'promote propaganda and education ... to show the benefits of living in a peaceful multiracial society'.[154] For the SWP, Lewisham showed that it was clear that 'many people outside the SWP were keen to oppose the National Front but wanted little to do with the SWP itself'.[155] As David Widgery wrote in *Beating Time*:

> The black community, who had successfully defended their patch, had had a glimpse of a white anti-racist feeling which was much bigger and more militant than the liberal community-relations tea parties might suggest. A lot of ordinary people thought it was a Good Thing that the Little Hitlers had taken a bit of stick. Every racialist was made smaller.[156]

---

150   *Morning Star*, 26 August 1977.
151   Ibid.
152   Minutes of NRRC meeting, 19 September 1977, in CPGB archives, CP/LON/RACE/02/06, LHASC.
153   Cook, *A Knife at the Throat of Us All*, 1978, London: CPGB, p. 23.
154   Ibid.
155   Copsey 2000, p. 130.
156   Widgery 1986, p. 49.

'The National Front is a Nazi Front': The Anti-Nazi League, 1977–9

In November 1977, the Anti-Nazi League was launched at the House of Commons by SWP District Organiser Paul Holborrow, alongside two Labour left MPs, Peter Hain and Ernie Roberts, who took up the three executive positions of National Organiser, Press Officer and Treasurer, respectively.[157] The Steering Committee also included SWP member Nigel Harris, as well as Maurice Ludmer of *Searchlight*, actress Miriam Karlin, former Young Liberal Simon Hebditch, plus four Labour MPs, Dennis Skinner, Audrey Wise, Martin Flannery and Neil Kinnock.[158] The purpose of the Anti-Nazi League was to counter the organisation and propaganda of the NF as the prospect of a General Election loomed closer. The ANL's founding statement gave the League's objectives: 'to organise on the widest possible scale against the propaganda and activities of the Nazis in Britain'.[159] The urgent need 'to alert the people ... to the growing menace by the New Nazis' meant that the ANL was narrowly focused in its purpose, reflected in the name of the organisation.[160] The ANL acknowledged that the immediate threat was the 'worrying prospect of a Nazi party gaining significant support in Britain' as the NF intended to put forward over 300 candidates at the next General Election.[161] They also acknowledged that the National Front used popular racism and dissatisfaction over unemployment, housing and cuts in social and welfare services to garner support for their fascist aims, stating that 'Ordinary voters must be made aware of the threat that lies behind the National Front'.[162] Thus, according to the SWP leader Tony Cliff, the target of the ANL was 'the hard racism of the NF which, if allowed to thrive, could convert the many more numerous soft racists in British society into the caches of a mass fascist movement'.[163]

The relationship between the Anti-Nazi League and the Communist Party was estranged at first, with a long tradition of mistrust between the CPGB and the Socialist Workers Party. In June 1977, the Central Committee of the SWP published an open letter in *Socialist Worker* to the Political Committee of the CPGB, appealing for 'united action on certain specific issues', such as the

---

157   Renton 2006, p. 77; Copsey 2000, p. 131.

158   Renton 2006, p. 77.

159   ANL, 'Anti-Nazi League Founding Statement', in CPGB archives, CP/CENT/SUBS/04/15, LHASC.

160   Ibid.

161   Ibid.

162   Ibid.

163   Cliff 2000, p. 164.

fight against the National Front, proposing a 'joint campaign within the Labour movement to drive the fascists off the streets'.[164] Bert Ramelson, the CPGB's National Industrial Organiser, replied that united action was needed, but it was the view of the Party that the SWP's 'activity and propaganda is divisive and disruptive, making more difficult the development of united mass struggle'.[165] The Communist Party considered 'the critical question' in the struggle against racism to be 'to win maximum support for the activities of the Labour Movement which oppose racism' and the SWP's criticisms of the movement were viewed as disruptive to this approach.[166] In the aftermath of the 'Battle of Lewisham', *Socialist Worker* criticised the leadership of the CPGB for its 'refusal to join the united demonstration' at Clifton Rise.[167] The SWP claimed that 'many individual members [of the CPGB] were with us, remembering Cable Street in the 1930s' and announced 'We ask those members of the Communist Party who disagree with the suicidal line of the leaders to demand its immediate change'.[168]

Although not making any public statements about the ANL at first, the CPGB leadership were wary of the League and its narrow focus, favouring broader based anti-racist organisations, and also were sceptical of the influence and direction of the SWP. The reporting of the foundation of the Anti-Nazi League in the *Morning Star* announced that the ANL was a 'broad-based campaign ... supported by over a hundred public figures, including 40 Labour MPs', not mentioning the SWP at all, but stating that the League was 'totally non-partisan and non-sectarian'.[169] Mike Luft, a founder of the Manchester Anti-Fascist Committee, was cited by Renton, stating that 'it was an extension of the hostile attitude which the Communist Party had always manifested towards rival left-wing traditions'.[170] Keith Laybourn has remarked in his study of the CPGB that 'its interests were not particularly concerned with the National Front', where the IS/SWP seemed to be much more active, but CPGB member Bob Stoker claimed that 'Week after week we were talking about the campaign against the National Front'.[171]

164   *Socialist Worker*, 16 June 1977.
165   *Socialist Worker*, 9 July 1977.
166   Ibid.
167   *Socialist Worker*, 20 August 1977.
168   Ibid.
169   *Morning Star*, 12 November 1977.
170   Cited in Renton 2002, p. 23.
171   Ward, Hellawell and Lloyd 2006, p. 124.

In early 1978, the *Morning Star* began to present the ANL favourably,[172] while the National Organiser of the CPGB and National Co-Ordinator of the Party's National Race Relations Committee, Dave Cook, produced the important anti-racist pamphlet, *A Knife at the Throat of Us All*. Cook acknowledged the 'valu-able job' the ANL were doing in emphasising the Nazi origins of the NF, but warned 'it is important to remember that more than this is needed'.[173] Cook emphasised that the Party's strategy 'must have the goal of bringing into the struggle the big battalions of the labour movement, the democratic organisa-tions of the people, black people – *all* who can be won to oppose the advocacy of racism, as a threat to democracy' and not the 'purely defensive strategies' of the SWP.[174] But most significantly, Cook had stated that the Communist Party supported the Anti-Nazi League in an important Party publication.[175] In April 1978, the Political Committee of the CPGB announced that it supported the ANL as a 'propaganda and campaigning organisation *against the National Front*', but reiterated that the ANL was not 'an appropriate body to carry out the detailed systematic work against racism ... for which *broad anti-racist committees* are the most appropriate'.[176] In her study of anti-fascism in *International Socialism*, Chanie Rosenburg claimed that the CPGB joined the ANL (incorrectly dating it after the RAR/ANL Carnival on 30 April 1978) because it was 'waning and afraid of being totally outflanked'.[177] This was the view of the SWP in 1978 when it asserted that the ANL Carnival confirmed 'the fact that the CP despite having about three times as many active members as we do, is not playing a leading role in the growing anti-racist movement'.[178] The 'tiny CP presence' at the Car-nival was considered by the SWP 'a major disaster for them' and highlighted the wider crisis within the Communist Party.[179] Geoff Brown, an ANL organiser in Manchester, has argued that the reason the CPGB joined was 'because large chunks of the Labour left and trade union bureaucracy had already decided to support the ANL' and with the Party's traditional allies enlisted, 'To stay out

---

172 *Morning Star*, 10 January 1978; 22 February 1978.

173 Cook, *A Knife at the Throat of Us All*, p. 27.

174 Cook, *A Knife at the Throat of Us All*, p. 19; p. 23.

175 Cook, *A Knife at the Throat of Us All*, p. 27; Italics are in the original text.

176 PC Weekly Letter, 6 April 1978, in CPGB archives, CP/CENT/PC/14/22, LHASC; Italics are in the original text.

177 C. Rosenburg, 'The Labour Party and the Fight Against Fascism', *International Socialism*, 39, 1988, p. 82.

178 SWP Central Committee, 'Crisis in the Communist Party', SWP *Internal Bulletin*, Pre-Con-ference Issue 2, May 1978, p. 8.

179 Ibid.

would mean the CP risking political isolation'.[180] Thus, Bill Dunn, the CPGB's London District Industrial Organiser, joined the Anti-Nazi League Steering Committee in spring 1978.[181]

The ANL began its campaign with a distribution of anti-NF propaganda in Bournemouth East during a NF-contested by-election in late 1977.[182] From this point until the General Election in May 1979, the Anti-Nazi League enjoyed immense success as a mass movement against the NF, with Anthony M. Messina writing, 'Not since the Campaign for Nuclear Disarmament in the 1960s had an extra-parliamentary organization mobilized such a mass following'.[183] The focus of the ANL was 'to erode popular support for the National Front', which it did through combining 'mass propaganda ... with militant action on the streets'.[184] Focusing on the electoral hopes of the NF to present themselves as a respectable party, the ANL publicised the Nazi elements of the NF, with slogans such as 'Stop the Nazi National Front' and 'Don't be taken for a ride – the National Front is Nazi'.[185] This involved a massive dissemination of anti-NF propaganda, with 5,250,000 leaflets and a million badges and stickers distributed during the first year of the ANL's existence.[186]

While the ANL was 'centred on electoral politics' as Paul Gilroy described it, there was still confrontation between ANL supporters and NF members as the ANL mobilised counter-demonstrations against a dwindling NF, but also its supporters 'occupied the public haunts of the National Front members' to prevent paper sales and public meetings.[187] In an internal bulletin produced in May 1979, the SWP Central Committee noted the success of the ANL on two points – the first being that 'a large and credible movement could be built quickly which firmly labelled the NF as Nazis' and the second being that 'the SWP had a much wider audience for our policy of physically confronting the Nazis whenever possible'.[188]

---

180   Geoff Brown, 'Not Quite the Full Picture', *London Socialist Historians Group Newsletter*, 28, Autumn 2006, p. 7.
181   Renton 2006, p. 191.
182   Copsey 2000, p. 131.
183   Messina 1989, p. 118. For narrative histories of the Anti-Nazi League, see Renton 2006; Widgery 1986; Copsey 2000, pp. 130–52.
184   Messina 1989, p. 111; Alexander 1987, p. 155.
185   ANL, 'Emergency Appeal!', *New Statesman*, 30 June 1978, p. 877; ANL, *The Liars of the National Front*, n.d., London: ANL flyer, in CPGB archives, CP/LOC/LEW/05/04, LHASC.
186   Messina 1989, p. 119.
187   Gilroy 2002, p. 171; Hiro 1992, p. 171.
188   SWP Central Committee, 'ANL – A Balance Sheet', *SWP Internal Bulletin*, 2, May 1979, p. 4.

Rock against Racism

Alongside the electoral campaigns, the ANL also co-operated with another initiative started by SWP members, Rock Against Racism (RAR). Rock Against
Racism and the Anti-Nazi League organised a series of carnivals, beginning
with a music festival in Victoria Park on 30 April 1978, combining a number of punk and reggae acts. Attended by around 80,000 people, *The Leveller* described the Carnival as 'the highest-decibel rejection of racism and
fascism ever to hit the UK'.[189] This was followed by 35,000 attending a carnival in Manchester, then 5,000 in Cardiff, 8,000 in Edinburgh, 2,000 in Har-
wich, 5,000 in Southampton, 2,000 in Bradford, before another 100,000 attended the second RAR/ANL Carnival in London on 24 September 1978.[190] The
SWP estimated that between the two carnivals in London, 'something like
400,000 people had been involved in some form of anti-racist anti-nazi activity'.[191]

There is already a growing body of literature on the history of Rock Against
Racism (RAR) and its use of music to raise awareness of racism and mobilise
an anti-racist response amongst British youth.[192] The immediate catalyst for
the launching of Rock Against Racism was a letter written by some younger
activists to the *New Musical Express*, *Melody Maker* and *Socialist Worker* in
response to racist remarks made onstage by Eric Clapton, but as Ian Goodyer
wrote in his study of RAR, 'they were aware that there were bigger fish to fry
than one hypocritical rock star'.[193] The letter declared:

Rock was and still can be a progressive culture not a package mail order
stick-on nightmare of mediocre garbage.
Keep the faith, black and white unite and fight.
We want to organise a rank and file movement against the racist poison
in rock music. We urge support for Rock Against Racism.[194]

---

189   Walker, 'Victoria Park. What Did You Do There? We Got High. We Touched The Sky', *The
       Leveller*, 16, June 1978.
190   Renton 2006, p. 131; Cliff 2000, p. 164.
191   SWP Central Committee, 'ANL – A Balance Sheet', p. 4.
192   See Widgery 1986; Renton 2006, pp. 32–50; pp. 115–35; Frith and Street 1992, pp. 67–80;
       Goodyer 2003, pp. 44–62; Dawson 2005; Goodyer 2002. For criticisms, see Gilroy 2002,
       pp. 151–77; Kalra, Hutnyk and Sharma 1996, pp. 127–55; Sabin 1999, pp. 199–218.
193   Goodyer 2003, p. 44.
194   *Socialist Worker*, 2 October 1976.

The major organisers behind RAR were David Widgery, a writer for *Socialist Worker* and the defunct *Oz*, Roger Huddle, a designer in the *Socialist Worker* artroom, Red Saunders, an 'IS fellow-traveller' and part of a theatre group called the Kartoon Klowns, and Ruth Gregory and Syd Shelton, who were both graphic designers.[195] This group was instrumental in the function of the movement, producing the fanzine *Temporary Hoarding* and other RAR merchandise, such as badges, co-ordinating efforts with the Anti-Nazi League and organising RAR shows, both at local level and the large RAR/ANL Carnivals. The major emphasis on music was based on the growing popularity of punk and reggae amongst British youth, but while this music was characterised as radical and confrontational, it was not inherently progressive or leftist, with the National Front attempting to recruit the white youth attracted to punk.

As the NF shifted towards trying to 'control' the streets, there was a focus on recruiting younger members and after initial discussions throughout 1977, the Young National Front (YNF), with its newspaper *Bulldog*, was established in early 1978.[196] While focussing on issues of race and immigration, the paper also heavily featured stories on football and popular music,[197] particularly punk. As Matthew Worley has shown, punk was 'a contested site of political engagement in the late 1970s'[198] and the YNF enthused about punk as a *white* working-class subculture. Both the SWP and CPGB understood that they needed to engage with youth more to prevent their flirtation with the fascist politics of the NF. In October 1977, the Political Committee of the Communist Party warned:

> The formation of a N.F. youth section should further alert the entire movement of the need to give much more specific and detailed attention and assistance to young people – particularly the unemployed.[199]

The PC suggested that the Party 'should hold discussions with the Y.C.L. at every level, ... to discuss how we can assist the League in its campaigning and reach out to more young people', but by the late 1970s, membership in the YCL was falling even more rapidly than in the CPGB, especially outside of London.[200] The SWP, having long eschewed separate structures for youth members (its youth

---

195   Goodyer 2002, p. 27; p. 23; Renton 2006, p. 33.
196   Shaffer 2013, p. 464.
197   Shaffer 2013, pp. 464–5.
198   Worley 2012, p. 334.
199   CPGB PC Weekly Letter, 20 October 1978, in CPGB archives, CP/CENT/CIRC/68, LHASC.
200   Smith 2012, p. 49.

journal, *Rebel*, had last appeared in 1966–7),[201] looked to Rock Against Racism and Anti-Nazi League to reach out to potential young socialists.

Recognising that punk was 'one of the most important *working class* cultural things to ever happen',[202] Rock Against Racism used the appeal of punk and reggae, which were ambiguous and wide-reaching cultural phenomena, to instil an anti-racist agenda in British youth. Like the Anti-Nazi League, Rock Against Racism was about spreading the anti-NF and anti-racist message and not necessarily about recruitment. 'The point of RAR', Simon Frith and John Street wrote in *Marxism Today* in the mid-1980s, 'was not to change a party but to destroy one, the National Front'.[203] The Socialist Workers Party was instrumental in the function of RAR, especially with the production of *Temporary Hoarding*, but unlike its prominent role in the ANL, the SWP was much more restrained in controlling Rock Against Racism. This allowed RAR to freely 'work with issues and ideas which fell outside the formal political agenda',[204] such as celebrating cultural radicalism, the use of punk and reggae music, Dada and Russian Constructivist inspired cut-and-paste fanzines, the influence of 1960s counter-culture and youthful language. However, RAR did not abandon traditional leftist politics entirely, with Dick Hebdige noting that RAR maintained an 'old sense of political priorities and tactics', such as 'marching, changing minds to change the world, exposing and explaining the historical roots of racism in *Temporary Hoarding*, identifying the enemy, "raising consciousness"'.[205] As Ian Goodyer has written, the original letter to *NME* called for a 'rank and file movement against the racist poison in rock music', which 'echoe[d] the language of the Left and reminds us of the socialist credentials of the letter's signatories'.[206]

While successful in distributing the anti-NF message amongst British youth, the momentum of RAR (and the ANL) was temporary, although the SWP did not see a broad coalition as useful in the long-term. Ian Birchall wrote of the lessons of Rock Against Racism and the Anti-Nazi League in *International Socialism*: 'how do the revolutionaries act to build a successful broad front, but at the same time recruit to their own organisation, the only effective way of constructing a barrier against reformist influence?'[207] This juxtaposition between

201 Birchall 2011, p. 255.
202 'Look Get It Straight', *Socialist Review*, July/August 1978, p. 14; Italics are in the original text.
203 Frith and Street, 'Party Music', *Marxism Today*, June 1986, p. 28.
204 Frith and Street 1992, p. 79.
205 Hebdige 1988, p. 214.
206 Goodyer 2002, p. 27.
207 Birchall, 'Only Rock and Roll? A Review of D. Widgery, *Beating Time*', *International Socialism*, 2/33, Autumn 1986, p. 127.

broad alliances and recruitment to a political organisation with a more defined
agenda was also experienced by the Communist Party. The Party had warned
in its other literature about attempting to promote explicit CPGB policies in
other broad organisations,[208] but it still emphasised amongst its members that
recruitment needed attention. After the first RAR/ANL Carnival in London in
April 1978, the London District Committee of the CPGB acknowledged that the
Carnival had brought out many working-class youth, but the Party's response
had been 'inadequate',[209] while the Lewisham CPGB Branch noted that this
lack of response showed the problems of the Young Communist League's work
amongst working-class youth.[210] As Graham Stevenson remarked in his study
of the postwar YCL, despite the mobilisation of many young people through
RAR/ANL, the YCL 'did not profit from these struggles'.[211]

The *Morning Star* had reported that unions, trade councils, the CPGB and the
SWP were all present at the Carnival, but Steve Munby, editor of the YCL's paper
Challenge in 1978, pointed out that these organisations 'constituted a clear
minority'.[212] The organisers of RAR had written in a letter to *Socialist Review*
that these traditional political organisations did not 'understand working class
kids NOW are political and fun without having to make 5 minute speeches to
prove it'.[213] Munby recognised that most young people attended the Carnival
for the music, but emphasised the potential 'strong progressive elements' of the
music, declaring that punk, reggae and new wave were 'of particular *political*
importance'.[214] In *Comment*, Paul Bradshaw, editor of *Challenge* from late 1975
to late 1977, wrote that the RAR/ANL Carnival was 'critical because they've
broken out of the traditional political approach', describing them as a 'fusion of
cultural rebellion and political action'.[215] Bradshaw saw the role of the Carnival
as important, but stated that local and regional RAR events were 'vital elements
in carrying the fight [against racism] forward'.[216] This point is not elaborated

208   NRRC, *Racism: How to Combat It*, 1978, London: CPGB pamphlet, p. 3.
209   Handwritten note of LDC meeting, 21 May 1978, in CPGB archives, CP/LON/DC/08/08,
      LHASC.
210   Diary Planner of Lewisham CPGB Branch, 15 May 1978, in CPGB archives, CP/LON/LEW/
      02/07, LHASC.
211   Stevenson, 'The YCL 1966–1980 – Anatomy of Decline', available at: http://graham
      .thewebtailor.co.uk/archives/000044.html, accessed 13 April 2005.
212   Munby, 'Close Encounters with the Third Reich', *Challenge*, 53, June 1978, p. 3.
213   'Look Get It Straight', p. 14.
214   Munby, 'Close Encounters with the Third Reich', p. 3.
215   Bradshaw, 'Carnivals & Confrontations', *Comment*, 14 October 1978, p. 328.
216   Ibid.

upon by Bradshaw and was rarely, if ever, mentioned in other CPGB literature on Rock Against Racism or the Anti-Nazi League.

The importance of Rock Against Racism was its focus upon local actions, with many smaller gigs organised that were not connected to the major RAR/ANL Carnivals. At the height of the RAR/ANL campaigns in 1978, there were 300 Rock Against Racism shows, alongside the major Carnivals, as well as another 23 shows on the 'Militant Entertainment Tour' in the months before the 1979 General Election.[217] However, young CPGB/YCL members were more likely to be involved in separate Communist Party run events, such as the People's Jubilee at Alexandra Palace in June 1977, than with Rock Against Racism. In a briefing document on anti-racist activities for Party branches produced by the CPGB's National Student Committee (NSC), the Party saw youth events as 'basically political or cultural', rather than being able to fuse the two elements.[218] Although the NSC advised contacting 'all the social, cultural, political and religious groups and societies' to seek contributions to the event, these anti-racist 'festivals' were very much seen as Communist Party run and there was little interaction with Rock Against Racism, besides the briefing document advising that RAR 'have a lot of good stuff including badges'.[219]

While the CPGB and YCL had debated the importance of youth culture in the pages of *Marxism Today* in 1973–4, the YCL (or the Party itself) were slow to acknowledge the role of new music, such as punk, in youth culture in the late 1970s. In June 1976, Paul Bradshaw claimed, 'Generally the music of the seventies, has ... not been of the youth and does not reflect the overt struggles they are involved in', although he stated that reggae was 'undoubtedly the most militant, political music around'.[220] At the same time that punk was emerging and a month before the riot at the 1976 Notting Hill Carnival, Bradshaw lamented, 'Certainly within the existing deep crisis of capitalism, one would expect new forms of culture, especially through music, to develop and give expression to the problems facing youth'.[221] While Bradshaw thought this 'ha[d] not been the case so far', he did warn, as did the organisers of Rock Against Racism,

---

217   Xerox, 'And They Still Say Wanking Will Turn You Blind', *Temporary Hoarding*, 8, March/April 1979, p. 2; 'RAR Militant Entertainment Tour '79', *Temporary Hoarding*, 8, March/April 1979, p. 6.

218   National Student Committee, 'Briefing Document', in CPGB archives, CP/LON/ADVS/13/03, LHASC.

219   Ibid.

220   Bradshaw, 'Trends in Youth Culture in the 1970's', *Cogito*, 3, 1976, p. 12, in CPGB archives, CP/YCL/21/01, LHASC.

221   Bradshaw, 'Trends in Youth Culture in the 1970's', p. 12.

of the 'danger of a rightward swing amongst young people'.[222] However, while the YCL worked within the traditional socialist 'festivals' arena, Rock Against Racism mobilised youth for an anti-racist movement, with its first letter published in September 1976 and the first RAR show performed on 10 December 1976.[223] An anonymous YCL member from London had written in *Challenge* in June 1976 that '[t]he left ignore popular culture at their peril',[224] but the YCL (and the CPGB) were slow to realise the potential of punk and reggae, as popular youth cultures, to mobilise anti-racist and anti-fascist activism. While having some presence in the Anti-Nazi League, the Communist Party, besides paper sales and strong coverage at the RAR/ANL carnivals, had little practical to do with Rock Against Racism. There were some Communist Party members who admired and supported RAR, viewing it as a demonstration of the broad democratic alliance, with the Political Committee describing the RAR/ANL Carnival as the 'biggest, most inspiring and politically important demonstration for some years',[225] but this support was different from actual involvement.

In his analysis of the shift towards Thatcherism in 'The Great Moving Right Show' that featured in *Marxism Today* in January 1979, Stuart Hall described Rock Against Racism as 'one of the timeliest and best constructed of cultural interventions' and the 'direct interventions against the rising fortunes of the National Front' was 'one of the few success stories' of a demoralised left.[226] One of the purposes of Hall's article was to depict the broad alliances formed against the NF, primarily the work of the Anti-Nazi League, as an example of the strategy outlined in *The British Road to Socialism* and to see the shift to the right as more than 'a simple expression of the economic crisis',[227] which needed different strategies than traditional class-based militancy. Hall argued that the Communist Party, like many on the left and within the labour movement, was unable to recognise the ideological and cultural activism that RAR epitomised had to be expanded to the ideological shift to the right, what Hall described as 'a decisive shift in the balance of hegemony', that was represented by the National Front and the much larger threat of Thatcherism.[228]

---

222   Ibid.
223   Renton 2006, p. 34.
224   'Bowie', *Challenge*, 35, June/July 1976, p. 8.
225   CPGB PC Weekly Letter, 3 May 1978, in CPGB archives, CP/CENT/CIRC/68/07, LHASC.
226   Stuart Hall, 'The Great Moving Right Show', p. 15.
227   Stuart Hall, 'The Great Moving Right Show', p. 14.
228   Stuart Hall, 'The Great Moving Right Show', p. 15.

The ANL and the Wider British Left

Although the SWP did have a significant presence within the ANL, it was the simplicity of the ANL's message of opposing the NF Nazis, easily identifiable and objected to by most, that helped the ANL succeed in destroying popular support for the NF. Because the ANL was geared towards quick mobilisation of massive numbers and the straightforward single issue of opposing the NF, the structure of the ANL was seen to be 'barely controlled at all', in particular to avoid sectarian differences obstructing swift action, although it was noted this lack of control did not hide the fact that the ANL had been 'efficient in producing and distributing its propaganda'.[229] With Paul Holborrow and Nigel Harris on its Steering Committee, the 'Socialist Workers' Party supplied the Anti-Nazi League with its organisational backbone',[230] but this was more indicative of the young and proactive nature of a lot of the SWP's members and not of an 'SWP front'.[231] The SWP stressed in its internal bulletin that the ANL was 'not a front for the SWP' and the ANL did 'not have a clear position at all ... on many things we regard as a matter of principle'.[232] However, it did emphasise maintaining 'our own independent SWP presence in the ANL' which meant not 'turning ANL meetings into SWP recruitment meetings'.[233] The structure of the ANL was a contentious issue from time to time and some felt that it needed some formalised direction, which then had the potential to alienate other supporters. The Communist Party also had reservations about the structure and organisation of the Anti-Nazi League. The CPGB supported the ANL as a 'propaganda and campaigning organisation *against the National Front*'.[234] In the important NRRC pamphlet produced by the Party in 1978, *Racism: How to Combat It*, the CPGB noted that the ANL was 'primarily an action organisation' and its structure 'lends itself to fast impressive mobilisation', acknowledging that at this task 'the ANL has shown itself first-class'.[235]

---

229   Weightman, 'Flogging Anti-Racism', *New Society*, 11 May 1978, p. 294.

230   Copsey 2000, p. 133.

231   Although Tony Cliff announced in *The Leveller*, 'The leadership of the ANL is in reality the SWP and we don't hide it, we don't give a damn'. Cliff, 'Sell the Paper! Build the Party!', *The Leveller*, 30 September 1979, p. 20.

232   SWP Central Committee, 'Perspectives for the 1978 Conference', *SWP Internal Bulletin*, Pre-Conference Issue 2, May 1978, p. 5; Italics are in the original text.

233   Ibid.

234   PC Weekly Letter, 6 April 1978; Italics are in the original text.

235   NRRC, *Racism: How to Combat It*, 1978, London: CPGB pamphlet, p. 2.

The fact that the ANL did not have a delegate structure and organisations could only become sponsors meant that 'Any group of people can constitute themselves as an Anti-Nazi League group ... and organise them how they wish', as described in the NRRC pamphlet.[236] These local ANLs had the potential to be marred by sectarianism between the leftist groups and the CPGB was still suspicious of the IMG 'using the ANL at local level as a front organisation'.[237] In the minutes of the Lewisham CPGB Branch, it was suggested that the Party's Political Committee had originally agreed to affiliate to the ANL in an attempt to 'counteract any ultra-left tendency' within the League.[238] The Party felt that 'it is up to us to turn [the local ANLs] into broad based committees which work alongside local anti-racialist committees'.[239] This point was stressed by the Party in the NRRC pamphlet that 'we need many more ANLs *and* a strengthening of the work of the anti-racism campaigns', declaring that, 'we do not need the one posed against the other'.[240] In an article in *Marxism Today* in July 1978, Gideon Ben-Tovim noted that the most 'imaginative and contemporary approach to anti-fascist struggle' was the ANL, 'in which the "old left" – Tribune MPs, the Communist Party and the trade union movement – have not been major forces'.[241] The ANL reflected the Broad Democratic Alliance espoused by *The British Road to Socialism* and, therefore, the CPGB could act as a 'major, though by no means, unifying force', due to its 'heterogeneous membership, its contacts and roots'.[242] The NRRC pamphlet instructed that CPGB branches and Area Committees 'should become co-sponsors of existing ANLs, becoming involved in their activities, and becoming individual ANL members'.[243] The Merseyside CPGB branch instructed that members 'join the ANL branch in their locality, work place or college' and '[i]f one doesn't exist – then set one up'.[244] In the Hackney branch, one of the most active branches on the issue of anti-racism, Branch Secretary Monty Goldman, noted that 12 CPGB members were

236   NRRC, *Racism*, p. 2.
237   NSC minutes, 19/20 May 1978, in CPGB archives, CP/LON/ADVS/13/03, LHASC.
238   Diary Planner of Lewisham CPGB Branch, 20 March 1978, in CPGB archives, CP/LON/LEW/ 02/07, LHASC.
239   'NSC Notes', 4, 23 May 1978, in CPGB archives, CP/LON/ADVDS/13/03, LHASC.
240   NRRC, *Racism*, p. 3.
241   Ben-Tovim, 'The Struggle Against Racism: Theoretical and Strategic Perspectives', *Marxism Today*, July 1978, p. 212.
242   Ben-Tovim, 'The Struggle Against Racism', p. 213.
243   NRRC, *Racism*, p. 3.
244   Merseyside CPGB Branch, 'Merseyside Against Racism and the Nazis', *Under the Bed*, 1, November 1978, p. 5, in CPGB archives, CP/LOC/NW/04/10, LHASC.

involved in ANL groups in Hackney,[245] while Tony Gilbert, member of the Hackney branch and the NRRC, attended the ANL conference as a representative of Liberation.[246]

The Lewisham CPGB Branch noted in its minutes on May 1978 that it was evident at the RAR/ANL carnival in Victoria Park that there was a problem with the CPGB's inability to implement its own strategy and remarked that the presence of the SWP 'shows [the] need to build [a] People's Front'.[247] The SWP stressed that the ANL was 'a *united front* [my emphasis] between us and many other people formed around a political programme that does not go nearly as far as our own'.[248] The emphasis of the united front, which combined 'mass propaganda ... with militant action', was contrasted by the SWP with the assertion that 'the CPGB always attempted to push the ANL towards Popular Frontism'.[249] The SWP saw the Anti-Nazi League as a united struggle by all those concerned with the rise of the National Front, but with the SWP maintaining its independence within the League. This was compared with the Broad Democratic Alliance of the CPGB where 'criticism must be muted and struggles restrained so as not to offend union bureaucrats, left MPs or churchmen'.[250] The Anti-Nazi League was praised by the CPGB reformers for its similarities to the Party's own Broad Democratic Alliance, the Popular Front strategy for the 1970s. The SWP, opposing the Popular Front, denied that the ANL was such a Front. The contrast between the ANL and 'the Communist Party-dominated popular fronts' was, according to Paul Holborrow, over the degree of action taken: 'It was a complete break from the other campaigns, which had been completely ruled by the pace of the most conservative groups. We were activists, we would do something quickly rather than deliberating and do nothing'.[251]

By the end of 1978, the Anti-Nazi League had begun to stagnate.[252] While 1977 had seen a temporary resurgence in the NF's electoral presence, the local

---

245 Monty Goldman, 'Secretary's Report', Hackney Borough Conference Report, 1978, in CPGB archives, CP/IND/KAY/03/06, LHASC.

246 'Minutes of LDCP Race Relations Advisory', 27 July 1978, in CPGB archives, CP/LON/RACE/02/06, LHASC.

247 Minutes of Lewisham CPGB Branch in Diary Planner, 15 May 1978, in CPGB archives, CP/LON/LEW/02/07, LHASC.

248 SWP Central Committee, 'Perspectives for the 1978 Conference', p. 5.

249 SWP Central Committee, 'Opposing the Nazis', SWP Discussion Bulletin, 1, 1984, p. 11.

250 Goodwin, 'The United Front', International Socialism, 1/104, January 1978, p. 19.

251 Cited in Renton 2006, p. 105.

252 Copsey 2000, p. 146.

government elections in the summer of 1978 saw their share of the vote fall significantly, with votes falling in Dudley by 5.6 percent, Wolverhampton by 5.1 percent, Solihull by 4 percent and Rotherham by 2.7 percent, alongside Bradford's vote falling from 12.3 percent in 1976 to 3.1 in 1978.[253] To counter this slide on the electoral front, the NF tried to emphasise its street presence, such as the laying of a wreath on Remembrance Sunday at the Cenotaph and attack on Brick Lane on the day of the second RAR/ANL Carnival in September 1978. Although the attack on Brick Lane was a tactical misjudgement by the ANL (and by the police who were guarding the Carnival), most of the attempts by the NF to mobilise on the street were still met by thousands of police and anti-fascist protestors. According to the Home Secretary Merlyn Rees, over 3,200 police were deployed to 'keep the peace' while NF members lay the Cenotaph wreath and the CPGB estimated that around 2,000 NF supporters attended this event.[254] The Political Committee of the Party warned the following week:

> This, together with their ability to maintain a number of centres of public activity and acquire premises is a warning that despite the public setbacks the Front has suffered in recent months their ability to secure a mobilisation of members and supporters is still much too great for the comfort of democrats and anti-racialists.[255]

Despite a massive decline in support, the NF still committed itself to electoral politics and in the General Election of May 1979, they put forward 303 candidates, 297 in England, five in Wales and one in Scotland.[256] As a result of the ANL's mobilisation and the unwillingness of local councils to hire out venues to the NF, the National Front 'pinned its hopes on a relatively small number of election meetings, marches and rallies'.[257] In the final days of the NF's election campaign, the NF decided to hold a meeting at Southall Town Hall on St George's Day, 23 April 1979. The reaction by the left and the local black community led to a major police operation, with the result being hundreds of injuries and the death of one anti-fascist protestor.

---

253   'An Analysis of NF votes', *Searchlight*, 36 June 1978, p. 4.
254   *Hansard*, House of Commons, 24 November 1978, col. 762w; CPGB PC weekly letter, 16 November 1978, p. 2, in CPGB archives, CP/CENT/CIRC/68/07, LHASC.
255   Ibid.
256   Husbands 1988, p. 67.
257   Copsey 2000, p. 146.

Southall and the Death of Blair Peach

To oppose the National Front's meeting at Southall Town Hall on 23 April 1979, a community meeting, called by the Southall IWA, was held on 11 April and decided on a course of action to petition the council to refuse the NF access to the Town Hall, march from Southall to Ealing Town Hall on 22 April and that 'all businesses, restaurants, shops, etc. should shut down on 23 April from 1 p.m. onwards'.[258] Sharma explained that this form of protest was called a 'Hartal' and was 'quite a common tactic in India'.[259] Sharma also emphasised that the 11 April meeting had 'decided not to resort to confrontation with the police' and organised a 'massive peaceful sitdown' outside the Town Hall.[260] The SWP, the ANL and Socialist Unity, an organisation led by Tariq Ali that incorporated the IMG, had called for a protest march on 23 April, but had been 'turned down by local groupings in favour of the sit-down protest'.[261]

The NF meeting was to begin at 7.30pm and the protest had been scheduled to commence from 5 p.m., but confrontations between police and youth had been occurring since the early afternoon. With over 2,700 police involved, around 2,000 demonstrators were confronted by the police and the Special Patrol Group (SPG), which began to prevent demonstrators from protesting outside the front of the Town Hall.[262] Dave Renton has written that 'Between 7.30 and 9 p.m., Southall witnessed a full-scale police riot'.[263] The SWP pamphlet, *Southall: The Fight For Our Future*, described the events:

> The first lines of foot police opened up and made way for SPG men with riot shields and hoards of baton-wielding police on horseback. Some demonstrators tried to defend themselves by throwing bricks. But it was useless. The mounties ran amock, joking, laughing and making racist remarks as they smashed skulls with their batons. The footmen followed up using riot shields as weapons and arresting anyone ... The police violence did nothing to control the situation.[264]

258　Cited in Renton 2006, p. 141.
259　'Interview with Vishnu Sharma', *Marxism Today*, December 1979, p. 22.
260　Ibid.
261　Grewal 2003, p. 3.
262　Renton 2006, p. 143; Grewal 2003, p. 4.
263　Renton 2006, p. 146.
264　SWP, *Southall: The Fight For Our Future*, n.d., London: SWP pamphlet, p. 3.

At around 7.45pm, Blair Peach, an ANL and SWP member, was 'struck on the head by an assailant widely believed to have been a member of the SPG', dying of his injuries after midnight.[265] By the end of the night, 342 people, 'mostly Asian and local', had been arrested.[266] Of those arrested, 23 percent were arrested for allegedly assaulting a police officer, 28 percent for obstruction, 26 percent for threatening behaviour and 15 percent for possessing an offensive weapon, with a handful charged with 'actual bodily harm, grievous bodily harm, malicious wounding, criminal damage, [and] abusive language'.[267] Of those charged, approximately 10 percent were facing more than one charge.[268]

The following day's *Morning Star*, having gone to press before Blair Peach's death was announced, reported the 'total shutdown' of Southall.[269] The paper reported the police claims of 250 demonstrators arrested during the evening and 77 arrested in the afternoon, along with 40 people taken to Ealing Hospital, including 18 policemen.[270] The next day's *Morning Star* contained the headline, 'Curb The Mad Dogs Of Racism!', declaring that 'Rees, McNee and Thatcher – All to Blame in Southall Tragedy'.[271] Home Secretary Merlyn Rees was accused of allowing the NF 'to spread its racist poison in clear violation of the Race Relations Act' and that the 'holding of an election does not annul the Race Relations Act, nor absolve Mr Rees of the responsibility to ensure that it is rigorously applied'.[272] Metropolitan Police Commissioner David McNee was also accused of 'protecting a handful of racist hoodlums', when it was McNee's 'duty to protect the freedom of the citizens of Southall', but he had failed to do so, and 'On the contrary, his men assaulted them, left, right and centre'.[273] Thatcher was also criticised for 'encouraging the growth of racism' and the *Morning Star* declared: 'it is sheer humbug for Mrs. Thatcher and Co. to prattle on about law and order when she talks about Britain being swamped by black people'.[274] The CPGB reiterated its line that 'throwing missiles at the police is not the way to fight racism', but understood 'the sense of frustration, anger and

---

265 Grewal 2003, p. 5.
266 CARF/Southall Rights, *Southall*, p. 60.
267 Southall Campaign Committee/Friends of Blair Peach Committee joint bulletin, n.d., MS 2141/C/1, in Indian Workers Association papers, Birmingham City Archive.
268 Ibid.
269 *Morning Star*, 24 April 1979.
270 Ibid.
271 *Morning Star*, 25 April 1979.
272 Ibid.
273 Ibid.
274 Ibid.

outrage' felt by the black community in Southall.[275] Whatever violent action was taken by the protestors on 23 April, the *Morning Star* stated that the 'real violence in Southall was the officially sponsored violence from mobs of police, apparently including the notorious Special Patrol Group, who simply went beserk [sic]'.[276] The death of Blair Peach and the violent clashes in Southall were 'the direct result of the toleration of the National Front provocations by the authorities', declared CPGB General Secretary Gordon McLennan, tolerance that the CPGB thought should be remedied by the use of the Race Relations Act to its full extent.[277] As the death occurred during the dissolution of Parliament, it fell to the incoming Conservatives to decide whether to hold a public inquiry into the events at Southall. On 25 May 1979, Conservative MP Leon Brittan announced that 'various inquiries' were underway and these internal inquiries were 'the right and proper course to establish the facts of what occurred and to deal with the allegations and complaints'. Syd Bidwell, the local Labour member for Southall, pushed for a judicial inquiry, but Brittan argued that a decision about this should be delayed until after a report was completed by Police Commissioner David McNee.[278]

Approximately 15,000 people marched through Southall on 28 April 1979 in memory of Blair Peach.[279] A public inquiry, like that held by Lord Scarman after Red Lion Square, was never held, but there was a coronial inquest and an unofficial inquiry held by the National Council of Civil Liberties (NCCL). Commander John Cass held an internal inquest into Peach's death for the Metropolitan Police, which uncovered a stash of illegal weapons held by officers of the SPG, which could have caused similar injuries to those sustained by Peach. Despite this, the results of this inquest were closed until 2010. David Renton's examination of the documents that Cass compiled and his final report shows that Cass identified three police officers that were likely to have been involved in the killing of Peach, but 'advised there was too little evidence to go on to identify any of them individually' before proposing that 'the officers involved had conspired to pervert the course of justice and to obstruct an investigation'.[280] However, shortly after the Cass report was completed, the Director of Public Proseuctions Sir Thomas Hetherington announced that

---

275   Ibid.
276   Ibid.
277   Ibid.
278   *Hansard*, 25 May 1979, col. 1404.
279   Grewal 2003, p. 6.
280   Renton 2014, p. 27.

no police officers would be charged with any offence relating to Peach's death or its investigation.[281]

According to files opened in 2007 by the National Archives, the Director of Public Prosecutions decided after reading the Cass Report that 'the available evidence was insufficient to justify any criminal proceedings', while the coroner's inquest, held at the same time, was 'prohibited by law from appearing to determine any matter of either civil or criminal liability'.[282] When it was announced that the National Council of Civil Liberties was to hold an unofficial 'people's inquiry' into the events of 23 April 1979 at Southall, the government retorted that there were five internal investigations already occurring and that the Home Secretary had concluded that 'there is no significant gap in the various inquiries which have taken place into Southall which a public inquiry could usefully fill'. The only public discussion would be a Green Paper on the effectiveness of the Public Order Act 1936.[283] A letter from the Home Office's Assistant Secretary, G.H. Phillips, to Stephen Boys-Smith further demonstrated that the government was able to use the possibility of Blair Peach's family launching a civil case to resist announcing a public inquiry. After the five internal reports recommended that no criminal action should be taken, the government felt by mid-1980 that this was the best time to 'draw a line under the issue of a public inquiry into Southall'.[284]

'Feeling Rather Swamped': Thatcher and the Exploitation of Popular Racism

In the May General Election, the National Front received only 1.3 percent of the vote out of the 303 electorates challenged.[285] Margaret Thatcher and the Conservatives won the election convincingly and ushered in 18 years of Conservative rule. As Maurice Ludmer warned in *Searchlight* the previous summer, 'The Front has suffered a major blow, but the racism on which it breeds is alive and well and living in Conservative Central Office'.[286] Alongside the important antifascist work done by the Anti-Nazi League, one of the other primary reasons for

---

281   Renton 2014, p. 28.
282   Letter to Arthur Lewis MP, July 1980, HO 299/114, in NA.
283   'NCCL Inquiry', 25 July 1980, HO 299/114, in NA.
284   'Blair Peach and Southall: After the Inquiry', memo from G.H. Phillips to S. Boys-Smith, 30 May 1980, HO 299/111.
285   Husbands 1988, p. 67.
286   'Editorial', *Searchlight*, 36, June 1978, p. 2.

the demise of the NF at the General Election was the appeal of Thatcher's right-wing populism to potential NF voters. As Richard Thurlow wrote, Thatcher's 'forceful aggressive leadership, her uncompromising stance on law and order, the stand against the unions and the illiberal attitude towards immigration' had demonstrated Thatcherism was a powerful alternative to the dwindling fortunes of the National Front and thus, 'Attacked by the left, undermined by the state and having its appeal to patriotism made unnecessary by the actions of Mrs Thatcher, the racial populist neo-fascist right had nowhere to go'.[287] The NF split into three different factions, while the openly neo-Nazi British Movement continued, recruiting heavily amongst the young skinheads left unemployed by Thatcher's economic policies.

It was an interview given to Granada Television's *World in Action* in January 1978 by Thatcher that explicitly declared her position on race relations and immigration, which saw her stake out ground on the populist right – a Powellite declaration that had the impact of siphoning off some people who were 'soft' NF supporters. In her interview, Thatcher repeated the dictum that had shaped British immigration law since the 1960s, that 'if you want good race relations, you have got to allay people's fears on numbers', claiming that around 45–50,000 immigrants were entering Britain per year, although two-thirds of immigrants accepted in 1976 were the wives or children of already working residents and this still represented fewer than four for every 100 people in Britain.[288] Playing the 'numbers game', Thatcher described this as 'an awful lot' and stated that 'people are really rather afraid that this country might be rather swamped by people with a different culture', thus the 'moment the minority threatens to become a big one, people get frightened'.[289] Thatcher declared that, 'We are a British nation with British characteristics' and to 'keep good race relations and ... fundamental British characteristics', the Conservatives planned a 'clear end to immigration'.[290] This was despite the fact that permanent migration of workers from the Commonwealth had already been brought 'to a halt' by the 1971 Immigration Act.[291] The CPGB's Political Committee described Thatcher's statements as 'the most sinister one on race relations since Powell's "Tiber running with blood" speech' and that she was 'now

---

287   Thurlow 1987, p. 286.
288   Margaret Thatcher, TV interview for Granada *World in Action*, available at: http://www
       .margaretthatcher.org/speeches/displaydocument.asp?docid=103485, accessed 13 July
       2006; *The Guardian*, 1 February 1978.
289   Ibid.
290   Ibid.
291   Spencer 1997, p. 143.

openly using the language of Powell and the National Front'.[292] By adopting
the language and policies of the NF, Thatcher's method was to get 'people who
now vote National Front to vote Tory', but the effect of Thatcher's statements,
claimed the Communist Party, was to 'increase [the NF's] prestige instead of
exposing it as a menace' and 'increase hostility to black people here'.[293] The
revival of 'race' and immigration as political issues for the Conservatives under
Thatcher was described by Vishnu Sharma in a 1979 Communist Party pamphlet:

> All along the line Labour and Conservative governments have retreated
> in the face of racist clamour. Now we have a government which is not
> being pushed. It is leading. Although the National Front, and other fascist
> groupings of the far right, continue to present a very real threat, the main
> racist injection into British politics over the next period is likely to be the
> new legislation of the government.[294]

This demonisation of black immigrants was part of a wider phenomenon
within Thatcherite populism that combined 'organic Toryism ... with the
aggressive theme of a revived neo-liberalism'.[295] This phenomenon of 'Thatcherism' was analysed by Stuart Hall and Martin Jacques in *Marxism Today* as
the Communist Party and the wider left attempted to arrest their decline after
the 'British upturn' of the early 1970s. Hall was not a member of the Communist Party, but had long been a fellow traveller of the Party, contributing
to *Marxism Today* and speaking at the Communist University of London, an
annual forum held by the CPGB in the 1970s, increasingly used to discuss the
ideas of the Party's reformers. As the reformers, such as Jacques, looked to
appeal to the wider left and activists under the strategy of the broad democratic
alliance, Hall became one of the most influential thinkers for the Communist Party, with significant impact on the Party's approach to race and cultural
politics. In January 1979, *Marxism Today* published Hall's 'The Great Moving
Right Show', which analysed the politics of Thatcherism, describing it as more
than just 'the corresponding political bedfellow of a period of capitalist reces-
sion',[296] but the result of a longer ideological shift away from the parameters

---

292   CPGB PC Weekly Letter, 2 February 1978, in CPGB archives, CP/CENT/PC/14/20, LHASC.
293   Ibid.
294   Sharma, *No Racist Immigration Laws*, 1979, London: CPGB pamphlet, p. 11.
295   Hall 1988, p. 48.
296   Hall 1979, p. 14.

of postwar social democracy. Thatcherism encompassed many themes of the right – 'law and order, the need for social discipline and authority in the face of a conspiracy by the enemies of the state, the onset of social anarchy, the "enemy within", the dilution of British stock by alien black elements'[297] – but found a greater reception for the repressive measures needed to deal with these concerns in the economic crisis of the late 1970s. Thatcherism inherited the ideas of Powellism and the far (radical) right, using the language of 'nation' and the 'people' against what it saw as dividing British society, 'class' and the 'unions'.[298] This is what Jacques described as 'the underlying crisis of hegemony', in which Thatcher asserted a 'popular *and* authoritarian rightism' as the solution to 'a more divided and polarised society'.[299] Written in the months following Thatcher's electoral victory, Jacques outlined two main themes within Thatcher's populist appeal. The first was an emphasis on traditional laissez-faire economics, 'the virtues of the market, competition, elitism, individual initiative, the iniquities of state intervention and bureaucracy'.[300] The other was using the right's traditional theme of 'law and order', 'reacting against trade union militancy, national aspirations, permissiveness, women's liberation', replacing it with 'an essentially regressive and conservative solution embracing such themes as authority, law and order, patriotism, national unity, the family and individual freedom'.[301] Thatcherism was significantly different from previous Conservative governments which saw its emphasis of 'law and order' as central to revitalising the British nation, which meant turning the repressive institutions of the state upon those elements of British society viewed as 'subversive', including Britain's black population. As Vishnu Sharma wrote in a 1979 CPGB pamphlet:

> The Thatcher government is not a re-run of the previous Tory Heath administration. What is under assault is every aspect of progressive achievement of the working class ... As part of this attack, as sure as night follows day, the Conservatives will turn their attention to immigration.[302]

Hall and Jacques's analysis was an important contribution to the political reassessment that the Party was undergoing as a reaction to what Geoff Andrews

297 Hall 1979, p. 16.
298 Hall 1979, p. 17.
299 Jacques 1979, p. 10; Italics are in the original text.
300 Ibid.
301 Ibid.
302 Sharma, *No Racist Immigration Laws*, p. 3.

described as 'the crisis of labourism',[303] the decline of the traditional industrial militant strategy. The reformers in the Party had influenced the redrafting of the Party's programme, *The British Road to Socialism*, in 1977, which proposed the broad democratic alliance in a move away from defensive industrial union-ism as its main focus. Trevor Carter wrote in *Shattering Illusions* that Thatcher's victory only compounded the upsurge in racism that had already begun in the mid-1970s, stating, 'You could say that the black community had a head-start of three years over the rest of the left in the battle against Thatcherism'.[304] While the left had great success with the Anti-Nazi League and drew mass support at Grunwick (although it was eventually defeated), there was still 'little involve-ment by the labour and trade union movement in the main concerns of black people'[305] and the black community was alienated from the political process of organised unionism that was failing the wider left by the time of Thatcher's election. As Carter wrote, 'it took Thatcher's defeat of Labour to drive the left into its first serious examination of the identity and whereabouts of the work-ing class and to accept that it was not only white and male'.[306] The impact of this upon the political activism of black Britons in the 1980s will be examined in the next chapter.

Conclusion

The late 1970s had seen the coming together of black and white workers to cam-paign against racism and fascism in Britain and serious in-roads had been made to overcome the bifurcation of the British working class, as Satnam Virdee described it,[307] that had been present in the late 1960s and early 1970s. The two-year strike at the Grunwick Photo Processing Plant and the struggle against the National Front (incorporating the Anti-Nazi League and Rock Against Racism) demonstrated that collective action between black and white activists was pos-sible and provided an example of how anti-racist and working-class solidarity could be expressed. The support that the striking Asian workforce received at Grunwick was very different from the trade unions' handling of other unorgan-ised strikes by Asian workers at Mansfield Hosiery Mills and Imperial Type-writers in the early 1970s, with APEX, the TGWU and other unions bringing

---

303   Andrews 2004, p. 202.
304   Carter 1986, p. 115.
305   Carter 1986, p. 116.
306   Carter 1986, p. 115.
307   Virdee 2014, p. 123.

their membership to the north London factory and reaching its zenith with the mass pickets in July 1977. The Anti-Nazi League and its sister organisation, Rock Against Racism, also mobilised people on an unprecedented scale against the National Front (and against racism more broadly) and this was highly successful in arresting the electoral fortunes of the NF, as well as challenging their determination to win 'the streets'. Nearly every public appearance by the NF in the late 1970s brought out a much larger counter-demonstration and soon it became almost impossible for the NF to organise visibly without a vocal anti-fascist presence, but also a large (and increasingly confrontational) police contingent. The success of the ANL saw the NF perform very badly at the 1979 election, but anti-racists and working-class activists were confronted with a much more powerful threat – a combative Conservative government under Margaret Thatcher.

But there were also tensions running through this period of increased solidarity and co-operation between black and white workers and activists. Despite the significant trade union support for the Grunwick strike, it ultimately failed as the owners of the factory refused to co-operate with the ACAS findings and the strike petered out in early 1978. Many were to blame the defeat of the strike on the TUC and the strategy of seeking a ruling from ACAS, instead of engaging in secondary picketing and blacking in other industries (which could have been effective, yet illegal). A number of black activists contended that the involvement of the trade union bureaucrats at Grunwick had led them away from support from the Asian community (which had sustained the earlier strikes at Mansfield Hosiery Mills and Imperial Typewriters), but also tied them to the machinery of the official labour movement, which left the strikers floundering when Grunwick's owners did not comply with it. As Paul Gordon wrote:

> More important, perhaps, than the defeat itself was the fact that Grunwick marked the end of an era of vibrant and creative black struggles which had threatened to bring a political dimension to industrial struggle. It was an end brought about by the invasion of official trade unionism, which had moved from a position of opposition or apathy towards black workers to a strategy of control through co-option.[308]

While successfully mobilising against the fascist NF, many were concerned that the anti-racist movement, especially the ANL, had no real strategy for taking on the racism of the new Thatcher government. Throughout 1979 and 1980, there

---

308   Gordon 1985, p. 172; p. 173.

was a debate within the ANL and with the wider anti-racist movement over whether the scope of the ANL should have been broadened to deal with issues such as immigration controls, police racism and racism in the workplace, or whether this was a role for other anti-racist organisations, leaving the ANL as purely an *anti-fascist* group. The dominance of the ANL in the preceding years probably hindered broad anti-racist bodies being developed in this crucial period, when the Thatcher government was perhaps in a more vulnerable situation than it was in later years.

One phenomenon that was more evident at both the Grunwick strike and in the fight against the National Front was a large and confrontational police presence. Examples of this can be seen with the 'Battle for Chapter Road' in July 1977 when the police descended on the mass pickets at Grunwick, the 'Battle of Lewisham' in August of the same year when the police and anti-fascist protestors clashed in the south-east London borough, and at Southall in April 1979 when the SPG attempted to break up an anti-fascist demonstration and killed one protestor. This confrontational and violent approach by the police can be viewed as a precursor to the hardline approach to policing undertaken in the 1980s, starting with the 1981 inner city riots through to the Miners' Strike of 1984–5 (and then to the Poll Tax riots in 1990). This coincided with a re-evaluation of the left's strategies by many different organisations, including the Communist Party (but also the Socialist Workers Party, the International Marxist Group, Militant, and the Labour Party itself), which sought new ways of confronting the state under Thatcher, as well as ways to incorporate many of those disillusioned by the status quo into the left and the labour movement. This re-evaluation will be discussed in more detail in the next chapter.

As discussed in this chapter, the Communist Party had already undergone substantial debate about its strategy in the late 1970s as many were convinced by the Eurocommunist idea of the 'broad democratic alliance' and extending the struggle beyond traditional class politics. Both traditional industrial milit-ants and the Eurocommunist reformers placed great importance on anti-racist activism, but there was disagreement over the centrality of the trade unions within the anti-racist struggle. By the late 1970s it seemed to be demonstrated that while the labour movement was important to the anti-racist movement, it also needed to go beyond it and not to rely on trade unions to be the sole representatives of black workers in Britain, with many broad-based anti-racist and community organisations playing an important role. Through these dif-ferent organisations and groups, individual CPGB members performed import-ant tasks within the anti-racist movement, with Party members involved in the Grunwick Strike Committee, the All London Committee Against Racism and Fascism, Liberation, the National Council of Civil Liberties, the Anti-Nazi

League, the Friends of Blair Peach and the Indian Workers Association (Southall) to name but a few – but anti-racist activities were not likely to be co-ordinated on a party-wide basis and often the Party members were instructed to make demands *as Communist Party members*. This created a widespread but incoherent anti-racist agenda for the CPGB and one that the Party did not benefit from in any considerable way. As for setting the Party's anti-racist agenda *ideologically*, this was probably communicated most effectively though the coverage given to anti-racist and anti-fascist activism in the pages of the *Morning Star*, but as discussed in the next chapter, in the early 1980s, the paper would become one of the key battlefields between the different factions of the Party, which undermined transmission of the Party's anti-racist platform.

Babylon's Burning: Into the 1980s

Margaret Thatcher's election victory in May 1979 was a watershed moment, emphatically pronouncing the end of the postwar social-democratic consensus of the role of the state that had been in decline since the late 1960s. Thatcher's victory was a demonstration of the ascendancy of the rightist populism that considered British society on the verge of collapse. The Thatcherite solution was to confront and control the 'subversive' elements in society, whether it was trade unionists, Irish republicans, youth or Britain's black population. As mentioned in the last chapter, Margaret Thatcher combined a social conservatism from the traditional Tory right (previously espoused by Enoch Powell and the Monday Club) with an economic liberalism that preached free markets and privatisation at its core – something that the Conservatives since the 1950s had shifted away from. This was a break with Britain's postwar social-democratic consensus and a realignment of state power around the framework of a market-led economic base – what is known to many now as 'neo-liberalism'. The Thatcherite model of neo-liberalism was more than classic laissez-faire liberal economics, but a rearrangement of the relationship between the state and the individual citizen to favour certain forms of economics. As Michel Foucault wrote in 1978, neo-liberalism is not merely Adam Smith or a market society, but assumes: 'the overall exercise of political power can be modeled on the principles of a market economy ... to discover how far and to what extent the formal principles of a market economy can index a general art of government'.[1]

Under neo-liberalism, the governance of the state favours market principles so that democratic concepts, such as 'freedom' and 'liberty', are defined by consumer 'choice', resulting in citizenship not being defined by an individual's obligations to and rights within a democratic society, but by their consumer power. Richard Seymour has argued that under Thatcher, while championing the idea of 'choice' for rational and informed consumer citizens, the state pushed individuals towards accepting certain rationalities of the free market in some circumstances and, on other occasions, intervened heavily to ensure an outcome preferable to the government.[2] This meant financial incentives for financial capitalist ventures in the City, a divestment in manufacturing, a drive

---

1 Foucault 2010, p. 131.
2 Seymour 2010, p. 31.

towards privatisation and most importantly in the first half of the decade, the use of state power, through legislation and police force, to 'tackle' the trade union 'problem'. This desire of Thatcher and other Conservatives to 'smash' the trade unions was borne out of the victory of the miners in 1972, where the Heath government was unable to stand up to the tactics taken by the labour movement, and the experience of the Grunwick strike, where the National Association For Freedom campaigned that the presence of a trade union was anathema to the freedom of the individual worker. This desire resulted in early confrontations with the unions, such as the 1980 Steel Strike, but did not really gain momentum until March 1984 when the Miners' Strike began. Before the confrontations with the trade unions, the first massive confrontation between the repressive apparatus of the state and the people was between the police and black and Asian youth in Britain's inner cities across the country in 1981.

As discussed previously, Stuart Hall and Martin Jacques first viewed 'Thatcherism' as a defining change in Conservatism in the late 1970s before the Conservatives were elected in May 1979. Hall and Jacques, writing in the Communist Party of Great Britain's theoretical journal *Marxism Today*, saw that the agenda put forward by Margaret Thatcher was the representation of a shift to the right that had been gathering momentum since the upturn in industrial militancy and cultural radicalism in the late 1960s. This shift to the right was as much an ideological shift as it was a response to the economic crisis conditions of the mid- to late 1970s. This analysis of Thatcherism and the emphasis upon ideology was part of a larger dynamic shift on the left that encompassed the Communist Party, of whom Jacques was an Executive Committee member and editor of *Marxism Today*. Jacques was a leading reformer within the CPGB, who was pushing that the Communist Party should have incorporated a wider political approach than focusing on industrial militancy and traditional class-based politics. The push to reform the Party's political strategy was encompassed in the redrafting of the CPGB programme, *The British Road to Socialism*, in 1977.

This redrafting of the Party manifesto came at a time in the late 1970s when the CPGB seemed to be in a severely weakened position. Despite having considerable influence in the trade union movement at the executive level during the previous decade of heightened industrial militancy, this had failed to produce any real political gains or stem its dramatically decreasing membership numbers. This decline in membership was exacerbated by the schisms that had formed within the Party after the introduction of the Social Contract between the Labour government and the Trades Union Congress (TUC). This schism was defined between the reformers, influenced by Gramscism and Eurocommunism, who believed that the Party's limited industrial approach had alienated potential allies within the new social movements, and on the other side, the traditional industrial militants, who viewed the centrality of class politics and the emphasis upon Labour-Communist unity in the trade unions as essential to the creation of a socialist Britain. The 1977 edition of *The British Road to Socialism* promoted the strategy of the broad democratic alliance, which signified the official, yet highly disputed, idea that the struggle for socialism needed 'not only ... to be an association of class forces, ... but of other important forces in society which emerge out of areas of oppression not always directly connected with the relations of production'.[3] The CPGB, 'as the organised Marxist political party', imbued itself as a vital organisation in mediating between the traditional labour movement and the other social forces to establish this alliance.[4]

For many of the reformers within the Party, it seemed as if the strategies put forward by the left (including the Communist Party) were from another era (principally the late 1960s and early 1970s) and this made them seem out of touch, particularly as the Conservative side of politics was mutating into a more confrontational and ideologically driven threat. It seemed evident that the traditional strategies of the left were not going to draw massive support from those who had been involved in the inner-city riots, despite a large disaffection with Thatcherism from both areas of British society. Hall and Jacques, along with others centred around *Marxism Today*, sought to reinvigorate the left and attempted to appeal to those who were disaffected by Thatcherism, but not part of the traditional left and the labour movement. To understand how the Conservatives were to be combated in the 1980s, Hall and Jacques were instrumental in determining what Thatcherism meant and how it differed from previous postwar Conservatism. Particularly, Hall and Jacques (along with others, such as Andrew Gamble, Paul Gilroy and Joe Sim) recognised the 'strong state' emphasis by Thatcher and the need to confront the 'enemies within', all the while using terms such as 'freedom' and 'choice' to describe the role of the individual in 1980s British society. As Stuart Hall wrote in 1980, 'Make no mistake about it: under this regime, the market is to be Free; the people are to be Disciplined'.[5]

The increasingly repressive measures undertaken by the police, especially with the introduction of the Special Patrol Group, had first been witnessed in Britain at Grunwick and Southall (based on policing techniques developed in Northern Ireland)[6] and became more involved in dealing with street crime in the urban inner cities. Between the anti-NF demonstration in Southall on

---

3 CPGB, *The British Road to Socialism*, 1977, London, p. 29.

4 CPGB, *The British Road to Socialism*, 1977, p. 34.

5 Hall 1980, p. 5.

6 Gordon 1985, p. 162.

23 April 1979 and the nationwide riots in July 1981, the police became more confrontational, especially with Britain's black communities and other sections of the working class, who were suffering under the economic and social policies of the Conservative government. Riots in Bristol, Brixton and across Britain over an 18-month period demonstrated a violent response to racism, the police and continuing economic despair, disconnected from the traditional political discourse of political and trade union activism, which was undergoing a period of serious introspection in the wake of Thatcher's victory. Amidst the pyrrhic victory of the 1980 steel strike, both the Labour Party and the far left groups, including the Communist Party, looked inwards and very quickly entered a state of pessimism that affected their relationships with workers and activists in the early 1980s. After James Callaghan resigned as Labour leader in late 1980, the Party was consumed by factional battles between the left and right wings of Labour – between Denis Healey and Michael Foot for party leadership in November 1980 and between Denis Healey and Tony Benn for deputy party leadership in 1981. The Communist Party, as discussed at length in this book, was engulfed in a debate over the future strategy of the Party, particularly after Eric Hobsbawm's 'The Forward March of Labour Halted?' appeared in *Marxism Today* in late 1978. The CPGB's far left rivals, the SWP and the IMG, also suffered from the shift in left thinking after Thatcher's victory, with the IMG becoming an entrist group into the Labour Party by 1982–3[7] and Tony Cliff, as leader of the SWP, claiming that the British labour movement was experiencing a 'downturn'.[8]

While the left, including the CPGB, had been successful as part of the Anti-Nazi League's defeat of the National Front, it had not made the same headway in combating other forms of popular and institutional racism. For the Communist Party, the proposition of the broad democratic alliance, envisioned to bring wider movements, such as black activists, into progressive leftist politics, failed to appeal to a disillusioned black community, who felt betrayed and patronised by the white left, which had for so long minimised the role of 'race' within the class struggle and the fight against racism. The coming together of black and white workers and activists in the late 1970s, characterised by the Anti-Nazi League and the Grunwick strike, papered over divisions that were able to reappear as Thatcherism began to bear down upon the working class and its organisations. By 1981, the relationship between the left and the black

---

7   Callaghan 1987, pp. 158–60.
8   Cliff 1979; Cliff, 'Building in the Dowturn', *Socialist Review*, April 1983, pp. 3–5; Birchall 2011, pp. 441–54.

communities seemed strained as ever, with some black activists, such as Darcus Howe, criticising the absence of the left in the demonstrations against the
lack of police action surrounding the New Cross Fire in early 1981, a major precursor to the 1981 riots. These riotous and unplanned actions by black and Asian
youth, first in Bristol in April 1980, then in Brixton in April 1981 and finally
across many urban areas in July 1981, were a response to a number of pressures,
including years of police harassment, high youth unemployment and a lack of
investment in inner city areas that led to poor housing and sub-standard social
services. Despite the government suspecting the involvement of various left-
wing groups as 'outside elements' in the riots,[9] the left were not involved in the
riots and were primarily a presence in the aftermath of the riots.

Further Defeats for the CPGB

In the final months of 1978, Dave Cook responded to the decline of the CPGB
after the 35th National Congress – defeats of union action at British Leyland
and Grunwick, the secession of the hardline Stalinists to the New Communist Party, hostile reaction by some traditionalists within the Party to the broad
democratic alliance, continuing decline in Party membership – by reaffirm-
ing the relevance of the Party's programme in an article in *Marxism Today*,
'The British Road to Socialism and the Communist Party'.[10] Cook argued that
the traditional labour movement was 'far from corresponding with the whole
working class' and that class exploitation was not the sole politicising force for
workers.[11] The 'renewal of Marxism over recent years [had] tended to remain
at abstract level' and it was the purpose of the 'broad democratic alliance' to
expand 'collective action' between the labour movement and the new social
movements for a 'much closer relationship between [the Party's] theoretical
work and practical activities'.[12] There were some in the Party who were sceptical
about the changes in *The British Road to Socialism* and Cook's article, alongside Eric Hobsbawm's 'The Forward March of Labour Halted?', presented at
the 1978 Marx Memorial Lecture, generated furious debate in *Marxism Today*

9   Shipley, 'Left-Wing Extremists and the Riots', Conservative Research Department
       Memorandum, 7 July 1981, *Margaret Thatcher Foundation*, available at: http://www
       .margaretthatcher.org/document/121332, accessed 20 January 2015.
10   Cook, 'The British Road to Socialism and the Communist Party', *Marxism Today*, Decem-
       ber 1978, pp. 370–9.
11   Cook, 'The British Road to Socialism and the Communist Party', p. 372.
12   Cook, 'The British Road to Socialism and the Communist Party', p. 374.

throughout 1979. In his study of the CPGB's industrial strategy, John McIlroy asked what these new social forces of action outside the 'old axis of the unions, Labour Party and CP' could achieve if the 'big industrial struggles of the 1970s had failed to qualitatively advance socialist consciousness'.[13]

However, it was not the intention of Cook or the other reformists to have the CPGB select either industrial militancy or the broad democratic alliance, but rather to attempt to synthesise the two strategies. In Cook's article, the ANL was used as an example of successful co-operation between the labour movement and the social movements, with a 'range of cultural sponsorship and involvement', such as 'Rock Against Racism, actors, sports, festivals' to 'trigger off such a response from predominantly working class youth'.[14] But this did not negate the importance placed on the labour movement and the trade unions by the CPGB within anti-racist politics, with the 1977 edition of *The British Road to Socialism* stating that it 'must play the decisive part in winning the working class to reject racialist ideas and practices, and in defending black people from discrimination'.[15] However, either strategy put forward by the Party in *The British Road to Socialism* could not overcome the fact that the Party was in decline. In 1979, the Party had 20,599 members, having lost over 10,000 in ten years and only 126 factory branches, having less than half than it did in the mid-1960s.[16] The Party had had no MPs since Phil Piratin and Willie Gallacher lost their seats in 1950 and only five candidates had been elected in local elections.[17]

Much of the optimism portrayed by the reformers around *The British Road to Socialism* was quashed by the convincing Conservative victory at the General Election in May 1979. The election of Margaret Thatcher saw the lowest share of the vote for the Labour Party since 1931 and a swing to the right by skilled working-class voters, with around a third of trade unionists voting for the Conservatives.[18] Martin Jacques saw this shift to the right as part of the 'crisis of hegemony' and while the Party developed the concepts of 'the broad democratic alliance, the mode of rule and the revolutionary process' in *The British Road to Socialism* as a response to this crisis, Jacques acknowledged in October 1979 that this 'reorientation is not yet complete'.[19] 'The biggest single

---

13   McIlroy 1999, p. 224.

14   Cook, 'The British Road to Socialism and the Communist Party', p. 378.

15   CPGB, *The British Road to Socialism*, 1977, p. 30.

16   Thompson 1992, p. 218; McIlroy 1999, p. 222.

17   Cross 2003, p. 314.

18   Hobsbawm, 'The Forward March of Labour Halted? – A Response', *Marxism Today*, September 1979, p. 265; Thompson 1993, p. 112.

19   Jacques, 'Thatcherism – The Impasse Broken?', *Marxism Today*, October 1979, p. 13.

weakness of the Party's practice', stated Jacques, was to 'underestimate the extent of the crisis and the range of issues around which popular support can be mobilised'.[20] After the 1979 election, Eric Hobsbawm, who had criticised the 'almost entirely *economist* militancy' of the traditional labour movement in 'The Forward March of Labour Halted?' in late 1978,[21] maintained that this Conservative victory demonstrated that the limits of 'trade union conscious-ness' had not been overcome and that unions '*by themselves* cannot offset the setbacks of the labour movement in other respects'.[22] Effectively Hobsbawm was arguing that trade union militancy by itself could not automatically create class-consciousness or organise a radical socialist advance. Ideally, this was the responsibility of the Communist Party. However, with membership just over 20,000 in 1979 (further declining to 18,458 in 1981),[23] diminished workplace presence and internal divisions between the traditionalists and the reformists, the CPGB was hardly in a position to, as Jacques hoped, 'transform the labour movement and popular consciousness'.[24]

The Police and the Black Communities

The rightward shift that occurred under Thatcher had a profound impact upon the relationship between the institutions of the state and Britain's black com-munities. While institutional racism had long existed (along with efforts to combat it), racism from state agencies, such as the police, the judiciary and the Home Office, came to the fore. By 1979, confidence in the institutions of the state had been severely damaged, particularly after the death of Blair Peach, the anti-fascist protestor believed to have been killed by the police during a demonstration against the National Front in Southall on 23 April 1979. Between the passing of the 1976 Race Relations Act and the 'race riots' across Britain in the summer of 1981, the role of the state in the struggle against racism moved from enforcing legislation to improve 'race relations' to being at the forefront of institutional racism, through the police, the judiciary and immigration con-trols, in what Stuart Hall described as the 'criminalisation' of the black commu-

---

20   Ibid.

21   Hobsbawm, 'The Forward March of Labour Halted?', *Marxism Today*, September 1978, p. 286.

22   Hobsbawm, 'The Forward March of Labour Halted? – A Response', p. 266; p. 267; Italics are in the original text.

23   Thompson 1992, p. 218.

24   Jacques 1979, p. 13.

nity.[25] The police did not just apply the law, but were now able to shape it, with Hall warning that they were 'the best organised and the most effective campaigning lobby for the expansion of police powers'.[26] Racism amongst the police was seen as an example of a wider shift to the right, embodied by the election of Margaret Thatcher in May 1979. The National Front had been defeated in the 1979 General Election, but as the Communist Party recognised at their 1981 National Congress, the left had failed to 'tackle racist ideology wherever it is expressed, at the workplace, in pubs, clubs' and to prevent the 'rightward shift in British politics affecting all aspects of life'.[27] Nowhere was this rightward shift felt more intensely than in the fractured and often openly hostile relationship between the police and Britain's black communities.

The issue of racism and the British police force has been discussed at length elsewhere,[28] but it is necessary here to note the repressive and alienating nature of the police upon Britain's black population. Racism within police dealings with the black communities 'stretches back to the beginnings of postwar settlement'[29] and was only exacerbated by the economic crisis of the 1970s. The urban black community was blamed for the increase in street crime, with the stereotype of 'black youth' equals 'black crime'.[30] Alongside this image of the black youth involved in street crime, there was a suspicion cast upon all black people of being illegal immigrants, with great powers of discretion and arrest given to police and immigration officers by the 1971 Immigration Act. The enforcement of this Act led to 'substantial numbers of people who were not in breach of immigration laws ... [being] asked to prove their innocence by establishing their right to be in the U.K. simply because of their colour'.[31] The reality of these controls was that black people had to succumb to the discretionary powers of immigration control and feared inquiry into their residency status by the police at any time. These laws were, Vishnu Sharma wrote, 'as much concerned with *control* of black people in Britain, as they are to do with "immigration"' and thus, 'Fear and insecurity exist in all black communit-

25   Hall, 'Policing the Police', in Cook and Rabstein, *Black & Blue: Racism and the Police*, 1981, London CPGB pamphlet, p. 7.

26   Hall, 'Policing the Police', p. 9.

27   'Branch Resolutions – Racism: Anti-Racist, Anti-Fascist Struggle', *Comment*, 5 December 1981, p. 37.

28   For analysis of the issue of racism within the British police force and the effects of institutional racism, see Hall et al. 1978; Holdaway 1996; Gilroy 2002, pp. 84–145.

29   Gilroy, 'The Myth of Black Criminality', *Socialist Register*, 1982, p. 49.

30   Gutzmore 1983, p. 21.

31   Cited in Joshua and Wallace with Booth 1983, p. 51.

ies as a consequence'.[32] As the economic downturn worsened, the 'imagery of alien violence and criminality personified in the "mugger" and the "illegal" immigrant [became] an important card in the hands of politicians and police officers'.[33]

The racism of the police had long been recognised by the Communist Party, although practical action by the CPGB in this area of the anti-racist struggle was severely limited. By the late 1970s, the racism of the police force was most recognisable in the use of 'sus' to prevent street crime. 'Sus' was an interpretation of a vagrancy law passed in 1824, which made it possible to arrest anyone in public suspected of intending to commit an offence. The police force, wrote Dave Cook, were 'shot through with racist elements and regard[ed] young blacks as their targets'[34] and 'sus' was the most potent weapon to use against them, as in the ideological criminalisation of black youth, all blacks had the potential to be involved in crime. The Hackney CPGB Branch noted in an internal policy document that 60 percent of those arrested on 'sus' charges in Hackney were black, although the black population in the borough was only 20 percent.[35] At the CPGB's 36th National Congress in December 1979, the Party put forward a resolution that, 'We demand the repeal of the SUS laws', which was part of a wider 'Scrap SUS campaign', which the Party urged people to join.[36] Martin Rabstein acknowledged that scrapping the 'sus' law would not 'end the racial tension', but it would 'help affirm the democratic rights of all people, and constitute the first substantial political victory for a struggle started by black people in this country'.[37]

The police force itself was seen as an alienating and repressive state institution that had little involvement of blacks within it and this was one of the reasons for the racism of its white majority. The Communist Party reported in the *Morning Star* in 1972 that by September 1971, only 41 out of 92,925 police officers in England and Wales were black and that recruitment attempts had

---

32   Sharma, *No Racist Immigration Laws*, 1979, London: CPGB pamphlet, p. 6; Italics are in the original text.

33   Gilroy, 'The Myth of Black Criminality', p. 48.

34   Cook, *A Knife at the Throat of Us All: Racism and the National Front*, 1978, London: CPGB pamphlet, pp. 28–9.

35   Hackney CP Branch Internal Policy Document, in CPGB archives, CP/LON/BRA/09/11, LHASC.

36   'Racism', *Comment*, 1 December 1979, p. 411; 'They Call it "Sus"', draft of CPGB flyer, in CPGB archives, CP/LON/RACE/02/06, LHASC.

37   Rabstein, 'Sus – When No Black People Are Above Suspicion', *Comment*, 27 May 1978, p. 173.

been 'haphazard and half-hearted'.[38] In the London Metropolitan Police, there had been a 100 percent increase in recruits in 1974, but still there were only 22 black police officers in the Met, with the total proportion for England and Wales being around 0.043 percent.[39] By the time of Lord Scarman's inquiry into the Brixton riots held in late 1981, there were still only 132 black police officers in the Metropolitan Police and 326 in the whole of England and Wales.[40] John Benyon calculated that, 'If the ethnic minorities were to be proportionately represented in the police, at least a fourteen-fold increase would be needed'.[41] The very whiteness of the police force presented a difficulty and an often-claimed indifference, bordering on hostility, in the police dealings with racist attacks upon Britain's black citizens. An investigation into the racist violence in East End London by the Bethnal Green and Stepney Trades Council stated that many had no confidence in the local police force and many considered them 'to be uninterested in their problems, or actively biased against Asians'.[42] The investigation concluded that there was a 'very high level of physical attacks on the immigrant families and their property', but there was 'considerable doubt within the immigrant community as to the interest and impartiality of the Police in handling complaints of racist attacks'.[43] The indifference or racist bias of the police, as perceived by Britain's black population, saw them feel increasingly alienated from and oppressed by the state and with the failure of traditional political opposition offered by the organised, and primarily white, labour movement, black activism took a much more confrontational approach.

At the heart of this confrontational approach was the 'criminalisation' of black youth.[44] Both Afro-Caribbean and Asian youth faced many of the hardships that had been experienced by their migrant parents, but they also had grown up in Britain, which altered their experiences, particularly in terms of cultural identity and their expectations. The children of postwar black migrants had experienced similar developments in their young lives as their white contemporaries and in many ways, shared closer ties with white British society than to the culture of their parents' homeland, but were still divorced from

---

38   *Morning Star*, 14 September 1972.

39   'Arm of the Law', *New Society*, 6 June 1974, p. 560.

40   Benyon 1984, p. 103.

41   Ibid.

42   Bethnal Green and Stepney Trades Council, *Blood on the Streets: A Report by Bethnal Green and Stepney Trades Council on Racial Attacks in East London*, 1978, London: BG & STC pamphlet, p. 7.

43   Bethnal Green and Stepney Trades Council, *Blood on the Streets*, p. 9.

44   See Gilroy, 'The Myth of Black Criminality', pp. 47–56; Gutzmore 1983, pp. 13–30.

CHAPTER 5

many of the opportunities offered by a white identity. Chris Mullard wrote of this as the 'black Britons' dilemma':

> He will be British in every way. He will possess understandable values and attitudes; he will wear the same dress, speak the same language, with the same accent; he will be as educated as any other Englishman; and he will behave in an easy relatable way. The only thing he will not be is white.[45]

Popular racist sentiment may have demanded for immigrants to return to where they came from, but for the children of black migrants, Britain was their home. The realisation that they would have to defend their right to remain where they had been for most of their lives led to a militant attitude amongst many black and Asian youth. Bhopinder Basi, a radicalised Asian youth in Birmingham, remarked, 'we started with such simple slogans as, "Here to stay. Here to fight" ... Our parents may have entertained some myth of going back to the *pind*, but we didn't'.[46] The acts of rebellion seen on the streets of Bristol, Brixton, Toxteth and Moss Side throughout the early 1980s were thus, in part, the violent reaction to a decade-long history of harassment and violence against the existence of black youth in Britain. It was also a *British* and *black* reaction that rejected the 'simple bipolar cleavage' of being either British *or* black/Asian.[47]

The first generation of Commonwealth migrants were viewed as potential agents for significant political, and revolutionary, action. These migrants were not encumbered by the 'labourist' and 'economistic' approaches of the left and trade union movement[48] and were, as demonstrated at strikes at Mansfield Hosiery Mills, Imperial Typewriters and Grunwick, willing to organise autonomously; but at the same time, there was a tendency to gravitate towards the traditional non-militant community organisations, as well as a sense of grudging timidity to accept the conditions of migrant life and some yearning to return to one's homeland. This is what Edward Said described as the paradox of the exile, where the 'positive benefit of challenging the system' by the migrant's position was always countered by a debilitating sense of loss and exclusion, 'between the old empire and the new state'.[49]

---

45 Mullard 1973, p. 145.

46 Bhopinder Basi, cited in Ramamurthy 2007, p. 18.

47 Brah 1996, p. 41.

48 Cambridge and Gutzmore, 'The Industrial Action of the Black Masses and the Class Struggle in Britain', *Black Liberator*, 2/3 (June 1974/January 1975), p. 207.

49 Said 1994, p. 404; p. 403.

Some on the left had traditionally believed that this feeling of exile and of being trapped between two cultures would also exist in the second generation of black Britons. Back in a 1974 discussion of youth culture in the CPGB journal *Marxism Today*, Imtiaz Chounara claimed that 'most young coloured people are caught in between two cultures – that of Britain and that of their parents'.[50] Chounara appealed for the CPGB to incorporate black youth (not just black workers in the industrial sector) into the Party, to counter the appeal of 'black power', which the CPGB believed to share an affinity with 'deviant' versions of Marxism, such as Maoism and Trotskyism.[51] Chounara suggested:

We must therefore fight for black youth to mix culturally with white youth but at the same time to retain their own cultural identity. This is an important part of the fight for black consciousness – to get respect for black people and their culture, not only amongst young white people but also amongst black people themselves. This cannot be done in a 'black power' manner, putting black above white, but in a true Marxist manner, fighting for the rightful place of black workers alongside their white brothers as equals.[52]

However, as shown in previous chapters, the Communist Party had to compete with other left-wing and black activist groups to entice black and Asian youth into politics, but many more rejected this or any other form of political activity. And without a viable political outlet, the anger felt by black and Asian youth in the early 1980s erupted into public disorder on the streets of Britain in 1980 and 1981.

From Southall to Brixton: The Violent Reaction to the Police under Thatcher

Between the events of Southall on 23 April 1979 and July 1981, there had been increasing riots in inner city areas across Britain, where black and white youth had reacted against the police and in some places, such as Southall, fascist agitation. Although there has been major emphasis in studies of the Thatcherite government from 1979 to 1990 on Thatcher's abhorrence of the trade unions and

---

50   Chounara, 'Trends in Youth Culture', *Marxism Today*, October 1974, p. 318.

51   International Affairs Committee, 'Racialism and "Black Power"', in CPGB archives, CP/ LON/RACE/02/01, LHASC.

52   Chounara, 'Trends in Youth Culture', pp. 318–19.

the focus of her government on destroying an organised labour movement, the riots that occurred across Britain in 1981 have been largely overlooked. While the anti-union legislation and the Miners' Strike are important elements of the dominance of Thatcher's neo-liberalism during the 1980s that involved high levels of confrontation between the state and the labour movement, the first major confrontation between the repressive institutions of the state and the 'subversive' sections of British society was not with the trade unions, but with Britain's black population, particularly black youth in the inner cities.

The first major riot was in Bristol on 2 April 1980, followed by a much larger outbreak in Brixton between 10–12 April 1981 before culminating in riots across Britain in July 1981. These riots can be seen as the reaction to the lack of a political voice by Britain's black communities and to the racism of the police directed primarily at black youth, as well as against the Conservative government. The riots were symptomatic of the wider disillusionment, shared by both black and white youth, with the Conservative government's repressive police tactics and monetarist economic policies, which contributed to high unemployment. The problem of police racism, at the centre of these riots, was, as Stuart Hall wrote, 'where blacks and others encounter a drift and a thrust towards making the whole of society more policed'.[53] By the early 1980s, the police strategy in the urban inner cities was making a strong and visible presence of police power under the auspices of maintaining 'law and order' and taking a strong stance against street crime. As the Communist Party declared in May 1980, 'the hawks are in control in the Metropolitan police force'.[54]

The first major confrontation was on 2 April 1980 in the St Paul's District of Bristol, when approximately fifty policemen raided a café that was patronised primarily by Afro-Caribbeans, which caused a confrontation between 2,000 mainly black citizens and over 100 policemen.[55] The confrontation was significant because of its scale and intensity, including burning and looting of private property and the racial aspect of the incident.[56] The clash was, Dilip Hiro wrote, a reaction to the confrontational tactics of the police against the black community.[57] The CPGB saw that the events in Bristol 'were no "spontaneous riot" because there was nothing spontaneous about racial oppression – or its response'.[58] What Bristol demonstrated, Neville Carey predicted in *Com-*

---

53   Hall, 'Policing the Police', p. 7.

54   Heywood, 'Police Hawks Come Out On Top', *Comment*, 10 May 1980, p. 151.

55   Hiro 1992, p. 85.

56   Joshua and Wallace with Booth 1983, p. 7.

57   Hiro 1992, p. 86.

58   Hackney CP Branch Internal Policy Document.

ment, was that 'we are heading towards open warfare in deprived areas containing large numbers of unemployed youth' as the police were being increasingly
used to deal with troubles caused by the combination of racism and unemployment.[59] A petition with these immediate demands was circulated by the
CPGB following the riot, but Carey admitted that the Communist Party was
'doing far too little' in working with the black communities, who mistrusted
the opportunism and arrogance of the white left.[60] Carey warned that it would
'take a great deal of mass pressure from the Left and progressive movements to
stop this Law and Order government from encouraging the use of even greater
force to deal with social discontent'.[61] But Bristol was only 'the shape of things
to come'.[62] As Harris Joshua and Tina Wallace wrote, 'the same basic pattern of
violence was to be repeated in almost every major city with a black population,
precipitating a crisis of race unprecedented in the postwar era, and a crisis of
law and order unprecedented since the 1930s'.[63]

On 10 April 1981, a riot broke out in Brixton after the police stopped an
injured youth on the street and the crowd reacted to the heavy police presence.
Two events preceded the Brixton riots that contributed to eruption of action
against the police. In January 1981, a fire on New Cross Road in Deptford led to
the deaths of 13 black youth. The fire was believed to have been started by a
white racist, but the police investigation failed to arrest anyone connected to
the fire, further angering the black community.[64] This resulted in large protests
by the black communities, with little involvement from the white left and
progressive movements, which was different from the political mobilisations of
the late 1970s around Grunwick and the Anti-Nazi League. The mobilisation of
thousands after the New Cross Fire 'indicated the extent to which they had been
frustrated ... from expressing themselves politically'.[65] This mobilisation was
against the disinterest and ineptitude of the initial police investigation and the
mainstream press until the black protest had 'drawn attention to the deaths and
the official silence by marching through central London'.[66] Paul Gilroy wrote,
'The tragic deaths set in motion a sequence of events which lead directly to the

---

59   Carey, 'Bristol Police Fail in Take Over Bid', *Comment*, 26 April 1980, p. 136.
60   Carey, 'Bristol Police Fail in Take Over Bid', p. 137.
61   Carey, 'Bristol Police Fail in Take Over Bid', p. 136.
62   Harman, 'The Summer of 1981: A Post-Riot Analysis', *International Socialism*, 2/14, Autumn
      1981, p. 1.
63   Joshua and Wallace with Booth 1983, p. 7.
64   Hiro 1992, p. 87.
65   Howe, 'Brixton Before the Uprising', *Race Today*, February/March 1982, p. 69.
66   Gilroy 2002, p. 130.

explosion in Brixton in April 1981, and provided a means to galvanize blacks from all over the country into overt and organized political mobilisation.[67]

Another event that contributed to the Brixton riots was the strategy launched by the police in the week before the riot. Operation 'Swamp 81' was launched by the Lambeth police on 6 April 1981. The purpose of 'Swamp 81' was to 'flood identified areas on "L" District [Lambeth] to detect and arrest burglars and robbers', with success, according to the police, depending on a 'concentrated effort of "stops", based on powers of surveillance and *suspicion proceeded by persistent and astute questioning*'.[68] In four days, the squads stopped 943 people and arrested 118, with only 75 charged, one with robbery.[69] The fact that so many police were deployed to street patrols in the immediate days preceding the riots contributed to the massive police response to the riots. Even after the first confrontations on 10 April, the operation continued with an extra 96 officers deployed to Brixton on 11 April. After the initial confrontation between police officers and a crowd of black youth on the evening of 10 April 1981, rumours of police violence and several other incidents involving police and youths erupted into rioting across Brixton on 11 April and was finally quelled the following day. In the course of the events over that weekend, around 7,000 police officers were deployed to Brixton to restore order, although as John Benyon claimed, 'during the worst night of violence on Saturday 11 April it seems that a few hundred people were involved'.[70] In the aftermath, 450 people, including many policemen, were injured, with 145 buildings and 207 vehicles damaged and the total damage bill amounting to £6.5 million.

After the Brixton riots, there was outrage from the government, high-ranking police officials and the mainstream press, with Lord Scarman appointed to launch an inquiry into the events. But as Dilip Hiro wrote, 'the root causes which led to the Brixton rioting persisted and Britain experienced a spate of violent disorders a few months later'.[71] Most major cities with black populations experienced rioting of some level, beginning on 3 July in Toxteth and Southall before spreading to Moss Side and then to most other cities over the weekend of 10–12 July 1981. 'The incidents which ignited the disturbances varied enormously from place to place' noted Chris Harman, with some incidents sparked by police harassment, others by racist attacks and fascist agitation or

---

67   Gilroy 2002, p. 129.
68   Cited in Scarman 1986, p. 95; my emphasis.
69   Hiro 1992, p. 87; Gilroy 2002, p. 132.
70   Hiro 1992, p. 88; Benyon 1985, p. 409.
71   Hiro 1992, p. 88.

elsewhere, 'the eruptions were "spontaneous" – youth on the streets just started looting and that was it'.[72] The official estimate of the total costs of damage caused during the July riots was £45 million, with £17 million caused to private property.[73] Around 4,000 people were arrested and 'of the 3,704 for whom data was available, 766 were described as West Indian or African, 180 as Asian, 292 as "other" and 2,466 or 67% were white', while around 66 percent were under the age of 21 and about half were unemployed.[74]

These riots were the result of institutional racism, police harassment and urban deprivation, although to what extent each factor contributed to the riots can never be measured exactly. Conservative MP John Stokes described the riots as 'something new and sinister in our long national history'[75] and the events were presented by many in the press as an end to 'law and order' or the 'British way of life'. John Benyon has contended that the riots were 'neither unique events nor racial disturbances ... which indicated serious social and political grievances and frustrations',[76] however, both the left and black activists have attempted to place the riots within wider historical narratives. For the left, these rebellious actions were to be placed in a narrative of the common people and class struggle in British history, stretching back to even the Peasants' Revolt of 1381. For black activists and journalists, the riots were part of a history of black people attempting to maintain their identity within the confines of a colonial legacy. The apparent continuance of colonial relations in Britain saw black immigrants resist the discrimination and hostility they faced, in a direct and spontaneous manner.

'Crisis in the Inner Cities': The Communist Party's Reaction

The CPGB's National Race Relations Committee (NRRC) had first begun preparing for a discussion conference, 'Racism and the Police' in October 1980, declaring that the 'role of the police has become a central issue of anti-racist politics ... loom[ing] large in any serious discussion of "institutionalised" racism and how to combat it'.[77] The NRRC invited representatives from black organisations,

---

72   Harman, 'The Summer of 1981: A Post-Riot Analysis', p. 5.

73   Hiro 1992, p. 90.

74   Benyon 1985, p. 410.

75   Hansard, 13 April 1981, col. 29.

76   Benyon 1985, p. 410.

77   Conference Invitation to 'Racism and the Police', October 1980, in CPGB archives, CP/LON/
     RACE/02/11, LHASC.

political parties, anti-racist, civil liberties and legal organisations, labour movement bodies and individuals to 'assist the process of drawing up clear proposals for which the labour, democratic and anti-racist movements can campaign'.[78] The N RRC acknowledged that it would 'not be a policy-making Conference', but felt that the issue of police racism 'urgently needs bringing down from the level of generalities to practical proposals'.[79] The conference was attended by around 160 delegates and put forward a 'Charter of Demands', published in *Comment* on 21 February 1981 and then reproduced, along with the conference speeches, in a pamphlet *Black and Blue*, published in November 1981.[80]

The editors of the pamphlet, Dave Cook and Martin Rabstein, emphasised the wide range of groups involved in the conference, although many of the groups were represented by members of the Communist Party. Through this conference, the Communist Party believed it was 'performing its key role of welding together ... toward[s] the construction of the broad democratic alliance'.[81] The Party hoped that the 'Charter of Demands' was 'one component part of a programme to democratise, to force democratic victories in the teeth of what will be the most powerful opposition in various parts of the apparatus of state'.[82]

Keeping with the framework of the broad democratic alliance, the 'Charter' called for consultation between the police and 'genuine representatives of black communities' as Britain's black communities needed 'community policing with democratic accountability and control, not saturation policing'.[83] 'Hard' policing, such as Operation 'Swamp 81', was seen as keeping the black communities under control, rather than protecting it and the 'Charter', like the resolutions put forward at the CPGB's National Congress, called for the removal of 'SUS' and the disbanding of the SPG.[84]

Included in the 'Charter of Demands' were proposals put forward by the Communist Party previously, calling for 'race relations and public order law' to be 'firmly enforced against racists' and 'given more teeth to outlaw the advocacy and practice of racism'.[85] As with the Party's stance on immigration control, the Race Relations Act and anti-fascism, the repressive and anti-left bias of

78 Ibid.
79 Ibid.
80 'Racism and the Police', *Comment*, 21 February 1981, pp. 6–7.
81 Cook and Rabstein, 'Inner City Crisis', in Cook and Rabstein, *Black & Blue*, p. 6.
82 Cook, 'Charter of Demands', in Cook and Rabstein, *Black & Blue*, p. 32.
83 'Racism and the Police', p. 6.
84 'Racism and the Police', p. 7.
85 Ibid.

the state was weighed against the practical use of the state to combat racism. The police, who were at the forefront of the fractious relationship between the black communities and the state, were widely seen as incapable of mending community relations, but, in line with the ideals of the broad democratic alliance, the CPGB stated its commitment to the 'rights of the "non-political" individual – the right to be free of harassment, the right to walk without fear on the streets', which the Party believed needed to be protected by some kind of police force.[86]

After the riots in July, the CPGB's Executive Committee released a statement, 'Crisis in the Inner Cities', describing the disturbances as a reaction to long-term problems that had developed in the urban inner-cities, 'in the context of both the deep crisis affecting our economy, and the particular consequences of Thatcher's policies'.[87] However, the Party noted that it was 'crude economic reductionism' to simplify the argument to 'economic crisis = disturbances on the streets', recognising the 'important racial dimension' of the riots.[88] The riots were not an isolated issue of 'law and order', but partly a wider reaction to the repressive actions of the police and the monetarist economic policies under Thatcherism, with the CPGB leadership stating:

> Thatcher is blind to the part played by her disastrous economic and social policies in causing the disturbances, and the police chiefs are blind to the connections between their everyday methods of policing and the violence they face.[89]

Therefore, the black and white youth were 'not rioting against society at large, but *were* rioting against the police, against unemployment, against racism'.[90] The Party saw the broad democratic alliance put forward in *The British Road to Socialism* as the necessary strategy for the working class 'to force democratic victories' within 'the most powerful opposition in various parts of the apparatus of state',[91] which looked to working within the present system for immediate victories while attempting to build popular opposition for long–

---

86   Cook and Rabstein, *Black & Blue*, p. 6.

87   'Crisis in the Inner Cities', Executive Committee Statement, 12–13 September 1981, p. 1, in
      CPGB archives, CP/CENT/CTTE/02/06, LHASC.

88   'Crisis in the Inner Cities', p. 2.

89   'Crisis in the Inner Cities', p. 6.

90   'Crisis in the Inner Cities', p. 9; Italics are in the original text.

91   'Crisis in the Inner Cities', p. 11.

term reform. The response by the labour movement and the left had to be, the Party declared, more than simply 'getting rid of the Tories', instead it was to 'respond to the immediate demands of the black community', as the Party urged these organisations to campaign at local level, 'linked to the need for left alternative policies nationally'.[92]

The 1981 Riots as Social Protest

For commentators, academics and activists on the left and within the black communities, these riots have been viewed as either part of a wider malaise by the lower classes against the neo-liberal policies of Thatcherism, or the unstructured reaction by black youth to years of racial harassment and discrimination that continued on from the black struggles of the 1970s.

For the far left, the 1981 riots were indicative of a widespread antipathy towards the socio-economic policies of the Conservative government. The SWP were adamant that the 1981 riots were '*class* riots' and not '*race riots*'.[93] Colin Sparks stated the riots were the work of 'a mainly *working class* community against the symbols of oppression and deprivation'.[94] The riots were the 'common result of unemployment and crisis', exacerbated by the experience of racism and the unequal distribution of economic hardship upon black youth.[95] What demonstrated the class aspect of the riots was, Chris Harman wrote, the fact that 'in *virtually all* the British riots there has been significant white involvement alongside blacks, and the involvement has not just been of white leftists, but of white working class youth'.[96] For Harman, the 'immediate background of the riots lies ... in a huge increase in unemployment',[97] with the result being a common experience of repression and economic hardship that contributed to the lower class rebellion. Harman portrayed the riots as a modern incarnation of previous rebellions by the lower classes in Britain. While there was a strong narrative of resistance flowing from the black industrial struggles of the 1970s and the disturbances at Notting Hill and Bristol, Harman linked

---

92   'Crisis in the Inner Cities', p. 10; p. 11.
93   SWP CC, 'The Riots and After'; Italics are in the original text.
94   Sparks, 'A Class Riot Not a Race Riot', *Socialist Review*, May 1981, p. 7; Italics are in the original text.
95   Sparks, 'A Class Riot Not a Race Riot', p. 9.
96   Harman, 'The Summer of 1981: A Post-Riot Analysis', p. 14; Italics are in the original text.
97   Harman, 'The Summer of 1981: A Post-Riot Analysis', p. 15.

the riots to previous unemployment struggles in 1886–7 and in 1931–2.[98] For the left, the riots were seen as a starting point for resistance to Thatcherism. The swp declared that the riots were the symptoms of a 'bitterness brewing ... from the experience of Tory government and economic crisis', which would 'sooner or later ... explode in the factories as well as on the streets'.[99] It was up to socialists to 'seize the opportunities to build unity in struggle'[100] that would present themselves as Thatcherism emboldened its attacks upon the 'subversive' elements of society.

While not denying the common economic causes of the riots or the involvement of white youth, black activists and journalists emphasised the role of black youth and the racial discrimination and harassment experienced by the black communities that were integral factors in the outbreak of the rioting. For the journal *Race & Class*, the reasons for the riots were clear, quoting a black youth interviewed for the *Sunday Telegraph*: 'It is not against the white community, it's against the police'.[101] The journal emphasised the repressive nature of the police and the continual harassment faced by black people in everyday life. The repeated harassment by the police formed a long narrative that heightened with the events of the late 1970s, before exploding with the riots of the early 1980s. The journal tried to emphasise the continuity between the events, stating, 'In many ways what happened during and after the 1976 Carnival was a premonition of the later "riots"'.[102]

The journal also drew a historical continuity between the hundreds of racial attacks that had occurred since the mid-1970s and the rioting; a process from which black people were 'attacked, ... criminalised ... and rendered second-class citizens' to the violent response against the racists and the police, who had failed to adequately protect the black communities.[103] Quoting the Hackney Legal Defence Committee, the journal portrayed the riots as the long awaited reaction to this continual racism: 'Black youth took to the streets to defend our communities against police and racial violence. From Brixton to Toxteth, Moss Side to Southall black youth said: "No more: enough is enough!"'[104]

Both *Race & Class* and *Race Today* portrayed the riots as the result of a lack of a political voice for Britain's black communities in conventional party

---

98   Harman, 'The Summer of 1981: A Post-Riot Analysis', pp. 15–16.

99   swp cc, 'The Riots and After'.

100   Harman, 'The Summer of 1981: A Post-Riot Analysis', p. 40.

101   Cited in 'The "Riots"', *Race & Class*, 23/2–3, Winter 1981–Autumn 1982, p. 225.

102   Cited in 'The "Riots"', p. 239.

103   'The "Riots"', p. 232.

104   Cited in 'The "Riots"', p. 231.

politics. As A. Sivanandan was quoted, 'The black community is a community under attack and, increasingly, a community without redress'.[105] Looking at the political situation for black Britons throughout the early 1970 and the early 1980s, both journals saw the long process of the black communities attempting to work within the system, but still facing exclusion – from the mainstream political parties, trade unions, local government and the left, amongst others – which could burst into spontaneous acts of rebellion. The riots were a forceful recognition of the limited space in which black people in Britain could enter the political sphere, as well as an unplanned reaction to years of racial discrimination, police harassment, violence and economic hardship. The left and black activists recognised that these riots had a political dimension, but there was disagreement on whether this dimension was characterised by notions of 'class' or 'race'.

Lord Scarman's Report and the Denial of Institutional Racism

Unlike the triumphalism of the state and strong government celebrated by the Conservatives after the Falklands War and the Miner's Strike, the aftermath of the 1981 riots saw the government having to temporarily retreat from its forceful 'law and order' position and make concessions that police tactics in the black communities did involve racist and alienating behaviour. Although there was much speculation over the cause of the riots and numerous objections to their violence, many acknowledged that the heavy-handed police actions in the black communities over the previous decade had been a principal factor in provoking such a violent reaction by black youth.[106]

Lord Scarman's Inquiry was primarily focused on the events in Brixton, although the government asked Scarman to take the July riots into account, but as Joe Sim noted, 'This request was not evident in the final draft'.[107] The Scarman Report, wrote Stuart Hall, 'was no panacea', but 'broke the prevailing law-and-order consensus' that left the police blameless,[108] instead arguing that the 'problem of policing a deprived, multi-racial area like Brixton cannot be considered without reference to the social environment in which the policing occurs'.[109] In reference to the environment of deprivation that existed in Bri-

---

105   Cited in 'The "Riots"', p. 236.
106   See Smith 2010, pp. 18–33.
107   Sim, 'Scarman: The Police Counter-Attack', *Socialist Register*, 1982, p. 58.
108   Hall 1999, p. 188.
109   Scarman 1986, p. 194.

tain's inner cities, which increasingly suffered from the monetarist policies of the Conservative government, the Scarman Report explicitly stated that there could be 'no doubt that unemployment was a major factor ... which lies at the root of the disorders in Brixton and elsewhere'.[110] Scarman acknowledged that the black community face similar problems to the wider working class in areas such as education, unemployment and discrimination, but on a much more severe scale. The result of this was that 'young black people may feel a particular sense of frustration and deprivation'.[111] Scarman also found the riots to be 'a spontaneous reaction to what was seen as police harassment'.[112]

However, while Scarman criticised some of the actions by the police, the Report, on the whole, stood in favour of the police force. Scarman concluded that 'the power to stop and search', one of the immediate factors for racial harassment by the police, was 'necessary to combat street crime'.[113] From this decision, Scarman found that 'the direction and policies of the Metropolitan Police *are not racist*', but did admit that 'racial prejudice does manifest itself occasionally in the behaviour of a few officers on the streets'.[114] What the Brixton riots did reveal for Lord Scarman was 'weakness in the capacity of the police to respond sufficiently firmly to violence in the streets', finding that 'the use of "hard" policing methods, including the deployment of the Special Patrol Group, is appropriate, even essential'.[115] Scarman concluded that 'racial disadvantage and its nasty associate, racial discrimination' still existed in British society, but controversially declared that '"Institutional racism" does not exist in Britain'.[116] This denial of institutional racism by Scarman demonstrated, according to Martin Barker and Anne Beefer, that Scarman's Report was 'a liberal Report, but one within entirely racist parameters'.[117]

The Scarman Report was criticised by the Communist Party's National Race Relations Committee for its failure to recognise the existence of institutional racism, describing the Report as 'full of contradictions'.[118] Some positive elements to the Report conceded by the Party were the connections between the

---

110   Scarman 1986, p. 205.

111   Scarman 1986, p. 194.

112   Scarman 1986, p. 195.

113   Scarman 1986, p. 207.

114   Scarman 1986, p. 198; my emphasis.

115   Scarman 1986, p. 201.

116   Scarman 1986, p. 209.

117   Barker and Beezer, 'The Language of Racism – An Examination of Lord Scarman's Report and the Brixton Riots', *International Socialism*, 2/18, p. 108.

118   'The Scarman Report', December 1981, in CPGB archives, CP/CENT/CTTE/02/06, LHASC.

disturbances and the economic crisis, racism within the police, community policing, the banning of racist marches and anti-racist training for the police, although many of these points included criticisms of their weaknesses.[119] Other parts of the Report were described as 'just plain bad', with the Party asserting that the Report contained 'no explicit criticism of the government's economic and social policies', the token gesture of a liaison committee with only 'consultative' powers, the negligent mention of racist attacks on black people and most importantly, the denial of institutional racism.[120]

At the CPGB's National Congress in December 1981, the Party repeated the call for an accountable and co-operative police force, working with the black community, while calling for greater Party work within local communities, particularly in response to unemployment, the police and racism.[121] On the issue of racism, the Party recognised the 'rightward shift in British politics affecting all aspects of life' and expressed 'great concern [at] the growing activities of racist and fascist organisations, and particularly the growing attacks on black people'.[122] The Anti-Nazi League had defeated the National Front electorally but fascists were 'now returning to [the] traditional policy of street terrorism and underground activity'.[123] In the struggle against racism, the Party stated that it 'must seek to win many more black members to its ranks', but recognised that this was difficult and would 'only happen inasmuch as the Party is consistently involved in fighting on the issues that the black community recognises as the most urgent'.[124] While the CPGB saw potential for the Party and the Young Communist League to help the youth, such as those involved in the riots, to 'become involved ... in non-anarchic, non-individualistic forms of mass action', the Party failed to make headway in the black community and the Party's membership continued to decline. Youth unemployment did not propel many youth towards the left, with the 'overwhelming majority of the young unemployed remain[ing] apolitical', and as Kenneth Roberts wrote, 'Rather than being channelled into party politics, their discontents are more likely to be expressed on the streets'.[125] By the time of the 1985 riots in London and Birmingham, Thatcher had defeated the trade unions in the Miners' Strike, had seen the British Army victorious in the Falklands War and had led a sustained campaign of

---

119   Ibid.
120   Ibid.
121   'Social and Economic Policy', *Comment*, 5 December 1981, p. 39.
122   'Racism', *Comment*, 5 December 1981, p. 37.
123   Ibid.
124   'Racism', p. 38.
125   Roberts 1984, p. 182.

privatisation of British industry – unlike the vulnerability experienced after the 1981 riots, Thatcherism was now at its hegemonic height.

The Broad Democratic Alliance and Municipal Anti-racism

While the CPGB still saw itself as a revolutionary party, its postwar programme proposed working within the capitalist system to implement socialism through a gradual and democratic process. This was defined by Betty Matthews back in the late 1970s as a 'process of many-sided democratic movements and demands which stage by stage bite into the economic, political, ideological and state power of monopoly capitalism and extend the power of the workers and people'.[126] This was extended to the Party's strategy within the anti-racist struggle. The Communist Party had looked to the Labour government to provide a positive role in combating racial discrimination (with the introduction and amendment of the Race Relations Act), but under the Conservatives, the CPGB, like other anti-racists, increasingly looked to more local organisations to help in the struggle against racism. As the Conservative government ruled at parliamentary level, the CPGB, through the strategy of the broad democratic alliance, saw that their part in the anti-racist movement was to be most effective at local level, co-operating with the CRCs and other community and ethnic organisations. The groundwork for this approach had been made in the late 1970s as the Race Relations Act 1976 had established local Community Relations Councils that the general public could be involved with, which allowed the Communist Party membership to join as individuals.

The 1978 pamphlet, *Racism: How to Combat It*, detailed how Party members, as well as fellow travellers, could combat racism at the practical and everyday level. The pamphlet was concerned with the role of the state, specifically outlining what local CRCs could do in the struggle against racism. CRCs, the Party complained, were haphazardly funded, with wide variation in the amount of grants received, which led to a great variance in the amount of staff involved and therefore, the effectiveness of the organisations to combat racism.[127] As the CRCs welcomed individual members, the Party encouraged its members to affiliate their branches to the organisations, to be involved in the elections for the general council and the executive committee, although there is no mention

---

126   CPGB Education Department, *The Revolutionary Party*, 1977, London: CPGB pamphlet, p. 10.

127   NRRC, *Racism: How to Combat It*, 1978, London: CPGB pamphlet, p. 5.

of converting these organisations to the politics of the CPGB.[128] As the pamphlet warned, 'be cautious of proposals to extend policy beyond [the] two issues' of multi-racialism and opposition to racism and fascism as 'many organisations could not affiliate to a body with more extensive statements of policy'.[129] The Party warned that:

> We should be quite clear that ... it would be damaging for any single organisation to try and set itself up as a sort of 'directing' centre ... as with the Women's Movement, such an attempt would instantly exclude those who, although willing to be part of a broad campaign, would feel that it no longer belonged to them if 'run' by a single organization.[130]

The CPGB had a long history of its membership joining (or forming) broader single-issue organisations with varying degrees of success. Within the anti-racist and anti-colonial movements, Party members had been involved in a number of organisations, such as the Movement for Colonial Freedom/Liberation, the Anti-Apartheid Movement, the Campaign Against Racial Discrimination, the Indian Workers Association, the Trade Unions Against Racialism and the Anti-Nazi League (amongst others). As Christopher Moores shows with the involvement of CPGB members in the National Council for Civil Liberties, this often led to accusations of these organisations being controlled by communists,[131] but in most cases, the Communists did not attempt to take over the direction of these organisations and the Party 'line' more or less reflected wider trends of thought within them. As the broad democratic alliance was promoted by the Party, it became even easier for the Communist Party members involved in these organisations to dispose of the concept that they were representatives of the Party and become 'regular' members of these pressure groups.

In 1981, Gideon Ben-Tovim, a member of the Party's National Race Relations Committee, along with other leftist academics wrote in *Politics and Power* that there had been a shift to a 'more authoritarian consensus' and while legislation had not changed, 'what has changed ... is in the interpretation and implementation of those statutes and legal precedents', with 'the courts and the judiciary, the police and the Civil Service' able to wield 'discretionary powers'

---

128   Ibid.
129   NRRC, *Racism*, p. 2.
130   NRRC, *Racism*, p. 3.
131   Moores 2009, p. 542.

open to abuse in the guise of racial discrimination.[132] The 'inaccessibility of such areas of state administration' had led to the left, in particular the CPGB, using the local levels of the state to fight racism.[133] Instead of rejecting aid programmes and projects offered by the state as 'forms of bribery', Ben-Tovim and his co-authors suggested that these could be used as 'weapons ... for the benefit of black interests, in terms of access to resources, a heightened political awareness and cohesion' and also part of a wider 'means of democratising the state apparatuses by opening them up by black participation and control'.[134] This was part of a push in the 1980s to see local councils as sites of resistance to the Thatcherite status quo and the rise of 'municipal anti-racism'.

In the early 1980s, several city councils under Labour control, primarily the Greater London Council under left-wing Labour leader Ken Livingstone, launched anti-racist campaigns and other initiatives to combat racism and racial discrimination. One of the primary aims of these Labour city councils was the channelling of funds into areas that were under attack from the Conservatives at the national level, including council housing, social services and employment, and this was certainly attempted by the councils. Under the GLC and then Labour-run councils in London boroughs, such as Hackney, Lambeth and Camden, the employment of black and Asian people by the local authorities rose significantly. Alongside this allocation of housing, social services and employment opportunities, these local councils were also important for the distribution of state funds to local initiatives and groups for various projects. While some anti-racists connected to the Communist Party and the Labour left, such as Gideon Ben-Tovim and those who wrote in *Politics & Power*, saw this as a way to fight state racism from below, others felt it made those who sought funding for anti-racist projects conform to the liberal anti-racism promoted by the Labour Party and also acted as a form of monitoring. In her history of the Asian Youth Movements, Anandi Ramamurthy described how the AYM in Bradford shifted as it became more involved in the local Labour-led council:

The new aims [of the AYM (Bradford)] focused on opposing discrimination, educating the youth about the relationship between discrimination and inequality and recognised the right of black people to organise independently, but there was no recognition in the new aims and objectives to the fact that 'the only real force capable of fighting racism was a workers

---

132   Ben-Tovim, Gabriel, Law and Stredder 1981, pp. 172–3.
133   Ben-Tovim, Gabriel, Law and Stredder 1981, p. 173.
134   Ben-Tovim, Gabriel, Law and Stredder 1981, p. 176.

movement, both black and white,' nor was there any commitment given to international solidarity.[135]

In addition to these material attempts to combat racial discrimination and to promote racial equality, these councils were heavily involved in anti-racist campaigns disseminated through the media and advertising, as well as encouraging Racial Awareness Training (RAT) for council employees and others. The anti-racist campaigns launched by the GLC's Ethnic Minorities Committee created a number of billboards, posters and pamphlets in the early to mid-1980s directed at tackling racism, along the lines of 'Nearly a million Londoners are getting a raw deal – simply because the other 6 million let it happen. Let's kick racism out of town', or 'If you're not part of the solution, you're part of the problem. You've got the power to challenge the damaging effects of racism. Use it'.[136] For Gilroy, these campaigns made racism seem like a solely ideological concept that could be combatted on an individual basis, without addressing the structural and material causes of it, and was simply a moral issue that people needed to rectify, individualising the issue and making mass anti-racist activism seem irrelevant. As he wrote in 1987:

> the GLC's tactics relied on isolated and individualized acts ... The problem of what connects one anti-racist to the next is not recognized as a substantive political issue. Municipal anti-racism solved it by providing signs, badges and stickers through which individuals could convey their affiliation to others without having to negotiate through collective activity the extent to which definitions of anti-racism were actually held in common.[137]

Another critic of this municipal anti-racism was A. Sivanandan, who argued that any 'positive action' done by local authorities was 'backed up by a system of monitoring'.[138] But the main target for Sivanandan's critique of municipal anti-racism was its use of RAT to 'train' people who were employed by the local authorities and other service providers about 'racial awareness'. For Sivanandan, RAT, like the GLC's anti-racism campaigns, saw racism as an ideological and individualised problem, with RAT unable (or unwilling) to tackle the

---

135   Ramamurthy 2013, p. 163.
136   Gilroy 2002, pp. 181–5.
137   Gilroy 2002, p. 191.
138   Sivanandan 2008, pp. 144–5.

underlying structural and material factors that led to racial discrimination in Britain, describing the RAT concept of racism as follows:

> Racism, according to RAT, has its roots in white culture, and white culture, unaffected by material conditions or history, goes back to the beginning of time. Hence, racism is part of the collective unconsciousness, the pre-natal scream, the original sin.[139]

The focus of RAT was therefore on changing attitudes and behaviours and not power relations, except when these power relations are redefined as 'personal relations'.[140] RAT was seen by Sivanandan as the antithesis of collective anti-racist action informed by an awareness of unequal power dynamics in British society and the material conditions that fostered these unequal relations, linking anti-racism with other struggles, such as working-class, women's liberation and anti-imperialist movements. Effective anti-racist action required, Sivanandan believed, a common denominator of a black political identity – 'as a common colour of colonial and racist exploitation'[141] – and argued that municipal anti-racism, by focussing on racism's ideological aspects, encouraged the fragmentation of a collective anti-racist movement into a number of ethnic communities informed by identity politics. As he protested:

> This 'vertical mosaic' of ethnic groups, so distanced from the horizontal of class politics, then became even more removed by the policies of 'left' Labour councils who, lacking the race-class perspective which would have allowed them to dismantle the institutional racism of their own structures, institutionalized ethnicity instead.[142]

In the pages of *Marxism Today*, many of the Party reformers who had embraced the 'broad democratic alliance' came to the defence of the strategy to municipal socialism and its extension, municipal anti-racism. David Edgar acknowledged that the anti-racist campaigns conducted by various local authorities had 'laid themselves open to caricature ... and may, in a more profound sense, have been fundamentally misconceived', but used council employment figures, for example, to argue that the promotion of an anti-racist agenda had had some

---

139   Sivanandan 2008, p. 163.
140   Sivanandan 2008, p. 162.
141   Sivanandan 2008, p. 165.
142   Sivanandan 2008, p. 144.

positive outcomes.[143] Furthermore, Edgar took umbrage with Sivanandan's criticisms, accepted that although there were 'undoubted misconceptions and misunderstandings' in the municipal anti-racism strategy, anti-racist activism at the local state level had fostered an awareness of other social and political issues, writing 'it could be argued that anti-racists have been quicker off the mark on global economic restructuring than some others'.[144]

On a similar note, Paul Corrigan, Trevor Jones, John Lloyd and Jock Young proposed in *Marxism Today* that although municipal socialism had 'now failed … at least municipal new leftists *tried*'.[145] Beatrix Campbell blamed the 'traditional institutions of labourism within civil society, primarily the trade union movement', as well as the mainstream Labour Party (accusing it of being 'inert or absent within civil society'), for its alleged refusal to partake in the campaigns for equal opportunities orchestrated by the local councils, such as those based on anti-racism and women's liberation.[146] For those writing *Marxism Today*, the councils, for all their misgivings, were still sites of resistance against Thatcherism and its neo-liberal policies and in this era of leftist retreat, the local councils were one area of the struggle where tangible gains could be made. As Satnam Virdee wrote in relation to Sivanandan's critique of municipal anti-racism, in these criticisms of the GLC's anti-racist strategy:

> there is little evidence of a systematic assessment of the relative effectiveness of the wide range of policies introduced by local councils to curb racial discrimination and inequality faced by working class black and Asian people in important areas of social life including housing, employment and social services.[147]

The 'Limits' of Trade Unionism in the 1980s

Beatrix Campbell's writings in *Marxism Today* represented the extreme end of the spectrum of those reformers inside the Communist Party and attached to the journal-cum-magazine in the 1980s, with Campbell heavily criticising the trade unions for ignoring women's issues, such as equal pay and sexism

---

143   Edgar, 'On the Race Track', *Marxism Today*, November 1988, p. 30.
144   Edgar, 'On the Race Track', p. 31.
145   Corrigan, Jones, Lloyd and Young, 'Citizen Gains', *Marxism Today*, August 1988, p. 18.
146   Campbell, 'Charge of the Light Brigade', *Marxism Today*, February 1987, p. 10.
147   Virdee 2014, p. 154.

in the workplace. On the other hand, most others connected to reform within the Party and *Marxism Today* were of the opinion that the traditional reliance of the labour movement on the trade unions had limited success and argued that this had been borne out by the events of the late 1970s and early 1980s. Eric Hobsbawm had argued in 'The Forward March of Labour Halted?' in 1978 that 'straight-forward economist trade union consciousness may at times actually set workers against each other rather than establish wider patterns of solidarity',[148] and for those who endorsed the CPGB's 'broad democratic alliance', these 'wider patterns of solidarity' could not be expended just to keep the trade unions onside. Despite the debates surrounding Hobsbawm's thesis and its links to the newly promoted 'broad democratic alliance', which filled the pages of *Marxism Today* between 1978 and 1980, the early 1980s saw an uneasy truce between the two main factions, the 'Euros' and the 'Tankies' (although two opposition factional journals started to appear that argued that both of these larger factions as 'anti-party' – *Straight Left* and *The Leninist*).[149]

The 'match on the blue touch paper', as Francis Beckett described it,[150] that reignited this division and led to irreparable damage within the Communist Party was an article in *Marxism Today* in late 1982 by Tony Lane, which criticised the trade union strategy promoted by some inside the CPGB, particularly censuring the trade union bureaucracy for failing to deal with the significant changes to the manufacturing industry in Britain and the decline of large-scale urban factories – traditionally the most organised workforces. For Lane, these long-term economic shifts had a more profound effect upon the trade union movement than 'resurgent *laissez-faire* Toryism', writing:

> Trade union leadership at all levels, from the local to the national, has been so stunned by the reactionary nature of shopkeeper Toryism that it often seems to take more notice of ideology than it does of material changes in its environment.[151]

Lane blamed 'sectional interests' and 'a lack of will to fight' for the trade unions' 'crisis of legitimacy', explaining that this had caused a schism between the trade union leaders (including the shop stewards) and the rank-and-file membership

---

148 Hobsbawm, 'The Forward March of Labour Halted?', *Marxism Today*, September 1978, p. 286.
149 Parker 2012, p. 104.
150 Beckett 1998, p. 194.
151 Lane, 'The Unions: Caught on the Ebb Tide', *Marxism Today*, September 1982, p. 7.

and the feeling that there was little democracy within the movement.[152] Unless there was a clear leadership over how to face the problems facing the unions in the 1980s, as well as more interactive democracy at the rank-and-file level, Lane argued, the rank and file would face 'uncertainty as to whether unions are worth fighting for'.[153]

Lane's was not particularly different from other criticisms made by Hobsbawm and others since the late 1970s and could not be seen as especially controversial – as Andrew Pearmain has written, '[i]t was a mildly populist critique of the trade union bureaucracy, which would not have seemed out of place in *The Sunday Times* or *Socialist Worker*'.[154] But the CPGB's Industrial Organiser Mick Costello and editor of the *Morning Star* Tony Chater used the article as an issue to force the centrist Party leadership under General Secretary Gordon McLennan to take action against the journal and its editor, Martin Jacques, as well as airing critiques of Lane, Jacques and the journal in the pages of the daily paper. Disciplinary action for Jacques and the journal by the Party's internal bodies was defeated (narrowly, according to Pearmain),[155] but the same bodies also severely rebuked Chater, Costello and the paper for, in the words of Willie Thompson, 'forming a cabal to attack another party journal and to use the party's name without reference to the EC [Executive Committee]'.[156] In the aftermath, Costello resigned from his post as Industrial Organiser and joined Chater at the *Morning Star*. The newspaper, nominally run independently from the CPGB by the People's Press Printing Society, was used by Chater as a base for criticising the Party and its leadership, who, it was believed, were unwilling to stand up to the 'Euros'. On the other hand, Jacques had, according to Francis Beckett, lost faith in reforming the Party[157] and moved towards transforming *Marxism Today* into a separate entity, although it still relied on funding from the Party. While two of the major Party organs drifted away from any form of oversight by the Party leadership, the Party itself fractured, unclear of its direction and role within the British political landscape. As Geoff Andrews wrote:

From this point on, the party was split in two; the leadership and Gramscian-Eurocommunists were in control of the party and the Costello/

152   Lane, 'The Unions', p. 13.
153   Ibid.
154   Pearmain 2011, p. 129.
155   Pearmain 2011, pp. 130–1.
156   Thompson 1992, p. 184.
157   Beckett 1998, p. 197.

Chater group controlled the *Morning Star*, and, with it, a notable list of trade union leaders, and contact with a declining trade union base. Neither side could be described as ultimate victors in this battle. The party was deprived of its daily paper and with it, what was left of its trade union base; and the 'hardliners' were now detached from the party, its political machine and its resources.[158]

At the 1983 AGM of the PPPS and Communist Party's National Congress in the same year, the issue of control of the newspaper became a heated one, leading to the expulsion of several Party members from the *Morning Star* group. By the time that the Miners' Strike broke out in March 1984, the industrial strategy of the Communist Party was in total disarray and at the national level the Party was slow to come up with a programme of action to help the National Union of Mineworkers, leaving it to local activists to take the initiative.

This loss of patience with the structures of the trade union movement was not just felt by the Eurocommunist wing of the CPGB, many black and Asian workers were similarly dissatisfied with the trade unions, particularly for their limited reaction to the problem of racism faced by these workers. In 1977, the PEP (Political and Economic Planning) report, *Racial Disadvantage in Britain*, outlined the problems that black workers faced in their relationship with the trade union movement, noting that while the 1970s had seen developments in most of the trade unions adopting anti-racist and equal opportunities policies, there was 'a contrast between this formal policy and its practical results'.[159] In interviews with eight of the largest unions in Britain, the report found 'little evidence that any definite action had been taken' by the trade union leadership to combat incidents of racial discrimination inside the unions.[160] The report revealed that the trade union leaders were likely to ignore cases of racial discrimination unless they reached the highest echelons of the unions' complaint structures and as 'very few complaints filtered up to head-office level, ... leaders tended to interpret this as meaning that there was very little trouble of this kind.'[161] As discussed in the previous chapter, the trade unions, along with the Labour Party, were spurred into anti-racist action by the mid- to late 1970s, as seen with the large-scale mobilisation of trade union support for the Grunwick strike and the labour movement backing of the Anti-Nazi League. However, as Phizacklea and Miles argued in 1987, the anti-racist campaigning

---

158   Andrews 2004, p. 207.
159   Smith 1977, p. 193.
160   Smith 1977, p. 202.
161   Smith 1977, p. 204.

by the trade unions (primarily the TUC) and the Labour Party 'seemed to die away with the collapse of the National Front vote in the general election of 1979'.[162]

In August 1976, the TUC formed its Race Relations Advisory Committee and in 1981 created a Black Workers Charter, but several studies conducted in the 1980s revealed that these initiatives had a limited impact upon the efforts of the trade unions to combat racism in the workplace and within their own organisations. Phizacklea and Miles cited a 1981 investigation by the Commission for Racial Equality into the AUEW that it was the policy of the union to condemn racial discrimination, 'no specific instructions about how such a policy should be implemented had been provided for either officials or members' and this principled opposition to racism was 'contradicted by both the open expression of racism' by some union members and 'the refusal of the officials to take any action to combat that racism'.[163] Gloria Lee stated that when interviewed, black members 'saw themselves as grossly under-represented within their unions' and 'felt that as black members, they [were] more poorly served by their union than white members'.[164] John Wrench cited in his 1986 paper that certain acts of explicit racism were still occurring in the trade union movement in the early 1980s, but there was also 'the more passive collusion of union officers in practices which were discriminatory in their outcomes, and a reluctance to change these practices', such as the use of word-of-mouth to hire people, which worked greatly against non-white applicants.[165]

As mentioned in Chapter 3, the traditional position of the trade unions was to have no specific policies to assist black workers integrate into the labour movement, arguing for 'equal treatment' for both black and white union members.[166] Despite the actions taken in the late 1970s and early 1980s, such as the aforementioned initiatives by the TUC, the 'equal treatment' argument still remained with the trade unions. In 1977, the PEP report stated that some union officials justified their poor record on combating racism 'by saying they make no distinction between black and white and that this means that no special action can be taken'.[167] Phizacklea and Miles claimed that this was still the case in the 1980s and declared '[r]acism can masquerade in the guise of colour-

---

162   Phizacklea and Miles 1987, p. 119.
163   Ibid.
164   Lee 1987, p. 151.
165   Wrench, *Trade Unions, Equal Opportunity and Racism*, Policy Papers in Ethnic Relations no. 5, 1986, pp. 11–12.
166   Wrench and Virdee 1996, p. 245.
167   Smith 1977, p. 193.

blindness, when there is clear evidence of cases containing discrimination and allegations of lack of support for Asian and Caribbean members from their unions.'[168]

As part of the TUC's efforts to combat racism, special education classes were created to inform trade unionists about the impact of racism upon black workers and how to tackle this, but critics asserted that as these classes were voluntary to attend, it had not reached the right audience and was not well supported by the unions.[169] Wrench argued that 'those ... who would benefit most from attending such courses tend to stay away as they feel that such provisions are a waste of time and money'.[170] A 1984 report by the Greater London Council's Anti-Racist Trade Union Working Group found that the GMWU, ACTT and NUT all held equal opportunities and 'racism awareness' training courses, but only the AUEW-TASS ran any 'positive action' programmes, which supported 'appointing officials with ethnic background, or females, to the union'.[171]

John Wrench wrote in 1986 about this GLC report, stating:

The findings of the GLC survey confirm the suspicions of many activists that despite the history of disputes and struggles, the research, the educational material, and the prosecutions, there remains a body of trade union officers who simply do not understand – or are unwilling to acknowledge – what racism and racial equality are, what their effects are, how they operate, and what sorts of measures are needed to oppose them.[172]

However, most of these reports from the 1980s pointed to areas where the trade unions were progressing on issues of 'race'. Phizacklea and Miles wrote that 'we have witnessed some concern amongst some unions to increase the participation and representation of Asian and Caribbean workers and restatement of a commitment amongst the same union to tackle racism within their own ranks and the wider society'.[173] John Wrench also noted that in the era of austerity and the Thatcherite onslaught against the trade union movement, 'there has been an awareness of common cause and common interest' between black and white workers and that this had been 'part of one positive development of

---

168   Phizacklea and Miles 1987, p. 123.
169   Lee 1987, p. 149.
170   Wrench 1986, p. 13.
171   GLC Anti-Racist Trade Union Working Group, *Racism Within Trade Unions*, 1984, London: GLC, p. 16.
172   Wrench, *Trade Unions, Equal Opportunity and Racism*, p. 22.
173   Phizacklea and Miles 1987, p. 121.

recent years – the increasing organisation of black workers and their success in making their influence felt within the labour movement.'[174]

The Push for Black Sections/Caucuses within the Labour Movement

At the same time, a push was made by some black activists for separate caucuses or sections within the trade unions (and within the Labour Party) for black people, similar to those developed for women in the early 1980s. Some within the Communist Party, such as Trevor Carter, argued for these black caucuses, with Carter proposing in his 1986 book *Shattering Illusions* that '[c]aucusing has developed as the main way in which black people have asserted their presence in trade unions'.[175] Arguing that these caucuses were not 'separatist', Carter wrote that the caucus 'simply aims to ensure that that wider body [the trade union] is more fully informed by and answerable to its whole membership.'[176] While the *Morning Star* opposed this strategy and had Bill Morris, the black Deputy General Secretary of the TGWU, denounce it as 'sectarian' and 'divisive', *Marxism Today* featured several articles in 1984 and 1985 that argued for black sections inside the Labour Party and in the trade unions (all from non-CPGB members). Trevor Phillips argued that the poor support given by the Labour Party to its black parliamentary candidates in the 1983 election demanded that its black members formally organise *within* the Party and that this was necessary to be taken seriously by Labour's National Executive Committee.[177] Iqbal Wahhab and Marc Wardsworth argued in the following issue that recognition of these proposed black sections (to be voted for at the forthcoming Labour Party conference) would be an example of 'real and credible power-sharing', but added that black sections were not 'a panacea' to the problems that black people faced in and outside the Labour Party, although they clarified that this was only 'part of a solution provided by black activists themselves'.[178] By this time, a few unions with a high number of black workers (such as the National and Local Government Officers' Association and the National Union of Public Employees) had established black caucuses and both articles proposed that this was a way forward for the Labour Party and other

---

174   Wrench, *Trade Unions, Equal Opportunity and Racism*, p. 24.
175   Carter 1986, p. 141.
176   Ibid.
177   Phillips, 'Labour's Black Sections', *Marxism Today*, September 1984, p. 2.
178   Wahhab and Wadsworth, 'Black Sections', *Marxism Today*, October 1984, p. 45.

trade unions. Wahhab and Wadsworth said that even if black sections were not officially recognised, 'caucusing' would probably be the best strategy to be employed by black workers to get 'a better deal'.[179] Phillips suggested that the trade unions 'may also find the black caucus approach too hard to take' and would reject the notion as it may highlight 'the relative weakness of trade union influence at local level', as well as provoke 'demands for the right to independent caucuses within the unions' on an even wider basis.[180] Despite opposition from Labour Opposition leader Neil Kinnock, the black sections motion was passed by the Labour Party conference and the Party, alongside several public service unions, established black caucuses or sections as part of their internal structures.

At the Communist Party's 1983 38th National Congress, the CPGB supported black caucuses within the trade unions. A resolution was passed that stated that black members' groups would 'enable the needs and problems of black workers to be expressed better' and would 'enrich the quality of struggle in defence of the trade union movement and in the interests of the working class as a whole'.[181] In the EC resolution, 'Key Issues for Trade Unions', it was acknowledged that black members' groups had been established in some unions, such as NALGO, and this was welcomed by the CPGB, purporting that these groups would 'help involve more black trade unionists in union affairs and press unions to tackle racism more decisively'.[182] Both resolutions made pronouncements that these black members' groups were favourable to separate trade unions for black workers. As the EC Resolution declared, 'These groups can lessen the dangers of separate trade unions for black workers, which would be divisive and isolate them'.[183] In a 1985 roundtable organised by *Marxism Today*, Stuart Hall and Vishnu Sharma argued that black caucuses and black sections were beneficial to the labour movement, while A. Sivanandan described them as a 'distraction from the struggle that the black community has to face today'.[184] Stuart Hall countered this by saying:

If you say that the real problem is maintaining the momentum of the black struggle then I can see that the black sections are a distraction.

---

179   Ibid.
180   Phillips, 'Labour's Black Sections', p. 3.
181   CPGB, 'Branch and District Resolutions: 1983 Congress', p. 12, in CPGB archives, CP/CENT/CONG/21/05, LHASC.
182   EC Resolution, 'Key Issues for Trade Unions', *Communist Focus*, December 1983, p. 16.
183   EC Resolution, 'Key Issues for Trade Unions', p. 15.
184   'Black Sections: Radical Demand or … Distraction?', *Marxism Today*, September 1985, p. 33.

But if you are concerned, and I am concerned, about the question of the white working class, you have to recognise that the Labour Party is a majority working class party. It has hegemonised the working class since the beginning of the twentieth century, whether we like it or not ... So the black struggle must have some idea about how to get into that organisationally, how to transform that organisation ...[185]

Similar to the idea of the broad democratic alliance and trying to use the labour movement, combined with the Communist Party and the new social movements, to create a counter-hegemony to challenge the capitalist system, Hall argued that bringing the black struggle to the Labour Party was a 'double struggle which is both with and against' and required taking the fight to the Labour Party's constituent elements, as well as the TUC – 'blowing it apart from the inside'.[186] To transform the ideas and actions of the labour movement, Hall proposed, one had to 'mak[e] the internal structured organisation of the labour movement aware of the impact and history of racism'.[187]

Despite their initial controversy, the general academic and political consensus is that the black caucuses within the trade unions and the black sections inside the Labour Party proved useful for promoting an awareness of issues of racial discrimination and equal opportunity within the labour movement. Existing to this day inside the Labour Party, these black sections outlasted the Communist Party (which dissolved in 1991) and NALGO and NUPE (which both merged into the union UNISON in 1993). At a time when Thatcherism seemed at its hegemonic peak and the labour movement was at one of its lowest ebbs, the formation of the black caucuses/sections in the face of fierce resistance was a victory that buoyed those in the anti-racist struggle and within the Communist Party, which was now in its final years as an organisation (and greatly suffering from the splits that reopened in 1983).

The End of the Party

The Thatcherite years also had a dramatic effect upon the Communist Party of Great Britain. As those reformers connected to *Marxism Today* argued in the late 1970s and early 1980s, Thatcherism was more than a stricter continuation of

---

185   'Black Sections', p. 34.
186   Ibid.
187   Ibid.

previous Conservative governments and represented a widespread ideological shift to the right that embodied strong notions of 'law and order', combined with the neo-liberalism of free market economics. The reformers believed that this shift to the right needed to be addressed by more than traditional class-based politics and demanded a greater emphasis on the long-term ideological aspects that had allowed this rightwards shift. This emphasis on ideology and the insufficiencies of class-based politics by the reformers has been viewed as a central reason for the eventual collapse of the CPGB. By the end of the 1980s, the 'New Times' approach, presented by Martin Jacques and Stuart Hall in *Marxism Today*,[188] was described by critics as a defeatist attitude and a vindication of Thatcherism. A. Sivanandan, who had previously criticised the left for its failure to address other issues outside the class politics of industrial militancy, wrote in *Race & Class* in 1989:

> New Times is a fraud, a counterfeit, a humbug. It palms off Thatcherite values as socialist, shores up the Thatcherite market with the pretended politics of choice, fits out the Thatcherite individual with progressive consumerism, makes consumption itself the stuff of politics. New Times is a mirror image of Thatcherism passing for socialism. New Times is Thatcherism in drag.[189]

With the Communist Party becoming increasingly divided between the reformers and the traditional industrialist wing, polarised through the respective publications of *Marxism Today* and the *Morning Star*, the Party also witnessed further defeats on the industrial front, experienced, along with the wider labour movement, during the 1984–5 Miners' Strike. For many in the labour movement, the defeat of the strike represented an end to the traditional approach of class politics through industrial actions and trade union militancy and was symptomatic of a wider crisis in the British left. Thatcher's monetarist policies had hastened the decline of heavy industry throughout Britain and the upheaval in many British towns caused by this decline, demonstrably felt through high levels of unemployment, was difficult for the left to counter. Raphael Samuel wrote that the 'disarray of the Left in the face of the miners'

---

188   The October 1988 edition of *Marxism Today* was dedicated to the 'New Times'. The *Manifesto for New Times* was the programme adopted by the CPGB at its 1989 National Congress that occurred as the Soviet bloc was collapsing. After the collapse of the CPGB in November 1991, some remnants of the Party formed the Democratic Left, which published the journal *New Times* throughout the 1990s. See Hall and Jacques 1990.

189   Sivanandan 1989, p. 1.

strike [was] ... part of a large discomfort both about the alternative to Thatcher-ism, and of the very possibility of a socialism which [was] in any sense repres-entative of popular desire and will'.[190]

The defeat of the strike further demoralised the remaining traditionalists within the CPGB, who were already in open conflict with the reformers in the Party leadership and had suffered from the leading traditionalists being expelled by the Executive Committee. Although the CPGB leadership and *Marxism Today* supported the strike, the assumptions of the reformers of the limited actions of industrial militancy seemed to be further validated by the strike's defeat. During the 1980s, the Communist Party's membership rapidly declined, hastened by the internal Party splits. In 1981, membership had been 18,458 and this had fallen to 12,711 in 1985, which then fell to a mere 7,615 in 1989 at the time of the collapse of the Soviet bloc.[191] Although those remaining in the Party launched a new Party programme in 1989 titled *A Manifesto for New Times* (expanding on a series of articles published in the October 1988 issue of *Marxism Today*), there was little enthusiasm for continuing the Party as a polit-ical organisation and at the December 1991 National Congress, the membership of the Communist Party of Great Britain, after more than seventy years of its existence, voted to dissolve itself.

Conclusion

In 1979, with the defeat of the National Front at the General Election and the mass support for the Anti-Nazi League, it may have seemed as if the anti-racist movement in Britain had gained a major victory. However, although the explicit fascism of the National Front had been curtailed, racism was still a widespread phenomenon in British society. Britain's black communities still faced many problems – harassment by the police, much higher unemployment rates under the monetarist policies of the Conservatives, continuing racial dis-crimination in the workplace, housing and social services and restrictions on citizenship under the 1981 British Nationality Act. The Thatcher governments that lasted from 1979 to 1990 fundamentally changed British society and this includes changing ideas of 'race' and nation, including further restrictions on citizenship, the patriotism evoked during the Falklands War, the lack of socio-economic support for Britain's black communities and the criminalisation of

---

190   Samuel 1986, pp. xiv–xv.
191   'Communist Party Membership', in CPGB archives, CP/CENT/ORG/19/04, LHASC.

black youth by the police and the judiciary. The disconnect between the government, the institutions of the state and the black communities resulted in episodes of public disorder across Britain throughout the Thatcher years – in 1980, 1981 and 1985. The confrontations that many sections of British society experienced under Thatcher were first experienced by black people, especially black youth, whose anger exploded after years of police harassment and racial discrimination (and abuse) at the hands of the state.

The Communist Party, which had played a significant, but not leading, role in the anti-racist and anti-fascist struggles of the 1960s and 1970s, saw its role in the anti-racist struggle in the early 1980s diminished even further. As this chapter has shown, anti-racist activity by CPGB activists was often interpreted as taking part in broad alliances and looking to build links between various organisations and movements through the involvement of Party personnel. For example, Vishnu Sharma was part of the CPGB's Executive Committee, but also played a leading role in the Indian Workers Association (Southall), the National Council for Civil Liberties, the Joint Council for the Welfare of Immigrants, the Anti-Nazi League and the Campaign Against Racist Laws. Emphasising this solidarity between movements and fostering a broad democratic alliance, as proposed by the redrafted *British Road to Socialism*, these Party members worked tirelessly to assist the anti-racist cause, but were warned not to alienate potential allies by pushing a communist agenda, which resulted in a dilution of the Communist Party's influence in the anti-racist movement. Another example of this is the 'Racism and the Police' conference organised in late 1980 by the Party's National Race Relations Committee, which brought together representatives from various anti-racist organisations, but also included a fair number of CPGB members. The resulting charter that was drawn up by the conference was vaguely in line with Communist Party policy, but shared its demands with most organisations in the anti-racist movement. This worked well for creating consensus, but sometimes this consensus came at the cost of the identity and influence of the Communist Party, which was now no longer the most significant group on the socialist left that was involved in the struggle against racism.

After the 'victories' that the anti-racist movement had in the late 1970s, particularly the solidarity expressed between black and white workers at the Grunwick strike and the contribution of the Anti-Nazi League to the electoral defeat of the National Front, many black activists criticised the left-wing groups and the labour movement for focusing on the political/economic threat of Thatcherism and forgetting about the problems of Britain's black communities. Darcus Howe and Paul Gilroy point to events such as the New Cross Fire in January 1981 as a time when the British left seem to have been absent from the anti-racist fight. The riots of 1980 and 1981 seemed to show the limits of the relationship built between black and white workers, activists and organisations in the previous few years and that resistance to Thatcher by black youth was going to be more direct than placing their faith in the institutions of the labour movement and the 'white left'. Like the rest of the left, the Communist Party reacted to the riots by trying to point rebellious youth towards the politics of the CPGB, but failed to redress the broader trend of black and Asian youth avoiding established political organisations and who were especially suspicious of those leftist groups who portrayed the riots as simple manifestations of a disapproval of Thatcherism.

Under the influence of *Marxism Today* and the Party positions developed by Stuart Hall and Martin Jacques (alongside others), it looked as if the Communist Party had something useful and unique to offer the labour movement and the anti-racist movement. However, this was overshadowed by developing schisms in Party, which brought the Party to the brink of collapse. Any hope that the Communist Party had to reshape Labour, the labour movement and the anti-racist movement, promised by the broad democratic alliance and the counter-hegemony outlined by *The British Road to Socialism* and in the pages of *Marxism Today*, disappeared along with its dwindling membership.

Conclusion

In 1957, Claudia Jones wrote in an article for *World News* discussing West Indians in Britain: 'Our Party is judged among colonial workers by its policy, but much more so by its deeds'.[1] This book has sought to examine both the anti-racist policies of the Communist Party of Great Britain and how it attempted to implement these policies. The CPGB spanned nearly the entire period of what Eric Hobsbawm called the 'short twentieth century'[2] and throughout its existence, had campaigned against colonialism, the 'colour bar' and racial discrimination (and racist violence) in the colonial sphere and in Britain. The Communist Party was one of the first organisations within the British labour movement to have an explicit anti-racist agenda, opposing the 'colour bar' in the British Empire/Commonwealth and later in the domestic sphere, but the question this book seeks to answer is how successful was the Party's effort to help fight racism faced by Britain's black and Asian communities and how successful was the Party in convincing other sections of the labour movement to take up the anti-racist struggle. As this book has shown, the CPGB were constantly performing a balancing act between looking to the trade unions and other labour organisations to spearhead the anti-racist movement, making white workers aware of the fight against racism, and working more closely with the black communities at the grassroots level, where there was increasing scepticism over the eagerness of the trade unions to combat racism. As a Liverpudlian Party member asked in a letter to *Comment* in 1981:

> On what terms do we involve the labour movement in the [anti-racist] struggle, as the vanguard taking over the direction of the struggle or as supporters of the black community bringing the power of the movement to bear where the black community itself feels the most urgent need?[3]

Since the reformation of factory branches during the Second World War, and particularly as the Party's postwar programme *The British Road to Socialism* saw them as key to any influence upon the Labour Party, the trade unions were central to the CPGB's agenda, including in the fight against racism. While the Party was attracting a number of black workers, activists and students from across

---

1 Jones, 'West Indians in Britain', *World News*, 29 June 1957, p. 416.
2 Hobsbawm 2004, p. 3.
3 'Letters', *Comment*, 17 October 1981, p. 14.

the Commonwealth in the 1950s, its literature focused on attempts to convince trade unionists to welcome these fellow workers and campaign against
'colour bars' in the labour movement and the workplace. In the pages of the
Daily Worker in the late 1950s, Kay Beauchamp stressed 'the need for the whole
Labour movement to take up the fight against colour discrimination, for the
trade unions to champion the rights of coloured workers and to make a special appeal to them to join the unions'.[4] Although the trade unions supported
campaigns, such as the Movement for Colonial Freedom, at bloc level, getting
individual trade unionists to take part in anti-racist activities was a much more
difficult task. As mentioned in the book, until the mid-1970s, trade unionists
favoured a 'colour blind' approach that promoted no 'special treatment' for
people based on ethnicity or nationality, but then offered little assistance to
those who needed help in overcoming racial discrimination in the workplace.

The elections of Labour in 1964 and 1966 highlighted the differences between
the labour movement and the needs of Britain's black communities, and the
problem that the Communist Party had in attempting to win the 'mass party'
towards a Labour-Communist alliance and maintaining a credible anti-racist
programme. Although Labour did introduce legislation against racial discrimination in public places, housing, employment and in social services in 1965 and
in 1968, this was done in conjunction with further restrictions on immigration
from the Commonwealth, which tied together the notions of integration with
restriction. As Dilip Hiro wrote, this signalled a convergence between Labour
and the Conservatives on the issues of immigration and racial justice – '[a]n
advance, albeit minor, on the front for ethnic minorities was conceded by the
Conservatives in exchange for a retreat by Labour in the matter of immigration
restrictions'.[5] It also signalled to black workers in Britain that Labour's anti-
racist idealism could be countered by the poll-driven necessity to be as 'tough
on immigration' as the Conservatives. A major part of the Communist Party's
anti-racist agenda throughout the 1960s and 1970s was to campaign for Labour
to repeal its commitment to racist immigration control measures and to place
further powers in the Race Relations legislation, but the two terms of Harold
Wilson in government showed that these were difficult demands to implement.
It was absolutely necessary for the Communist Party to oppose these racist
actions by the Labour Party, just as much as it opposed those perpetrated by
the Tories, but this was juxtaposed with the CPGB's support for Labour in many
other areas, especially in the electoral sphere. This inconsistency convinced

---

4   Beauchamp, 'Democracy v Racial Prejudice', *Daily Worker*, 16 May 1957.
5   Hiro 1992, p. 211.

a number of black activists and workers that it was better to join black community or single-issue organisations, rather than be a minority in the primarily
'white' labour organisations. This went away from the strategy put forward by
the CPGB, who were wary that these black community organisations would
feed into the 'black power' movement and turn black workers away from the
importance of the class struggle.

Even in the 1970s, as the trade unions became more aware of the issues of
racism faced by black workers and new networks of solidarity were formed
between the labour movement and the black communities, there were still tensions over the direction of political activity in these areas (such as the strike
at Grunwick between 1976 and 1978 or the Anti-Nazi League campaign from
1977 to 1981) and what issues were focused on in these actions of working-
class solidarity. For example, was strike action at Grunwick primarily about
defending the right to strike or combating racial discrimination and harassment in the workplace (or fighting the sexist treatment of South Asian women
by the management at Grunwick)? Was the anti-fascist movement more concerned with the threat that the National Front posed to the working class, or
did it concentrate on the racial violence and harassment experienced by black
Britons at the hands of NF and other fascist sympathisers? As the ideas of Antonio Gramsci and of Eurocommunism developed within the Communist Party
during this period, a number of those involved in anti-racist activities acknowledged these tensions and promoted engaging with black workers, activists and
youth in other ways, but by this time, the CPGB's influence within the anti-racist
movement had diminished. Other black activist and far left groups, such as the
Asian Youth Movements and the Race Today Collective on the one hand and
the International Marxist Group and the Socialist Workers Party on the other,
had emerged that were more radical, confrontational and less beholden to the
trade unions and the Labour Party. The middle ground that the Communist
Party was holding on to was growing ever smaller.

The isolated position of the Communist Party from others within the anti-
racist movement was exacerbated by its acceptance, as laid out in *The British
Road to Socialism*, of the potentially positive role of the state. Many on the left
eschewed any co-operation with the structures of the capitalist state and this
extended to their anti-racist activism, whilst numerous black activists argued
that most black people in Britain had experienced the racism of the state in
some form and therefore could not be relied upon to support an anti-racist
agenda. This was particularly the case with the more radical organisations that
appeared in the 1970s, such as the British Black Panther Movement and the
Asian Youth Movement. As the book has shown, the Communist Party routinely
called for the strengthening of the Race Relations Act and for prosecution of

those who incited racial hatred or committed racially discriminatory actions. However, the uneven prosecutorial history of the Act, which saw black power activist Michael x jailed in 1967, but no case brought against Enoch Powell in 1968,[6] made the case for others that were sceptical about progressive political movements encouraging the use of the repressive apparatuses of the state to intervene on their behalf. This was reinforced by the violence wreaked by the police against the mass pickets at Grunwick, at the Notting Hill Carnival in 1976 and against the anti-fascist movement on numerous occasions (which resulted in the deaths of two protestors in 1974 and 1979). By the early 1980s, the CPGB was promoting the popular idea (amongst the Gramscian and Eurocommunist left, at least) that the Thatcher government had ushered in a new era of author-itarianism and that the working class, particularly black people, suffered at the hands of the police and other state agencies, but still pushed in its 'Charter of Demands' for greater state interventions in some areas, such as

 – Existing race relations and public order law must be firmly enforced against racists. These laws must be given more teeth to outlaw the advocacy and practice of racism.[7]

The revised version of *The British Road to Socialism* that was drafted in 1977 also promoted greater co-operation with the state at the local level, with a number of CPGB activists proposing that local councils, particularly those controlled by the Labour Party, could serve as sites of resistance to the Thatcherite neo-liberal state at the national level. These local councils became involved in what was described as 'municipal anti-racism', which tried to redistribute funding and services to ethnic minority communities and organisations, as well as pro-moting an 'acceptable' form of anti-racism. This was criticised by some, such as the AYMs, for only giving funds to those organisations and campaigns that were willing to acquiesce to the rules of the local council, arguing that this meant that the anti-racism of certain radical organisations was blunted. Others cri-ticised the anti-racist training for buying into the Thatcherite paradigm and viewing racism as a solely ideological and individualistic problem, which over-looked the structural and socio-economic basis for racial inequality and racial discrimination. The result of this was, as Alana Lentin has argued, that inde-pendent anti-racist organisations and campaigns became increasingly institu-

---

6   Bunce and Field 2015, p. 30; Schofield 2013, pp. 251–2.
7   Cook, 'Charter of Demands', in Cook and Rabstein, *Black & Blue: Racism and the Police*, 1981, London: CPGB pamphlet, p. 29.

tionalised, co-ordinated (and co-opted) by local government agencies.[8] This dissipated many of the radical sections of the anti-racist movement during the 1980s, including the role of the Communist Party, which, for other reasons, was already on the verge of collapse.

In his discussion of the British left and the fight for gay rights, Graham Willett wrote about looking at how these Marxist groups dealt with movements that fought other types of oppression (rather than class oppression) from today's perspective:

> Deciding on these positions depends on whether one assumes that social-ists can be expected to transcend the limitations of their own times; whether they should be expected to hold to or, alternatively, to move bey-ond the most advanced politics available.[9]

Although anti-racism was a much more accepted political objective than gay rights, with the socialist left promoting opposition to racial discrimination since the 1920s, Willett reminds us that those involved in anti-racist activism had to work within a labour movement (and wider political landscape) where racism was not taken as seriously as it is today and we cannot transpose con-temporary political values onto the past. Whatever their actions, it is import-ant to remember that the Communist Party of Great Britain was one of the most vocal anti-racist organisations from the 1920s to the 1980s. When black workers started to migrate to Britain in the 1940s and 1950s, it was one of the few organisations to consistently campaign for the inclusion of black workers into the labour movement, as well as promoting a broader campaign against racial discrimination in British society. There were certainly limitations to this approach, particularly as the CPGB focused heavily upon the trade unions as a force for change within the anti-racist movement, while it seems that the trade unions lagged behind other sections of the movement to wholeheartedly put their weight behind the issue. From the late 1960s onwards, other left-wing and black activist organisations were able to surpass the position put forward by the CPGB, but their reach beyond the anti-racist movement, the far left and Britain's substantial black communities was limited, while the CPGB *had the potential* to reach into the more centrist labour movement. The *Morning Star*, as a widely read daily newspaper amongst many trade unionists, covered anti-racist issues on a regular basis, forming a significant action on behalf of the Communist

---

8 Lentin 2004, p. 143.
9 Willett 2014, p. 175.

Party's anti-racist programme. The fact that the Communist Party had its feet in both the trade union movement, but also inside radical left milieu and other progressive movements meant that in some ways it was in an advantageous position, potentially reaching a broad audience for its programme, as outlined in *The British Road to Socialism*. But it also meant that the CPGB's message often fell through the cracks – too radical for some, not radical enough for others – and its actions were diluted by this, with its activists being subsumed into larger social movements and organisations (and in the process losing any identity as CPGB members). This was the case for the Party's cohort of dedicated anti-racist activists.

At the 38th National Congress of the CPGB in 1983 (the Congress that saw the *Morning Star* faction break away from the CPGB over the political line put forward by *Marxism Today*), the Party's resolution on the issue of racism criticised the Party for its lack of black membership:

> The Congress is concerned at the under-representation of black people in the CPGB and believes that this is in part due to residual racialist attitudes and practices inside the Party.[10]

From looking at the material published by the Communist Party and examining its internal records, it is hard to agree with the assumption made in this resolution that racist attitudes existed within the CPGB. It is more likely that while nearly all members of the CPGB were committed to an anti-racist programme, only a number were dedicated to anti-racist activism and the preceding sentence in the resolution is more accurate, that Congress 'is aware that the [anti-racist] campaigning issues referred to [in the resolution] *have not become an essential part of regular activity of every Party branch*'.[11] Parallel to John Callaghan's response when Marika Sherwood criticised the CPGB of being racist in the 1930s, while the Party had 'undoubted shortcomings' in its recruitment of black members, it was just 'not very good at recruiting any section of the population' during the 1980s.[12] Its membership in 1983 was 15,691 (a loss of more than 14,000 members over the previous decade) and as Willie Thompson wrote, the Party was 'being rendered incapable of doing anything very much apart from operating on its own body'.[13] The resolution continued to state that '[w]hilst Congress welcomes the work of white comrades involved in anti-racist

10 'Racism', *Communist Focus*, December 1983, p. 31.
11 Ibid.; my emphasis.
12 Callaghan 1997–8, p. 520.
13 Thompson 1992, p. 218; p. 190.

organisations such as CARL, this is no substitute for the task of bringing more black comrades into the Party'.[14] This highlights the crux of the problem for the CPGB anti-racist activists in the early 1980s – a section of its membership was heavily involved in various anti-racist campaigns and organisations, but this did not translate into tangible gains for the Party, which was in a downward spiral by now. But it also highlights some over-optimistic feelings within the Party at the same time as it was unrealistic to expect many new members to join the Party during this period, particularly from a demographic that had been traditionally overlooked within the broader structures of the CPGB and the labour movement.

From the late 1940s onwards, as large-scale immigration from the Commonwealth commenced, the CPGB had attempted to incorporate anti-racism within the wider struggle for socialism. As an influential body within the trade union movement and the largest leftist party in postwar Britain, the Communist Party had the potential to be an important force in the struggle against racism. The Party's anti-colonial legacy had originally drawn black activists towards the CPGB in the 1950s, but for over a decade, the Party still viewed the issue of racism and the problems facing black immigrants in the context of anti-colonialism. The Party slowly formulated an effective strategy against racism as the Marxist ideology of the CPGB subordinated 'race' to the more immediate issues of class politics. Alongside this was a shift towards a less confrontational position of working within the capitalist state system, as outlined in *The British Road to Socialism*. This saw the Communist Party more willing to appeal to state agencies to fight racism, although the state itself was a fundamental and central part of institutional racism, through the police, the judiciary and the Home Office. The CPGB's position on race relations changed as black activists, both inside and outside the Party, expanded the concepts of 'race' and racism away from the simple construct of class organisation, alongside moves within the Party by younger members and intellectuals, inspired by the new social movements, to re-evaluate the CPGB's focus on class-based politics. This push for ideological and strategic reform was predicated by declining Party membership and a waning of industrial influence. At the same time, the black communities were wary of the white left and the labour movement, who had for so long minimised the role of 'race' within class politics. Despite the initial influence the Communist Party of Great Britain had within the anti-racist movement, this had largely evaporated by the early 1980s, through falling membership numbers and internal divisions, as well as a failure to effectively incorporate black

---

14   'Racism', p. 31.

workers into the political processes of the labour movement or to enlist white workers into the anti-racist struggle. This book has attempted to outline the importance of the Communist Party of Great Britain in the history of anti-racism in postwar Britain and its legacy, but also to highlight the difficulties faced by the Party and the limitations of its strategies. Without understanding the role that the CPGB played in the formation of the modern anti-racist movement in Britain, we cannot understand how the anti-racist movement has developed in the decades since then. The Communist Party was a pioneering force in the anti-colonialist and anti-racist movements from its birth in the 1920s until its slow demise in the 1980s, but it was also a 'prisoner' of this time and although sections of the Party promoted reform, it was unable to survive the seismic domestic and international political shifts of the 1980s and early 1990s and thus was transcended by a new wave of anti-racist, radical and black activist groups – the forward march of the Communist Party had been, in the words of Eric Hobsbawm, halted.

References

Archives

Birmingham City Archive – Indian Workers Association papers, Avtar Johul papers.
Black Cultural Archives, London – Stella Dadzie Papers.
Glasgow Caledonian University Archives – Scottish TUC archive.
Labour History Archive and Study Centre, Manchester – Communist Party of Great Britain archive.
Marx Memorial Library, London.
Modern Records Centre, University of Warwick: APEX papers, Grunwick Dispute archive, International Marxist Group papers, Alvaro de Miranda papers, Alastair Mutch papers, Trade Unionism in British Docks collection, TUC papers.
National Archives, London.
School of Oriental and African Studies Archives, London – Liberation papers.
Working Class Movement Library, Manchester.

Newspapers and Magazines

Black Liberator
Broad Left
Challenge
Cogito
Comment
Comment Supplement
Communist Focus
Communist Review
Daily Worker
International Socialism
Kala Tara
Labour Monthly
The Leveller
Marxism Today
Morning Star
New Society
Race Today
Red Pepper
Searchlight

Socialist Register
Socialist Review
Spare Rib
Speak Out
Temporary Hoarding
World News
World News and Views
World News Discussion Supplement

Books

Adi, Hakim 1998, *West Africans in Britain 1900–1960: Nationalism, Pan-Africanism and Communism*, London: Lawrence & Wishart.

Adi, Hakim 2013, *Pan-Africanism and Communism: The Communist International, Africa and the Diaspora, 1919–1939*, Trenton: Africa World Press.

Alexander, Peter 1987, *Racism, Resistance and Revolution*, London: Bookmarks.

Alleyne, Brian 2002, *Radicals Against Race: Black Activism and Cultural Politics*, London: Bloomsbury.

Anders, Władysław 1981, *An Army in Exile: The Story of the Second Polish Corps*, Nashville, TN: The Battery Press.

Andrews, Geoff 2004, *Endgames and New Times: The Final Years of British Communism*, London: Lawrence & Wishart.

Andrews, Geoff, Nina Fishman and Kevin Morgan 1995, *Opening the Books: Essays on the Social and Cultural History of the British Communist Party*, London: Pluto Press.

Anthias, Floya and Nira Yuval-Davis with Harriet Cain 1993, *Racialized Boundaries: Race, Nation, Gender, Colour and Class and the Anti-Racist Struggle*, London: Routledge.

Beckett, Francis 1998, *Enemy Within: The Rise and Fall of the British Communist Party*, London: Merlin Press.

Beckman, Morris 1993, *The 43 Group*, London: Centerprise Publications.

Birchall, Ian 2011, *Tony Cliff: A Marxist for His Time*, London: Bookmarks.

Birchall, Sean 2010, *Beating the Fascists: The Untold Story of Anti-Fascist Action*, London: Freedom Press.

Bornstein, Sam and Al Richardson 2007, *Two Steps Back – Communists and the Wider Labour Movement, 1935–1945: A Study in the Relations between 'Vanguard' and Class*, Monmouth: Merlin Press

Brah, Avtar 1996, *Cartographies of Diaspora: Contesting Identities*, London: Routledge.

Branson, Noreen 1985, *The History of the Communist Party of Great Britain, 1927–1941*, London: Lawrence & Wishart.

Branson, Noreen 1997, *The History of the Communist Party of Great Britain, 1941–1951*, London: Lawrence & Wishart.

Bunce, Robin and Paul Field 2015, *Darcus Howe: A Political Biography*, London: Bloomsbury.

Burkett, Jodi 2013, *Constructing Post-Imperial Britain: Britishness, 'Race' and the Radical Left in the 1960s*, Basingstoke: Palgrave Macmillan.

Butler, David and Dennis Kavanagh 1974, *The British General Election of February 1974*, London: Macmillan.

Callaghan, John 1987, *The Far Left in British Politics*, Oxford: Basil Blackwell.

Callaghan, John 1994, *Rajani Palme Dutt: A Study in British Stalinism*, London: Lawrence & Wishart.

Callaghan, John 2003, *Cold War, Crisis and Conflict: The CPGB 1951–68*, London: Lawrence & Wishart.

Callinicos, Alex 1993, *Race and Class*, London: Bookmarks.

Carrillo, Santiago 1977, *'Eurocommunism' and the State*, London: Lawrence & Wishart.

Carter, Trevor 1986, *Shattering Illusions: West Indians in British Politics*, London: Lawrence & Wishart.

Cesarani, David 2001, *Justice Delayed: How Britain Became A Refuge for Nazi War Criminals*, London: Phoenix Press.

Chater, Tony 1966, *Race Relations in Britain*, London: Lawrence & Wishart.

Cliff, Tony 2000, *A World to Win: Life of a Revolutionary*, London: Bookmarks.

Copsey, Nigel 2000, *Anti-Fascism in Britain*, Basingstoke: Macmillan.

Crick, Michael 1984, *Militant*, London: Faber & Faber.

Crossman, Richard 1975, *The Diaries of a Cabinet Minister, Vol. 1: Minister of Housing 1964–66*, London: Hamish Hamilton.

Darke, Bob 1952, *The Communist Technique in Britain*, London: Penguin Books.

Dromey, Jack and Graham Taylor 1978, *Grunwick: The Workers' Story*, London: Lawrence & Wishart.

Dummett, Ann and Andrew Nicol 1990, *Subjects, Citizens, Aliens and Others: Nationality and Immigration Law*, London: Weidenfeld and Nicholson.

Durkin, Tom 2006, *Grunwick: Bravery and Betrayal*, London: Brent Trades Council.

Dutt, R. Palme 1957, *The Crisis of Britain and the British Empire*, London: Lawrence & Wishart.

Eaden, James and David Renton 2003, *The Communist Party of Great Britain since 1920*, Basingstoke: Palgrave.

Eatwell, Roger 1997, *Fascism*, New York: Penguin Books.

Featherstone, David 2012, *Solidarity: Hidden Histories and Geographies of Internationalism*, London: Zed Books.

Foot, Paul 1965, *Immigration and Race in British Politics*, Harmondsworth: Penguin Books.

Foot, Paul 1969, *The Rise of Enoch Powell: An Examination of Enoch Powell's Attitude to Immigration and Race*, Harmondsworth: Penguin Books.

Foucault, Michel 2010, *The Birth of Biopolitics: Lectures at the College de France 1978–1979*, Basingstoke: Palgrave Macmillan.

Fox, Ralph 1933, *The Colonial Policy of British Imperialism*, London: Martin Lawrence Ltd.

Fryer, Peter 1984, *Staying Power: The History of Black People in Britain*, London: Pluto Press.

Gilroy, Paul 2002, *There Ain't No Black in the Union Jack: The Cultural Politics of Race and Nation*, London: Routledge.

Gilroy, Paul 2009, *Crisis Music: The Cultural Politics of Rock Against Racism*, Manchester: Manchester University Press.

Guha, Ranajit and Gayatri Chakravorty Spivak (eds.) 1988, *Selected Subaltern Studies*, New York: Oxford University Press.

Hall, Stuart 1978, *Policing the Crisis: Mugging, the State and Law and Order*, London: Macmillan.

Hall, Stuart 1980, *Drifting into a Law and Order Society*, Amersham: Cobden Trust.

Hall, Stuart 1988, *The Hard Road to Renewal: Thatcherism and the Crisis of the Left*, London: Verso.

Hall, Stuart and Martin Jacques 1990, *New Times: The Changing Face of Politics in the 1990s*, London: Verso.

Hann, Dave 2013, *Physical Resistance: A Hundred Years of Anti-Fascism*, London: Zed Books.

Harman, Chris 1988, *The Fire Last Time: 1968 and After*, London: Bookmarks.

Hebdige, Dick 1988, *Hiding in the Light: On Images and Things*, London: Comedia.

Hiro, Dilip 1992, *Black British, White British: A History of Race Relations in Britain*, London: Paladin.

Hobsbawm, Eric 2004, *The Age of Extremes: 1914–1991*, London: Abacus.

Holdaway, Simon 1996, *The Racialisation of British Policing*, Houndsmills: Macmillan.

Howe, Stephen 1993, *Anti-Colonialism in British Politics: The Left and the End of Empire, 1918–1964*, Oxford: Clarendon Press.

Jacobs, Joe 1978, *Out of the Ghetto: My Youth in the East End, Communism and Fascism 1913–1939*, London: Janet Simon.

Jefferson, Tony and Roger Grimshaw 1984, *Controlling the Constable: Police Accountability in England and Wales*, London: Frederick Muller/The Cobden Trust.

Joshua, Harris and Tina Wallace with Heather Booth 1983, *To Ride the Storm: The 1980 Bristol 'Riot' and the State*, London: Heinemann.

Kay, Diana and Robert Miles 1992, *Refugees or Migrant Workers? European Volunteer Workers in Britain 1946–1951*, London: Routledge.

Klugmann, James 1968, *The History of the Communist Party of Great Britain: Volume 1, Formation and Early Years, 1919–1924*, London: Lawrence & Wishart.

Klugmann, James 1969, *The History of the Communist Party of Great Britain: Volume 2, The General Strike 1925–1926*, London: Lawrence & Wishart.

Knowles, Caroline 1992, *Race, Discourse and Labourism*, London: Routledge.

Layton-Henry, Zig 1992, *The Politics of Immigration: Immigration, 'Race' and 'Race' Relations in Post-War Britain*, Oxford: Blackwell.

Lentin, Alana 2004, *Racism and Anti-Racism in Europe*, London: Pluto Press.

Lewis, D.S. 1987, *Illusions of Grandeur: Mosley, Fascism and British Society, 1931–81*, Manchester: Manchester University Press.

Lyddon, Dave and Ralph Darlington 2001, *Glorious Summer: Class Struggle in Britain 1972*, London: Bookmarks.

Macleod, Alison 1997, *The Death of Uncle Joe*, Woodbridge: Merlin Press.

Messina, Anthony M. 1989, *Race and Party Competition in Britain*, New York: Clarendon Press.

Miles, Robert 1982, *Racism and Migrant Labour*, London: Routledge & Kegan Paul.

Miles, Robert 1991, *Racism*, London: Routledge.

Miles, Robert and Annie Phizacklea 1977, *The TUC, Black Workers and New Commonwealth Immigration, 1954–1973*, Bristol: SSRC Research Unit on Ethnic Relations.

Miles, Robert and Annie Phizacklea 1984, *White Man's Country: Racism in British Politics*, London: Pluto Press.

Moore, Robert 1975, *Racism and Black Resistance in Britain*, London: Pluto Press.

Morgan, Kenneth O. 1990, *The People's Peace: British History 1945–1990*, Oxford: Oxford University Press.

Morgan, Kevin, Gideon Cohen and Andrew Flinn 2007, *Communists and British Society 1920–1991*, London: Rivers Oram Press.

Mullard, Chris 1973, *Black Britain*, London: Allen & Unwin.

Neocleous, Mark 1997, *Fascism*, Buckingham: Open University Press.

Newton, Kenneth 1969, *The Sociology of British Communism*, London: Allen Lane.

Parker, Lawrence 2012, *Revolutionary Opposition in the CPGB, 1960–1991*, London: November Publications.

Paul, Kathleen 1997, *Whitewashing Britain*, Ithaca, NY: Cornell University Press.

Pearmain, Andrew 2011, *The Politics of New Labour: A Gramscian Analysis*, London: Lawrence & Wishart.

Phillips, Mike and Trevor Phillips 1998, *Windrush: The Irresistible Rise of Multi-Racial Britain*, London: Harper Collins.

Piratin, Phil 1978, *Our Flag Stays Red*, London: Lawrence & Wishart.

Ramamurthy, Anandi 2007, *Kala Tara: A History of the Asian Youth Movements in Britain in the 1970s and 1980s*, Preston: Second Generation Asians Resisting Racism Project, available from: http://www.tandana.org/pg/resources, accessed 14 March 2007.

Ramamurthy, Anandi 2013, *Black Star: Britain's Asian Youth Movements*, London: Pluto Press.

Ramdin, Ron 1987, *The Making of the Black Working Class in Britain*, Aldershot: Gower.

Renton, David 2000, *Fascism, Anti-Fascism and Britain in the 1940s*, London: Macmillan.

Renton, David 2001, *This Rough Game: Fascism and Anti-Fascism*, Stroud: Sutton Publishing.

Renton, David 2006, *When We Touched the Sky: The Anti-Nazi League 1977–1981*, Cheltenham: New Clarion Press.

Renton, David 2014, *Who Killed Blair Peach?*, London: Defend the Right to Protest.

Renton, David and James Eaden 2002, *The Communist Party of Great Britain since 1920*, Basingstoke: Palgrave Macmillan.

Richardson, Brian (ed.) 2013, *Say It Loud! Marxism and the Fight Against Racism*, London: Bookmarks.

Said, Edward W. 1994, *Culture and Imperialism*, London: Vintage.

Scarman, Lord 1986, *The Scarman Report: The Brixton Disorders 10–12 April 1981*, Harmondsworth: Penguin Books.

Schofield, Camilla 2013, *Enoch Powell and the Making of a Postcolonial Britain*, Cambridge: Cambridge University Press.

Seymour, Richard 2010, *The Meaning of David Cameron*, Winchester: Zero Books.

Sherwood, Marika 1999, *Claudia Jones: A Life in Exile*, London: Lawrence & Wishart.

Shubin, Vladimir 1999, *ANC: A View from Moscow*, University of the Western Cape: Mayibuye Books.

Shukra, Kalbir 1988, *The Changing Pattern of Black Politics in Britain*, London: Pluto Press.

Sivanandan, Ambalavaner 1982, *A Different Hunger: Writings on Black Resistance*, London: Pluto Press.

Sivanandan, Ambalavaner 2008, *Catching History on the Wing: Race, Culture and Globalisation*, London: Pluto Press.

Smith, David J. 1977, *Racial Disadvantage in Britain: The PEP Report*, Harmondsworth: Penguin Books.

Solomos, John 1988, *Black Youth, Racism and the State: The Politics of Ideology and Policy*, Cambridge: Cambridge University Press.

Solomos, John 1989, *Race and Racism in Contemporary Britain*, Basingstoke: Macmillan.

Solomos, John 2003, *Race and Racism in Britain*, Basingstoke: Palgrave.

Spencer, Ian R.G. 1997, *British Immigration Policy Since 1939: The Making of a Multi-Racial Britain*, London: Routledge.

Spivak, Gayatri Chakravorty 2003, *A Critique of Postcolonial Reason: Towards a History of the Vanishing Present*, London: Harvard University Press.

Srebrnik, Henry 1994, *London Jews and British Communism, 1935–1945*, London: Vallentine Mitchell.

Thompson, Willie 1992, *The Good Old Cause: British Communism 1920–1991*, London: Pluto Press.

Thompson, Willie 1993, *The Long Death of British Labourism: Interpreting a Political Culture*, London: Pluto Press.

Thurlow, Richard 1987, *Fascism in Britain: A History 1918–1985*, Oxford: Basil Blackwell.

Tompson, Keith 1988, *Under Siege: Racial Violence in Britain Today*, London.

Turner, Alwyn W. 2008, *Crisis? What Crisis? Britain in the 1970s*, London: Aurum Press.

Virdee, Satnam 2014, *Racism, Class and the Racialized Outsider*, Basingstoke: Palgrave Macmillan.

Walker, Martin 1977, *The National Front*, London: Harper Collins.

Widgery, David 1986, *Beating Time: Riot 'n' Race 'n' Rock 'n' Roll*, London: Chatto & Windus.

Wilson, Amrit 1981, *Finding a Voice: Asian Women in Britain*, London: Virago.

Winder, Robert 2005, *Bloody Foreigners*, London: Abacus.

Woddis, Jack 1960, *Africa: The Roots of Revolt*, London: Lawrence & Wishart.

Worley, Matthew 2002, *Class Against Class: The Communist Party in Britain Between the Wars*, London: IB Tauris.

Wrench, John 1986, *Unequal Comrades: Trade Unions, Equal Opportunity and Racism*, University of Warwick: Centre for Research in Ethnic Relations.

Articles

Adi, Hakim 2006, 'Forgotten Comrade? Desmond Buckle: An African Communist in Britain', *Science & Society*, 70, no. 1: 22–45.

Ben-Tovim, Gideon, John Gabriel, Ian Law and Kathleen Stredder 1981, 'Race, Left Strategies and the State', *Politics and Power*, 3: 153–81.

Benyon, John 1985, 'Going Through The Motions: The Political Agenda, the 1981 Riots and the Scarman Inquiry', *Parliamentary Affairs*, 38, no. 4: 409–22.

Bhabha, Homi K. 1988, 'The Commitment to Theory', *New Formations*, 5: 5–23.

Brownell, Josiah 2007, 'The Taint of Communism: The Movement for Colonial Freedom, the Labour Party, and the Communist Party of Great Britain, 1954–70', *Canadian Journal of History*, 42, no. 2: 235–58.

Callaghan, John 1997–8, 'Colonies, Racism, the CPGB and the Comintern in the Inter-War Years', *Science & Society*, 61, no. 4: 513–25.

Callaghan, John 2004, 'Industrial Militancy, 1945–79: The Failure of the British Road to Socialism?', *Twentieth Century British History*, 15, no. 4: 388–409.

Cambridge, A.X. and Cecil Gutzmore, 'The Industrial Action of the Black Masses and the Class Struggle in Britain', *Black Liberator*, 2, no. 3.

Carter, Bob, Clive Harris and Shirley Joshi 1987, 'The 1951–55 Conservative Government and the Racialization of Black Immigration', *Immigrants and Minorities*, 6, no. 3: 335–47.

Collins, Matthew 1999, 'Smashing Against Rocks', *The Australian/Israel Review*.

Crenshaw, Kimberle 1989, 'Demarginalizing the Intersection of Race and Sex: A Black Feminist Critique of Antidiscrimination Doctrine, Feminist Theory and Antiracist Politics', *University of Chicago Legal Forum*, 139–68.

Crenshaw, Kimberle 1991, 'Mapping the Margins: Intersectionality, Identity Politics, and Violence against Women of Color', *Stanford Law Review*, 43, no. 6: 1242–300.

Dawson, Ashley 2005, '"Love Music, Hate Racism": The Cultural Politics of the Rock Against Racism Campaigns, 1976–1981', *Postmodern Culture*, 16, no. 1.

Duffield, Mark 1985, 'Rationalization and the Politics of Segregation: Indian Workers in Britain's Foundry Industry, 1945–62', *Immigrants and Minorities*, 4, no. 2: 142–72.

Edele, Mark 2015, 'The Second World War as a History of Displacement', *History Australia*, 12, no. 2: 17–40.

Flewers, Paul 1995, 'From the Red Flag to the Union Jack: The Rise of Domestic Patriotism in the Communist Party of Great Britain', *New Interventions*, 6, no. 2.

Flewers, Paul 1996, 'Hitting the Pits: The Communist Party of Great Britain and the National Union of Miners', *New Interventions*, 7, no. 1.

Flinn, Andrew 2002, 'Cypriot, Indian and West Indian Branches of the CPGB, 1945–1970', *Socialist History*, 21: 47–66.

Foot, Paul 1965, 'Immigration and the British Labour Movement', *International Socialism*, 1, no. 22.

Foot, Paul 1992, 'David Widgery: Obituary', *New Left Review*, 196: 120–4.

Gilroy, Paul and Joe Sim 1985, 'Law, Order and the State of the Left', *Capital & Class*, 25: 15–51.

Goodyer, Ian 2003, 'Rock Against Racism: Multiculturalism and Political Mobilization, 1976–81', *Immigrants & Minorities*, 22, no. 1: 44–62.

Grewal, Shivdeep Singh 2003, 'Capital of the 1970s? Southall and the Conjuncture of 23 April 1979', *Socialist History*, 23: 1–34.

Gupta, Anirudha 1974, 'Ugandan Asian, Britain, India and the Commonwealth', *African Affairs*, 73, no. 292: 312–24.

Gutzmore, Cecil 1983, 'Capital, "Black Youth" and Crime', *Race & Class*, 25, no. 2: 13–30.

Hall, Stuart 1999, 'From Scarman to Stephen Lawrence', *History Workshop Journal*, 48: 187–97.

Hinton, James 1988, 'Self-Help and Socialism: The Squatters' Movement of 1946', *History Workshop Journal*, 25: 100–26.

Huntley, Eric 1982, 'The Left, Liberals and the Police', *Race Today*.

Husbands, C. 1988, 'Extreme Right-Wing Politics in Great Britain', *West European Politics*, 11, no. 2: 65–79.

Hyman, Richard 1990, 'Trade Unions, the Left and the Communist Party in Britain', *Journal of Communist Studies*, 6, no. 4: 143–61.

Kirk, Neville 2008, 'Traditionalists and Progressives: Labor, Race and Immigration in Post-World War II Australia and Britain', *Australian Historical Studies*, 39, no. 1: 64–7.

Kushner, Tony 1990, 'Jewish Communists in Twentieth-Century Britain: The Zaidman Collection', *Labour History Review*, 55, no. 2: 66–75.

Lal, Vinay 2001, 'Subaltern Studies and Its Critics: Debates over Indian History', *History and Theory*, 40, no. 1: 135–48.

Lindop, Fred 2001, 'Racism and the Working Class: Strikes in Support of Enoch Powell in 1968', *Labour History Review*, 66, no. 1: 79–100.

Mahon, John 1953, 'New Perspectives for Unity in the British Labour Movement', *Modern Quarterly*, 8, no. 4.

McDowell, Linda 2003, 'Workers, Migrants, Aliens or Citizens? State Constructions and Discourses of Identity Among Post-War European Labour Migrants in Britain', *Political Geography*, 22, no. 8: 863–86.

McDowell, Linda, Sundari Anitha and Ruth Pearson 2012, 'Striking Similarities: Representing South Asian Women's Industrial Action in Britain', *Gender, Place and Culture*, 19, no. 2: 133–52.

McDowell, Linda, Sundari Anitha and Ruth Pearson 2014, 'Striking Narratives: Class, Gender and Ethnicity in the "Great Grunwick Strike", London, UK. 1976–1978', *Women's History Review*, 23, no. 4: 595–619.

McGowan, Jack 2008, '"Dispute", "Battle", "Siege", "Farce"? – Grunwick 30 Years On', *Contemporary British History*, 22, no. 3: 383–406.

Miles, Robert 1984, 'The Riots of 1958: Notes on the Ideological Construction of "Race Relations" as a Political Issue in Britain', *Immigrants and Minorities* 3, no. 3: 252–75.

Miles, Robert and Annie Phizacklea 1978, 'The TUC and Black Workers 1974–1976', *British Journal of Industrial Relations*, 16, no. 2: 195–207.

Moores, Christopher 2009, 'The Progressive Professionals; The National Council for Civil Liberties and the Politics of Activism in the 1960s', *Twentieth Century British History*, 20, no. 4: 538–60.

Payling, Daisy 2014, '"Socialist Republic of South Yorkshire": Grassroots Activism and Left-Wing Solidarity in 1980s Sheffield', *Twentieth Century British History*, 25, no. 4: 602–27.

Petersson, Frederik 2014, 'Hub of the Anti-Imperialist Movement: The League Against Imperialism and Berlin, 1927–1933', *Interventions*, 16, no. 1: 49–71.

Radin, Beryl 1966, 'Coloured Workers and British Trade Unions', *Race*, 8, no. 2: 157–73.

Ramamurthy, Anandi 2006, 'The Politics of Britain's Asian Youth Movements', *Race & Class*, 48, no. 2: 38–62.

Redfern, Neil 2004, 'British Communists, the British Empire and the Second World War', *International Labor and Working Class History*, 65: 117–35.

Redfern, Neil 2002, 'A British Version of "Browderism": British Communists and the Teheran Conference of 1943', *Science & Society*, 66, no. 3: 360–80.

Renton, David 2002, 'Anti-Fascism in the North West: 1976–1982', *North West Labour History Journal*, 27.

Rose, John 1976, 'The Southall Asian Youth Movement', *International Socialism*, 1, no. 91.

Rosenburg, C. 1988, 'The Labour Party and the Fight Against Fascism', *International Socialism*, 2, no. 39: 55.

Sendziuk, Paul 2015, 'Forgotten People and Places: "Stalin's Poles" in Persia, India and Africa, 1942–50', *History Australia*, 12, no. 2: 41–61.

Shaffer, Ryan 2013, 'The Soundtrack of Neo-Fascism: Youth and Music in the National Front', *Patterns of Prejudice*, 47, nos. 4–5: 458–72.

Sherwood, Marika 1996, 'The Comintern, the CPGB, Colonies and Black Britons, 1920–1938', *Science & Society*, 60, no. 2: 137–63.

Shipley, Peter 1978, 'The National Front', *Conflict Studies*, 97: 1–16.

Shukra, Kalbir 1995, 'From Black Power to Black Perspectives: The Reconstruction of a Black Political Identity', *Youth and Policy*, 5–19.

Sivanandan, Ambalavaner 1985, 'RAT and the Degradation of Black Struggle', *Race & Class*, 25, no. 4: 1–33.

Sivanandan, Ambalavaner 1989, 'All that Melts Into Air is Solid: The Hokum of New Times', *Race & Class*, 31, no. 3: 1–30.

Smith, Evan 2008, '"Class Before Race": British Communism and the Place of Empire in Post-War Race Relations', *Science & Society*, 72, no. 4: 455–81.

Smith, Evan 2010, 'Conflicting Narratives of Black Youth Rebellion in Modern Britain', *Ethnicity and Race in a Changing World*, 1, no. 3: 18–33.

Smith, Evan 2012, 'When the Party Comes Down: The CPGB and Youth Culture, 1977–1991', *Twentieth Century Communism*, 5: 38–74.

Smith, Evan and Marinella Marmo 2014, 'The Myth of Sovereignty: British Immigration Control in Policy and Practice in the 1970s', *Historical Research*, 87/236: 344–69.

Trivedi, Parita 1984, 'To Deny Our Fullness: Asian Women in the Making of History', *Feminist Review*: 35–70.

Virdee, Satnam 2000, 'A Marxist Critique of Black Radical Theories of Trade-Union Racism', *Sociology*, 34, no. 3: 548–60.

Ward, Paul, Graham Hellawell and Sally Lloyd 2006, 'Witness Seminar: Anti-Fascism in 1970s Huddersfield', *Contemporary British History*, 20, no. 1: 119–33.

Watson, Don, 2014, 'Poles Apart: The campaign Against Polish Settlement in Scotland After the Second World War', *Scottish Labour History*, 49: 107–23.

Worley, Matthew 2012, 'Shot By Both Sides: Punk, Politics and the End of "Consensus"', *Contemporary British History*, 26, no. 3: 333–54.

Book Chapters

Adi, Hakim 1995, 'West Africans and the Communist Party in the 1950s', in *Opening the Books*, edited by Nina Fishman, Geoff Andrews and Kevin Morgan, London: Pluto Press.

Ben-Tovim, Gideon and John Gabriel 1982, 'The Politics of Race in Britain, 1962–79: A Review of the Major Trends and of Recent Debates', in *'Race' in Britain: Continuity and Change*, edited by Charles Husband, London: Hutchinson.

Benyon, John 1984, 'The Policing Issues', in *Scarman and After: Essays Reflecting on Lord Scarman's Report, the Riots and their Aftermath*, edited by John Benyon, Oxford: Pergamon Press.

Birchall, Ian 2014, ' "Vicarious Pleasure?": The British Far Left and the Third World, 1956–79', in *Against the Grain: The British Far Left from 1956*, edited by Evan Smith and Matthew Worley, Manchester: Manchester University Press.

Branson, Noreen 1985, 'Myths from Right and Left', in *Britain, Fascism and the Popular Front*, edited by Jim Fyrth, London: Lawrence & Wishart.

Callaghan, John 1995, 'The Communists and the Colonies: Anti-Imperialism Between the Wars', in *Opening the Books: Essays on the Social and Cultural History of the British Communist Party*, edited by Geoff Andrews, Nina Fishman and Kevin Morgan, London: Pluto Press.

Catterall, Stephen and Keith Gildart 2005, 'Outsiders: Trade Union Responses to Polish and Italian Coal Miners in Two British Coalfields, 1945–54', in *Towards a Comparative History of Coalfield Societies*, edited by Stefan Berger, Andy Croll and Norman LaPorte, Aldershot: Ashgate.

Clarke, John, Stuart Hall, Tony Jefferson and Brian Roberts 1976, 'Subcultures, Cultures and Class', in *Resistance Through Rituals*, edited by Stuart Hall and Tony Jefferson, New York: Holmes & Meier.

Eatwell, Roger 1998, 'Continuity and Metamorphosis: Fascism in Britain since 1945', in *Modern Europe After Fascism 1943–1980s*, edited by Stein Ugelvik Larsen, Boulder: Social Science Monographs.

Frith, Simon and John Street 1992, 'Rock Against Racism and Red Wedge: From Music to Politics, from Politics to Music', in *Rockin' the Boat: Mass Music and Mass Movements*, edited by Reebee Garofalo, Boston: South End Press.

Gollan, John 1975, 'From "Consensus" to Confrontation', in *British Trade Unionism: A Short History*, edited by Allen Hutt, London: Lawrence & Wishart.

Gordon, Paul 1985, ' "If They Come in the Morning ...": The Police, the Miners and Black People', in *Policing the Miners' Strike*, edited by Bob Fine and Robert Millar, London: Lawrence & Wishart.

Hindess, Barry 1977, 'The Concept of Class in Marxist Theory and Marxist Politics', in *Class, Hegemony and Party*, edited by Jon Bloomfield, London: Lawrence & Wishart.

Jones, Claudia 1985, 'The Caribbean Community in Britain', in *I Think of My Mother: Notes on the Life and Times of Claudia Jones*, edited by Buzz Johnson, London: Karia Press.

Kalra, Virinder S., John Hutnyk and Sanjay Sharma 1996, 'Re-Sounding (Anti)Racism, or Concordant Politics? Revolutionary Antecedents', in *Dis-Orienting Rhythms: The Politics of New Asian Dance Music*, edited by Sanjay Sharma, John Hutnyk and Ashwani Sharma, London: Zed Books.

Kushner, Tony 2000, '"Long May Its Memory Live!": Writing and Rewriting "the Battle of Cable Street"', in *Remembering Cable Street: Fascism and Anti-Fascism in British Society*, edited by Tony Kushner and Nadia Valman, London: Valentine Mitchell.

Lee, Gloria 1987, 'Black Members and Their Unions', in *The Manufacture of Disadvantage*, edited by Gloria Lee and Ray Loveridge, Milton Keynes: Open University Press.

Lunn, Kenneth 1985, 'Race Relations or Industrial Relations?: Race and Labour in Britain, 1880–1950', in *Race and Labour in Twentieth-Century Britain*, edited by Kenneth Lunn, London: Frank Cass and Co. Ltd.

Lunn, Kenneth 1999, 'Complex Encounters: Trade Unions, Immigration and Racism', in *British Trade Unions and Industrial Politics, Vol. II: The High Tide of Trade Unionism, 1964–79*, edited by John McIlroy, Nina Fishman and Alan Campbell, Aldershot: Ashgate.

Lyddon Dave and Ralph Darlington 2003, 'Industrial and Political Strategy in the 1972 British Strike Wave', in *New Approaches to Socialist History*, edited by Keith Flett and David Renton, Cheltenham: New Clarion Press.

MacFarlane, Gary 2013, 'From Confrontation to Compromise: Black British Politics in the 1970s and 1980s', in *Say It Loud! Marxism and the Fight Against Racism*, edited by Brian Richardson, London: Bookmarks.

McIlroy, John 1999, 'Notes on the Communist Party and Industrial Politics', in *British Trade Unions and Industrial Politics, Vol. II: The High Tide of Trade Unionism, 1964–79*, edited by John McIlroy, Nina Fishman and Alan Campbell, Aldershot: Ashgate.

Munslow, Barry 1983, 'Immigrants, Racism and British Workers', in *Socialist Arguments*, edited by David Coates and Gordon Johnson, Oxford: Martin Robertson.

Ovendale, Ritchie 1984, 'Introduction', in *The Foreign Policy of the British Labour Governments, 1945–1951*, edited by Ritchie Ovendale, Leicester: Leicester University Press.

Parmar, Pratibha 1986, 'Gender, Race and Class: Asian Women in Resistance', in *The Empire Strikes Back: Race and Racism in 70s Britain*, Centre for Contemporary Cultural Studies, London: Hutchinson.

Phizacklea, Annie and Robert Miles 1987, 'The British Trade Union Movement and Racism', in *The Manufacture of Disadvantage*, edited by Gloria Lee and Ray Loveride, Milton Keynes: Open University.

Pilkington, Edward 1996, 'The West Indian Community and the Notting Hill Riots of

1958', in *Racial Violence in Britain in the Nineteenth and Twentieth Centuries*, edited by Panikos Panayi, Leicester: Leicester University Press.

Powell, Enoch 1991, 'To the Annual General Meeting of the West Midlands Area Conservative Political Centre', in *Reflections of a Statesman: The Writings and Speeches of Enoch Powell*, selected by Rex Collings, London: Bellew Publishing.

Roberts, Kenneth 1984, 'Youth Unemployment and Urban Unrest', in *Scarman and After*, edited by John Benyon, Oxford: Permagon Press.

Sabin, Roger 1999, '"I Won't Let That Dago By": Rethinking Punk and Racism', in *Punk Rock: So What? The Cultural Legacy of Punk*, edited by Roger Sabin, London: Routledge.

Samuel, Raphael 1986, 'Preface', in *The Enemy Within: Pit Villages and the Miners' Strike of 1984–85*, edited by Raphael Samuel, Barbara Bloomfield and Guy Boanas, London: Routledge & Kegan Paul.

Smith, Elaine R. 2000, 'But What Did They Do? Contemporary Jewish Responses to Cable Street', in *Remembering Cable Street: Fascism and Anti-Fascism in British Society*, edited by Tony Kushner and Nadia Valman, London: Valentine Mitchell.

Solomos, John, Bob Findlay, Simon Jones and Paul Gilroy 1982, 'The Organic Crisis of British Capitalism and Race: The Experience of the Seventies', in *The Empire Strikes Back: Race and Racism in 70s Britain*, Centre for Contemporary Cultural Studies, London: Hutchinson.

Srebrnik, Henry 1995, 'Sidestepping the Contradictions: The Communist Party, Jewish Communists and Zionism, 1935–48', in *Opening the Books: Essays on the Social and Cultural History of the British Communist Party*, edited by Geoff Andrews, Nina Fishman and Kevin Morgan, London: Pluto Press.

Stalin, Joseph 1953, 'Marxism and the National Question', in *Works, Vol. 2*, by Joseph Stalin, London: Lawrence & Wishart.

Stevens, Richard 1999, 'Cold War Politics: Communism and Anti-Communism in the Trade Unions', in *British Trade Unions and Industrial Politics, Vol. II: The High Tide of Trade Unionism, 1964–79*, edited by John McIlroy, Nina Fishman and Alan Campbell, Aldershot: Ashgate.

Thurlow, Richard C. 2000, 'The Straw that Broke the Camel's Back: Public Order, Civil Liberties and the Battle of Cable Street', in *Remembering Cable Street: Fascism and Anti-Fascism in British Society*, edited by Tony Kushner and Nadia Valman, London: Valentine Mitchell.

Virdee, Satnam 1999, 'Racism and Resistance in British Trade Unions, 1948–79', in *Racializing Class, Classifying Race: Labour and Difference in Britain, the USA, and Africa*, edited by Peter Alexander and Rick Halpern, Basingstoke: Macmillan.

Virdee, Satnam 2014, 'Anti-Racism and the Socialist Left, 1968–79', in *Against the Grain: The British Far Left from 1956*, edited by Evan Smith and Matthew Worley, Manchester: Manchester University Press.

Walker, Martin 1979, 'The National Front', in *Multi-Party Britain*, edited by H.M. Drucker, London: Macmillan Press.

Willett, Graham 2014, 'Something New Under the Sun: The Revolutionary Left and Gay Politics', in *Against the Grain: The British Far Left from 1956*, edited by Evan Smith and Matthew Worley, Manchester: Manchester University Press.

Worley, Matthew 2004, 'Courting Disaster? The Communist International in the Third Period', in *In Search of Revolution: International Communist Parties in the Third Period*, edited by Matthew Worley, London/New York: IB Tauris.

Wrench, John and Satnam Virdee, 'Organising the Unorganised: "Race", Poor Work and Trade Unions', in *The New Workplace and Trade Unionism*, edited by Peter Ackers, Chris Smith and Paul Smith, London: Routledge.

Unpublished Theses

Cross, Richard 2003, 'The CPGB and the "Collapse of Socialism", 1977–1991', PhD thesis, University of Manchester.

Goodyer, Ian 2002, 'The Cultural Politics of Rock Against Racism', MA thesis, Sheffield Hallam University.

Index*

---

* Communist Party of Great Britain referred to throughout book.

CPSIA information can be obtained
at www.ICGtesting.com
Printed in the USA
LVHW01s1354280918
591626LV00002B/2/P